10th SIGHUM Workshop on Language Technology for Cultural Heritage, Social Sciences, and Humanities (LaTeCH 2016)

Held at ACL 2016

Berlin, Germany
11 August 2016

ISBN: 978-1-5108-2773-8

LaTeCH 2016

**Proceedings of the 10th SIGHUM Workshop on
Language Technology for Cultural Heritage,
Social Sciences, and Humanities
(LaTeCH 2016)**

August 11, 2016
Berlin, Germany

Production and Manufacturing by
Taberg Media Group AB
Box 94, 562 02 Taberg
Sweden

Introduction

The LaTeCH workshop series, which started in 2007, was initially motivated by the growing interest in language technology research and applications to the cultural heritage domain. The scope quickly broadened to also include the humanities and the social sciences. LaTeCH is currently the annual venue of the ACL Special Interest Group on Language Technologies for the Socio-Economic Sciences and Humanities (SIGHUM).

LaTeCH 2016 is the tenth instalment of the LaTeCH workshop series. Fittingly, LaTeCH received the best birthday present a workshop can hope for: A record number of submissions. 48 papers have been submitted in total, 23 of them being long papers (8 pages). Overall, 21 papers have been accepted for presentation, giving this workshop an acceptance rate of about 44% (long: 47%, short: 40%, previous years: about 60%).

While we did not set a specific topic for this workshop, there is one thematic group that can be easily identified among the accepted papers: Historic languages and their processing. Apart from that, several papers deal with political/social issues and diachronic development in general.

We would like to thank all authors for the hard work that went into their submissions. We are also grateful to the members of the programme committee for their thorough reviews. Reviewing this many papers in time would not have been possible without the additional reviewers who were able to join the programme committee on a short notice and those who volunteered to review a few papers more than anticipated. We also thank the ACL 2016 organisers, in particular the Workshop Co-chairs Jun Zhao and Sabine Schulte im Walde.

Beatrice Alex and Nils Reiter

Organizers:

Nils Reiter (co-chair), Stuttgart University, Germany
Beatrice Alex (co-chair), University of Edinburgh, UK
Kalliopi A. Zervanou, Utrecht University, The Netherlands

Program Committee:

Nikolaos Aletras, University College London, UK
JinYeong Bak, KAIST Daejeon, South Korea
Chris Biemann, TU Darmstadt, Germany
André Blessing, Stuttgart University, Germany
Toine Bogers, Aalborg University Copenhagen, Denmark
Gosse Bouma, Groningen University, The Netherlands
Paul Buitelaar, Insight Centre for Data Analytics, NUI Galway, Ireland
Mariona Coll Ardanuy, Trier University, Germany
Gerard de Melo, Tsinghua University, Beijing, China
Thierry Declerck, DFKI, Germany
Stefanie Dipper, Ruhr-Universität Bochum, Germany
Jacob Eisenstein, Georgia Institute of Technology, USA
Mark Finlayson, Florida International University, USA
Antske Fokkens, VU University Amsterdam, The Netherlands
Serge Heiden, ENS de Lyon, France
Aurélie Herbelot, University of Trento, Italy
Iris Hendrickx, Radboud University Nijmegen, The Netherlands
Gerhard Heyer, Leipzig University, Germany
Yufang Hou, IBM Research, Ireland
Amy Isard, University of Edinburgh, UK
Adam Jatowt, Kyoto University, Japan
Richard Johansson, University of Gothenburg, Sweden
Jaap Kamps, Universiteit van Amsterdam, The Netherlands
Vangelis Karkaletsis, NCSR Demokritos, Athens, Greece
Mike Kestemont, Antwerp University/Research Foundation Flanders, Belgium
Dimitrios Kokkinakis, University of Gothenburg, Sweden
Stasinos Konstantopoulos, NCSR Demokritos, Athens, Greece
Jonas Kuhn, Stuttgart University, Germany
John Lee, City University of Hong Kong
Chaya Liebeskind, Bar Ilan University, Israel
Clare Llewellyn, University of Edinburgh, UK
Shervin Malmasi, Harvard Medical School, USA
Ruli Manurung, University of Indonesia, Depok, Indonesia
Barbara McGillivray, Nature Publishing Group, UK
Yusuke Miyao, National Institute of Informatics, Japan
Joakim Nivre, Uppsala University, Sweden
Pierre Nugues, Lund University, Sweden
Mick O'Donnell, Universidad Autonoma de Madrid, Spain
Petya Osenova, Bulgarian Academy of Sciences, Bulgaria

Table of Contents

Brave New World: Uncovering Topical Dynamics in the ACL Anthology Reference Corpus Using Term Life Cycle Information
Anne-Kathrin Schumann 1

Analysis of Policy Agendas: Lessons Learned from Automatic Topic Classification of Croatian Political Texts
Mladen Karan, Jan Šnajder, Daniela Sirinic and Goran Glavaš 12

Searching Four-Millenia-Old Digitized Documents: A Text Retrieval System for Egyptologists
Estíbaliz Iglesias-Franjo and Jesús Vilares 22

Old Swedish Part-of-Speech Tagging between Variation and External Knowledge
Yvonne Adesam and Gerlof Bouma 32

Code-Switching Ubique Est - Language Identification and Part-of-Speech Tagging for Historical Mixed Text
Sarah Schulz and Mareike Keller 43

Dealing with word-internal modification and spelling variation in data-driven lemmatization
Fabian Barteld, Ingrid Schröder and Heike Zinsmeister 52

You Shall Know People by the Company They Keep: Person Name Disambiguation for Social Network Construction
Mariona Coll Ardanuy, Maarten van den Bos and Caroline Sporleder 63

Deriving Players & Themes in the Regesta Imperii using SVMs and Neural Networks
Juri Opitz and Anette Frank 74

Semi-automated annotation of page-based documents within the Genre and Multimodality framework
Tuomo Hiippala 84

Nomen Omen. Enhancing the Latin Morphological Analyser Lemlat with an Onomasticon
Marco Budassi and Marco Passarotti 90

How Do Cultural Differences Impact the Quality of Sarcasm Annotation?: A Case Study of Indian Annotators and American Text
Aditya Joshi, Pushpak Bhattacharyya, Mark Carman, Jaya Saraswati and Rajita Shukla 95

Combining Phonology and Morphology for the Normalization of Historical Texts
Izaskun Etxeberria, Iñaki Alegria, Larraitz Uria and Mans Hulden 100

Towards Building a Political Protest Database to Explain Changes in the Welfare State
Çağıl Sönmez, Arzucan Özgür and Erdem Yörük 106

An Assessment of Experimental Protocols for Tracing Changes in Word Semantics Relative to Accuracy and Reliability
Johannes Hellrich and Udo Hahn 111

Universal Morphology for Old Hungarian
Eszter Simon and Veronika Vincze 118

Automatic Identification of Suicide Notes from Linguistic and Sentiment Features
    Annika Marie Schoene and Nina Dethlefs 128

Towards a text analysis system for political debates
    Dieu-Thu Le, Ngoc Thang Vu and Andre Blessing 134

Whodunit... and to Whom? Subjects, Objects, and Actions in Research Articles on American Labor Unions
    Vilja Hulden 140

An NLP Pipeline for Coptic
    Amir Zeldes and Caroline T. Schroeder 146

Automatic discovery of Latin syntactic changes
    Micha Elsner and Emily Lane 156

Information-based Modeling of Diachronic Linguistic Change: from Typicality to Productivity
    Stefania Degaetano-Ortlieb and Elke Teich 165

Conference Program

Thursday, August 11, 2016

9:00–10:30   **Session 1**

09:00   *Brave New World: Uncovering Topical Dynamics in the ACL Anthology Reference Corpus Using Term Life Cycle Information*
Anne-Kathrin Schumann

09:30   *Analysis of Policy Agendas: Lessons Learned from Automatic Topic Classification of Croatian Political Texts*
Mladen Karan, Jan Šnajder, Daniela Sirinic and Goran Glavaš

10:00   *Searching Four-Millenia-Old Digitized Documents: A Text Retrieval System for Egyptologists*
Estíbaliz Iglesias-Franjo and Jesús Vilares

11:00–12:30   **Session 2**

11:00   *Old Swedish Part-of-Speech Tagging between Variation and External Knowledge*
Yvonne Adesam and Gerlof Bouma

11:30   *Code-Switching Ubique Est - Language Identification and Part-of-Speech Tagging for Historical Mixed Text*
Sarah Schulz and Mareike Keller

12:00   *Dealing with word-internal modification and spelling variation in data-driven lemmatization*
Fabian Barteld, Ingrid Schröder and Heike Zinsmeister

Thursday, August 11, 2016 (continued)

13:30–14:00   SIGHUM Business Meeting

14:00–15:00   Session 3

14:00   *You Shall Know People by the Company They Keep: Person Name Disambiguation for Social Network Construction*
Mariona Coll Ardanuy, Maarten van den Bos and Caroline Sporleder

14:30   *Deriving Players & Themes in the Regesta Imperii using SVMs and Neural Networks*
Juri Opitz and Anette Frank

15:00–16:00   Poster Session

Semi-automated annotation of page-based documents within the Genre and Multimodality framework
Tuomo Hiippala

Nomen Omen. Enhancing the Latin Morphological Analyser Lemlat with an Onomasticon
Marco Budassi and Marco Passarotti

How Do Cultural Differences Impact the Quality of Sarcasm Annotation?: A Case Study of Indian Annotators and American Text
Aditya Joshi, Pushpak Bhattacharyya, Mark Carman, Jaya Saraswati and Rajita Shukla

Combining Phonology and Morphology for the Normalization of Historical Texts
Izaskun Etxeberria, Iñaki Alegria, Larraitz Uria and Mans Hulden

Towards Building a Political Protest Database to Explain Changes in the Welfare State
Çağıl Sönmez, Arzucan Özgür and Erdem Yörük

An Assessment of Experimental Protocols for Tracing Changes in Word Semantics Relative to Accuracy and Reliability
Johannes Hellrich and Udo Hahn

Universal Morphology for Old Hungarian
Eszter Simon and Veronika Vincze

Automatic Identification of Suicide Notes from Linguistic and Sentiment Features
Annika Marie Schoene and Nina Dethlefs

Towards a text analysis system for political debates
Dieu-Thu Le, Ngoc Thang Vu and Andre Blessing

Whodunit... and to Whom? Subjects, Objects, and Actions in Research Articles on American Labor Unions
Vilja Hulden

16:00–17:30   Session 4

16:00   *An NLP Pipeline for Coptic*
Amir Zeldes and Caroline T. Schroeder

16:30   *Automatic discovery of Latin syntactic changes*
Micha Elsner and Emily Lane

17:00   *Information-based Modeling of Diachronic Linguistic Change: from Typicality to Productivity*
Stefania Degaetano-Ortlieb and Elke Teich

Brave New World
Uncovering Topical Dynamics in the ACL Anthology Reference Corpus Using Term Life Cycle Information

Anne-Kathrin Schumann

`annek_schumann@gmx.de`

Abstract

One of the main interests in the analysis of large document collections is to discover domains of discourse that are still actively developing, growing in interest and relevance, at a given point in time, and to distinguish them from those topics that are in stagnation or decline. The present paper describes a terminologically inspired approach to this kind of task. The inputs to the method are a corpus spanning several decades of research in computational linguistics and a set of single-word terms that frequently occur in that corpus. The diachronic development of these terms is modelled by means of term life cycle information, namely the parameters *relative frequency* and *productivity*. In a second step, k-means clustering is used to identify groups of terms with similar development patterns. The paper describes a mathematical approach to modelling term productivity and discusses what kind of information can be obtained from this measure. The results of the clustering experiment are promising and well motivate future research.

1 Introduction

The discovery of trends and other kinds of topical dynamics is one of the central aims of applied computational linguistics research. It is also of great interest to the digital humanities community for which large text collections are typical sources of information: Which of the many topics mentioned in the corpus are relevant at a given moment in time? How to sort them diachronically, how to model their interplay? These and similar questions, directed towards the ACL Anthology Reference Corpus (ACL ARC) (Bird et al., 2008), form one part of the motivation for the present paper.

A rather more pronounced source of motivation, however, is related to *terminology*, i.e. the study of the specialised lexicon (Wüster, 1979). In terminology, text-linguistic and lexico-semantic approaches (see, for example, Faber and L'Homme (2014)) have been contrasted to knowledge management and its need for abstract, static representations of (specialised) knowledge. Well-known, even if rather different examples of such representations are the Saffron system[1] (Bordea, 2013) and the EcoLexicon[2] (Faber et al., 2016).

The present paper takes a new perspective on terminology by stressing the importance of *temporal dynamics*: Knowledge evolves constantly and this evolution obviously affects concepts and terms as well as the relations that they form. *Term life cycles*, then, are indicative of the evolution of knowledge and a better understanding of them might be helpful in tasks such as information extraction, semantic relatedness analysis, temporal text classification, or trend analysis. Therefore, the present paper aims at finding (preliminary) answers to, at least, one of the following research questions.

1. What are the parameters by which the diachronic development of terms and topics can be described? Is it possible to model diachronic term development patterns or even a term life cycle (e.g. creation, growth, consolidation, and decline)?

2. Is it possible to use knowledge about this life cycle for extracting information (e.g. by distinguishing growing/trending terms from consolidated or dying ones)?

---

[1] `http://saffron.insight-centre.org`.
[2] `http://ecolexicon.ugr.es/en/index.htm`.

Proceedings of the 10th SIGHUM Workshop on Language Technology for Cultural Heritage, Social Sciences, and Humanities (LaTeCH), pages 1–11,
Berlin, Germany, August 11, 2016. ©2016 Association for Computational Linguistics

3. Is it possible to identify terms that exhibit similar development patterns? If yes, are these terms semantically related?

2 Related Work

The present investigation is related to various strands of research in terminology and computational linguistics. In a general way, it forms a part of the growing body of scientific work dedicated to the *analysis of scientific text corpora*, an area that has developed a multitude of different approaches (compare, for example, Atanassova et al. (2015)). Text-analytical studies, in their majority, aim at the exploitation of scientific data as a source of knowledge. Typical use cases are term extraction, the analysis of citation networks and co-authorship graphs as well as text classification. Interesting terminological variations on these common themes are the studies by Monaghan et al. (2010), who use terminological methods for the identification of domain experts, and the analysis of the LREC Anthology carried out by Mariani et al. (2014).

Trend analysis research is related to our study insofar as we hope to draw conclusions on "trending" or "growing" topics or terms on the basis of term life cycle modelling. Terminology is considered to varying degrees in this kind of research. An example that explicitly accounts for a whole range of term features is the system described by Babko-Malaya et al. (2015). Their complex tool models the emergence of new technologies from a corpus of scientific patents mainly on the basis of non-linguistic sources of information (authors, H-index, affiliation, etc.). However, terms are extracted, too, and characterised, among many other parameters, by the status of authors using them and their maturity as measured by linguistic usage patterns. By far simpler approaches to trend analysis are the studies by Francopoulo et al. (2016) and Asooja et al. (2016). Francopoulo et al. (2016) use machine learning techniques to predict the relative term frequencies of terms extracted from the NLP4NLP corpus (Francopoulo et al., 2015). The work carried by out by Asooja et al. (2016) is similar in that it uses Saffron to extract terms from LREC papers and then combines tf-idf scores with regression modelling to predict the future growth or decline of terms.

Terminological studies dedicated to uncovering diachronic aspects of term development are relatively rare. Picton (2011) is an innovative study dedicated to the description of term life cycles. Working on two very small corpora, Picton uses features such as term frequency, linguistic patterns, term variation, and term productivity to identify term life cycle patterns that can be classified into four categories:

- Novelty and obsolescence (various types of neology and necrology, that is, the disappearance of a concept and its denomination)

- Implantation of terms and concepts, that is, the fact of their being accepted as familiar units in a given domain – the next step after neology

- Centrality: this is a topic-related category containing patterns such as "central topic" and "topic disappearance", that is, terms become obsolete because the dominant paradigm in a given field of expertise changes

- Changes related to the structure of specialised documents, that is, changes caused by terminologically uninteresting reasons

Unfortunately, Picton does not describe a robust analysis or evaluation method for her model. Other related terminological studies are Schumann and QasemiZadeh (2015) as well as Schumann and Fischer (2016). Schumann and QasemiZadeh model the development of the term "machine translation" in the ACL ARC by extracting related terms at two distinct time periods. Schumann and Fischer annotate terms in a diachronic corpus of scientific English and present a pilot study arguing that terms undergo semantic and morpho-syntactic development processes over time.

The present study clearly extends and adds to the cited investigations: The presented approach is not just an attempt at extracting "growing" or "trending" terms, but, in fact, represents a more principled effort towards modelling the evolution of the specialised lexicon. The paper also presents a novel parameter for the description of temporal dynamics in terminology. The scientific goal consists in a better understanding of the evolution of knowledge through the evolution of terms.

3 Modelling the Term Life Cycle

This study aims at modelling the life cycles of individual terms in order to learn more about their diachronic development. This is done with the help of just two parameters, namely term frequency and term productivity. Another important decision is to work on the level of single-word terms. This is not just a pragmatic decision related to the fact that single-word terms have a sufficient amount of occurrences, whereas many multi-word terms may not. We also view single-word terms as representatives of semantic clusters of related, more specific terms or, in the words of Bordea (2013), candidates for "domain models". Consequently, by modelling the life cycles of single-word terms, we hope to model the life cycle of their multi-word child terms as well.

3.1 Parameters

As pointed out before, we try to model term life cycles with the help of two parameters, namely term frequency and term productivity, and analyse these parameters in the form of a time series:

- **Term frequency**, that is, the absolute frequency of occurrence of a given term in a given year, normalised by the number of word tokens available from the corpus for that year.

- **Term productivity**, that is, a measure for the ability of a concept (lexicalised as a single-word term) to produce new, subordinated concepts (lexicalised as multi-word terms).

While our take on frequency, though probably unorthodox, may not require any further explanation, a more detailed discussion of "productivity" seems in order here. First of all, productivity is defined only for simple terms, e.g. "word". Productivity, then, is the ability of "word" to participate in the formation of new multi-word terms, e.g. "target word", "input word", etc. We decided to formalise this feature in terms of entropy. In particular, for each year y and single-word term t, we calculated the entropy of the conditional probabilities of all n multi-word terms m containing t. This is shown in Formula 1:

$$e_{(t,y)} = - \sum_{i=1}^{n} log_2(p_{m_i,y}) \cdot p_{m_i,y} \qquad (1)$$

Entropy is a measure of dispersion and, therefore, adequate for measuring productivity:

- If a term has many derived multi-word terms (MWTs) with similar probabilities, it is very productive and has a high entropy.

- If a term has only a few MWTs, it is not very productive and has a low entropy.

- If a term has only one dominant MWT, it occurs in the form of a fixed expression and has a low entropy.

For calculating the conditional probabilities, we simply took the frequency of a multi-word term m matching the simple-word term t and divided this frequency by the frequency, for a given year, of all n multi-word units pertaining to t. This is shown in Formula 2. Here, $f(m)$ denotes the absolute frequency of m.

$$p_{m,y} = \frac{f(m)}{\sum\limits_{i=1}^{n} f(m_i)} \qquad (2)$$

3.2 Data

All work was carried out on the ACL ARC (Bird et al., 2008), analysed for term occurrences by Zadeh and Handschuh (2014). The corpus was encoded into CWB (Evert and Hardie, 2011) and annotated for terminology from the reference list provided by Zadeh and Handschuh (2014) by means of simple, context-insensitive string matching. This data set was then queried for occurrences of single-word terms. For each year, we extracted frequency information for all single-word terms with an overall absolute frequency of at least 100. This yielded a list of 679 term lemmas. We also extracted frequency-per-year information for multi-word terms, using a regular expression. For calculating productivity, we then had to map multi-word onto single-word units. This was again done with a rather simple string matching procedure and reduced the list of single-word terms under study to 424, since for many terms (e.g. "adaboost", "adjunction", "axiomatization") we did not find any dependent multi-word unit.

3.3 Pilot Study

Picton's typology of diachronic term development patterns does not seem fully convincing since it is, at least, in danger of mixing various levels of analysis (terms, topics, textual aspects). We therefore decided to carry out a pilot study on our data to develop a better understanding of the kinds of dynamics that can be expected to be found. This was done by plotting term frequency and productivity for a number of terms. As a result of this study, we

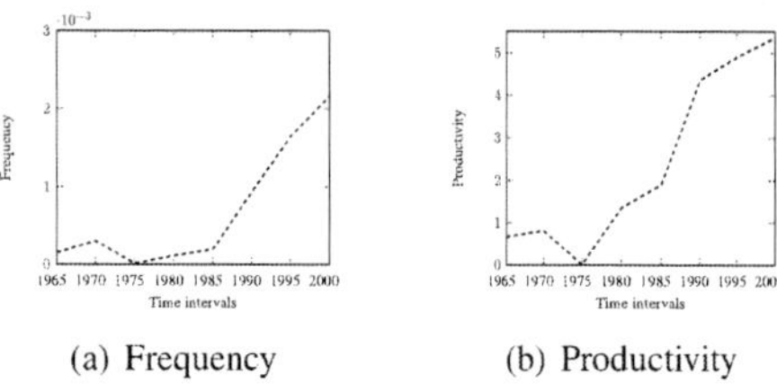

(a) Frequency   (b) Productivity

Figure 1: Frequency and productivity graphs for "corpus".

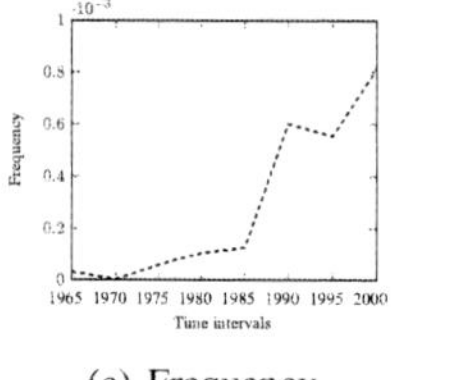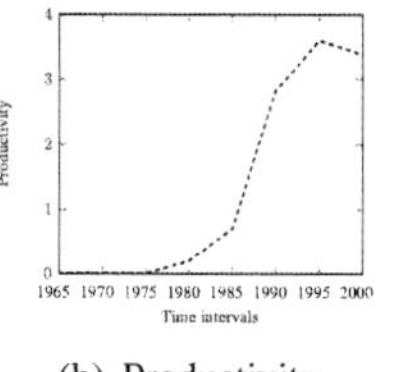

(a) Frequency   (b) Productivity

Figure 2: Frequency and productivity graphs for "score".

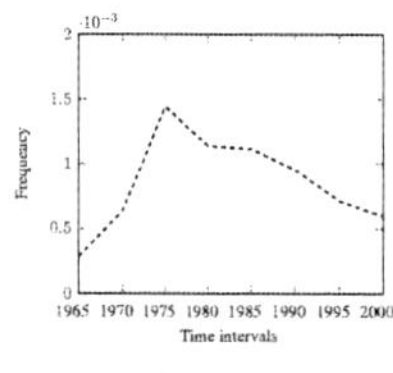

(a) Frequency   (b) Productivity

Figure 3: Frequency and productivity graphs for "representation".

expect to find three types of dynamics: growing terms, consolidated terms, and terms in decline.

3.3.1 Growing Terms

Growing terms exhibit an ongoing increase of both productivity and frequency in 2006, the last year of data in the ACL ARC, that is, none of the two curves has yet started to visibly converge to some maximum. Figure 1 shows frequency and productivity values for "corpus", averaged over intervals of 5 years.[3] Besides "corpus", "cluster", "classification" and "feature" show a similar pattern.

3.3.2 Consolidated Terms

Consolidated terms still grow in frequency, but not in productivity. One could interpret these terms as belonging to the standard paradigm of computational linguistics (in 2006). Figure 2 exemplifies this for "score": "Scores" are widely cited in many publications, but not many new scores are being developed, while scoring has been the dominant evaluation paradigm already for a while and promises to remain such for the near future. Besides "score", "training" and "translation" exhibit similar patterns.

3.3.3 Terms in Decline

Terms in decline seem to have reached an upper bound of productivity and are being used less in terms of frequency. Figure 4 shows this for "representation". Such terms might rise again in the future, but in that case, they may already belong to another paradigm, that is, they may have taken on new shades of meaning. Besides "representation", "reasoning" and "grammar" follow a similar pattern.

---

[3]6 years for 2000-2006. In the plot, x axis ticks denote the first year of the interval.

4 Clustering Experiment

4.1 Algorithm and Data Representation

To investigate the usefulness of our model for the study of the research questions posed above and to verify the hypotheses derived from the pilot study, we carried out a clustering experiment. The aim was to check whether it is possible to sort the data into three clusters of terms, namely "growing", "consolidated", and "in decline". For this purpose, we used the R implementation (R Core Team, 2013) of the Hartigan and Wong k-means clustering algorithm (Hartigan and Wong, 1979) with 3 centres. Standardized frequency and productivity values for each year and term were passed to the algorithm as a feature vector, each value representing a distinct feature.

4.2 Evaluating Clustering Quality

A series of 20 models with 3 centers was calculated. To select the optimal model, we manually labelled all of our 424 observations according to the criteria shown in Table 1. Table 2 shows the distribution of the labels in our data. We do not believe these labels to represent real classes of terms, since the criteria "largest frequency" and "largest productivity" are certainly insufficient for classification. However, we used these labels for approximating the true class distribution when selecting the most reliable from our series of 20 models.

Year	Largest Frequency	Largest Productivity	Label
Year	2005-2006	2005-2006	g(rowing)-g
		1990-2004	g-c(onsolidated)
		earlier than 1990	g-d(ying)
	1990-2004	2005-2006	cg
		1990-2004	cc
		earlier than 1990	cd
	earlier than 1990	2005-2006	dg
		1990-2004	dc
		earlier than 1990	dd

Table 1: Manual labels for data.

Label	Number	%
cc	118	28 %
dc	105	25 %
cd	58	14 %
dd	51	12 %
cg	36	8 %
dg	31	8 %
gg	15	4 %
gc	7	1 %
gd	3	1 %

Table 2: Label distribution in data.

Label	Cluster 1	Cluster 2	Cluster 3
cc	15	20	83
cd	4	54	0
cg	5	0	31
dc	69	18	18
dd	14	37	0
dg	20	4	7
gc	0	0	7
gd	0	3	0
gg	0	0	15
Terms	**127**	**136**	**161**

Table 3: Best model clustering result.

Evaluation of clustering results was then performed by means of a simple variation of accuracy calculation: For each label, we assumed that the cluster with the majority of observations represented the "real" class for this label. Accuracy was calculated for each label as the proportion of correct class assignments and overall accuracy was calculated as the average over all 9 labels. Since this leads to overestimation for labels with only a few observations (e.g. *gd*), we also devised a weighted accuracy score.

4.3 Best Model

Our best model reached 84 % of accuracy (weighted accuracy: 75 %) and distributes labels over clusters as shown in Table 3. From the table it appears that there is a rather neat distinction between cluster 1 – terms with "dying" frequencies, that is, terms whose largest relative frequency was observed before 1990 – and cluster 3: terms with active or, at least, consolidated productivity values. Cluster 2 is more difficult to interpret. The last row of the table also shows that the terms are distributed relatively evenly over the three clusters.

4.4 Typical Terms

So far, our results seem to confirm the existence of a term life cycle with distinct stages such as growth and decline. However, from a digital humanities point of view, it is more interesting to identify "typical" terms for each cluster. We did this by calculating, for each term, its Euclidean distance from the center of its respective cluster. This is shown in Formula 3, where e is the Euclidean distance for each term, f is its feature vector and c is the vector representing the cluster center. n is the number of features passed to the function.

$$e = \sqrt{\sum_{i=1}^{n}(f_i - c_i)^2} \qquad (3)$$

Table 4 gives an overview of the resulting typicality ranking for each of the three clusters. The table displays the terms with the 10 shortest distances from the center (for each cluster) and the terms with the 5 largest distances. The distance values are also given. Columns F and P display the year in which a given term reached its highest frequency or productivity value, respectively. Figures 4 and 5 plot standardised frequency and productivity values for the top-3 terms for clusters 1 and 3 against the cluster centers (labelled as "Cluster 1" and "Cluster 3", respectively).

5 Interpretation of Results

5.1 Results of First Experiment

The results presented in the previous sections confirm that "typical" terms for cluster 1 are indeed terms with a long-standing history. Many of them were used more actively in the 1970s and 1980s than in later years. Some of them indeed exhibit

Cluster 1				Cluster 2				Cluster 3			
Terms	Distance	F	P	Terms	Distance	F	P	Terms	Distance	F	P
interpretation	5.16	1981	2006	report	4.50	2005	1965	annotation	3.33	2004	2004
parsing	5.38	1983	1992	anchor	4.51	1995	1965	corpus	3.40	2005	2006
representation	5.43	1975	1998	lexicalization	4.59	1994	1965	cluster	3.41	2002	2006
process	5.44	1975	2004	internet	4.60	2004	1965	smooth	3.49	2006	2006
syntax	5.45	1980	2005	unigram	4.60	2003	1965	classifier	3.50	2003	2006
formalism	5.49	1987	1992	synset	4.65	1998	1965	ranking	3.51	2004	2004
case	5.56	1983	1994	perplexity	4.69	1989	1965	method	3.61	2003	2006
backtrack	5.59	1987	1965	collocate	4.71	1998	1965	n-gram	3.64	2005	2004
semantic	5.61	1982	2006	pcfg	4.72	1999	1965	measure	3.70	2006	2000
understanding	5.62	1975	1994	cd-rom	4.73	1999	1965	corpora	3.71	2002	2006
...				...				...			
device	8.23	1965	2003	grammaticality	8.19	1989	2004	character	7.56	1980	2003
transformation	8.33	1967	1998	phrasing	8.21	1967	2002	hownet	7.60	2002	2002
natural-language	8.33	1982	1983	array	8.26	1967	1992	paragraph	7.62	1991	2004
linguist	8.51	1969	1983	grouping	8.32	1965	1996	morph	7.64	1965	2001
comprehension	8.61	1978	1983	concordance	8.37	1969	1997	summarizer	7.64	2000	2002

Table 4: Typical terms for all three clusters.

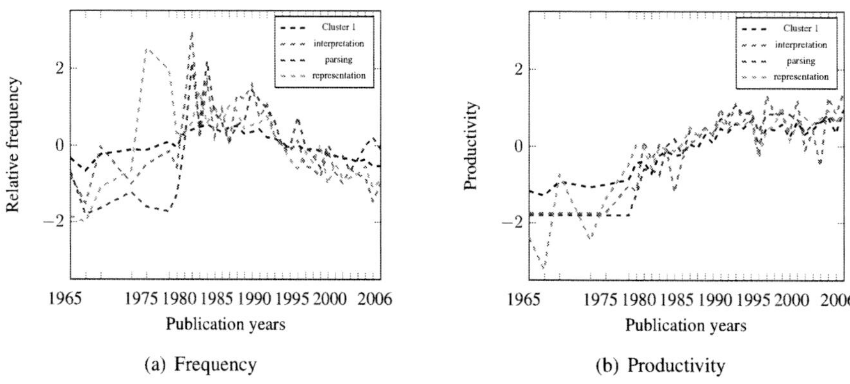

(a) Frequency

(b) Productivity

Figure 4: Frequency and productivity development for typical terms in cluster 1.

decreasing productivity, so they can really be considered terms "in decline". Others, such as "syntax" or "interpretation", seem to have lost importance in terms of frequency, however, they continue to give rise to multi-word terms and they may also have taken on new or other shades of meaning over the intervening years[4]. For these reasons, it might be reasonable to consider them "consolidated" terms rather than terms "in decline", that is, these terms form a part of the standard vocabulary of computational linguistics. Table 5 in the appendix seems to support this interpretation. While some of the top-50 terms for cluster 1 seem indeed outdated (e.g. "prolog"), others denote research topics that were more active in the past (e.g. "formalism", "grammar"), but still cannot be considered irrelevant today. Still others seem to be part of the background vocabulary without which computational linguistics cannot exist (e.g. "sentence", "meaning").

The terms typical for cluster 3 exhibit a very different pattern of development. Their history starts in the 1990s (at any rate, not earlier than in the second half of the 1980s). They then rise quickly and steadily and continue to grow in 2006 when our period of observation ends. It seems straightforward to predict further growth for them and, indeed, today, 10 years later, we know that terms like "corpus", "classifier", and "n-gram" still play an important role in computational linguistics research. In fact, Table 5 confirms that the top-50 terms of cluster 3 almost exclusively represent the statistical paradigm of computational linguistics and we are actually surprised that they are so easily identifiable. These terms almost seem to constitute a kind of newspeak that is associated not only to new topics, but also to new methods and, possibly, a new generation of researchers.

Last but not least, cluster 2 is not as easily in-

---

[4]Note that terms with 1965 as the most "productive" year actually have 0 productivity over the whole period of observation.

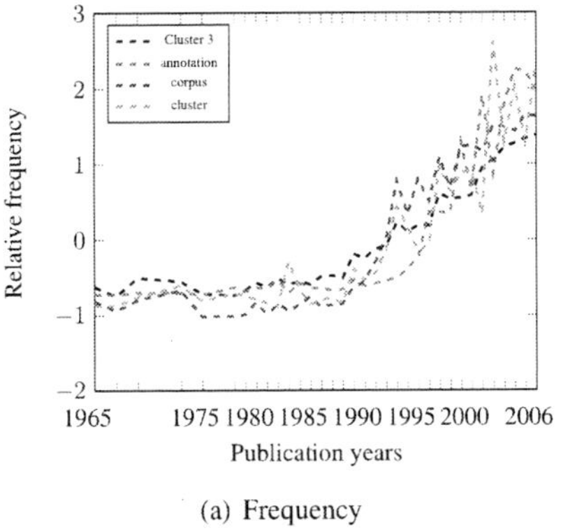

(a) Frequency

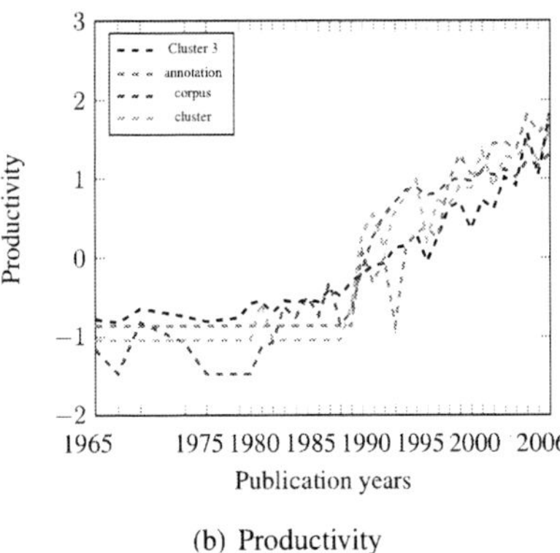

(b) Productivity

Figure 5: Frequency and productivity development for typical terms in cluster 3.

terpretable. Many of the terms in this cluster actually have zero productivity over the whole period of observation (for example, "unigram" has 1965 as the year of its "largest" productivity, meaning that the 0 value (=0 or 1 collocation(s)) set for this year was not overwritten by any larger value in any of the following years). We believe that this is, at least, in part a result of our processing decision to attribute multi-word terms to only one simple term (see Section 3.2 for more detailed information) in order to avoid double-counting. However, it seems that this leads to a loss of relevant information.

5.2 Double-Counting

To check the effect of this detail, we ran the experiment a second time, with the double-counting option set: Now, multi-word units could be assigned to more than one single-word term. First of all, this lead to a very considerable increase of the data set that now holds 592 terms[5]. It also contains more "growing" terms (labels containing the letter g) and less clearly "dying" ones (label dd). Moreover, this slight shift in the data set seems to be echoed in the clustering result in the sense that the cluster of "growing" terms now holds a larger share of the data. Accuracy slightly decreased to 0.80 (weighted: 0.73).

In fact, however, changing how multi-word units are attributed to single-word terms does not affect the general result of the experiment. Table 6 shows that clusters 1 and 3 exhibit only slight changes in comparison to the first experiment. Still, the result looks more convincing than

in the first experiment. For example, terms like "internet", "unigram", "synset", and "perplexity" are now are in cluster 3, as we would expect. Cluster 2 also turns out to be more interesting in this experiment, at least in the sense of being more readily interpretable. Already among the top-10 terms for this cluster we now find:

- Terms with non-standard orthography (e.g. "word-net"). The example term's counterpart "wordnet" is in cluster 3.

- Regional variants of terms that are less popular. An example is "tokenisation". The term has 196 corpus hits. Its counterpart "tokenization" is in cluster 3 and has 1256 corpus hits.

- Infrequent terms such as "sbar" with only 242 hits in the corpus.

- "Terms" that are the result of defective lemmatisation (e.g. "classifiers"). The example term's counterpart "classifier" is in cluster 3.

- Terms that are actually proper names and, therefore, less likely to form multi-word units (e.g. "umls").

Cluster 2, then, really is a residual class of unproductive rather consolidated terms, as was expected after the pilot study. However, it provides interesting insights into the features that distinguish preferred terms from their non-preferred variants. We also believe that the finding that proper names are less likely to form multi-word units – if it can be shown to hold in general – can be useful in entity recognition.

---

[5]Note, however, that this does not mean that fewer multi-word units were considered in the first experiment. They were just attributed to a smaller set of single-word terms.

6 Conclusion

It is tempting to discuss the 2006-state of computational linguistics on the basis of our results, however, we leave this discussion to digital humanities researchers. As a side note, we only remark that our results clearly illustrate the rise of the statistical paradigm and the extent to which it has lead to the creation of not only new methods for doing computational linguistics, but also of a new language to talk about it. In fact, the right-hand sides of Tables 5 and 6 seem to be slightly more uniform in their concentration on mathematical methods than the left-hand sides of the tables which present a mixture of linguistic topics, discussions of processing problems ("prolog", "disk", "processor", etc.), and methods that used to be more important in the more distant past. It would be an interesting research task to investigate whether this apparent increase in uniformity can be confirmed in a large-scale study and, if this is the case, how it relates to the Kuhnian notion of "normal science" (Kuhn, 1962). With regard to the research questions posed in the beginning of this paper we find the following:

1. Our study confirms that terms, their semantics and relevance for a domain, change over time, and that frequency and productivity are useful parameters for the description of such changes. Consolidation and growth seem to be common term development patterns. However, there certainly must be more features than the two used here (e.g. those used in trend research), or more types of development patterns, since our clustering experiment did not result in a clean separation of the three expected classes. We also find that terms remain productive in many cases even if they are used less. Extinction, then, may actually be an exceptional case: Knowledge develops continuously and complete ruptures are uncommon.

2. It seems relatively straightforward to predict future growth for terms with a stable growth pattern. In our experiments, growth patterns were identified with simple methods, however, our approach is not able to predict disruptive, sudden changes in a domain. On the other hand, there is no reason why state-of-the-art terminological methods should not be combined with our method for an in-depth analysis of terms, their development, and their relations. In our current experiments, we did not even look at features such as term co-occurrence, linguistic patterns, etc., but we plan to do so in the future. Finally, studying the interactions between various features might be beneficial for the development of more powerful applications. For example, one might hypothesize that a sudden increase of term productivity is a predictor of a future frequency increase. Clearly, more work is wanted in that direction.

3. Clustering seems to be quite useful for finding terms with similar trajectories and we believe that our method can be used in conjunction with co-occurrence-based approaches, in particular, for the purpose of search space reduction. We expect that more sophisticated modelling will lead to even more interesting results – especially with respect to the modelling of semantically related terms.

Acknowledgments

The research described in this paper was partly funded by the Deutsche Forschungsgemeinschaft through the Cluster of Excellence "Multimodal Computing and Interaction". Moreover, the author would like to acknowledge helpful discussions on related topics with Tatjana Gornostaja and Peter Fankhauser.

References

Kartik Asooja, Georgeta Bordea, Gabriela Vulcu, and Paul Buitelaar. 2016. Forecasting Emerging Trends from Scientific Literature. In *Proceedings of the 10th International Conference on Language Resources and Evaluation (LREC 2016)*, Portorož, Slovenia. European Language Resources Association.

Iana Atanassova, Marc Bertin, and Philipp Mayr, editors. 2015. *Mining Scientific Papers: Computational Linguistics and Bibliometrics*. Co-located with ISSI 2015. CEUR Workshop Proceedings.

Olga Babko-Malaya, Andy Seidel, Daniel Hunter, Jason C. HandUber, Michelle Torrelli, and Fotios Barlos. 2015. Forecasting Technology Emergence from Metadata and Language of Scientific Publications and Patents. In *Proceedings of the 15th International Conference on Scientometrics and Informetrics (ISSI 2015)*, Istanbul, Turkey. Boğaziçi Universitesi.

Steven Bird, Robert Dale, Bonnie Dorr, Bryan Gibson, Mark Joseph, Min-Yen Kan, Dongwon Lee, Brett Powley, Dragomir Radev, and Yee Fan Tan. 2008. The ACL Anthology Reference Corpus: A Reference Dataset for Bibliographic Research in Computational Linguistics. In *Proceedings of the 6th International Conference on Language Resources and Evaluation (LREC 2008)*, Marrakech, Morocco. European Language Resources Association.

Georgeta Bordea. 2013. *Domain adaptive extraction of topical hierarchies for Expertise Mining*. Ph.D. thesis, National University of Ireland, Galway.

Stefan Evert and Andrew Hardie. 2011. Twenty-first century Corpus Workbench: Updating a query architecture for the new millennium. In *Proceedings of the Corpus Linguistics 2011 Conference*, Birmingham, UK. University of Birmingham.

Pamela Faber and Marie-Claude L'Homme. 2014. Lexical semantic approaches to terminology. Special issue of Terminology, 20 (2).

Pamela Faber, Pilar León-Araúz, and Arianne Reimerink. 2016. Ecolexicon: New Features and Challenges. In *GLOBALEX 2016: Lexicographic Resources for Human Language Technology*, co-located with LREC 2016, Portorož, Slovenia. European Language Resources Association.

Gil Francopoulo, Joseph Mariani, and Patrik Paroubek. 2015. Nlp4nlp: The Cobbler's Children Won't Go Unshod. *D-Lib Magazine: The magazine of Digital Library Research*, 21(11/12).

Gil Francopoulo, Joseph Mariani, and Patrick Paroubek. 2016. Predictive Modeling: Guessing the NLP Terms of Tomorrow. In *Proceedings of the 10th International Conference on Language Resources and Evaluation (LREC 2016)*, Portorož, Slovenia. European Language Resources Association.

J. A. Hartigan and M. A. Wong. 1979. Algorithm AS 136: A K-Means Clustering Algorithm. *Journal of the Royal Statistical Society, Series C (Applied Statistics)*, 1(28):100–108.

Thomas S. Kuhn. 1962. *The Structure of Scientific Revolutions*. University of Chicago Press.

Joseph Mariani, Patrick Paroubek, Gil Francopoulo, and Olivier Hamon. 2014. Rediscovering 15 Years of Discoveries in Language Resources and Evaluation: The LREC Anthology Analysis. In *Proceedings of the 9th International Conference on Language Resources and Evaluation (LREC 2014)*, Reykjavik, Iceland. European Language Resources Association.

Fergal Monaghan, Georgeta Bordea, Krystian Samp, and Paul Buitelaar. 2010. Exploring Your Research: Sprinkling some Saffron on Semantic Web Dog Food. In *Proceedings of the 9th International Semantic Web Conference, Semantic Web Challenge*, Shanghai, China.

Aurelie Picton. 2011. Picturing short-period diachronic phenomena in specialised corpora: A textual terminology description of the dynamics of knowledge in space technologies. *Terminology*, 17(1):134–156.

R Core Team, 2013. *R: A Language and Environment for Statistical Computing*. R Foundation for Statistical Computing, Vienna, Austria.

Anne-Kathrin Schumann and Stefan Fischer. 2016. Compasses, Magnets, Water Microscopes: Annotation and Analysis of Terminology in a Diachronic Corpus of Scientific Texts. In *Proceedings of the 10th International Conference on Language Resources and Evaluation (LREC 2016)*, Portorož, Slovenia. European Language Resources Association.

Anne-Kathrin Schumann and Behrang QasemiZadeh. 2015. Tracing Research Paradigm Change Using Terminological Methods: A Pilot Study on "Machine Translation" in the ACL Anthology Reference Corpus. In *Proceedings of 11th International Conference on Terminology and Artificial Intelligence*, Granada, Spain. CEUR Workshop Proceedings.

Eugen Wüster. 1979. *Einführung in die allgemeine Terminologielehre und terminologische Lexikographie*, volume 1: Textteil of *Schriftenreihe der Technischen Universität Wien; 8*. Springer, Wien.

Behrang Q. Zadeh and Siegfried Handschuh. 2014. The ACL RD-TEC: A Dataset for Benchmarking Terminology Extraction and Classification in Computational Linguistics. In *Proceedings of the 4th International Workshop on Computational Terminology (Computerm)*, co-located with COLING 2014, Dublin, Ireland. Association for Computational Linguistics and Dublin City University.

Cluster 1	Cluster 3
interpretation	annotation
parsing	corpus
representation	cluster
process	smooth
syntax	classifier
formalism	ranking
case	method
backtrack	n-gram
semantic	measure
understanding	corpora
mechanism	optimization
logic	estimation
theory	regression
knowledge	precision
prolog	learn
concept	annotator
interface	validation
instantiation	document
ambiguity	evaluation
meaning	entropy
user	model
parse	score
analyser	prune
grammar	token
predicate	train
implementation	label
structure	algorithm
verb	summarization
reasoning	training
denotation	approach
hardware	sampling
discourse	ontology
signal	statistic
generation	distribution
debug	probability
quantifier	weighting
inferencing	co-occurrence
procedure	approximation
disk	tag
event	markup
unification	disambiguation
utterance	chunk
sentence	word
synthesis	nlp
vocabulary	mining
inheritance	bigram
fact	technique
linguistic	likelihood
conjunct	bootstrapping
inference	voting

Table 5: Top-50 terms for clusters 1 and 3 in first experiment.

Cluster 1	Cluster 2	Cluster 3
grammars	word-net	clustering
parsing	sbar	annotation
interpretation	svms	ranking
logic	bagging	smooth
formalism	grounding	precision
mechanism	classifiers	learning
process	tf-idf	classifier
theory	umls	corpus
case	runtime	n-gram
interface	tokenisation	rank
parser	negra	bootstrap
semantic	k-nn	cluster
representation	retrieve	method
structure	minipar	regression
understanding	collocate	measure
knowledge	interoperability	treebank
unification	hmms	cross-validation
parse	f-score	entropy
ambiguity	adaboost	wordnet
processing	caching	corpora
prolog	technologies	segmentation
meaning	knn	optimization
concept	recogniser	learn
user	ptb	annotator
grammar	basque	bootstrapping
implementation	comlex	label
generation	tokenizer	unigram
verb	cd-rom	estimation
reasoning	genia	weighting
mean	television	document
predicate	collapse	tagging
message	word-segmentation	validation
syntax	usability	model
discourse	synchronization	evaluation
database	standardization	prune
synthesis	nucleus	token
signal	superarv	chunk
lambda	key-word	backoff
spell	measuring	ontology
processor	pagerank	nlp
understand	parse-tree	sampling
composition	lemmatization	summarisation
utterance	hypothesize	summarization
vocabulary	timeml	score
inheritance	nonterminal	chunking
natural-language	silence	bigram
text-to-speech	questionnaire	training
morphologic	translations	algorithm
linguistic	katakana	tag
event	retirieving	approach

Table 6: Top-50 terms for clusters 1, 2, and 3 in second experiment.

Analysis of Policy Agendas: Lessons Learned from Automatic Topic Classification of Croatian Political Texts

Mladen Karan*   Jan Šnajder*   Daniela Širinić†   Goran Glavaš*
*Faculty of Electrical Engineering and Computing, University of Zagreb, Croatia
{mladen.karan, jan.snajder, goran.glavas}@fer.hr
†Faculty of Political Science, University of Zagreb, Croatia
dsirinic@fpzg.hr

Abstract

Policy agenda research is concerned with measuring the policymaker activities. Topic classification has proven a valuable tool for policy agenda research. However, manual topic coding is extremely costly and time-consuming. Supervised topic classification offers a cost-effective and reliable alternative, yet it introduces new challenges, the most significant of which are the training set coding, classifier design, and accuracy-efficiency trade-off. In this work, we address these challenges in the context of the recently launched Croatian Policy Agendas project. We describe a new policy agenda dataset, explore the many system design choices, and report on the insights gained. Our best-performing model reaches 77% and 68% of F_1-score for major topics and subtopics, respectively.

1   Introduction

Understanding politics means understanding what political actors are saying and writing (Grimmer and Stewart, 2013), i.e., understanding the *content* of the messages. Accordingly, *content analysis* plays an important role in political science (Holsti, 1969; Weber, 1990; Krippendorff, 2012). Probably the most prominent form of content analysis is *topic classification*. In topic classification, the individual documents are assigned to a limited set of categories. Once documents have been assigned categories, they can be searched more efficiently than when using traditional keyword-based methods. Moreover, categories are a prerequisite for the analysis of patterns and changes in political content across time. As noted by, among others, Hillard et al. (2007), reliable topic classification can save significant research time.

One strand of research in which topic classification has proven beneficial is the analysis of policy agendas (Kingdon and Thurber, 1984): the set of issues arising in the decision-making process. The main idea is that the frequency with which the issues occur in political texts can be used as a measure of policy attention. This strand of research has been particularly influenced by the Policy Agendas Project (PAP), initiated by Bryan Jones and Frank Baumgartner in 1993, with the intention to track changes in policy activity within particular areas of policy-making over longer periods of time (John, 2006).[1] The main issue PAP addressed is that of reliably measuring the policymaker activities across time. To this end, PAP developed an exhaustive and consistent codebook comprised of 19 major topic and 225 subtopic codes, by which all policymaker activities were categorized. Building on this idea, the Comparative Agendas Project (CAP) (Bevan, 2014) extended the PAP codebook, originally developed for the United States.[2] While PAP was focused on ensuring longitudinal measurement reliability, CAP extended this methodological framework to also study policy changes comparatively, across time and space (countries). The CAP codebook consists of 21 major topics and more than 200 subtopics, used for coding of political texts for over 18 countries. Consequently, CAP-coded data have been used as the primary source for a number of policy agenda studies (e.g., Baumgartner et al. (2006)), and have been a foundation for one of the largest and most productive research networks in political science.

The perennial problem of topic classification – and content analysis in general – is the sheer volume of political texts. Manual coding is extremely time-consuming and costly, and thus does not scale

---

[1]http://www.policyagendas.org
[2]http://www.comparativeagendas.info

Proceedings of the 10th SIGHUM Workshop on Language Technology for Cultural Heritage, Social Sciences, and Humanities (LaTeCH), pages 12–21,
Berlin, Germany, August 11, 2016. ©2016 Association for Computational Linguistics

to large text collections. Consequently, as pointed out by Grimmer and Stewart (2013), analyzing large text collections is impossible for all but the most well-funded projects. Moreover, manual coding can be unreliable and inconsistent. For this reason, social scientists are increasingly relying on automated topic classification (ATC) (Purpura and Hillard, 2006; Quinn et al., 2006; Hillard et al., 2008; Quinn et al., 2010). ATC has two compelling advantages over human coding (Benoit, 2011): reliability and efficiency.

From a computational perspective, ATC is an instance of a more general text categorization task (Sebastiani, 2002), which falls within the purview of natural language processing and machine learning. The task is typically framed as a supervised machine learning problem, either multi-class (a single topic per document) or multi-label (multiple topics per document). Note that policy agenda research typically adopts the single-topic approach.

While arguably more efficient than human coding, ATC does come with its problems. First and foremost, ATC does not get around the problem of validity: ATC generally cannot detect nuances in the text as well as a human can, thereby limiting the validity of content analysis results. Secondly, there are a number of practical challenges involved in setting up a high-performance ATC system. Building an ATC system requires a high-quality manually coded dataset with a sufficiently large coverage. Furthermore, there are a lot of design choices involved, which greatly affect the system's performance. In the end, one does typically not want to compromise the quality otherwise obtainable by human coding, which means that a trade off has to be found between accuracy and human coding effort. This can be done by estimating the confidence of classifier decisions for each individual document, and then forwarding to a human coder the (hopefully small) subset of documents for which the decision confidence is low. For this to work, however, we need reliable estimates of classifier confidence, which turns out to be far from trivial.

In this work, we address the above challenges in the context of automatic topic classification of Croatian political texts. We first present a new dataset, built within the Croatian Policy Agendas Project, and a first such dataset for Croatian. The dataset has been manually coded according to the CAP codebook, with additional measures taken to ensure reliability. An additional challenge lies in the fact that the dataset consists only of titles, which further exacerbates the data sparsity problem. We use this dataset to train and evaluate a number of text classification models, also experimenting with two problem-specific extensions. Finally, we consider various confidence estimation strategies. The main research questions we answer are as follows: (1) Can we use the hierarchical structure of our topic scheme to improve classification performance?; (2) Can we make use of idiosyncratic coding rules?; and (3) What confidence estimation strategy gives best accuracy-efficiency trade-off? We hope that the lessons learned from these experiments will be useful to others working on the same or similar task for other languages.

The rest of the paper is structured as follows. In the next section, we briefly review the related work on ATC. In Section 3, we describe the Croatian Policy Agendas Project and the corresponding dataset. Section 4 focuses on the classification models. In Section 5, we present the experimental results. Section 6 concludes the paper and outlines future work.

2   Related Work

The use of supervised topic classification for policy agenda research has been introduced by Purpura and Hillard (2006). The authors presented a system that classifies the Congressional Bills according to the PAP codebook. Their system is a two-level support vector machine (SVM) with word features weighted by pointwise mutual information. The authors conclude that the system performs "about as well as humans would be expected to perform."

In subsequent work, Hillard et al. (2008) experiment with a number of classifiers (Naïve Bayes, SVM, BoosTexter, and MaxEnt), achieving high prediction accuracies across the different algorithms, with SVM emerging as the winner (88.7% and 81.0% accuracy on major topics and subtopics, respectively). Furthermore, they experiment with voting ensembles and investigate the accuracy-efficiency trade-off. While their experiments indicate that the improvement by ensemble voting is negligible, they also indicate that combining classifier decisions provides a key indication of classification confidence, which in turn can be used to lower the cost of improving accuracy. In particular, they demonstrate that inspecting and manually coding 20% of bills (about 1300 documents) where all three classifiers disagree boosts accuracy from

78% to 87%. Similarly, Collingwood and Wilkerson (2012) show that accepting decisions where at least three classifiers agree results in 86% average agreement at about 85% coverage.

The key idea behind the accuracy-efficiency trade-off is to reject the automatic classification of documents on which the classifiers exhibit low confidence. The alternative way to mitigate the cost of human coding is to incorporate the classifier in the coding process up front, in a so-called active learning setup. In active learning, the classifier confidence is used as a signal to guide the human coder which documents to code next, yielding larger accuracy improvements with lower coding effort. Hillard et al. (2007) show that, when compared to random sampling, active learning leads to a statistically significant 3% accuracy increase on the Congress Bills dataset.

Albeit our work focuses on supervised topic classification, for completeness we note that there exists a valuable body of work on the use of unsupervised topic classification from political texts. This strand of research mostly revolves around the use of topic models (Blei, 2012), e.g., (Quinn et al., 2006; Quinn et al., 2010; Grimmer, 2010). Other lines of research consider the estimation of category proportions instead of assigning single topics to documents (Hopkins and King, 2010), as well as the use of dictionaries for single- and multi-topic classification (Albaugh et al., 2013).

3 The Croatian Policy Agendas Project

The Croatian Policy Agendas project was launched with the aim of better understanding the changes in policy activity and policy priorities in a new democracy. The project is part of a large body of political agenda research that started with the Policy Agendas and Congressional Bills projects in the United States (E Adler and Wilkerson, 2006; John, 2006), and which has recently evolved into the Comparative Agendas Project (CAP) – a growing network of national projects in 17 countries. All national projects focused on manual topic coding of various policy documents such as legislation, political speeches, judicial decisions, media content, or public opinion. Regardless of the type of documents and observations, all materials were coded according to the CAP master codebook with 21 top-level (major) topic codes (shown in Table 1) and over 200 subtopic codes. The standardized coding system enables (1) the capturing of the policy focus of

Code	Major topic
1	Domestic Macroeconomic Issues
2	Civil Rights, Minority Issues, and Civil Liberties
3	Health
4	Agriculture
5	Labor and Employment
6	Education
7	Environment
8	Energy
9	Immigration and Refugee Issues
10	Transportation
12	Law, Crime, and Family Issues
13	Social Welfare
14	Community Development and Housing Issues
15	Banking, Finance, and Domestic Commerce
16	Defense
17	Space, Science, Technology, and Communications
18	Foreign Trade
19	International Affairs and Foreign Aid
20	Government Operations
21	Public Lands, Water Management, and Territorial Issues
23	Cultural Policy Issues

Table 1: Top-level policy topics (major topics)

each observation, regardless of its source (Bevan, 2014), and (2) comparison of policy agendas across countries and regions.

3.1 Data Collection

The data gathering for the Croatian Policy Agendas project began in June 2015 and has so far resulted in a collection consisting of titles[3] of (1) all documents published by the National Gazette from January 1990 to December 2015 (all legal acts of the Parliament, the Government, and the President), (2) all agendas of the Croatian Parliament and Croatian Government, and (3) parliamentary questions. All document titles were merged into a single dataset, totaling over 100,000 title units. A subset of these were chosen for manual topic coding. It is worth pointing out that a large portion of documents from our collection are restricted access documents (e.g., minutes of the Government cabinet meeting), hence working with titles is the only option in such cases. In contrast, for publicly accessible documents, the content analysis could also be extended to full texts; we leave this option for future work.

---

[3]Whenever possible, CAP datasets include a link to original documents and complementary text that was used for classification. In some countries, full access to digitized documents was possible. In most cases, however, including Croatia, only document titles were available.

Measure	CS #1	CS #2	CS #3	CS #4
Percent agreement	81.5	81.2	80.6	85.4
Fleiss' κ	0.61	0.61	0.60	0.70
Krippendorff's α	0.61	0.62	0.60	0.70

Table 2: Calibration inter-annotator agreement

Measure	Phase #1	Phase #2	Phase #3
Percent agreement	51.2	79.7	83.0
Cohen's κ	0.51	0.79	–
Fleiss' κ	–	–	0.87
Number of coders	2	2	3

Table 3: Inter-annotator agreement

3.2 Coding Procedure

We devised the coding procedure so to ensure high reliability of the data. To this end, we split the coding procedure into several sessions, with checkpoints between them. The coding was carried out by thirteen students of political science and legal studies. After the initial training session, whose purpose was to introduce the students to the task and explain the coding guidelines, all thirteen students coded four small calibration sets, each consisting of 50 titles (a total of 200 titles). The calibration step allowed us to (1) identify which topics require a more detailed explanation and provision of examples from the codebook and (2) measure the inter-annotator agreement (IAA). We show the IAA on the four calibration sets (CS) in Table 2.

After the calibration session, we prepared a sample of document titles for further coding. To ensure that there is a sufficient variation across subtopics, we used stratified random sampling to select 7300 titles, accounting also for the source of the document (National Gazette, parliamentary sessions agenda, government weekly meetings agenda, or parliamentary questions). This introduces a variance across the topics and document types, which differ greatly in vocabulary and form of the titles.

The main coding session was carried out in four phases. First, each document title was coded independently by two out of thirteen students, where students were asked to take notes and tag the examples they consider problematic. In the second phase, we split the thirteen students into four groups and considered only the titles where coders disagreed in the first coding phases, as well as titles tagged as problematic by at least one of the coders (even if they agreed on the code). Each title on which the coders disagreed or which was tagged as problematic in the second phase was independently coded by two out of four groups. In the third coding phase, three political sciences experts independently coded all titles where codings by two student groups differed. Finally, the disagreements remaining after the third coding phase were discussed and resolved by consensus by the three experts. Table 3 shows the IAA measures for each of the coding phases. We make the manually coded dataset freely available.[4]

Table 4 gives some examples from the dataset. Particularly interesting are the titles that belong to the 00 subtopic (General): these are either (1) too general to be categorized in any of the more specific subtopics or (2) pertaining to two or more different subtopics. Also interesting is the 99 subtopic (Other), assigned to titles on a well-defined subtopic not covered by the CAP codebook.

4 Topic Classification Models

Following Purpura and Hillard (2006) as well as Hillard et al. (2008), we frame the topic classification task as a supervised multi-class classification problem. Solving this problem involves a number of design choices: choosing from among different machine learning algorithms, multi-class classification schemes, and methods to handle hierarchy. While our study is far from exhaustive, we do explore a reasonable number of options.

4.1 Text Preprocessing

We apply the typical text categorization preprocessing pipeline: we tokenize all documents, lemmatize the words using an automatically acquired morphological lexicon built by Šnajder et al. (2008), and remove all stopwords (non-content words). We chose to lemmatize because Croatian is an inflectionally rich language, and prior research (Malenica et al., 2008) has shown that lemmatization improves classifier performance. We do not apply any further preprocessing such as parsing, as syntactic features are very sparse and would require much more data to yield any benefits.

4.2 Algorithms and Schemes

There are three approaches to multi-class classification. One option is to use a classifier that can naturally handle multiple classes, such as the Naïve Bayes. The other two options rely on decomposing

---

[4] http://takelab.fer.hr/data/apa

Title (Croatian)	Title (English)	Code	Major topic / Subtopic
Odluka o imenovanju ministra financija	Appointment decision for the finance minister position	1500	Finance / General
Odluka o suglasnosti za povećanje cijena električne energije	Decision of approval for the increase in electricity prices	802	Energy / Electrical Energy
Pravilnik o socijalnom zbrinjavanju useljenika i povratnika	Regulation of social care for immigrants and returnees	1399	Social Welfare / Other
Zakon o postupanju s nezakonito izgradenim zgradama	Law on the treatment of illegally constructed buildings	1401	Community Development / Housing
Pravilnik o praćenju emisija onečišćujućih tvari u zrak iz nepokretnih izvora	Regulation of tracking air pollutants emissions from immobile sources	705	Environment topic / Air Pollution

Table 4: Example titles and their codes from the Croatian Policy Agendas Project data set

a multi-class problem into a series of binary classification problems. The one-vs-one (OVO) scheme works by training one binary classifier for each pair of classes. The prediction for an instance is obtained by voting of the individual binary classifiers. In contrast, in the one-vs-rest (OVR) scheme, we train for each class one binary classifier separating that class from all the other classes. An instance is classified into the class for which the corresponding classifier confidence is the highest.[5] The OVO and OVR schemes apply a divide-and-conquer strategy as they break up one difficult multi-class problem into many smaller and simpler binary problems. However, the downside of these schemes is that they introduce a large number of classifiers, consequently making the training resource-intensive.

In this work we consider a number of different algorithms and schemes, as follows.

LR-OVO. For this model, we use a binary logistic regression classifier implemented in the LIBLINEAR package (Fan et al., 2008), coupled with the OVO scheme.[6] To avoid overfitting, we optimize the hyperparameter C on a held-out validation set. Moreover, we perform implicit feature selection using L1-regularization, enforcing feature sparsity. The logistic regression classifier predicts class probability, which can be used directly as a measure of classification confidence. To accommodate the multi-class setup, we compute the confidence for class c as the average of confidences of all pairwise classifiers that include c.

LR-OVR. This model is the same as LR-OVO, but employs the OVR multi-class scheme. The confidence for class c is simply the confidence of the binary classifier corresponding to that class.

GNB. A Naïve Bayes (NB) model with numerical feature vectors, where the class likelihoods are modeled using Gaussian distributions. We make the usual simplifying assumption of a diagonal and shared covariance matrix. We note that for text classification a multinomial NB is more often used than a Gaussian NB. The motivation for using a Gaussian version is that we wanted all our classifiers to work with identical (numeric) feature vectors.

XGB. We experiment with the extreme gradient boosting algorithm (Chen and Guestrin, 2016). It is a decision tree-based algorithm, which aims to obtain "strong" classifiers by combining a large number of "weaker" ones. To avoid overfitting, we optimize the *eta* and *numrounds* hyperparameters on a held-out validation set.

4.3 Hierarchical Classification

The CAP codebook is a two-level taxonomy, featuring 21 major topics and more than 200 subtopics. Although we are ultimately interested in classifying documents into subtopics, we can leverage the hierarchical structure to decompose the multi-class problem into two separate classification problems, one for each hierarchy level. The assumption is that the separate problems are easier to solve than the original joint problem.

In line with common practice, we use the top-down level-based approach, in which one flat classifier is trained for each level of the hierarchy. We train a classifier to discriminate between major topics and, for each major topic, one classifier to discriminate between its subtopics. At prediction time, the straightforward approach would be to apply the

---

[5]We note that there are many variants of the OVO and OVR schemes; the interested reader is referred to (Galar et al., 2011) for an overview.

[6]We also experimented with the SVM algorithm from the same library and found the logistic regression to perform slightly better on our dataset. For the sake of brevity, we omit the SVM results.

top-level classifier first to obtain the major topic, and then apply the corresponding second-level classifier to obtain the subtopic. The obvious downside is that the error propagates: if the model makes a mistake at the major topic level, it cannot be undone. To mitigate this, we linearly combine the confidences from both levels:

$$f(t, s_t) = conf_1(t) + \alpha \cdot conf_2(s_t) \qquad (1)$$

where t is a major topic, s_t is its subtopic, and $conf_n$ is the confidence of the classifier at level n. Using the joint confidence derived by f softens the strict two-level split and may alleviate error propagation issues. Furthermore, it allows us to weigh decisions from different levels differently. The intuition behind this is that we expect decisions on the first level to be more confident as (1) there is more training data and (2) the differences between major topics are more prominent than the differences among subtopics within one major topic.

In our models, we calculate f for all possible major topic/subtopic pairs and classify the document into the subtopic that maximizes f. We optimize α on a held-out validation set. We denote the hierarchical versions of our models as LR-OVO-H, LR-OVR-H, LR-GNB-H, and LR-XGB-H. To account for the possibility that a non-hierarchical approach works better on our dataset, we also build a flat LR-OVR model trained directly on all 208 subtopics, denoted LR-OVR-F.

4.4 Features

We use the same set of features for our models:

- Lemmas – we weigh each lemma l using the tf-idf weighting scheme:

$$\textit{tfidf}(l) = \textit{freq}(l) \cdot \frac{|D|}{|\{d \mid l \in d\}|} \qquad (2)$$

  where *freq* is the frequency of l in the document, while D is the set of all documents;

- Bigrams – binary features for 300 most frequent bigrams in the data set;

- Word2vec – we use distributed word representations proposed by Mikolov et al. (2013), derived by applying the *word2vec* tool on the hrWaC web-corpus (Ljubešić and Erjavec, 2011). Following Mitchell and Lapata (2010), we compute the composed semantic representation of a document as the sum the vectors of its content words. The resulting vector of length 300 is fed as input to our models.

While we do not perform explicit feature selection, it is performed implicitly by the L1-regularization in LR-based models, and also in the XGB model, which embeds feature selection.

4.5 Postprocessing Rules

The second extension we consider is the application of postprocessing rules. These are meant to enforce two specific coding principles, also prescribed in the coding guidelines:

1. If two or more subtopics are equally represented in a document, or the document content is rather general, then it should be assigned the General (00) subtopic;

2. If a document does not fit well into any of the existing subtopics, but the document content is not general, then it should be assigned the Other (99) subtopic.

We map these to two postprocesing rules:

1. If, for a given document, the ratio of confidences for the top two subtopics is above a threshold θ_1, the document is labeled with the General (00) subtopic;

2. If the highest confidence subtopic for a given document is below θ_2, then the document is labeled with the Other (99) subtopic.

Each rule is parametrized by a threshold that is tuned on a held-out validation set.

4.6 Confidence Estimation

Validity is of central concern to any content analysis study. To preserve validity, researchers will often be willing to trade off coding efficiency for topic classification accuracy. As demonstrated by Hillard et al. (2008), as well as Collingwood and Wilkerson (2012), significant improvements in accuracy can be obtained by leveraging the insights about classification confidence.

In machine learning parlance, the accuracy-efficiency trade-off is known as *classification with reject option* (Herbei and Wegkamp, 2006). In many practical applications, it is better if the classifier refrains from making a prediction unless it is sufficiently confident. Intuitively, the accuracy and rejection are related; according to Chow (1970), the error rate decreases monotonically with increasing the rejection rate. The key, then, is devising the optimal optimal rejection rule.

In our experiments, we wish to control the number of documents, N, rejected by the classifier. These documents will be forwarded to a human coder, and hence directly determine the coding costs. We implemented four rejection strategies.

Single threshold. This simple strategy relies on classifier confidence estimates. Documents are ranked by confidences and the bottom-ranked N documents are rejected.

Ensemble disagreement. Classifier ensembles (Dietterich, 2000) provide a natural way of estimating confidences by means of agreement levels. The main idea is to reject the instances on which a certain number of classifiers disagree. While this strategy has been shown efficient by Collingwood and Wilkerson (2012), it does not control for the number of rejections. We therefore use a slightly different strategy, also considered by Hillard et al. (2008): using a 3-classifier ensemble, we sample the desired number of documents from the set of document on which at least one classifier disagrees. In the experimental section, to account for the randomness of the sampling, we run the procedure 100 times and report the average performance.

Ensemble threshold. Inspired by Fumera and Roli (2004), we compute the total confidence of a 3-classifier ensemble as a product of the individual classifiers' confidences.

Optimized thresholds. This is a more elaborate rejection strategy that leverages the hierarchical structure as well as confidences between subtopics. A document is rejected if either:

1. Its major topic confidence is less than a threshold p_1. The intuition here is that, if a prediction has low confidence on the major topic level, then it is most likely erroneous;

2. Both its subtopic confidence is less than p_2 and the difference to the second-highest confidence subtopic is less than p_3. The intuition is that, in addition to the classifier confidence, what signals classification error are the situations in which the confidences for the two most confident classes are too close.

We optimize thresholds p_1, p_2, and p_3 on a held-out validation set to maximize accuracy score, while fixing the maximum number of documents the model is allowed to reject.

5 Experimental Evaluation

In this section, we report on the results for the different classification models and rejection strategies on the Croatian Policy Agendas Project dataset.

5.1 Setup

To obtain more reliable performance estimates, we use 5-fold cross-validation, and report the mean and standard deviation of each evaluation measure across the five folds. We report micro- and macro-averaged F1-scores (denoted F_1^{μ} and F_1^{M}, respectively), Cohen's kappa coefficient (Cohen, 1960), and the AC1 coefficient (Gwet, 2002). All model hyperparameters are tuned using grid search on a held-out validation set.

5.2 Classification Accuracy

Classification performance for all our models is given in Table 5. The LR-based models outperform the other two considered models on both hierarchy levels. We observe that, on the major topic level, the OVR-based models considerably outperform OVO-based models. However, on the subtopic level, both approaches perform comparably. Another observation is that, on the subtopic level, the best models are those that use hierarchy.

In addition to the individual models, we also experiment with an ensemble comprised of LR-OVR-H, LR-OVO-H, and XGB-H classifiers. The ensemble employs the majority voting strategy, while in case of ties it falls back to the prediction of the best-performing individual classifier (LR-OVR-H). The ensemble performs comparably to, or numerically outperforms, the LR-OVR-H model. The best micro F1-score is 0.77 and 0.68 for the major topic and subtopics, respectively.

In Table 6 we present results of the best-performing individual model (LR-OVR-H) for the major topics. We observe that those major topics on which the classifier performs the worst are also those with the least number of training instances. Table 7 shows the performance of LR-OVR-H on the 10 best-performing subtopics. As for the worst-performing subtopics, these have a score of 0 due to data sparsity (less than 15 training instances). These include, e.g., *Juvenile Crime (1206)* and *Rural Housing (1404)*, each with only 7 instances.

5.3 Thresholds

Our models use a number of thresholds for hierarchical classification and postprocessing rules, op-

Model	Subtopics				Major topics			
	F_1^μ	F_1^M	κ	AC1	F_1^μ	F_1^M	κ	AC1
GNB-H	$0.41 \pm .01$	$0.31 \pm .01$	$0.40 \pm .01$	$0.41 \pm .01$	$0.57 \pm .01$	$0.50 \pm .01$	$0.53 \pm .01$	$0.57 \pm .01$
LR-OVO-H	$0.61 \pm .01$	$0.50 \pm .01$	$0.61 \pm .01$	$0.61 \pm .01$	$0.75 \pm .01$	$0.69 \pm .02$	$0.72 \pm .01$	$0.75 \pm .01$
XGB-H	$0.58 \pm .02$	$0.46 \pm .03$	$0.57 \pm .02$	$0.58 \pm .02$	$0.71 \pm .01$	$0.69 \pm .03$	$0.68 \pm .01$	$0.71 \pm .01$
LR-OVR-H	$0.65 \pm .01$	$0.55 \pm .02$	$0.65 \pm .01$	$0.65 \pm .01$	$\mathbf{0.77} \pm .01$	$\mathbf{0.75} \pm .01$	$\mathbf{0.75} \pm .01$	$\mathbf{0.77} \pm .01$
LR-OVR-F	$0.65 \pm .01$	$0.54 \pm .01$	$0.65 \pm .01$	$0.65 \pm .01$	$0.74 \pm .01$	$0.71 \pm .02$	$0.72 \pm .01$	$0.74 \pm .01$
Ensemble	$\mathbf{0.68} \pm .01$	$\mathbf{0.56} \pm .01$	$\mathbf{0.67} \pm .01$	$\mathbf{0.68} \pm .01$	$\mathbf{0.77} \pm .01$	$\mathbf{0.75} \pm .02$	$\mathbf{0.75} \pm .01$	$\mathbf{0.77} \pm .01$

Table 5: Classifiers' performances and standard deviations on major topics (22) and subtopics (208)

Topic	# docs	F_1	κ
Macroeconomics (1)	410	$0.72 \pm .05$	$0.71 \pm .05$
Civil Rights ... (2)	224	$0.76 \pm .05$	$0.75 \pm .05$
Health (3)	295	$0.82 \pm .01$	$0.82 \pm .01$
Agriculture (4)	397	$0.77 \pm .03$	$0.75 \pm .03$
Labor ... (5)	202	$0.76 \pm .04$	$0.75 \pm .04$
Education (6)	222	$0.84 \pm .04$	$0.83 \pm .04$
Environment (7)	199	$0.73 \pm .04$	$0.72 \pm .04$
Energy (8)	225	$0.87 \pm .03$	$0.86 \pm .03$
Immigration ... (9)	29	$0.51 \pm .15$	$0.51 \pm .15$
Transportation (10)	356	$0.80 \pm .02$	$0.79 \pm .02$
Law, Crime ... (12)	711	$0.82 \pm .02$	$0.80 \pm .02$
Social Welfare (13)	191	$0.68 \pm .06$	$0.67 \pm .06$
Community (14)	245	$0.76 \pm .03$	$0.75 \pm .03$
Banking (15)	566	$0.75 \pm .01$	$0.73 \pm .02$
Defense (16)	437	$0.75 \pm .04$	$0.74 \pm .04$
Space, Science (17)	184	$0.75 \pm .02$	$0.74 \pm .02$
Foreign Trade (18)	206	$0.73 \pm .03$	$0.73 \pm .03$
International (19)	623	$0.77 \pm .02$	$0.75 \pm .02$
Government op. (20)	1253	$0.74 \pm .01$	$0.68 \pm .01$
Public lands (21)	298	$0.84 \pm .03$	$0.84 \pm .04$
Cultural Policy ... (23)	91	$0.67 \pm .09$	$0.67 \pm .09$
Other (99)	14	$0.59 \pm .10$	$0.59 \pm .10$

Table 6: Results by topic on the major topic level

Topic	# docs	F_1	κ
Drugs ... (342)	21	$0.96 \pm .05$	$0.96 \pm .05$
Gender ... (202)	22	$0.95 \pm .10$	$0.95 \pm .10$
Court ... (1204)	344	$0.92 \pm .02$	$0.92 \pm .02$
Alternative ... (806)	22	$0.91 \pm .11$	$0.91 \pm .11$
Price control ... (110)	26	$0.89 \pm .05$	$0.89 \pm .05$
Trade ... (1802)	19	$0.87 \pm .19$	$0.87 \pm .19$
Census ... (2013)	25	$0.86 \pm .17$	$0.86 \pm .16$
Monetary ... (104)	30	$0.86 \pm .03$	$0.86 \pm .03$
Drinking water ... (701)	20	$0.85 \pm .11$	$0.85 \pm .11$
Water ... (2104)	171	$0.85 \pm .04$	$0.84 \pm .04$

Table 7: Results for 10 best-predicted subtopics

timized on held-out datasets. Some insights into model behavior and nature of the task can be obtained by inspecting the optimal threshold values.

The optimal values for the postprocessing rules' thresholds are such that the rules are effectively never activated. This is likely because the cases where the rules could improve the accuracy are much less frequent than those where they could harm, so overall it is better never to activate them.

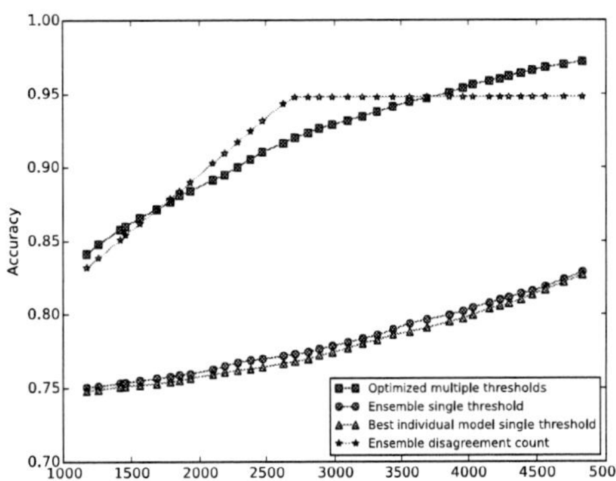

Figure 1: Acceptance-rejection curves for the different rejection strategies

The optimal value for the hierarchy threshold is very low (α=0.01). This suggests that, when calculating the joint confidence, much more weight is given to the major topic decision. This result is in line with the expectation that major topic classifiers are more reliable than subtopic classifiers.

5.4 Rejection Strategy

We evaluate the different rejection strategies to see which one offers the best accuracy-effort trade-off. To quantitatively assess this trade-off, we adopt the Accuracy-Rejection curves (ARC) proposed by Nadeem et al. (2010). The ARC shows the accuracy of a classifier as a function of its rejection rate (number of documents forwarded to human coders). A good rejection strategy will reach high accuracy levels even for low rejection rates.

The plots for various strategies described in Section 4.6 are given in Figure 1. The strategy of optimizing several thresholds to yield maximum accuracy significantly outperforms the two single-threshold strategies. Moreover, it performs comparably to the ensemble disagreement-based approach, even though it requires only a single classifier. The ensemble disagreement approach levels out at about 2600 documents because that is the number of documents that satisfy its agreement condition; even if the maximal allowed number of documents to reject is higher, it can never reject more than 2600. Before that point, however, it provides the optimal rejection strategy. These results suggest that it might be beneficial to combine the ensemble disagreement and optimized thresholds strategies. The results also show that, if relying on the ensemble disagreement strategy, manually checking about 30% of the data set (2300/7300) would yield a substantial improvement in accuracy from 77% to 90%.

6 Conclusion

We addressed the task of supervised topic classification of Croatian political texts, undertaken as part of the recently launched Croatian Policy Agendas Project. We built a new dataset consisting of 7300 titles, manually coded according to the Comparative Agendas Project codebook. On this dataset, we experimented with a number of machine learning models, and investigated to what extent the models can benefit from including hierarchy information or postprocessing rules. We learned that, on this dataset, a hierarchical approach indeed performs better. Rules however, did not bring any improvement to our models. We also experimented with different rejection strategies, aiming to optimize the accuracy-efficiency trade-off. We find that an ensemble disagreement-based method and our proposed method that optimizes multiple thresholds perform comparably well.

A possible venue of future work is the combination of different rejection strategies. Another promising possibility is the use of the most recent state-of-the-art models for text classification such as convolutional neural networks (CNN) or recurrent neural networks (RNN). Finally, it would be interesting to see whether the performance could be improved further by supplying full document texts and additional meta-data.

Acknowledgments. The Croatian Policy Agendas Project is funded by the European Social Fund; more details can be found on www.cepis.hr. This work was also in part supported by the Unity Through Knowledge Fund of the Croatian Science Foundation, under the grant 19/15: "EVEnt Retrieval Based on semantically Enriched Structures for Interactive user Tasks (EVERBEST)". We thank the reviewers for their helpful suggestions.

References

Quinn Albaugh, Julie Sevenans, Stuart Soroka, and Peter John Loewen. 2013. The automated coding of policy agendas: A dictionary-based approach. In *6th Annual Comparative Agendas Conference, Atnwerp, Beligum.*

Frank R Baumgartner, Christoffer Green-Pedersen, and Bryan D Jones. 2006. Comparative studies of policy agendas. *Journal of European Public Policy*, 13(7):959–974.

William L Benoit. 2011. Content analysis in political communication. *The sourcebook for political communication research: methods, measures, and analytical techniques*, pages 268–279.

Shaun Bevan. 2014. Gone fishing: The creation of the comparative agendas project master codebook. Technical report, Mannheim: Mannheimer Zentrum für Europäische Sozialforschung.

David M Blei. 2012. Probabilistic topic models. *Communications of the ACM*, 55(4):77–84.

Tianqi Chen and Carlos Guestrin. 2016. Xgboost: A scalable tree boosting system. *arXiv preprint arXiv:1603.02754.*

Chao K Chow. 1970. On optimum recognition error and reject tradeoff. *Information Theory, IEEE Transactions on*, 16(1):41–46.

Jacob Cohen. 1960. A coefficient of agreement for nominal scales. *Educational and psychological measurement*, 20(1):37–46.

Loren Collingwood and John Wilkerson. 2012. Trade-offs in accuracy and efficiency in supervised learning methods. *Journal of Information Technology & Politics*, 9(3):298–318.

Thomas G Dietterich. 2000. Ensemble methods in machine learning. In *Multiple classifier systems*, pages 1–15. Springer.

Scott E Adler and John Wilkerson. 2006. Congressional bills project - technical report. Technical report, University of Washington.

Rong-En Fan, Kai-Wei Chang, Cho-Jui Hsieh, Xiang-Rui Wang, and Chih-Jen Lin. 2008. LIBLINEAR: A library for large linear classification. *Journal of Machine Learning Research*, 9:1871–1874.

Giorgio Fumera and Fabio Roli. 2004. Analysis of error-reject trade-off in linearly combined multiple classifiers. *Pattern Recognition*, 37(6):1245–1265.

Mikel Galar, Alberto Fernández, Edurne Barrenechea, Humberto Bustince, and Francisco Herrera. 2011. An overview of ensemble methods for binary classifiers in multi-class problems: Experimental study on one-vs-one and one-vs-all schemes. *Pattern Recognition*, 44(8):1761–1776.

Justin Grimmer and Brandon M Stewart. 2013. Text as data: The promise and pitfalls of automatic content analysis methods for political texts. *Political Analysis*, 21(3):267–297.

Justin Grimmer. 2010. A bayesian hierarchical topic model for political texts: Measuring expressed agendas in senate press releases. *Political Analysis*, 18(1):1–35.

Kilem Gwet. 2002. Kappa statistic is not satisfactory for assessing the extent of agreement between raters. *Statistical methods for inter-rater reliability assessment*, 1(6):1–6.

Radu Herbei and Marten H Wegkamp. 2006. Classification with reject option. *Canadian Journal of Statistics*, 34(4):709–721.

Dustin Hillard, Stephen Purpura, and John Wilkerson. 2007. An active learning framework for classifying political text. In *Annual Meeting of the Midwest Political Science Association, Chicago*.

Dustin Hillard, Stephen Purpura, and John Wilkerson. 2008. Computer-assisted topic classification for mixed-methods social science research. *Journal of Information Technology & Politics*, 4(4):31–46.

Ole R Holsti. 1969. *Content analysis for the social sciences and humanities*. Addison-Wesley.

Daniel J Hopkins and Gary King. 2010. A method of automated nonparametric content analysis for social science. *American Journal of Political Science*, 54(1):229–247.

Peter John. 2006. The policy agendas project: a review. *Journal of European Public Policy*, 13(7):975–986.

John W Kingdon and James A Thurber. 1984. *Agendas, alternatives, and public policies*, volume 45. Little, Brown Boston.

Klaus Krippendorff. 2012. *Content analysis: An introduction to its methodology*. Sage.

Nikola Ljubešić and Tomaž Erjavec. 2011. hrWaC and slWac: Compiling web corpora for Croatian and Slovene. In Ivan Habernal and Václav Matousek, editors, *Text, Speech and Dialogue - 14th International Conference, TSD 2011, Pilsen, Czech Republic, September 1-5, 2011. Proceedings*, Lecture Notes in Computer Science, pages 395–402. Springer.

Mislav Malenica, Tomislav Šmuc, Jan Šnajder, and Bojana Dalbelo Bašić. 2008. Language morphology offset: Text classification on a Croatian–English parallel corpus. *Information processing & management*, 44(1):325–339.

Tomas Mikolov, Ilya Sutskever, Kai Chen, Greg S Corrado, and Jeff Dean. 2013. Distributed representations of words and phrases and their compositionality. In *Advances in neural information processing systems*, pages 3111–3119.

Jeff Mitchell and Mirella Lapata. 2010. Composition in distributional models of semantics. *Cognitive science*, 34(8):1388–1429.

Malik Sajjad Ahmed Nadeem, Jean-Daniel Zucker, and Blaise Hanczar. 2010. Accuracy-rejection curves (arcs) for comparing classification methods with a reject option. In *MLSB*, pages 65–81.

Stephen Purpura and Dustin Hillard. 2006. Automated classification of congressional legislation. In *Proceedings of the 2006 international conference on Digital government research*, pages 219–225. Digital Government Society of North America.

Kevin M Quinn, Burt L Monroe, Michael Colaresi, Michael H Crespin, and Dragomir R Radev. 2006. An automated method of topic-coding legislative speech over time with application to the 105th-108th us senate. In *Midwest Political Science Association Meeting*, pages 1–61.

Kevin M Quinn, Burt L Monroe, Michael Colaresi, Michael H Crespin, and Dragomir R Radev. 2010. How to analyze political attention with minimal assumptions and costs. *American Journal of Political Science*, 54(1):209–228.

Fabrizio Sebastiani. 2002. Machine learning in automated text categorization. *ACM computing surveys (CSUR)*, 34(1):1–47.

Jan Šnajder, Bojana Dalbelo Bašić, and Marko Tadić. 2008. Automatic acquisition of inflectional lexica for morphological normalisation. *Information Processing & Management*, 44(5):1720–1731.

Robert Philip Weber. 1990. *Basic content analysis*. Number 49. Sage.

Searching Four-Millenia-Old Digitized Documents:
A Text Retrieval System for Egyptologists

Estíbaliz Iglesias-Franjo and **Jesús Vilares**
Grupo Lengua Y Sociedad de la Información (LYS), Departamento de Computación
Facultade de Informática, Universidade da Coruña
Campus de A Coruña, 15071 – A Coruña (Spain)
{estibaliz.ifranjo, jesus.vilares}@udc.es

Abstract

Progress made in recent years has led to a growing interest in Digital Heritage. This article focuses on Egyptology and, more specifically, the study and preservation of ancient Egyptian scripts. We present a Text Retrieval system developed specifically to work with hieroglyphic texts. We intend to make it freely available to the research community. To the best of our knowledge this is the first tool of its kind.

1 Introduction

Until recently, the development of Information Retrieval (IR) systems has mainly focused on contemporary languages. From a socio-economic point of view, this makes perfect sense since our needs, as users, are connected to our everyday tasks, which we develop in our languages. Why should we pay attention to dead languages such as Ancient Egyptian? Our civilization was born in Mesopotamia and Egypt, and the culture of Pharaohs has fascinated us for decades and even centuries. Even nowadays, Egyptology continues to be one of the major branches of Archaeology and it is not unusual to find, from time to time, that new discoveries in this field open our news bulletins. Moreover, Egyptian is the longest-attested language, it thus becoming a particularly valuable object of research for Diachronic Linguists (Loprieno, 1995). However, neither should we forget its intrinsic value as one of the most representative elements of one of the most important human civilizations of all time. Egyptian Hieroglyphic script is a major component of our cultural heritage and, for that very reason, we should put particular emphasis on its preservation and study.

At this point, we need to introduce *Digital Heritage*, the scientific area that focuses on the use of computing and information technologies for the preservation and study of the human cultural legacy for current and future generations.

In this context, this work describes an open source Text Information Retrieval (TIR) system designed specifically for the processing of Egyptian Hieroglyphic scripts. To the best of our knowledge this is the first tool of its kind.

The rest of the paper is structured as follows. Firstly, Section 2 makes an introduction to Ancient Egyptian. Secondly, Section 3 describes how to encode hieroglyphic texts. Previous related work is outlined in Section 4. Next, the requirements of our system are analysed in Section 5, which is then described in Section 6. Finally, Section 7 presents our contributions and future work.

2 Language and Writing System

2.1 History

As previously commented, Egyptian (Allen, 2014; Loprieno, 1995; Cervelló-Autuori, 2015) is the longest-attested human language, with a documented history that spans several millenia, from about 3300 BC until the present day, when it is still used by the Coptic Christian Church in its rituals. Of course, it has undergone profound changes throughout its lifetime. So, we can distinguish two main phases in its development: *Earlier Egyptian*, whose writing system corresponds to the stereotypical image we have of Egyptian and that lasted as a spoken language from its origins until after 1300 BC; and *Later Egyptian*, which started to be used at that time and, after continuous evolution, survived until the 11th century AD as a productive language and until today as the ritual language of the Coptic Church. Our work focuses on Earlier Egyptian because of its archaelogical interest, in particular in the so-called *Middle or Classic Egyptian*, which remained as the traditional language

Proceedings of the 10th SIGHUM Workshop on Language Technology for Cultural Heritage, Social Sciences, and Humanities (LaTeCH), pages 22–31,
Berlin, Germany, August 11, 2016. ©2016 Association for Computational Linguistics

of hieroglyphic inscriptions until the fifth century AD, thus still being widely used in royal inscriptions, religious literature and monuments. From now on, unless we specify the contrary, we will be referring to *Middle Egyptian* when using the terms "Ancient Egyptian" or just "Egyptian" for short.

2.2 Characteristics

Egyptian belongs to the Afro-Asiatic language family, the same as contemporary languages such as Arabic, Hebrew and Berber, although Egyptian constitutes a subfamily of its own.

As in the case of early Arabic and Hebrew, Egyptian is a *consonantal* language since its words are formed from a consonantal root with vowels being used to indicate inflectional or derived forms. For the same reason, only consonants are written.

Its writing system is *pictographic* since its signs, or *hieroglyphs*, consist of symbols portraying beings and elements of the Egyptian world: parts of the human body (⊙: an *eye*), plants (⌡: a *reed*), animals (⍦: a *pintail duck*), objects (⍦: a *mast with sail*), etc.

It is also *logographic* since some, but not all, symbols have a meaning that corresponds, directly or indirectly (e.g. through a cultural, metonymic or metaphoric relation), to the same real-word element they reproduce. For example: ⊙, an *eye* for *eye*; and ⍦, a *mast with sail* for *wind*.

Egyptian writing system is *phonographic* too, since part of its signs depict sounds. For example, ⊙ for the phoneme /χ/, transliterated as *ḫ*.

Finally, Ancient Egyptian had an *inherently "open"* writing system with no fixed alphabet. The number of available signs progressively increased from about 800 hieroglyphs in the Old Kingdom period to more than 5,000 in the Greco-Roman period. Moreover, new symbols and variants continue to be discovered when ancient texts are analyzed (Rosmorduc, 2003a).

2.3 Sign Types

In contrast with the formerly-held common belief that Egyptian writing system is a purely symbolic one, its script is mainly phonetical and combines different types of signs.

The first group are the *phonograms* or *phonetic signs*. In these signs the image carries no meaning whatsoever, being used by convention to represent the sounds of language. We can distinguish

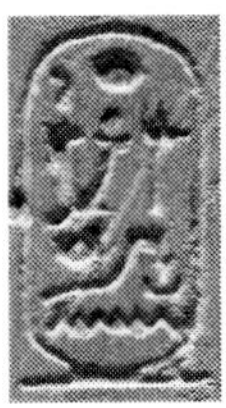

Figure 1: The four possible ways of writing the prenomen of Ramesses II by varying its direction.

three types of phonograms according to the number of consonantal sounds represented, from one to three: *uniliterals*, e.g. ⊙ (*ḫ*),[1]; *biliterals*, e.g. ⍦ (*s3*); and *triliterals*, e.g. ⍦ (*ḫpr*).

The other group are the *semagrams*. In this case, the image of the sign participates directly in the codification and the significance of the linguistic message. In turn, we can distinguish two types of semagrams. Firstly, the *ideograms* (aka *logograms*) or *lexical signs*. They represent the things they actually depict and, consequently, are read that way. For example ⊙, that depicts an eye and represents the word *irt*, which means "*eye*"; and ⍦, which depicts a scribe's kit and is read *sḫ3*, used for "*write*" and related words. The second type are the *determinatives* or *semantic signs*. These signs are placed at the end of a word to indicate that it corresponds to a given semantic group. They are of great importance since they allow the reader to differentiate between words that have the same consonantal representation but different meaning. Unlike ideograms, determinatives are silent so they are not read. As an example, given the above-mentioned ideogram ⍦, and the determinatives ⊙ (category [WRITING - ABSTRACT NOTIONS]) and ⍦ (category [MAN - HUMAN BEING]), the word ⍦ means "*to write*" while the word ⍦ means "*scribe*".

It should be noted that the same glyph may belong to more than one category at once. For example, depending on the context, ≈ can be interpreted as the biliteral phonogram *mw*, the ideogram *mw* (which means "*water*") or the determinative [WATER - LIQUIDS].

2.4 Writing Direction

Egyptian writing system is very flexible with regard to its *direction of writing*, which is not fixed.

---

[1]Where appropriate we will indicate the transliteration corresponding to the hieroglyphic text in question.

Hieroglyphic texts can be found written in horizontal rows, as with English and Arabic, or in vertical columns, as with traditional Japanese, Chinese and Mongolian. Moreover, although they are always read from top to bottom, they may follow a left-to-right ordering, as with English and Mongolian, or a right-to-left ordering, as with Arabic and Japanese. The reason for such a variety comes from the fact that Egyptian hieroglyphic script had a marked artistic nature (Cervelló-Autuori, 2015). It was intended to be carved or painted in monuments, walls, jewels, etc., even taking part of the scene itself (Rosmorduc, 2003a), and since one of the main characteristics of Egyptian art was its symmetry, they required their writing to adapt to it. Figure 1 presents a good example of its variety.

2.5 Sign Arrangement

Another remarkable feature is *continuous writing*, in which all the words run together with no dividers to separate words or phrases. This is also characteristic of some contemporary languages such as Chinese or Japanese, where no word separators are used. For example, in the case of the text ⟨hieroglyphs⟩ (*iw ꜣpdw ḥr nht*), it stands for *"The birds are on the sycamore"*.

Additionally, hieroglyphs were not arranged one after the other, in a linear way, as in the case of our writing system. Instead, scribes gathered them in so-called *groups*, trying to fill the space available neatly, in a way which resembles contemporary Hangul Korean script. Thus, as shown above, *"sycamore"* was not written ⟨hieroglyphs⟩ (*nht*), but ⟨hieroglyphs⟩ instead.

This arrangement depended, of course, on the words to be written, but also on several principles or heuristics (Cervelló-Autuori, 2015) the scribe followed in order to obtain the most harmonious and aesthetic arrangement possible.

3 Encoding Hieroglyphic Texts

Egyptologists and Linguists needed a practical way to represent hieroglyphic texts without having to re-draw their signs. The problem was solved by using regular characters to encode those texts.

3.1 Gardiner's List and the Extended Library

Named after its creator, the Egyptologist Sir Alan Gardiner (1957), *Gardiner's List*, a standard reference in the study of Egyptian, classifies its signs

Symbol	Operation	Example
−	concatenation	Q3-X1-Z4-N1
:	subordination	X1:Z4:N1
*	juxtaposition	Q3*X1:Z4
( )	grouping	Q3*(X1:Z4):N1

Table 1: Sign arrangement operators in MdC.

into 26 categories according to their drawing, each one identified with a letter: category A corresponds to *"Man and his occupations"* (⟨hieroglyphs⟩...); B to *"Woman and her occupations"* (⟨hieroglyphs⟩...); etc. In turn, hieroglyphs within each category are numbered sequentially so a given sign can be coded using the letter of its category and its corresponding number. For example, the code E8 corresponds to the sign ⟨hieroglyph⟩ (*"goat kid"*), the eigth element of category E (*"Mammals"*). This classification includes the most common hieroglyphs (743 signs and 20 variants), enabling us to encode a significant proportion of the texts.

In the 1990s, this list was largely extended to include newly identified signs and variants, thus becoming the so-called *Extended Library* (Grimal et al., 2000), with 4706 symbols. Gardiner's classification was not modified since new signs were numbered after the existing ones, and variants of existing signs were codified by attaching an extra letter to its code. For example, the symbol ⟨hieroglyph⟩ (code E8a) was added as variant of ⟨hieroglyph⟩ (code E8).

3.2 Manuel de Codage and its Dialects

In the 1980s, the *International Association of Egyptologists (IAE)*[2] formed a committee with the aim of developing a standard encoding system for the digitalization of hieroglyphic texts. The resulting document was the *Manuel de Codage (MdC)* (Buurman et al., 1988), an evolution of *Gardiner's List* (later adapted to the *Extended Library*) where new codes and rules were added for the accurate representation of hieroglyphs and other features of Egyptian writing system by using ASCII text. Next, we introduce an overview of the most significant additions.

3.2.1 Sign Operators

Table 1 shows, in order of precedence, the basic operators for arranging the signs. Thus, returning to our previous example, ⟨hieroglyphs⟩ (*"sycamore"*) is N35:O4*X1-M1.

---

[2] http://www.iae-egyptology.org/

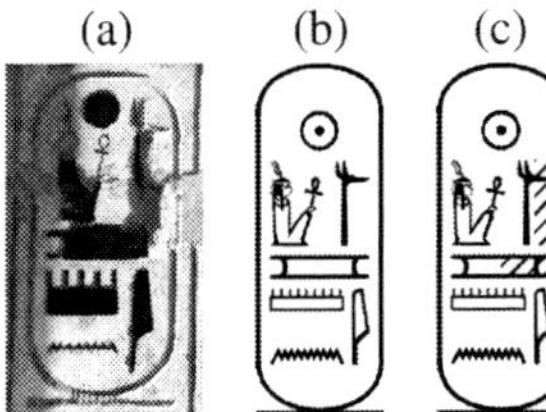

(b)   `<-N5-F12*C10-N36-M17*(Y5:N35)->`

(c)   `<-N5-(F12#13)*C10-N36#13-M17*(Y5:N35)->`

Figure 2: *(a)* Photo of a damaged cartouche showing the prenomem of Pharaoh Ramesses III; *(b)* MdC code corresponding to the undamaged cartouche and the output obtained from it with JSESH; and *(c)* MdC code corresponding to the shaded cartouche and its corresponding output.

Figure 3: Example of a handwritten entry, then printed lithographically, from Faulkner (2006).

3.2.2 Damaged Texts

The majority of the hieroglyphics that have survived until the present day have suffered the effects of time, exposure, vandalism, etc. So, one of the specific problems to be faced in this context was the representation of these texts in the most informative way. This matter was solved by the use of *shades*, implemented as special marks attached to the sign codes and which allow us to express whether the sign or even its presence is recognizable or not, how many signs are affected, which parts of them are damaged, etc. Figure 2 shows a simple example of their use.

3.2.3 Non-Hieroglyphic Text

MdC includes encoding support for combining hieroglyphs, transliterations, translations and other types of annotation within the same text. It assumes that all text is hieroglyphic unless it is enclosed between a given set of marks; for example '+l' (opening) and '+s' (closing) for enclosing regular text encoded in Latin script.

3.2.4 Dialects

Although the MdC should have been taken as the encoding standard for hieroglyphic text editors (see Section 4), the developers of these systems instead established their own particular spec-

ifications taking the MdC as their base, thus giving birth to different *dialects*. This meant that, in practice, with a few exceptions, a text written with a given program can not be opened and edited with another one unless it has been previously rewritten in the new notation. This fact not only makes it difficult to share documents between researchers and establish common corpora (Gozzoli, 2013), but also decreases the lifespan of those dialects and their encoded documents because of their dependence on that particular software they were created with and the fonts they use (Nederhof, 2013).

3.3 Unicode

As stated by Mark-Jan Nederhof (2013), the case of the inclusion of Egyptian Hieroglyphs in Unicode is a very good illustration of the troubles derived from trying to adapt other writing systems to Egyptian and its peculiarities. The process took more than a decade from the first proposal to its inclusion in Unicode 5.2. The list of available signs contains 1071 hieroglyphs (range U+13000..U+1342F) including the original Gardiner's List, its supplements and some other symbols (Everson and Richmond, 2007). Unfortunately, Unicode hieroglyphs encoding is limited by the lack of important features such as the availability of shading mechanisms, sign grouping or varied writing directionality (Richmond, 2015), thus making it a non-practical choice for many tasks.

3.4 Revised Encoding Scheme

Seeking to solve the current limitations of MdC, the above-mentioned software- and font-dependence of its dialects, and the formatting limitations of Unicode hieroglyphs, Mark-Jan Nederhof (2013) proposed the so-called *Revised Encoding Scheme (RES)*, which lacks such dependences and includes new sign operators. Although it requires more sophisticated processing than the MdC because of its added complexity, future hieroglyphic text processing systems will be probably influenced by this new scheme (Rosmorduc, 2015).

4 Related Work

The research community working on the application of Computer Science to Egyptology is small (Polis et al., 2013b). In the case of the computer processing of hieroglyphic text, it has been closely linked to the development of classic-style text editors (Gozzoli, 2013; Diop, 1992; Grimal, 1990). Since there were no hieroglyphic typewriters, scholars had to rely on handwritten texts when writing and sharing documents, a practical limitation that could easily lead to misinterpretations. Even in the case of books, the hieroglyphic texts printed in their pages were very complex and costly typographical transcriptions or, most of the time, mere lithographical copies of those handwritten by their authors, as shown in Figure 3, for example. Thus, the need for hieroglyphic text processing software was peremptory.

Among the specialized, and scarce, text processor software developed for this purpose, we should highlight two tools in particular. Firstly, GLYPH (Gozzoli, 2013), developed by Jan Buurman, which laid the foundations of future hieroglyphic text processors. It was published for DOS in 1986 and subsequently evolved and migrated to other operating systems: MACSCRIBE for Macintosh and WINGLYPH for Windows (3.1 and 95). The second tool we want to cite is JSESH, developed by Serge Rosmorduc (2014), which is, currently and in all probability, the most widely used word processor in Egyptology.

With regard to Text Mining and Natural Language Processing (NLP), Egyptian is, basically, a virgin territory waiting to be explored, namely because of the lack of computer corpora to work with (Rosmorduc, 2015). The reason for it is that hieroglyphic encoding is very time-consuming (Rosmorduc, 2015; Nederhof, 2015). However, those advances recently made in projects *Thesaurus Linguae Aegyptiae (TLA)* (Dils and Feder, 2013) and *Ramsès* (Polis et al., 2013a; Polis and Rosmorduc, 2013) are promising. Anyway, a few works about automatic transliterion (Barthélemy and Rosmorduc, 2011), language modeling (Nederhof and Rahman, 2015a) and text categorization (Gohy et al., 2013) can be found.

Recent advances in Egyptian OCR are of interest (Franken and van Gemert, 2013; Nederhof, 2015), since OCR would greatly reduce the cost of encoding these texts (Piotrowski, 2012, Ch. 4).

5 Requirements of the System

Our goal has been to develop an IR system capable of operating on Egyptian texts. For this purpose, we have studied the nature of this language and its writing system, and consulted an expert Egyptologist to better understand the application domain. As a result, we established the following requirements:

1. **Simplicity**: It should be intuitive and easy to use, with a minimum learning curve.

2. **Content indexing**: The system must be able to index documents containing conventional text and hieroglyphic text. At first we will focus on those documents written with JSESH, thus covering a significant proportion of the digitalized contents currently available.

3. **Querying using MdC encoding**: In the case of hieroglyphs, users will input the query using MdC encoding, with which they are already familiarized.

4. **Display the query using glyphs**: In order to make it easier for the user, the system will display, in parallel, the input MdC query using pictograms.

5. **Querying using conventional text**: Since the documents contain both hieroglyphic and conventional text (encoded in Latin script), we also want to be able to submit conventional text queries.

6. **Submission of mixed queries**: The possibility of making queries combining both hieroglyphic and conventional text.

7. **Relevant documents retrieval**.

8. **Display of document contents**: The user should be able to access the content of the documents retrieved by the system and check why they have been retrieved.

6 Description of the System

The architecture of our IR system, currently available under a free license at `http://github.com/estibalizifranjo/hieroglyphs`, corresponds, in general, to a classic Text Retrieval system, as shown in Figure 4. Two main phases of functioning can be distinguished: firstly, the indexing of the document collection on which searches are to be performed and, secondly, the querying–retrieval process. Next, we describe those modules of the system involved in each of these phases.

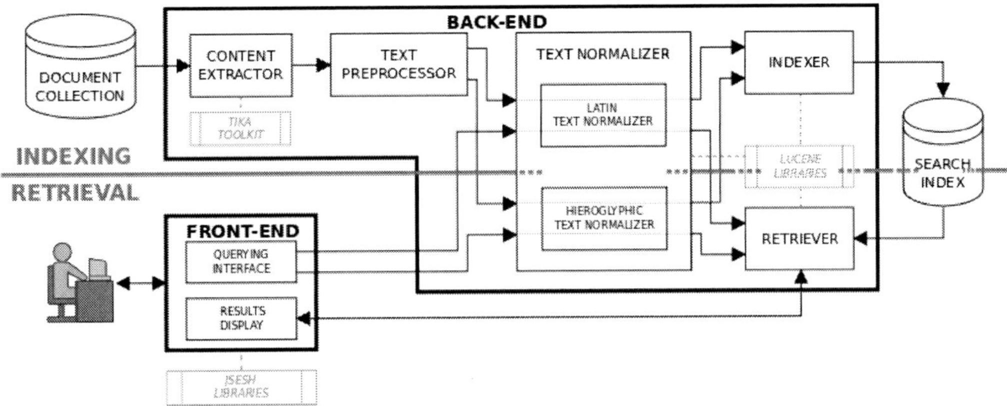

Figure 4: Schematic representation of the system: indexing and retrieval processes.

6.1 Phase 1: Indexing

It consists of extracting and indexing the content of the documents on which searches will be performed later.

6.1.1 Content Extraction

This module uses the Tika toolkit[3], which can detect and extract both text and metadata from a wide range of different file types (ODT, DOC, PDF, etc.), to extract the text of the documents.

6.1.2 Text Preprocessing

The obtained text is then preprocessed to separate conventional text from hieroglyphic text and to filter out irrelevant data. For this task the system applies a *pattern matching* approach. For instance, in the case of detecting pieces of unformatted conventional text, it uses a regular expression for identifying sequences of characters enclosed between the marks '+l' and '+s', corresponding to regular unformatted text, as explained in Section 3.2.3.

6.1.3 Conventional Text Normalization

The normalization components apply a series of *text operations* for tokenizing, conflating and generating the index terms of the input texts. The nature of such operations varies according to the type of text: regular text or hieroglyphs. For its implementation we have taken as our basis Apache Lucene.[4] In the case of conventional text, a standard processing is performed (Manning et al., 2008): firstly, a standard lexical analysis is applied for tokenizing the text, and the resulting terms are then conflated by lowercasing them and removing both stopwords and diacritics.

6.1.4 Hieroglyphic Text Normalization

Due to its peculiarities, hieroglyphic text is processed in a completely different way. The first problem is the lack of delimiters to separate words or phrases. Although MdC provides special markers for this purpose, in practice they are not used since they have no effect on the text graphical representation. As an initial solution, we have used *sign groups* (Section 2.5) as a working unit since they are delimited by '-' at encoding level. For example, the word $\overline{}$ (N35:O4*X1-M1) is composed of four signs but only two groups, so it would be tokenized into $\overline{}$ (N35:O4*X1) and (M1). This time input text will not be lowercased, since MdC encoding is case-sensitive, neither the punctuation marks will be removed, since they form part of MdC encoding.

6.1.5 Index Generation

Finally, the index structure is generated. In the case of the hieroglyphic text, the sign groups are indexed together with their occurrence positions within the text. This module has also been implemented using Lucene.

6.2 Phase 2: Querying–Retrieval

Two main sub-processes can be distinguished in this second phase, the querying process and the retrieval process, which can be controlled through the front-end interface of the system.

---

[3]http://tika.apache.org
[4]http://lucene.apache.org/core/

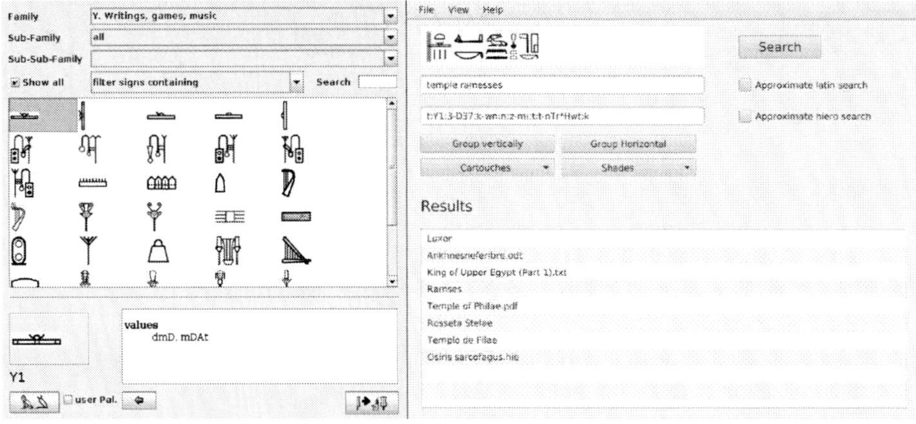

Figure 5: Screenshot of the front-end querying interface. A mixed query containing both Latin and hieroglyphic text (*top of right-hand panel*) has been composed, the latter with the assistance of the symbol palette (*left-hand panel*). The list of relevant documents retrieved by the system is already available (*bottom of right-hand panel*).

6.2.1 Querying

The user can query the indexed collection by using either hieroglyphics, regular text (in the Latin script) or a combination of both (*mixed* queries), that is, a query containing both hieroglyphic text and conventional text at the same time, such as that one shown in Figure 5, for example. The query normalization process is parallel to that performed during the indexing. In the case of hieroglyphic text, the *exact matching* mode requires the documents to contain exactly the same group sequence specified in the query (i.e. the same signs with the same arrangement), while the *approximate matching* mode allows the user to sub-specify the composition of a group (e.g. to require that a given group of the sequence contains a given sign but without specifying whether it contains any more symbols or their arrangement within the group).

6.2.2 Retrieval

Once the query has been normalized, the recovery module accesses the index looking for matches and identifies those documents of the collection that are relevant to the query. The current implementation combines two retrieval models (Manning et al., 2008): firstly, the relevant documents are selected by using a Boolean model and, then, a Vector Space model is used to score and rank those previously selected documents. The resulting document list will be returned and presented to the user.

6.2.3 Front-End Interface

Particular attention has been paid to the design of the interface to make its use as easy and intuitive as possible. As shown in the top of the right-hand panel of Figure 5, separate search forms are provided for conventional text (in the Latin script) and hieroglyphic text queries. In the case of the latter, those pictograms corresponding to the MdC code text being introduced will be automatically displayed so that the user can check them on the fly.

At this point, we decided to integrate additional features not considered in the original requirements, in order to improve the usability and flexibility of the interface. Following the example of the JSESH editing tool, our interface provides users, if required, with a palette of hieroglyphic signs that enables them to add symbols to the query by clicking on them, as shown in the left-hand panel of Figure 5. This palette also functions as a catalog of symbols organized according to Gardiner's List classification (Section 3.1), so the user can navigate through it and consult the information and variants associated with each symbol. The interface also provides several options for handling the hieroglyphic text, such as adding shadows or creating personalised palettes.

In the case of hieroglyphic queries, another possible choice for its input would have been to use a similar approach to that one proposed by Tetsuo Minohara (2010), which is based on the

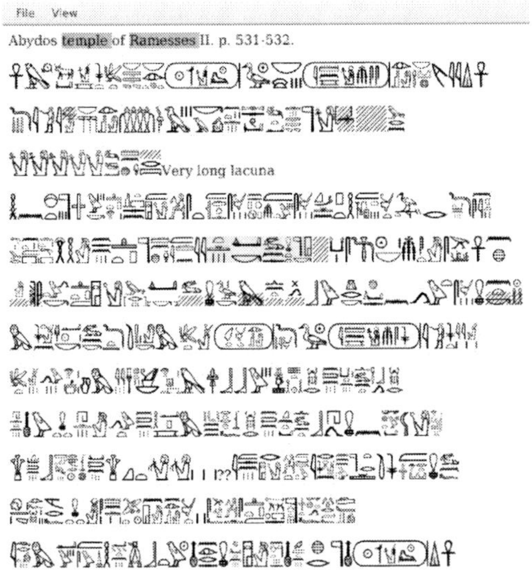

Figure 6: Content of one of the documents retrieved for our sample query, as presented by the system interface, which is highlighting the matchings found during the retrieval process.

Japanese Kanji writing method. However, this approach, although interesting, was not intuitive and too complex for a non-Japanese user.

At the same time, the interface is also responsible for presenting the user with the result of the search, as shown in the bottom of the right-hand panel of Figure 5. Moreover, it enables the user to access the content of these documents, which, if so required, will be displayed highlighting the matchings found during the retrieval process, as can be seen in Figure 6. Thus, the system provides the user with useful feedback about why the document has been retrieved.

For its implementation we have made use of the libraries provided with JSESH, including its symbol palette. This was intentional since, as previously explained in Section 4, JSESH is, currently, the most popular editing tool among the Egyptology community. This way, novice users of our system will find an interface with a very similar appearance and behavior to that of the editing tool they are already familiar with, thus greatly facilitating its use and minimizing the learning curve.

7   Conclusions and Future work

Ancient Egyptian Text Mining is still in the initial stages of development. We have presented in this work a Text Information Retrieval system specif-

ically designed to manage Egyptian hieroglyphic texts which, to the best of our knowledge, is the first tool of its kind. For its development we have taken into account the lexical and encoding characteristics of this language and its writing system. Apart from the conflation process to be applied in the case of the Egyptian text, we have taken special care with the design of the front-end interface in order to make it as intuitive and easy to use as possible for novel users, paying particular attention to the case of Egyptologists, its intended future users. Our first distribution have been released under a free license.

We intend to continue adding new features to the system. New input filters, for example, would allow the system to extend the range of source document types accepted as input: documents created with other hieroglyphic text editors, Unicode hieroglyphic text or, as in the case of this article, HieroTeX LaTeX documents (Rosmorduc, 2003b).

From an IR perspective, we would like to continue studying how to improve performance. One possible choice is the application of a more flexible retrieval solution using a single retrieval model instead of the current double-model 2-stage retrieval process. Classic Vector Space and Probabilistic models (Manning et al., 2008) are the first options. However, the very special and noisy nature of Egyptian writing system and the application context may suggest the use of other approaches: the use of standard character n-grams as a working unit, a solution successfully applied in both noisy contexts (Vilares et al., 2011) and languages whose writing systems share characteristics with Egyptian, such as Japanese (Ogawa and Matsuda, 1999), Chinese (Foo and Li, 2004), Korean (Lee and Ahn, 1996) or Arabic (Mustafa and Al-Radaideh, 2004); the use of so-called character s-grams (Järvelin et al., 2008), a generalization of the concept of n-gram by allowing *skips* during the matching process; the application of locality-based models (de Kretser and Moffat, 1999); or phonetic matching (Yasukawa et al., 2012). Closer to the NLP field, the development of *conflation mechanisms* based on lemmatization or morphological analysis (Piotrowski, 2012, Ch. 7) would be very useful. However, many of these solutions would require a further study of the language and its writing system, and the development of resources such as evaluation corpora, which were beyond the scope of this initial project, although

we intend to contact, in a close future, experts in
the field to try to solve these questions.

Acknowledgments

This research has been partially funded by the Spanish Ministry of Economy and Competitiveness (MINECO) through project FFI2014-51978-C2-2-R. We would like to thank Dr. Josep Cervelló Autuori, Director of the Institut d'Estudis del Pròxim Orient Antic (IEPOA) of the Universitat Autònoma de Barcelona for introducing us to the Ancient Egyptian script and acting as our fictional client. We would also like to thank Dr. Serge Rosmorduc, Associate of the Conservatoire National des Arts et Métiers (CNAM) for all his support when working with JSESH.

References

James P. Allen. 2014. *Middle Egyptian: An Introduction to the Language and Culture of Hieroglyphs (3rd Edition)*. Cambridge University Press.

François Barthélemy and Serge Rosmorduc. 2011. Intersection of multitape transducers vs. cascade of binary transducers: The example of Egyptian hieroglyphs transliteration. In *Proc. of the 9th International Workshop on Finite State Methods and Natural Language Processing (FSMNLP 2011)*, pp. 74–82. ACL.

Jan Buurman, Nicolas-Christophe Grimal, Michael Hainsworth, Jochen Hallof, and Dirk van der Plas. 1988. *Inventaire des signes hiéroglyphiques en vue de leur saisie informatique: manuel de codage des textes hiéroglyphiques en vue de leur saisie sur ordinateur*, volume 8 of *Mémoires de l'Académie des Inscriptions et Belles-Lettres*. De Boccard, Paris.

Josep Cervelló-Autuori. 2015. *Escrituras, Lengua y Cultura en el Antiguo Egipto*. El espejo y la lámpara. Edicions UAB.

Owen de Kretser and Alistair Moffat. 1999. Effective document presentation with a locality-based similarity heuristic. In *Proc. of 22nd Annual International ACM SIGIR Conference on Research and Development in Information Retrieval (SIGIR'99)*, pp. 113–120. ACM Press. DOI 10.1145/312624.312664.

Peter Dils and Frank Feder, 2013. In (Polis et al., 2013b), chapter The Thesaurus Linguae Aegyptiae. Review and Perspectives, pp. 11–23. Project website: http://aaew.bbaw.de/tla/ (visited on May 2016).

Cheikh M'Backé Diop. 1992. Hiéroglyphes et informatique. *ANKH: Revue d'Egyptologie et des Civilisations Africaines*, (1):105–121, February.

Michael Everson and Bob Richmond. 2007. Proposal to encode Egyptian Hieroglyphs in the SMP of the UCS. Working Group Document ISO/IEC JTC1/SC2/WG2 N3237 [L2/07-097]. Technical report, UTC (Unicode Technical Committee), Unicode Consortium, April. Unicode 8.0 hieroglyphs table available at: http://www.unicode.org/charts/PDF/U13000.pdf (visited on May 2016).

Raymond Oliver Faulkner. 2006. *Concise Dictionary of Middle Egyptian*. Griffith Institute.

Schubert Foo and Hui Li. 2004. Chinese word segmentation and its effect on Information Retrieval. *Information Processing and Management*, 40(1):161–190.

Morris Franken and Jan C. van Gemert. 2013. Automatic Egyptian hieroglyph recognition by retrieving images as texts. In *Proc. of the 21st ACM International Conference on Multimedia (MM'13)*, pp. 765–768. ACM.

Alan Henderson Gardiner. 1957. *Egyptian grammar: being an introduction to the study of hieroglyphs*. Griffith Institute, Ashmolean Museum, Oxford, 3rd ed., revised edition. A complete on-line version is available at: http://en.wikipedia.org/wiki/Gardiner's_sign_list (visited on May 2016).

Stéphanie Gohy, Benjamin Martin Leon, and Stéphane Polis, 2013. In (Polis et al., 2013b), chapter Automated text categorization in a dead language. The detection of genres in Late Egyptian, pp. 61–74.

Roberto Gozzoli, 2013. In (Polis et al., 2013b), chapter Hieroglyphic Text Processors, Manuel de Codage, Unicode and Lexicography, pp. 89–101.

Nicolas Grimal, Jochen Hallof, and Dirk van der Plas. 2000. *HIEROGLYPHICA: Sign List– Liste des Signes – Zeichenliste (2nd Edition)*, volume 1^2. Publications Interuniversitaires de Recherches Égyptologiques Informatisées, Utrecht–Paris. Second edition revised and enlarged by Jochen Hallof, Hans van den Berg and Gabriele Hallof. Online list available on: http://hieroglyphes.pagesperso-orange.fr/CCER-Hieroglyphica.htm (visited on May 2016).

Nicolas Grimal. 1990. Hiéroglyphes et ordinateurs. *BRISES. Bulletin de Recherches sur l'Information en Sciences Économiques Humaines et Sociales*, (15):57–60.

Antti Järvelin, Tuomas Talvensaari, and Anni Järvelin. 2008. Data driven methods for improving mono- and cross-lingual IR performance in noisy environments. In *Proc. of the Second Workshop on Analytics for Noisy Unstructured Text Data (AND'08)*, volume 303 of *ACM International Conference Proceeding Series*, pp. 75–82. ACM.

Joo Ho Lee and Jeong Soo Ahn. 1996. Using n-grams for Korean text retrieval. In *Proc. of the 19th Annual International ACM SIGIR Conference on Research and Development in Information Retrieval (SIGIR'96)*, pp. 216–224. ACM.

Antonio Loprieno. 1995. *Ancient Egyptian: A Linguistic Introduction.* Cambridge University Press.

Christopher D. Manning, Prabhakar Raghavan, and Hinrich Schütze. 2008. *Introduction to Information Retrieval.* Cambridge University Press.

Tatsuo Minohara. 2010. A writing system for the Ancient Egyptian hieroglyphs. In *Proc. of the 7th International Conference on Informatics and Systems (INFOS 2010)*, pp. 1–7. IEEE.

Suleiman H. Mustafa and Qasem A. Al-Radaideh. 2004. Using n-grams for Arabic text searching. *Journal of the American Society for Information Science and Technology (JASIST)*, 55(11):1002–1007.

Mark-Jan Nederhof and Fahrurrozi Rahman. 2015a. A probabilistic model of Ancient Egyptian writing. In *Proc. of the 12th International Conference on Finite State Methods and Natural Language Processing (FSMNLP 2015)*. ACL.

Mark-Jan Nederhof, 2013. In (Polis et al., 2013b), chapter The Manuel de Codage Encoding of Hieroglyphs Impedes Development of Corpora, pp. 103–110.

Mark-Jan Nederhof. 2015. OCR of handwritten transcriptions of Ancient Egyptian hieroglyphic text. In *Altertumswissenschaften in a Digital Age: Egyptology, Papyrology and Beyond (DHEgypt15). Leipzig, Germany, November 4-6, 2015.*

Yasushi Ogawa and Toru Matsuda. 1999. Overlapping statistical segmentation for effective indexing of Japanese text. *Information Processing and Management*, 35(4):463–480.

Michael Piotrowski. 2012. *Natural Language Processing for Historical Texts.* Synthesis Lectures on Human Language Technologies. Morgan & Claypool Publishers.

Stéphane Polis and Serge Rosmorduc, 2013. In (Polis et al., 2013b), chapter Building a Construction-Based Treebank of Late Egyptian. The Syntactic Layer in Ramses, pp. 45–59.

Stéphane Polis, Anne-Claude Honnay, and Jean Winand, 2013a. In (Polis et al., 2013b), chapter Building an Annotated Corpus of Late Egyptian. The Ramses Project: Review and Perspectives, pp. 25–44. Project website: http://www.egypto.ulg.ac.be/Ramses.htm. Beta online system: http://ramses.ulg.ac.be/ (both visited on May 2016).

Stéphane Polis, Jean Winand, and Todd Gillen, editors. 2013b. *Texts, Languages & Information Technology in Egyptology: Selected Papers from the Meeting of the Computer Working Group of the International Association of Egyptologists (Informatique & Égyptologie), Liège, 6-8 July 2010*, volume 9 of *Collection Ægyptiaca Leodiensia.* Presses Universitaires de Liège, Liège.

Bob Richmond. 2015. Egyptian Hieroglyphs in Unicode plain text: A note on a suggested approach [L2/15-069]. Technical report, UTC (Unicode Technical Committee), Unicode Consortium, February.

Serge Rosmorduc. 2003a. Codage informatique des langues anciennes. *Document numérique*, 6(3-4):211–224.

Serge Rosmorduc. 2003b. HieroTeX: A LaTeXperiment of hieroglyphic typesetting. Package available at: http://www.ctan.org/tex-archive/language/hieroglyph (visited on May 2016).

Serge Rosmorduc. 2014. JSESH documentation. Software available at: http://jsesh.qenherkhopeshef.org/ (visited on May 2016).

Serge Rosmorduc. 2015. Computational linguistics in egyptology. In Julie Stauder-Porchet, Andréas Stauder, and Willeke Wendrich, editors, *UCLA Encyclopedia of Egyptology.* UCLA, Los Angeles, USA.

Jesús Vilares, Manuel Vilares, and Juan Otero. 2011. Managing Misspelled Queries in IR Applications. *Information Processing & Management*, 47(2):263–286.

Michiko Yasukawa, J. Shane Culpepper, and Falk Scholer. 2012. Phonetic matching in Japanese. In *Proc. of SIGIR 2012 Workshop on Open Source Information Retrieval (OSIR 2012)*, pages 68–71.

A Third-Party Pictures

Figure 1, left (cropped picture): original by *Khruner*; available in Wikipedia under the Creative Commons Attribution-Share Alike 3.0 Unported license. **Figure 1, top** (cropped picture): original by *Hans Ollermann*; available in Wikipedia under the Creative Commons Attribution 2.0 Generic license. **Figure 1, right and bottom** (cropped pictures): originals by *Francesco Gasparetti*; available in Wikipedia under the Creative Commons Attribution 2.0 Generic license. **Figure 2, left** (cropped picture): original by *Lord-of-the-Light*; available in Wikipedia under the Creative Commons Attribution-Share Alike 3.0 Unported license.

Old Swedish Part-of-Speech Tagging
between Variation and External Knowledge

Yvonne Adesam
Språkbanken
Department of Swedish
University of Gothenburg
`yvonne.adesam@gu.se`

Gerlof Bouma
Språkbanken
Department of Swedish
University of Gothenburg
`gerlof.bouma@gu.se`

Abstract

We present results on part-of-speech and morphological tagging for Old Swedish (1225–1526). In a set of experiments we look at the difference between within-corpus and across-corpus accuracy, and explore ways of mitigating the effects of variation and data sparseness by adding different types of dictionary information. Combining several methods, together with a simple approach to handle spelling variation, we achieve a major boost in tagger performance on a modest test collection.

1 Introduction

Old Swedish is defined as the language stage that starts with the oldest preserved texts in the Latin alphabet (ca 1225) and ends with early print, in particular with the publication of the new testament of Gustav Vasa's bible (1526). The texts of this period are interesting as an example of a low resource and high variability material.

Compared to contemporary Swedish, Old Swedish had a different and more variable word order and a richer morphology, with nominal and verbal inflection systems resembling those of modern German or Icelandic: a nominal system with 3 genders and 4 cases and a verbal system with person and number agreement. Contemporary Swedish has 2 nominal genders,[1] at most 2 cases,[2] and no verbal agreement. Additionally, due to cultural differences and the effects of document topics/genres, the vocabulary used in Old Swedish texts may differ considerably from contemporary Swedish. We therefore expect the languages to lie too far apart

to use a part-of-speech tagger trained on contemporary Swedish on Old Swedish texts.

However, until recently there have been no annotated Old Swedish texts available for training a tagger, nor any complete grammatical descriptions (i.e. computational descriptions) for inducing an annotation tool. In addition, there are a number of particularities of Old Swedish texts that are a challenge for most annotation tools and tool development methods. For example, sentence splitting cannot be handled with standard tools, as sentence boundaries are marked, if at all, in a number of ways, such as by period, slash, comma, or capitalization. Also, lack of a standardized orthography results in a wide variety of spellings for the same word, especially between texts but also within. This makes them difficult to handle with statistical methods. These problems are inflated by the fact that we are dealing with texts from wildly different genres, with different geographic origins and from a time span of roughly three centuries.

There is a long tradition of printed editions of the Old Swedish texts, for instance in the form of the editions of the medieval provincial laws by Collin and Schlyter (published 1827–1877), the publications of *Svenska fornskriftsällskapet* (The Swedish society for historical texts, 1843–present), and the *Diplomatarium Suecanum* collection of the Swedish National Archives (1820–present). More recently, electronic editions and/or electronic versions of printed editions have also become available, for instance through the Fornsvenska Textbanken project (see Delsing (2002), ∼3M tokens of Old Swedish) and the ongoing digitization efforts of the National Archives (presently ∼1M tokens of Old Swedish). The availability of such quantities of electronic text and the potential for more provides an extra motivation for our research into NLP methods for this language stage.

Although little work has previously been done

---

[1] Nouns only know 2 genders, adjectives may in special cases inflect for masculine in addition to common and neuter.

[2] Whether Swedish has a case distinction or not depends how one considers the genitive suffix and the subjective/objective pronominal forms.

Proceedings of the 10th SIGHUM Workshop on Language Technology for Cultural Heritage, Social Sciences, and Humanities (LaTeCH), pages 32–42,
Berlin, Germany, August 11, 2016. ©2016 Association for Computational Linguistics

on automatic annotation of Old Swedish, there is related work for historical material in general. First, there exists extensive work on Modern Swedish (16th–19th c) (Pettersson, 2016, and references therein). The main difference between this work and ours is that the Modern Swedish texts are normalized to make them more similar to contemporary text, so that tools developed for contemporary material can be used. We, on the other hand, explore developing dedicated tools for the historical material by training on manually annotated historical text and using dedicated resources for the historical language variety. Since Old Swedish is more different from Contemporary Swedish than Modern Swedish is, we expect to get more mileage out of this approach than out of a transfer method.[3]

Secondly, quite a lot of work has been done for historical language variants other than Swedish, see e.g. the overview in Piotrowski (2012). Many of these also approach the historical texts by applying tools trained on the modern language variety, after adaptation of the historical texts to make them more similar to modern texts. However, for example Dipper (2011) explores normalizing the historical text to an artificial historical standard form, before training on the annotated historical text.

In this paper, we explore automatic part-of-speech (POS) tagging based on manually annotated historical text. We examine how much annotated data is needed and experiment with various ways of improving the tagging results, especially in the context of applying a tagger to documents from another domain and time. This can be achieved by handling spelling variation through a simple spelling simplification, as well as adding extra information such as manually and automatically derived lemmata, and POS and morphological information from a lexicon describing the historical language variant.

2 Materials and Tools

For our experiments, we rely on almost 20 000 tokens of text from Fornsvenska textbanken, consisting of one large and three small fragments from different texts. Around 18 000 come from the *Östgötalagen* ('The Ostrogothic law', based on manuscript Codex Holmiensis B50), a provincial law dating back to ~1290 in a manuscript from ~1350. This fragment will be used as training material. The other fragments are around 500 tokens each: the

beginning of *Äldre Västgötalagen* (the 'Elder Westrogothic law', Cod Holm B59), the text marking the start of the Old Swedish period, dating back to ~1220 in a manuscript from ~1280; the complete *Skämtan om abbotar* ('A joke on abbotts', Cod Holm D4a), a short satire from ~1450; and the initial chapter from *Pentateukparafrasen* ('A paraphrase of the Books of Moses', Cod Holm A1), from a manuscript from 1526, supposedly reflecting a text from ~1330. These will serve as evaluation material, in part representing different genres and periods. The electronic versions of *Östgötalagen*, *Äldre Västgötalagen* and *Pentateukparafrasen* have been taken from Fornsvenska textbanken, *Skämtan om abbotar* was digitized by us from the print edition of Klemming (1887–1889).

The corpora were manually segmented, lemmatized, and annotated for POS and morphological features. We mainly followed the guidelines for Old Norwegian from the Menotec project (Haugen and Øverland, 2014), which in turn are based on the PROIEL scheme for morpho-syntactic annotation of historical text (Haug and Jøhndal, 2008). The PROIEL scheme and its associated annotation and corpus exploration environment have been used for annotating corpora of 16 other historic languages.

The manual segmentation step includes sentence segmentation, which is a non-trivial problem for automatic analysis, see Bouma and Adesam (2013), and occasionally combining or splitting graphic tokens into minimal annotation units (words). The need to combine graphic tokens into words occurs frequently for compounds which may be written as two tokens. Splitting is more rare – it is among other things needed for pronominal clitics that form one graphic token with their host. An example of a compound is *niþings værk* 'atrocity' in (1) below.

(1) Uerder maþer .i. kyrkiu dræpin þet ær
    becomes person in church killed it is

    niþings værk. þa er kyrkia al vuighz.
    atrocity   then is church all deconsecrated

    'If a person is killed in church, this is an atrocity, then the whole church is deconsecrated.'

We currently do not have a way of recognizing such compounds automatically. Compounds are not always clearly morphologically recognizable as such. Having an entry in one of the Old Swedish dictionaries could be taken as a pragmatic opera-

---

[3]A proper, direct comparison of these methods for Old Swedish will have to await future work.

tionalization of compound-hood, but because of orthographic variation, matching against a dictionary is a non-trivial matter, which we return to in the case of single-token words below. We thus use our manual segmentation as the basis in our experiments.

Example (1) also shows the use of a period in three different positions: to mark the end of a clause, the end of a sentence and to demarcate the short word *i* 'in'. Because the function and use of punctuation in the Old Swedish material varies greatly, and is not always well-understood, we remove punctuation completely for the purpose of our experiments. A similar reasoning concerns the use of uppercase, which was removed before the experiments. Finally, we also applied a light (automatic) character normalization for cases which are more at the level of character encoding than spelling differences.[4]

For the manual annotation of lemma information, we use the entries in Söderwall's (1884–1918) dictionary of Old Swedish as lemmata. New lemmata were created for those cases not covered by the dictionary, which mostly concerned names and occasionally compounds. Söderwall's dictionary is available in electronic form.[5] Lemmata, both in the form of these manually annotated gold-standard level lemmata and in the form of the output of a lemmatizer that automatically links words to entries in the electronic Söderwall, will be used in the experiments in Sections 3–5. In addition, POS- and morphology tagging hints extracted from the electronic dictionary will be used in Section 6.

We use 19 POS-tags from the PROIEL/Menotec POS-tag set and morphological features encoding person, number, tense, mood, voice, gender, case, degree, adjectival/nominal declension (definiteness). The size of the morphological tag space is about 11 500 POS-morphology combinations. In our annotated data, a total of 358 different POS-morphology combinations are used. An overview of the tagset is given in Appendix A.

For the tagging experiments we use Marmot (Müller et al., 2013), a CRF framework for large tag sets like those in morphological tagging. We use Marmot's default settings[6] and have not in-vestigated optimization of settings and hyperparameters, instead focusing on the effects of adding/removing information on tagging accuracy.

3 Within corpus performance

We start by considering the accuracy of tagging on extremely within-domain data: data from the same corpus. This will provide us with a background to interpret the cross-document (both within and outside-of domain) results. All results will be reported for both full morphological tagging (assigning both POS-tag and morphological features) and the less fine-grained task of POS-tagging. In this paper, all averages are arithmetic means and macro averages.

3.1 Cross-validation

Cross-validation results of training and evaluating a basic model on Östgötalagen, with only the token layer as information, are given in Table 1. The table gives averages over different cross-validation regimes to get an idea of the homogeneity within the corpus as seen from the tagger. When randomly spreading sentences over ten data splits (10-fold random), the model will have seen material from all parts of the corpus, and if there are any differences with Östgötalagen that affect tagging, like systematic changes in orthography or vocabulary, these will be evened out in this way of evaluating. The tagger reaches an average POS-tagging accuracy of 94.2% under this regime, with relatively minor differences between the folds.

By taking ten consecutive parts from the corpus as splits, we get the '10-fold contiguous' regime. There is now a possibility that the tagger is confronted with evaluation data sections of the corpus it hasn't seen before. Performance drops a little bit, to 92.8%. We interpret this as an indication that the tagger has relatively little trouble generalizing to different parts of the corpus, a sign that the corpus is rather homogeneous. Note that the differences between folds has increased, with the minimum belonging to the fold with test data from the beginning of Östgötalagen.

Finally, we try to maximize the differences between folds by defining them on the text structure. Each split now corresponds to one of the

---

[4]In particular we neutralized the differences between *æ* and *ä*, *ø* and *ö* and *þ* and *ð*. Note that usage of *ð* is very rare in Old Swedish material, and *þ* may encode voiced as well as unvoiced dental fricatives.

[5]`https://spraakbanken.gu.se/resources`

[6]In the default settings, Marmot trains a trigram model without any regularization. Morphological tags are split into their parts by the tagger rather than treating them as atomic. The tagger automatically creates suffix and prefix features based on the token input layer. It will not predict morphological labels not seen in the training data.

		Min	Mean	Max
POS	10-fold random	.931	.942	.947
	10-fold contiguous	.897	.928	.958
	4-fold per chapter	.893	.915	.924
Morph	10-fold random	.819	.832	.841
	10-fold contiguous	.725	.805	.864
	4-fold per chapter	.751	.787	.808

Table 1: Cross-validation results for the basic model on Östgötalagen under different regimes.

major subdivisions of the legal text, the so called *balk*. We only use the four largest from our annotated material, each 3,500 to 5 000 tokens, to avoid large variations in training data size between folds. The average performance drops further to 91.5%. The lowest accuracy is achieved on the first balk, *Kyrkobalken*, concerning the church – in agreement with the 10-fold contiguous regime. We are not aware of any obvious differences, like provenance, that might explain this.

The picture for morphological tagging is the same as for POS-tagging, with average accuracy between 11 and 13 percentage-points lower. The drop in accuracy between regimes is a bit larger than for POS-tagging, meaning that the tagger is more sensitive to corpus differences in this task. It seems likely that this is directly related to the larger tag set and therefore increased data sparseness.

3.2 Lemmata and spelling

A major obstacle when working with historical text is spelling variation. For Swedish, there was no written standard until several hundred years after the Old Swedish period. When training a parser or any other statistical natural language processing tool, spelling variation leads to data sparseness, which for instance presents itself in the form of very high out-of-vocabulary (OOV) rates and large amounts of features that have to be weighted on the basis of low counts.

In this paper we investigate two orthogonal ways of remedying this: First, we add a word's lemma as a feature. We might expect this to have more of an effect on POS-tagging than on morphology tagging, as the lemma in it self does not provide explicit information about the morphology in the way for instance inflection does.[7] In this and the

next section, we use the manually annotated lemmata as features, in Section 5 we investigate the effectiveness of adding the output of an automatic lemmatizer.

Secondly, we apply the spelling simplification method described in Bouma and Adesam (2013), which uses a handful of rewriting rules intended to remove differences between spellings. For instance, it replaces many repeated characters by a single character (e.g. $aa \rightarrow a$), removes a restricted number of digraphs (e.g. $ck \rightarrow k$, $gh \rightarrow g$) and reduces certain characters denoting similar sounds to one (e.g. $u, v, w \rightarrow v$). We have previously shown this crude method to be effective in a sentence segmentation task (ibid), even though the simplification can easily conflate words that are not spelling variants and at the same time may fail to bring obvious variants together.[8] The simplification rules are directly applied to the token layer. Unlike adding a lemma, spelling simplification thus strictly removes information.

Simplifying the spelling has no effect on the within-corpus tagging accuracy on Östgötalagen (average for POS remains at 92.8% under the 10-fold contiguous regime, morphology is at 80.4%), adding a lemma gives a nominal increase (93.9% POS, 81.2 morphology). Combining the two does not lead to a change with respect to just adding a lemma (see Figure 2 in Section 4).

The absence of any real effect does not come as a surprise, given our remarks about the homogeneity of the corpus in the section above. In addition, it is interesting to note that the spelling simplification has only little impact on the lexical statistics of Östgötalagen: the average OOV-rate in cross-validation is basically unaffected (see also Table 2 in Section 4), and the number of rare types, with a token frequency of ≤ 10, drops with only 2.5% points, even though 55% of the types are affected by the spelling simplification.

3.3 Training data size

Figure 1 shows the effect of training size on accuracy, for using the train-test split of one of the 10-fold contiguous folds. Within-corpus learning curves are interesting from the point of view of

---

[7]One of the design goals of the Menotec scheme is to avoid having the same lemma with different POS-tags, which makes having the lemma particularly informative for a POS-tagger.

[8]Spelling simplification therefore shares characteristics with stemming: a fast method to reduce variation in a corpus. But whereas stemming mainly reduces variation due to inflection and derivation, spelling simplification maintains morphological information and aims at reducing variation due to orthographic variation.

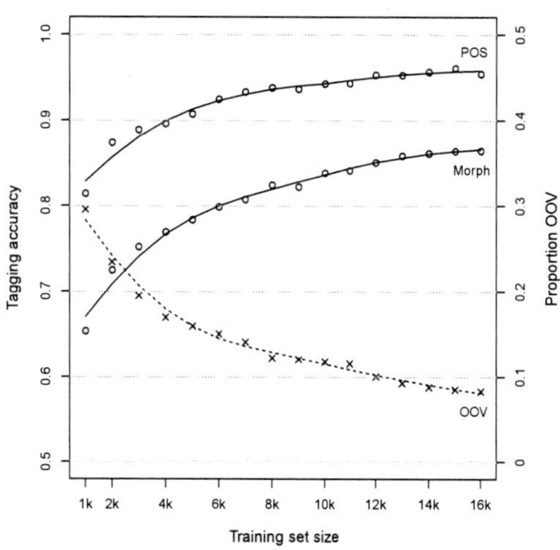

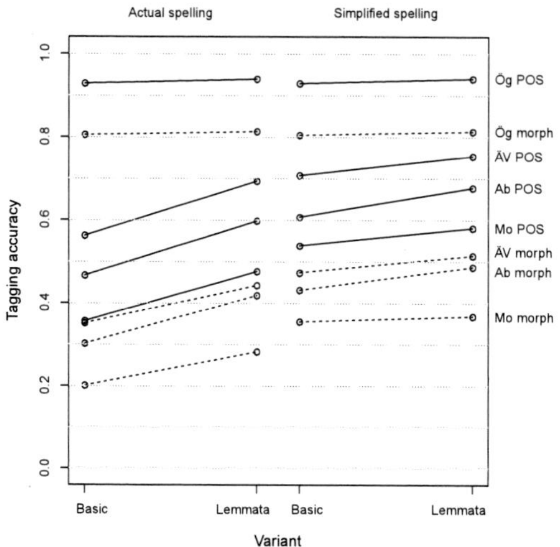

Figure 1: Learning curves for within-corpus accuracy (left axis) and related OOV proportions (right axis) on Östgötalagen for the basic model.

Figure 2: Effect of spelling simplification (left vs right column) and adding lemma information on tagging accuracy.

tagger-assisted manual annotation. Earlier studies on this topic (see Fort and Sagot (2010) on Penn Treebank-style POS-tagging, and Skjærholt (2011) on tagging Latin morphology using the PROIEL tagset) show that a pre-tagging accuracy of .8 and upwards can be beneficial to manual annotation speed and (to a lesser extent) accuracy, although the effect is stronger for less experienced annotators. For our Östgöta corpus, it would thus seem that a tagger trained on as little as 1 000 tokens (around one week's work for a medium-experienced annotator annotating POS, morphology and lemmata) can be of help for POS-tagging, and 7 000 tokens for morphology tagging.

4 Lemmata and spelling simplification across corpora

Let us now turn to the cross-document experiments, which will give us a better picture of what happens when we automatically annotate new texts. We train on the whole Östgötalagen data and evaluate the models on the three other texts, Äldre Västgötalagen (ÄV), Abota (Ab), and Moses (Mo) from Pentateukparafrasen. The results can be compared to the average results when performing tenfold evaluation on Östgötalagen (Ög).

The results are in Figure 2 (see Appendix B for the actual numbers). As we can see, while spelling simplification and lemma information does not help much when tagging Östgötalagen (as stated in Sec-

tion 3.2), we get a large improvement from both approaches when tagging other texts. Interestingly, in all cases, spelling simplification on its own contributes more than providing the tagger with the correct lemma, for both POS-tagging and morphological tagging. Combining spelling simplification and providing a lemma gives the best results, suggesting the enhancements supply complementary information.

Over all, we get a large increase in accuracy, rendering a quite acceptable POS-tagging accuracy for all texts, if we consider a semi-automatic annotation process where we automatically tag Old Swedish text before manually checking it. Morphological tagging is lagging behind, as is to be expected, as it is a more difficult task because of the larger tag set. However, a particular problem is the occurrence of unseen morphological labels in the testing data, which because of the used tagger settings cannot be predicted correctly. For Äldre Västgötalagen, Abota and Moses, the proportion of types with an unseen morphological label is 7%, 4% and 15%, respectively.

Let us also look at the improved number of tokens (i.e. the change in number of correct tokens) between the basic tagging, without extra information, and tagging with both lemma and spelling simplification, per POS. For Äldre Västgötalagen we have a larger change (more than 10 tokens, i.e., more than 2% of all tokens) for conjunctions,

	Actual		Simplified		Lemmata	
	Tok	Typ	Tok	Typ	Tok	Typ
Ög	.11	.30	.11	.29	.05	.20
ÄV	.65	.73	.50	.64	.14	.29
Ab	.75	.82	.60	.76	.31	.51
Mo	.79	.84	.54	.71	.35	.53

Table 2: OOV-rates for words (actual and simplified orthography) and lemmata, given Östgötalagen.

nouns, and verbs, while Abota has a large change for conjunctions, adverbs, nouns, and prepositions. For Moses we see a large change for conjunctions, nouns, demonstrative pronouns, and prepositions.

For conjunctions and prepositions, most improvements come from the spelling simplification, while nouns get their improvement from both lemma and spelling simplification. Verbs also get their improvement from both, but to a larger extent from lemma. The improvements for demonstrative pronouns come from the lemma. These results are not surprising. While we get an overall large improvement from spelling simplification, lemma may be more helpful for inflected POS categories.

Exploring the data further, one reason for the difference in impact of spelling simplification and lemma may be the rate of out-of-vocabulary words (OOV) between the texts. The OOV-rates for the different test sets are given in Table 2. Not surprising, the rate of OOV is lowest for Östgötalagen, since the test data comes from the same text as the training data. The OOV-rate in Äldre Västgötalagen, being the closest to the training data in genre, is a lot higher. Abota and Moses have the highest levels of OOV for the actual spelling. However, while the spelling simplification significantly lowers the OOV-rates for all texts but Östgötalagen, it has the largest impact on the OOV-rates for Moses, lowering the percentage of OOV by 25 percentage-points at token-level and almost 15 percentage-points at type-level.

5   Automatically assigned lemmata

We have seen that adding lemma information has a beneficial effect on tagging accuracy across corpora. In a realistic setup, we do not have access to gold standard lemmata. This raises the question whether automatically assigned lemmata also will boost accuracy. To this end we have implemented a simple lexicon linking method, which assigns one or more lemmata from Söderwall's dictionary to each token. Before discussing the effect of using automatically assigned lemmata, we describe our lexicon linking strategy.

5.1   Linking tokens to lemmata

Many entries in Söderwall's dictionary contain a list of form variants, to illustrate – rather than fully document (Djärv, 2009) – the different forms due to inflection and orthographic convention. In our electronic version, we have a total of 24 000 form variants for 8 000 (out of 27 000) lemmata. A straightforward linking strategy uses these as a simple look-up table. A token is linked to any lemma that a) matches the token exactly, or b) lists a form variant that matches the token exactly. We rank multiple lemmata in this order and use alphabetical order as a further tie breaker.

Average linking scores (i.e. recall) of this method on our four corpora is given in Table 3. We see that considering only the best suggestion from the dictionary retrieves a correct lemma for 45% of the tokens (28% of types). Considering whether the correct lemma is among all returned matches raises the score, but it remains low. The reason for this is the low proportion of cases in which this method applies, that is, the cases when we get a link to the dictionary at all (61% tokens, 42% types). This low application rate motivates a combination with a method with higher recall, like a fuzzy matching-based approach that assigns a lemma to every token. Pettersson (2016) and Bollmann (2013) have shown the effectiveness of a combination of look-up and fuzzy matching for different historical languages.

Our fuzzy matching method builds on Adesam et al. (2012). A word form is matched against the lemma that gives the lowest weighted edit distance, where edit operations may map several characters at once. Edit costs are calculated from the form variants listed in Söderwall's dictionary as follows: First, each variant is character aligned with its lemma using the EM specification given in Oncina and Sebban (2006).[9] In a second step, sequences of character mappings are taken from these alignments to give counts of n-to-m-gram mappings. Source and target sequences do not have to have the same effective length, as either of them may contain ϵ-s. Finally, we assign a cost

---

[9] For convenience, we use a hard-EM variant of Oncina and Sebban's method. See also Wieling et al. (2012) for a similar iterative method to obtain character alignments.

		Tokens	Types
Dictionary look-up	best	.45	.28
	all	.54	.33
	applies	.61	.42
Edit distance	best	.54	.48
	top 3	.69	.67
Combo	best	.62	.55
	top 3	.78	.73
Coverage		.92	.91

Table 3: Lexicon linking scores per method and dictionary statistics

of $-\log p(\text{target}|\text{source})$ to each mapping. For our final model, we include edits that map up to 5 characters. On a held-out development set from the dictionary listed form variants, this method retrieves the correct lemma 54% of the time, with the correct lemma being among the best 3 in 72% of the cases. Models that allowed wider edits did not give clear improvements on the held-out data.

As shown in Table 3, the model retrieves the correct lemma for 54% of the tokens (48% of types) in our corpora when considering the best match only. Among the top 3 of matches, the correct lemma is found 69% of the time (67% at type level). The Moses text is an outlier here with a mere 47% token score (43% types; neither shown in the table) for the best match. Its low linking accuracy must be explained from the high incidence of proper names (see also Section 6). Indeed, this is also reflected in the low coverage of our lemma list with respect to the text, which is up to 22 percentage-points lower than for the other texts (token- and type-level).

We combine these two methods by first taking all lemmata from the dictionary look-up method, and then adding the ranked lemmata from the edit distance method. This combined approach finds the correct lemma for 62% of the tokens (55% of types). The correct lemma is among the 3 best candidates in 78% of the cases (73% type-level).

5.2 Tagging with automatically assigned lemmata

We automatically add lemma information using the method just described as features in the test and training data. We explore two ways of adding lemma information: using only the single top-ranked lemma, and taking the top 3 suggestions so that each token receives multiple possible lemmata. In the latter case, the three suggestions are values of the same key, so that the model cannot distinguish for a given lemma whether it is the first or third ranked suggestion.[10]

As before, we compare tagging results using the data in its actual spelling and in a simplified version. The results are summarized in Figure 3 (see also Appendix B). Compared to a model with access to manually annotated lemma information, a model with a single automatic lemma loses tagging accuracy, both on the POS and the morphology tasks. This effect can be seen both in the actual spelling and the simplified spelling versions, although the effect is smaller for the Äldre Västgöta and Moses subcorpora in the simplified spelling experiment.

Interestingly enough, in the actual spelling version, using multiple automatically assigned lemmata not only improves upon using a single automatically assigned lemma but also upon using the manually assigned lemma. We do not currently understand the nature of this effect, especially since it disappears in the simplified spelling setup. We hope future investigations will give us better insight into this matter.

Overall, adding automatically assigned lemmata does not hurt performance (0–5 percentage points improvement for simplified spelling) and may potentially be very helpful (5–10 percentage points for actual spelling). Most importantly, however, having a lemma gives us access to more detailed and useful information from the dictionary, as we will see in the following section.

6   Adding tagging clues from the lexicon

Entries in Söderwall's dictionary contain information about POS and in some cases information pertaining to morphological properties. This information may be the POS itself (e.g. *adv.* for an adverbial or *v.* for verb), but it may also just give us e.g. the gender for a noun (*m.* for masculine). In some cases we get further specifications (e.g. *pron. pers.* for a personal pronoun or *adj. komp.* for an adjective in comparative form). Although Söderwall's label inventory is not directly mappable to ours, we can use this information as tagging clues by including Söderwall's labels as features in the data (cf Müller et al., 2013).

---

[10]We also experimented using different feature keys for the first, second and third suggestion. This gave similar but slightly worse results.

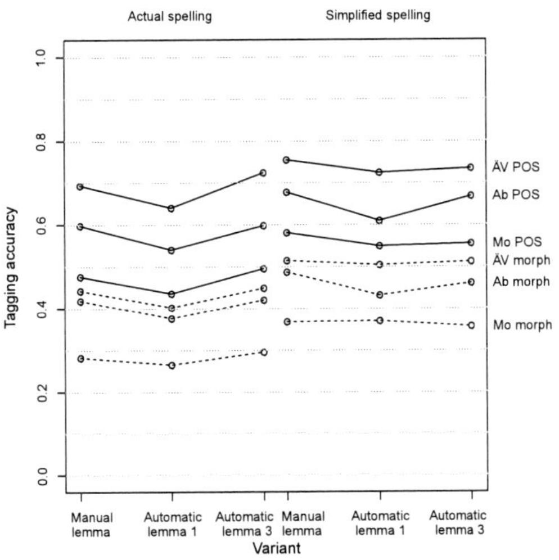
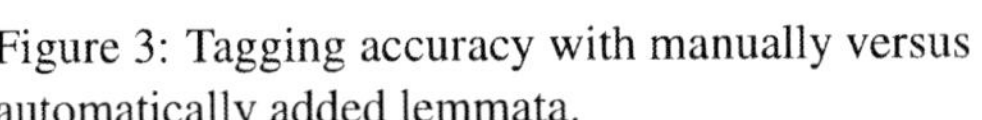
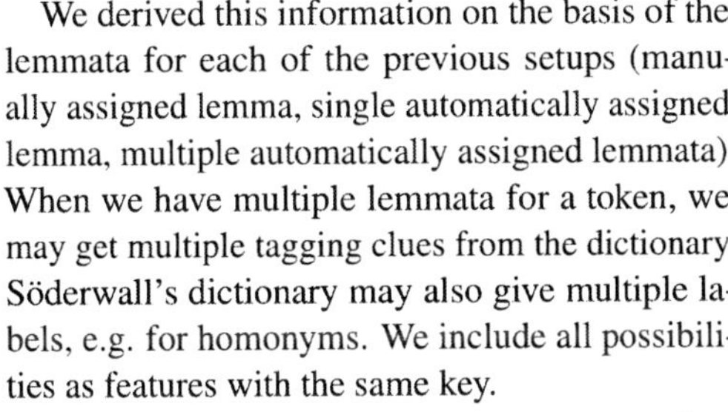
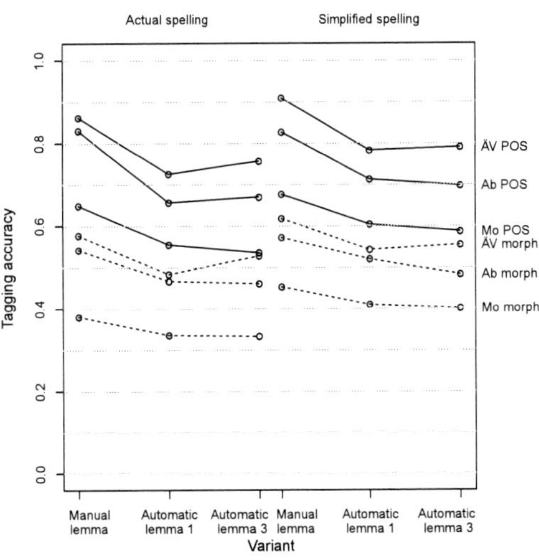

Figure 3: Tagging accuracy with manually versus automatically added lemmata.

Figure 4: Tagging accuracy for manually versus automatically added lemmata with tagging hints.

We derived this information on the basis of the lemmata for each of the previous setups (manually assigned lemma, single automatically assigned lemma, multiple automatically assigned lemma). When we have multiple lemmata for a token, we may get multiple tagging clues from the dictionary. Söderwall's dictionary may also give multiple labels, e.g. for homonyms. We include all possibilities as features with the same key.

We can extract at least one tagging clue per token (manually assigned lemma) in most cases, except for the Moses text, where we only have a coverage of ∼75%, due to proper names and numerals.

The results of using these extra tagging clues in POS and morphology tagging can be found in Figure 4 (see also Appendix B). Overall, accuracy goes up compared to the models without tagging clues (see Figure 3). Here it is clear that the models with manually assigned lemmata fare much better than those with automatically assigned lemmata. The previously seen advantage of having multiple automatically assigned lemmata has disappeared. As in each of the previous experiments, using simplified spelling improves accuracy.

On average, the best model without any manual input in the test data achieves 69.9% accuracy on the POS task and 49.0% on the morphology task (single automatic lemma with tagging clues, spelling simplification). This is a huge improvement over the initial 46.1% POS and 28.4% morphology (no lemma, actual spelling).

As mentioned, Moses achieves lower scores because it contains a lot of proper names: 72 occurrences (15% of the tokens) compared to one or two in the other two shorter texts, and 12 in the much longer Östgötalagen. Not only are individual proper names OOV, but the tagger assigns a very low probability to the word class as a whole. Indeed, the tagger never predicts the proper name label for any token in the evaluation, even under the best model. For Moses, this means that 15% of the tokens cannot be correctly tagged. Correcting only names would boost accuracy to almost 83% for POS-tags, on par with results for the Abota text.

Two other clearly problematic POS-tags are demonstrative pronouns and quantifiers. Demonstrative pronouns are tagged with low precision and recall in the Abota and Moses texts, in particular when using automatically derived lemmata. The quality of the automatically assigned lemmata cannot be the sole explanation for this effect, as it is fairly good for Abota, whereas it is low for Moses.

The label of quantifier is not only used for items expressing meanings like *all*, *each* and *some*, but also for cardinal numerals. In Moses, most of the numbers are written using roman numerals, which our tagger currently does not recognize. In Abota, it is the low quality of the automatic lemma assignment that causes problems specifically for this category. A possible reason for this is the irregular inflection paradigms for these items.

7 Conclusions

In this paper we have explored several approaches to automatic annotation of POS and morphology for Old Swedish text. These approaches have mainly been linguistically informed, and we have shown that adding clues about lemma and morphological information from a dictionary greatly improves results, together with a simplistic method for removing spelling variation.

With a training set of less than 18 000 words, we start out with an average accuracy of around .45 for coarse POS-tags (less than .30 with morphological classification) when testing on other texts. The overall best final results give us an average of .80 for POS-tags (.55 with morphological classification), using spelling simplification, manually annotated lemmata, and morphological information from the dictionary based on those lemmata. The best results with automatically induced extra information were .70 for POS-tags (.50 with morphological classification), when a single lemma was automatically selected, together with spelling simplification and morphological information from the dictionary based on the automatically extracted lemma.

We have also seen that a fairly small amount of manually annotated data, maybe as little as 1 000 words, is necessary for training a POS-tagger for aiding manual annotation, although more, above 7 000 words, is necessary for a morphology tagger.

Comparing results between the within-corpus and across-corpus experiments, we find it striking that even at the smallest within-text data set size (1 000 tokens), accuracy lies well above the accuracy of the basic model in the across-corpus setup. It is even slightly better than our best model using automatically assigned lemma information on Äldre Västgötalagen. The within-corpus learning curve underlines the severity of the differences between corpora.

We have seen that, on the one hand, spelling simplification gives better tagging results across corpora than adding lemmata, while on the other hand lemma OOV-rates are much lower than simplified spelling word OOV rates. The rate of OOV is therefore clearly not the only reason for low tagger performance across corpora. An important difference lies in the ways we added the lemmata and simplified spelling. The former was added as a feature linked to a single token, whereas for the latter we changed the token layer itself. This means that the simplified spelling also affected the suffix-/prefix-based features and the token context features the CRF tagger constructs automatically under the default settings we used. It seems plausible that this difference makes the simplified spelling much more effective. More experimentation is needed to see if lemma information is more effective when derived features are also added to the model. In any case, the effectiveness of simplified spelling also suggests that investigating proper spelling normalization may be well worth the effort.

Acknowledgments

This research is funded by Stiftelsen Marcus och Amalia Wallenbergs Minnesfond (project "MAÞiR", nr MAW 2012.0146).

References

Yvonne Adesam, Malin Ahlberg, and Gerlof Bouma. 2012. *bokstaffua, bokstaffwa, bokstafwa, bokstaua, bokstawa...* Towards lexical link-up for a corpus of Old Swedish. In Jancsary, editor, *Empirical Methods in Natural Language Processing: Proceedings of KONVENS 2012 (LThist 2012 workshop)*, page 365–369, Vienna.

Marcel Bollmann. 2013. Spelling normalization of historical German with sparse training data. Technical report, BLA: Bochumer Linguistische Arbeitsberichte 13.

Gerlof Bouma and Yvonne Adesam. 2013. Experiments on sentence segmentation in Old Swedish editions. In *Proceedings of the workshop on computational historical linguistics at NODALIDA 2013*, volume 18 of *NEALT Proceedings Series*.

Lars-Olof Delsing. 2002. Fornsvenska textbanken. In Lagman, Olsson, and Voodla, editors, *Nordistica Tartuensia 7*, pages 149–156, Tallinn. Pangloss.

Stefanie Dipper. 2011. Morphological and part-of-speech tagging of historical language data: A comparison. *Journal for Language Technology and Computational Linguistics, Special Issue: Proceedings of the TLT-Workshop on Annotation of Corpora for Research in the Humanities*, 26(2):25–37. http://www.jlcl.org/2011_Heft2/2.pdf.

Ulrika Djärv. 2009. *Fornsvenskans lexikala kodifiering i Söderwalls medeltidsordbok [The lexical codification of Old Swedish in Söderwall's medieval dictionary]*. Number 91 in Samlingar utgivna av Svenska fornskriftsällskapet. Serie 1. Svenska skrifter. Svenska fornskriftsällskapet, Uppsala.

Karën Fort and Benoît Sagot. 2010. Influence of pre-annotation on POS-tagged corpus development.

In *Proceedings of the Fourth Linguistic Annotation Workshop*, pages 56–63, Uppsala, Sweden, July. Association for Computational Linguistics.

Dag Haug and Marius Jøhndal. 2008. Creating a parallel treebank of the Old Indo-European bible translations. In Caroline Sporleder and Kiril Ribarov, editors, *Proceedings of the Second Workshop on Language Technology for Cultural Heritage Data (LaTeCH)*, pages 27–34.

Odd Einar Haugen and Fartein Thorsen Øverland. 2014. *Guidelines for Morphological and Syntactic Annotation of Old Norwegian Texts*, volume 13(2) of *Bergen Language and Linguistic Studies (BeLLS)*.

Thomas Müller, Helmut Schmid, and Hinrich Schütze. 2013. Efficient higher-order CRFs for morphological tagging. In *Proceedings of the 2013 Conference on Empirical Methods in Natural Language Processing*.

Jose Oncina and Marc Sebban. 2006. Learning stochastic edit distance: Application in handwritten character recognition. *Pattern Recognition*, 39(9):1575–1587.

Eva Pettersson. 2016. *Spelling Normalisation and Linguistic Analysis of Historical Text for Information Extraction*. Ph.D. thesis, Uppsala University.

Michael Piotrowski. 2012. *Natural Language Processing for Historical Texts*. Morgan & Claypool.

Arne Skjærholt. 2011. More, faster: Accelerated corpus annotation with statistical taggers. *JLCL*, 26(2):153–165.

Knut Fredrik Söderwall. 1884–1918. *Ordbok öfver svenska medeltids-språket*. Number 54 in Samlingar utgivna av Svenska fornskriftsällskapet. Serie 1. Svenska skrifter. Svenska fornskriftsällskapet, Lund & Uppsala.

Martijn Wieling, Eliza Margaretha, and John Nerbonne. 2012. Inducing a measure of phonetic similarity from pronunciation variation. *Journal of Phonetics*, 40(2):307–314.

A Overview of the Menotec POS-tagset

Part-of-speech	Morph features
Noun	gender, number, case, definiteness
Proper noun	gender, number, case, definiteness
Adjective	degree, gender, number, case, definiteness
Personal pronoun	case
Reflexive pronoun	case
Interrogative pronoun	gender, number, case
Indefinite pronoun	gender, number, case
Demonstrative pronoun	gender, number, case
Quantifier	gender, number, case
Possessive pronoun	gender, number, case
Verb	finiteness, tense, mood, person, number, voice
Adverb	degree
Interrogative adverb	–
Preposition	–
Coordinator	–
Subordinator	–
Interjektion	–
Unanalyzed	–
Foreign word	–

Based on Haugen and Øverland (2014).

B   Overview of experimental results

	ÄV		Ab		Mo	
	Pos	Mor	Pos	Mor	Pos	Mor
Basic	.562	.350	.465	.301	.356	.200
With lemmata:						
Manual	.692	.442	.597	.418	.475	.281
Auto 1	.640	.401	.540	.375	.435	.264
Auto 3	.723	.448	.597	.420	.495	.294
With lemmata and hints:						
Manual	.862	.576	.830	.542	.648	.380
Auto 1	.725	.483	.656	.466	.554	.335
Auto 3	.756	.527	.669	.460	.535	.333

Accuracies for POS- and morphology tagging on material in the actual spelling.

	ÄV		Ab		Mo	
	Pos	Mor	Pos	Mor	Pos	Mor
Basic	.707	.473	.606	.431	.537	.354
With lemmata						
Manual	.754	.513	.677	.486	.580	.367
Auto 1	.723	.503	.608	.431	.548	.369
Auto 3	.733	.511	.667	.460	.554	.356
With lemmata and hints						
Manual	.908	.617	.826	.571	.676	.452
Auto 1	.782	.542	.712	.519	.603	.409
Auto 3	.790	.554	.697	.482	.586	.401

Accuracies for POS- and morphology tagging on material in the simplified spelling.

ÄV: *Äldre Västgötalagen* (490 tokens)
Ab: *Skämtan om abbotar* (541 tokens)
Mo: *Pentateukparafrasen* (469 tokens)

Code-Switching Ubique Est - Language Identification and Part-of-Speech Tagging for Historical Mixed Text

Sarah Schulz
Institute for Natural Language Processing (IMS)
University of Stuttgart
70569 Stuttgart, Germany
schulzsh@ims.uni-stuttgart.de

Mareike Keller
Institute for English Linguistics
University of Mannheim
60131 Mannheim, Germany
markelle@mail.uni-mannheim.de

Abstract

In this paper, we describe the development of a language identification system and a part-of-speech tagger for Latin-Middle English mixed text. To this end, we annotate data with language IDs and Universal POS tags (Petrov et al., 2012). As a classifier, we train a conditional random field classifier for both sub-tasks, including features generated by the TreeTagger models of both languages. The focus lies on both a general and a task-specific evaluation. Moreover, we describe our effort concerning beyond proof-of-concept implementation of tools and towards a more task-oriented approach, showing how to apply our techniques in the context of Humanities research.

1 Introduction

Code-switching is often described as a phenomenon highly frequent in spoken language. In today's multi-cultural society, addressing mixed language in natural language processing appears to be inevitable, as the development of methods close to real-world data touches a nerve in recent computational linguistics. Especially social media as a form of written language close to spontaneous speech has recently been focused on code-switching research (e.g. Das and Gambäck (2013)).

However, code-switching is not just a recent phenomenon but can already be observed in medieval writing. As has been pointed out in several studies (Wenzel, 1994; Schendl and Wright, 2012; Jefferson et al., 2013), historical mixed text is an interesting, yet still widely unexplored, source of information concerning language use in multilingual societies of Medieval Europe. Even though some studies use text corpora in order to qualitatively describe the phenomenon (cf. Nurmi and Pahta (2013)), a deeper analysis of the underlying structures has not been carried out due to the lack of adequate resources.

In order to pave the way for an in-depth corpus-based analysis, we promote the systematic annotation of resources and concentrate on developing and implementing automatic processing tools. To this end, combining forces from Humanities and Computer Science seems promising for both sides. As an additional challenge, joint work in this context and with a specific purpose in mind does not just require the developing proof-of-concept tools. We need to tackle the issue of how to make tools available to Humanities scholars. Consequently, we do not just focus on developing techniques for automatic processing but also take into consideration how to share tools and make them useful for interpreting and analyzing data.

For the project presented in this study, we annotate Macaronic sermons (Horner, 2006)[1] with language information and part-of-speech (POS), respectively and use this resource to develop tools for automatic language identification (LID) on the word level and POS tagging of mixed Latin-Middle English text. The resulting tools allow for the automatic annotation of larger quantities of text and thus for the investigation of code-switching constraints within specific syntactic constructions on a larger scale. In particular, we aim at an analysis of code-switching rules within nominal phrases.

In the following example, determiner and modifier (*þe briʒt / the bright*) are written in Middle English whereas the head of the noun

---

[1] We are greatly endebted to the Pontifical Institute of Mediaeval Studies (PIMS), Toronto, for their support and kind permission to use a searchable PDF version of the sermon transcripts.

Proceedings of the 10th SIGHUM Workshop on Language Technology for Cultural Heritage, Social Sciences, and Humanities (LaTeCH), pages 43–51,
Berlin, Germany, August 11, 2016. ©2016 Association for Computational Linguistics

phrase (*sol / sun*) is written in Latin. Keller (2016) provides an analysis of adjectival modifiers in the framework of the Matrix Language Frame model introduced by Myers-Scotton (2001).

þe	briȝt	sol	sapiencie	subtrahit	lumen	suum
the	bright	sun	wisdom	withdraws	light	its
eng.	eng.	lat.	lat.	lat.	lat.	lat.

The focus of our work lies on the extraction of such phrases with the help of POS patterns along with the language information for all words of each phrase.

The body of this paper is organized as follows. Section 2 gives an overview of work that has been done in the context of code-switching. In Section 3, we describe the data set that serves as a basis for the experiments described in Sections 4 and 5. Section 6 concludes with an outline of how our tools will be made available for wider use by the academic community.

2 Related Work

Previous work on automatic processing of mixed text can be divided into two main areas: research on LID and work on POS tagging.

LID for written as well as for spoken code-switching has been tackled for a wide range of language pairs and with different methods. Lyu and Lyu (2008) investigate Mandarin-Taiwanese utterances from a corpus of spoken language. They propose a word-based lexical model for LID integrating acoustic, phonetic and lexical cues. Solorio and Liu (2008a) predict potential code-switching points in Spanish-English mixed data. Different learning algorithms are applied to transcriptions of code-switched discourse. Jain and Bhat (2014) present a system on using conditional posterior probabilities for the individual words along with other linguistically motivated language-specific as well as generic features. They experiment with a variety of language pairs, e.g. Nepali-English, Mandarin-English or Spanish-English. Yeong and Tan (2011) use morphological structure and sequence of syllables in Malay-English sentences to identify language. Barman et al. (2014) investigate mixed text including three languages: Bengali, English and Hindi. They experiment with word-level LID, applying a simple unsupervised dictionary-based approach, supervised word-level classification with and without contextual clues, and sequence labeling using CRFs.

So far, not much work has been published on POS tagging of code-switching text. Solorio and Liu (2008b) present results on POS tagging Spanish-English code-switched discourse. They investigate methods ranging from simple heuristics to an algorithm combining features from the output of an English and a Spanish POS tagger. Rodrigues and Kübler (2013) show POS tagging for speech transcripts containing multilingual intra-sentenial code-mixing. They compare a tagging model trained on a heterogeneous-language data set to a model that switches between two homogeneous-language tagging models dynamically using word-by-word LID. Jamatia et al. (2015) use both a coarse-grained and a fine-grained POS tag set for tagging English-Hindi Twitter and Facebook chat messages. They compare performance of a combination of language specific taggers to that of applying four machine learning algorithms using a range of different features.

Considering the rather limited number of automatic processing tools for our languages at hand, we focus on those methods suggesting the application of shallow features for written language. Thus, we renounce morphological processing as described in Yeong and Tan (2011) and prosodic features since we are working with written text.

3 Data

The texts addressed in the following are so-called Macaronic sermons (Horner, 2006), a text genre containing diverse code-switching structures of Middle English and Latin which is thus highly informative both for historical multilingualism research and for computational linguistics. Our aim is to investigate phrase-internal code-switching. This requires language information on the token level on one hand and a basic understanding of the syntax of a sentence on the other. We aim at POS tagging as a basis for a pattern-extraction-based approach. In particular, we are interested in extracting mixed-language nominal phrases with a focus on determiners, attributive adjectives and adjective phrases as adnominals.

Since we are often dealing with a critically low data situation in Digital Humanities focusing on historical topics, we experiment with a data set which can realistically be acquired with just a few hours of annotation effort. This implies that our approach is easily applicable to language pairs for

label	explanation	%
l	Latin	60.5
e	Middle English	24.6
a	word in both languages	1.8
n	Named Entity	1.0
p	punctuation	12.1

Table 1: Labels annotated for LID along an explanation for each label and the occurrence in percent.

label	explanation	%
ADJ	adjective	8.0
ADP	adposition (pre- and post)	7.9
ADV	adverb	6.0
CONJ	conjunction	7.9
DET	determiner	6.8
NOUN	noun (common and proper)	29.1
NUM	cardinal number	0.03
PRON	pronoun	4.3
PRT	particle or other function word	3.2
VERB	verb (all tenses and modes)	14.4
X	foreign word, typo, abbrev.	0.06
.	punctuation	12.3

Table 2: Labels annotated for POS tagging along with the explanation for each label and the occurrence in percent.

which there is only a limited amount of annotated data. Our annotated corpus comprises about 3000 tokens.

In a first step, we annotate the tokens for the following language information, mostly Latin and Middle English. The two languages share a small part of their vocabulary. Those words can e.g. be simple function words like *in*. For these items the attribution to one or the other language is not possible. We label these words with a separate tag to preserve the information that no decision on language could be made. Moreover, we mark named entities since they are often not part of the vocabulary of a language, as well as punctuation. Just about 25% of the tokens are Middle English compared to more than 60% of Latin words (cp. Table 1). Our data set comprises 159 sentences with an average length of 19.4 tokens. Overall we observe 316 switch points, which means an average number of two code-switching points per sentence.

In a second step, we annotate coarse-grained POS using the Universal Tagset (UT) suggested by Petrov et al. (2012). This choice facilitates a consistent annotation across languages since language specificities are conflated into more comprehensive categories. Nouns constitute by far the most frequent POS (cp. Table 2), which makes our data set a promising source for the investigation of nominal phrases.

4 Automated Processing of Mixed Text

We model LID and POS tagging as both two subsequent tasks in which POS tagging builds upon the results of the LID and two independent tasks where POS tagging and LID do not inform each other. LID can be understood as a step to facilitate POS tagging and any further processing of mixed text. In order to be used as a feature for POS tagging, it needs to be solved with a high accuracy to avoid error percolation through the entire processing pipeline.

4.1 Language Identification

We use an approach similar to the one described by Solorio and Liu (2008a). Since there is no available lemmatizer for Middle English, in contrast to Solorio and Liu (2008b) we cannot add lemma information to our training. To compensate for the lack of lemmas, we include POS informed word lists for both languages extracted from manually annotated corpora. Following the POS introduced by the universal dependency initiative (Nivre et al., 2016), we extract lists for the following POS: adjectives, adverbs, prepositions, proper nouns, nouns, determiners, interjections, pronouns, verbs, auxilary verbs and conjunctions. For Middle English we extract these lists from the Penn Parsed Corpora of Historical English (Kroch and Taylor, 2000). For Latin, we revert to the Latin corpora included in the Universal Dependency treebank namely Latin Dependency Treebank 2.0 (LDT) (Bamman and Crane, 2011), Latin-PROIEL UD treebank (Haug and Jøhndal, 2008) and the Latin-ITTB UD treebank (McGillivray et al., 2009). In case a word is found in one of the lists, we add its POS as a feature.

CRF classifiers are known to be successful for sequence labeling tasks. Based on features extracted from the results given by monolingual taggers for our data, we train a CRF classifier (Lafferty et al., 2001) combining those features with several other features. The features we implement are the following:

1. surface form
2. POS tag TreeTagger Latin
3. TreeTagger confidence Latin
4. POS tag TreeTagger Middle English
5. TreeTagger confidence Middle English
6. POS from Middle English word list
7. POS from Latin word list
8. character-unigrams prefix
9. character-bigrams prefix
10. character-trigrams prefix
11. character-unigram suffix
12. character-bigram suffix
13. character-trigram suffix

Features 2-5 are generated by the Latin and Middle English TreeTagger (Schmid, 1995), respectively. This means that this method is only an option for languages for which a TreeTagger model is available or can be trained[2]. We include character-n-gram affixes from length 1-3 to account for the fact that Latin is characterized by a relatively restricted suffix assignment. In addition, we use a context window of 5 tokens on all features.

4.2 Part-of-speech Tagging

For POS tagging, we use the same features as described in Section 4.1 (CRF_{base}). In order to investigate the influence of LID as a feature on POS Tagging, we also train the CRF classifier ($CRF_{predLID}$) using information generated by the LID system (feature 14.a). Since we cannot assume perfect LID, we evaluate the performance of a CRF classifier ($CRF_{goldLID}$) having the gold standard LID (feature 14.b) at its disposal. In this way, we can investigate to which degree differences in the quality of LID influence the POS tagging quality.

14.a LID label predicted by the system described in Section 4.1

14.b gold LID label manually annotated for our corpus

[2]We want to thank Achim Stein, University of Stuttgart, for providing the parameter file for Middle English.

	label	l	e	a	n	p	all
P	BL	68.9	0.0	0.0	0.0	100	33.8
	CRF	93.1	93.9	45.5	0.0	98.7	66.0
R	BL	100	0.0	0.0	0.0	99.4	40.0
	CRF	97.6	92.1	7.1	0.0	98.9	59.2
F	BL	81.6	0.0	0.0	0.0	100	36.3
	CRF	95.3	93.0	14.9	0.0	99.3	59.9

Table 3: Performance of the CRF system for langouage identification compared to the baseline (BL). Precision, recall and F-score per class and macro-average of all classes.

5 Results

We evaluate our systems in a 10-fold cross-validation setting using 80% for training, and 10% each for development and testing. We tune the hyper-parameter settings of our learning algorithm on our development set by testing different manually chosen parameter settings. The CRF classifier is trained with the CRF++ toolkit (Lafferty et al., 2001) using L2-regularization and a c-value of 1000. We report average results over all sets.

5.1 Language Identification

Since the sermons are primarily written in Latin featuring Middle English insertions, we use a combination of Latin and perfect punctuation labeling as a majority baseline (BL) for our LID system. We report per class precision, recall and F-score along with macro-averages for the overall system. We do not report accuracy since the number of instances per class highly varies.

As was to be expected, our system reliably finds the right label for Latin text and just a little less so for English. We attribute the poor performance for named entities and words appearing in both languages to the low number of training instances in

label	% err	% l	% e	% a	% n	% p
l	2.4	-	84.1	6.8	0.0	9.1
e	7.9	95.0	-	3.3	0.0	1.7
a	92.9	90.4	9.6	-	0.0	0.0
n	100	90	10.	0.0	-	0.0
p	0.5	100	0.0	0.0	0.0	-

Table 4: Percentage of incorrectly labeled tokens per class along with the distribution of incorrect labels among the other labels.

	label	ADJ	ADP	ADV	CONJ	DET	NOUN	NUM	PRON	PRT	VERB	X	.	all
	BL1	43.3	92.0	72.9	85.1	25.0	71.1	0.0	30.5	0.0	55.8	5.1	100	48.4
	BL2	55.7	83.1	68.6	87.2	37.5	82.5	0.0	34.5	23.2	78.2	7.1	100	54.8
P	CRF_{base}	68.1	92.0	81.2	88.8	79.3	85.2	0.0	82.2	71.4	85.9	0.0	98.2	69.4
	$CRF_{predLID}$	69.2	92.8	79.5	89.7	78.9	85.3	0.0	82.2	72.5	86.2	0.0	98.2	69.5
	$CRF_{goldLID}$	69.4	92.4	80.0	90.4	77.8	85.6	0.0	82.2	72.5	86.4	0.0	98.4	69.6
	BL1	51.0	80.6	56.8	63.1	3.3	79.4	0.0	45.1	0.0	76.5	1.0	98.4	46.3
	BL2	51.8	89.7	68.6	81.1	8.6	90.6	0.0	53.4	23.2	84.4	100	98.4	65.8
R	CRF_{base}	60.0	86.0	67.6	88.1	82.3	95.3	0.0	66.2	60.6	86.9	0.0	98.7	66.0
	$CRF_{predLID}$	60.4	85.5	69.2	88.9	82.3	95.4	0.0	66.2	58.6	87.6	0.0	98.4	66.0
	$CRF_{goldLID}$	65.1	89.1	74.2	89.4	80.0	90.3	0.0	73.3	64.8	87.0	0.0	98.7	66.2
	BL1	46.9	85.9	63.8	72.5	5.9	75.0	0.0	36.4	0.0	64.5	9.8	99.2	46.7
	BL2	53.7	86.3	68.8	84.1	14.0	86.4	0.0	41.9	36.5	81.2	13.3	99.2	55.5
F	CRF_{base}	**63.8**	88.9	73.7	88.5	**80.8**	**90.0**	0.0	73.3	65.6	86.4	0.0	98.4	67.4
	$CRF_{predLID}$	**64.5**	89.0	74.0	89.3	**80.6**	**90.1**	0.0	73.3	64.8	86.9	0.0	98.3	67.6
	$CRF_{goldLID}$	**65.1**	89.1	74.2	89.4	**80.0**	**90.3**	0.0	73.3	64.8	87.0	0.0	98.7	67.7

Table 5: Performance of the CRF systems for POS tagging compared to the majority baseline (BL1), the confidence baseline (BL2). CRF_{base}: system with the 13 basic features, $CRF_{predLID}$: system with predicted LID as an additional feature, $CRF_{goldLID}$: system with gold-standard LID as an additional feature. Precision (P), Recall (R) and F-score (F) per class and macro-average of all classes are given. The task-relevant results are emphasized in bold.

our corpus.

In order to investigate the primary sources of errors, we inspect the incorrectly labeled tokens per class. Table 4 shows that all but 2.4% of the Latin tokens are labeled correctly. The erroneous labels can be attributed to about 84% to English, 7% to the class that can appear in both languages. The remaining 9% contain wrong labels for punctuation. The performance for English tokens is slightly lower with a error rate of 7.9% incorrect labels which are almost all tagged as Latin. This can be due to the fact that our data contains more Latin tokens overall. The same effect is observable for the labels *a* (word in both languages) and *n* (named entities). Since the corpus contains just a few instances with those labels, they get incorrectly assigned to Latin. The small error in classifying punctuation appears in one of our cross-validation sets where colons are not part of the training but the test set.

5.2 Part-of-speech Tagging

For the evaluation of our POS tagger, we use two baselines. We compare the output of our systems to the output of the monolingual Latin tagger after mapping the Latin tagset to the UT. Moreover, we add a strong baseline, drawing on the confidence feature of the monolingual TreeTagger models. We choose the POS label of the monolingual tagger with a higher level of confidence. In case the label indicates that a word is a foreign word, we choose the label from the other language (in our case Middle English). We map all POS tags to the UT. Per-class results along with macro-F-score are shown in Table 5.

All our systems beat the baseline systems for almost all classes (except for BL2 adverb and verb) (cf. Table 5). With overall F-scores between 67.4 and 67.7 our systems achieve better F-scores than the baseline systems with an F-score of 46.7 and 55.5, respectively. In the further analysis we leave the results for NUM and X aside cause they appear just once and three times in the entire corpus, respectively. Even though the average scores for all classes combined range just between about 60 and 90, we achieve good results for classes with a high number of tokens in our corpus (e.g. nouns and verbs), and also for adpositions and conjunctions. Since macro-F-score gives equal weight to all classes the numbers might be misleading, depending on the purpose of the system. Given that we built the POS tagger with a specific task in mind, namely the extraction of nominal phrases, we calculate the F-score for the POS classes relevant to this task (determiners, adjectives and nouns). This gives a task-specific macro F-score of 78.2 (CRF_{base}), 78.4 ($CRF_{predLID}$) and 74.5 ($CRF_{goldLID}$), respectively. Those F-scores are noticeably above the average F-scores for the overall systems and also beat the task-specific F-scores of BL1 (42.6) and BL2 (51.4). The relatively high average recall of almost 80 for these three labels combined for all three systems is important for the task whereas precision has lower priority, since the extracted phrases are manually inspected afterwards. Since our LID system performs well, the system with automatically predicted labels shows a slight increase in performance compared to the system without LID information. The system with manually annotated LID information yields the best performance. However, according to McNemar's test the differences are not statistically significant.

The analysis of the incorrectly labeled tokens shows which POS tags are difficult to distinguish (cf. Table 6). Since we are especially interested in adjectives, an error rate of 40% is rather high. Out of these, about 63% have been incorrectly labeled as nouns, which has considerable negative effect on our objective, especially since most of the incorrectly labeled nouns are labeled as adjectives. Almost 70% of the adjectives that are incorrectly labeled as nouns are Latin. This can be explained by the morphology of adjectives in Latin. As Latin adjectives and nouns have often similar, if not the same suffixes of case marking, the two classes cannot be distinguished using the suffix as a defining feature. These difficulties are also observed by vor der Brück and Mehler (2016) who present a morphological tagger for Latin.

	þis	made	hom	to	lede
	this	made	them	to	lead
lang.	eng.	eng.	eng.	eng.	eng.
gold	PRON	VERB	PRON	PRT	VERB
pred	PRON	VERB	PRON	PRT	VERB
	super	terram	celestem	conuersacionem
	on	earth	heavenly	regime
lang.	lat.	lat.	lat.	lat.
gold	ADP	NOUN	ADJ	NOUN
pred	ADP	DET	NOUN	NOUN

The first half of the sentence [3] is written in Middle English. The assigned POS tágs are correct and also the first Latin word after the code-switching point is labeled correctly. The phrase *terram clestem conuersacionem* is tagged in the pattern of a noun phrase with a determiner and a compounded noun instead of a prepositional phrase *super terram* (Engl.: on earth) and a noun phrase (Engl.: heavenly behavior) consisting of an adjective and a noun. The similar syntactic function of pronouns (in case of possessive pronouns

---

[3]Translation by Horner (2006): *this made them lead on earth a heavenly regime.*

	LID			POS		
size	pre	rec	f-score	pre	rec	f-score
800	56.3	56.8	56.5	60.8.1	54.6	56.8
1600	56.6.0	57.8	57.2	66.7	63.0	64.6
2400	66.0	59.2	59.9.3	69.5	66.0	67.6

Table 7: Different portions of the training set along with precision, recall and F-score for LID and POS tagging.

and demonstrative pronouns) and determiners leads to a source of error.[4]

	In	isto	non	est	fiducia
	In	this	not	is	confidence
lang.	lat.	lat.	lat	lat.	lat.
gold	ADP	PRON	PRT	VERB	NOUN
pred	ADP	DET	PRT	VERB	NOUN

On closer inspection, we find that many of the incorrectly tagged words appear in POS sequences which are either rarely or not at all contained in the training data. We predict that adding more training data will significantly decrease errors of this kind. Since data sparsity in general is an issue dealing with historical text, we investigate how different sizes of the training set influence the results. We compare results for 800 tokens, 1600 tokens, and for the complete training set (around 2400 tokens).

With an increase of training instances, the results improve for both tasks (cf. Table 7). The increase from 800 to 1600 is higher than from 1600 to 2400. This suggests that the F-score might grow logarithmically with increasing training size.

6 Tools for Digital Humanities

Since the aim of our project is not only to build a proof-of-concept system but to enable Humanities scholars to automatically process their data with the help of our tools, we implement a simple web service in Java to offer an easily accessible interface to our tool.[5]. The data is returned in a format compatible with ICARUS, a search and visualization tool which primarily targets dependency trees (Gärtner et al., 2013). Despite the present lack of a dependency-parsed syntax layer, ICARUS offers the opportunity to inspect the data and pose complex search requests, combining the three layers

---

[4]Translation by Horner (2006): *in it there is no confidence.*

[5]The web service is hosted at `https://clarin09.ims.uni-stuttgart.de/normalisierung/mixed-pos.html` For access, please contact the author.

label	% err	ADJ	ADP	ADV	CONJ	DET	NOUN	PRON	PRT	VERB	.
ADJ	39.6	-	2.1	3.1	0.0	9.3	**62.9**	0.0	1.0	20.6	1.0
ADP	14.6	11.4	-	8.6	6.5	5.7	11.4	0.0	**37.1**	**14.3**	2.9
ADV	30.8	19.3	5.3	-	10.5	5.3	**33.3**	7.0	1.8	14.0	0.0
CONJ	11.1	0.0	0.0	**37.0**	-	11.1	7.4	22.2	11.1	7.4	3.7
DET	17.7	16.2	10.8	10.8	2.7	-	**32.4**	10.8	8.1	8.1	0.0
NOUN	4.6	**56.1**	0.0	9.8	0.0	0.0	-	2.4	0.0	26.8	4.9
PRON	33.8	8.8	0.0	2.2	15.5	**31.1**	20.0	-	2.2	17.8	2.2
PRT	41.4	4.9	12.2	14.6	17.1	**22.0**	14.6	2.4	-	12.2	0.0
VERB	12.4	25.5	3.6	1.8	0.0	7.3	**54.5**	5.5	0.0	-	1.8
.	1.6	33.3	0.0	0.0	16.7	0.0	**50.0**	0.0	0.0	0.0	-

Table 6: Percentage of incorrectly labeled tokens per class along with the distribution of incorrect labels among the other labels for the $\mathrm{CRF}_{predLID}$ system.

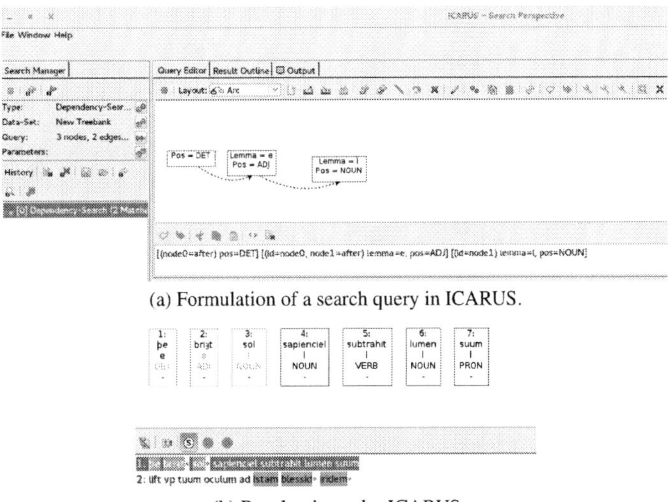

(a) Formulation of a search query in ICARUS.

(b) Results shown by ICARUS

Figure 1: Search interface of ICARUS returning results on a query for an English adjective followed by a Latin noun within the next 3 tokens.

of token, language information and POS tag. Figure 1 shows a query that extracts all sequences of a determiner in either of both languages followed by a Middle English adjective followed by a Latin noun. ICARUS shows the results within the sentence of origin. ICARUS also allows searches including gaps. This is helpful, since nominal phrases vary according to the number of adjectives and as to whether or not they contain an overt determiner. Thus, flexibility in formulating the search query facilitates an in-depth search of all possible constructions.

Our method can easily be adapted to other languages by inserting the fitting monolingual taggers (TreeTagger) and POS related word lists (if available). For this purpose, the code is publicly available on Github[6].

7 Conclusion and future work

We show the implementation and application of two systems developed for a specific purpose. We get reasonable results given the very low number of annotated training instances. Considering the detailed error analysis for our system, we can purposefully extend our training data in order to correct the sources of error in the future by for example adding monolingual data from the Penn-Helsinki Parsed Corpus of Middle English (Kroch and Taylor, 2000).

Subsequently, we will look into the possibility of jointly modeling LID and POS tagging. Eventually, we aim at a dependency parser for mixed

---

[6]`https://github.com/sarschu/CodeSwitching`

text in order to get deeper insights into the constraints on intra-sentinal code-switching.

We aim to show that not just the development of tools but also the support with respect to applying them constitutes an important component of successful collaboration between Humanities and Computer Science. In return, a task-oriented tool development along with immediate feedback on the performance and analysis of error from the Humanities side facilitate the implementation of systems that do not only serve the proof of a concept but are applied to real-world data. We believe that this kind of collaboration is the way to give Computer Science the chance to support other fields in their research and find new and interesting challenges throughout this work.

Acknowledgments

We want to thank André Blessing for his support with setting up the web service and Achim Stein for providing us with a TreeTagger model for Middle English. We are greatly endebted to the Pontifical Institute of Mediaeval Studies (PIMS), Toronto, for their support and kind permission to use a searchable PDF version of the sermon transcripts. This research has been performed within the CRETA project which is funded by the German Ministry for Education and Research (BMBF).

References

David Bamman and Gregory Crane. 2011. The ancient greek and latin dependency treebanks. In Caroline Sporleder, Antal Bosch, and Kalliopi Zervanou, editors, *Language Technology for Cultural Heritage*, Theory and Applications of Natural Language Processing, pages 79–98. Springer Berlin Heidelberg. 10.1007/978-3-642-20227-8$_5$.

Utsab Barman, Amitava Das, Joachim Wagner, and Jennifer Foster. 2014. Code-mixing: A challenge for language identification in the language of social media. In *In Proceedings of the First Workshop on Computational Approaches to Code-Switching*.

Amitava Das and Björn Gambäck. 2013. Code-mixing in social media text. the last language identification frontier? *TAL*, 54(3):41–64.

Markus Gärtner, Gregor Thiele, Wolfgang Seeker, Anders Björkelund, and Jonas Kuhn. 2013. Icarus – an extensible graphical search tool for dependency treebanks. In *Proceedings of the 51st Annual Meeting of the Association for Computational Linguistics: System Demonstrations*, pages 55–60, Sofia, Bulgaria, August. Association for Computational Linguistics.

Dag T. T. Haug and Marius L. Jøhndal. 2008. Creating a parallel treebank of the old indo-european bible translations. In Caroline Sporleder and Kiril Ribarov, editors, *Proceedings of the Second Workshop on Language Technology for Cultural Heritage Data (LaTeCH 2008)*, pages 27–34.

Patrick J. Horner. 2006. *A Macaronic Sermon Collection from Late Medieval England: Oxford, MS Bodley 649*. Pontifical Institute of Mediaeval Studies Toronto: Studies and texts. Pontifical Institute of Mediaeval Studies.

Naman Jain and Riyaz Ahmad Bhat. 2014. Language identification in code-switching scenario. In *Proceedings of The First Workshop on Computational Approaches to Code Switching*, pages 87–93, Doha, Qatar.

Anupam Jamatia, Björn Gambäck, and Amitava Das. 2015. Part-of-speech tagging for code-mixed english-hindi twitter and facebook chat messages. In *Recent Advances in Natural Language Processing, RANLP 2015, 7-9 September, 2015, Hissar, Bulgaria*, pages 239–248.

Judith A. Jefferson, Ad Putter, and Amanda Hopkins. 2013. *Multilingualism in Medieval Britain (c. 1066-1520): Sources and Analysis*. Medieval texts and cultures of Northern Europe. Brepols.

Mareike Keller. 2016. Code-switched adjectives and adverbs in macaronic sermons. In Elise Louviot and Catherine Delesse, editors, *Proceedings of the Biennial Conference on the diachrony of English (CBDA4)*. forthcoming.

Anthony Kroch and Ann Taylor. 2000. The penn-helsinki parsed corpus of middle english (ppcme2). Department of Linguistics, University of Pennsylvania. CD-ROM, second edition, release 4 (http://www.ling.upenn.edu/ppche-release-2016/PPCME2-RELEASE-4).

John D. Lafferty, Andrew McCallum, and Fernando C. N. Pereira. 2001. Conditional random fields: Probabilistic models for segmenting and labeling sequence data. In *Proceedings of the Eighteenth International Conference on Machine Learning*, ICML '01, pages 282–289, San Francisco, CA, USA. Morgan Kaufmann Publishers Inc.

Dau-Cheng Lyu and Ren-Yuan Lyu. 2008. Language identification on code-switching utterances using multiple cues. In *INTERSPEECH 2008, 9th Annual Conference of the International Speech Communication Association, Brisbane, Australia, September 22-26, 2008*, pages 711–714.

Barbara McGillivray, Marco Passarotti, and Paolo Ruffolo. 2009. The index thomisticus treebank project: Annotation, parsing and valency lexicon. *TAL*, 50:103–127.

Carol Myers-Scotton. 2001. The matrix language frame model: Development and responses. *Codeswitching Worldwide II*, pages 23–58.

Joakim Nivre, Marie-Catherine de Marneffe, Filip Ginter, Yoav Goldberg, Jan Hajic, Christopher D. Manning, Ryan McDonald, Slav Petrov, Sampo Pyysalo, Natalia Silveira, Reut Tsarfaty, and Daniel Zeman. 2016. Universal dependencies v1: A multilingual treebank collection. In Nicoletta Calzolari (Conference Chair), Khalid Choukri, Thierry Declerck, Sara Goggi, Marko Grobelnik, Bente Maegaard, Joseph Mariani, Helene Mazo, Asuncion Moreno, Jan Odijk, and Stelios Piperidis, editors, *Proceedings of the Tenth International Conference on Language Resources and Evaluation (LREC 2016)*, Paris, France, may. European Language Resources Association (ELRA).

Arja Nurmi and Päivi Pahta. 2013. Multilingual practices in the language of the law: Evidence from the lampeter corpus. In Olga Timofeeva Jukka Tyrkkö and Maria Salenius, editors, *Ex Philologia Lux: Essays in Honour of Leena Kahlas-Tarkka (Mémoires de la Société Nophilologique de Helsinki XC)*, pages 187–205. Société Nophilologique.

Slav Petrov, Dipanjan Das, and Ryan McDonald. 2012. A universal part-of-speech tagset. In Nicoletta Calzolari (Conference Chair), Khalid Choukri, Thierry Declerck, Mehmet Uur Doan, Bente Maegaard, Joseph Mariani, Asuncion Moreno, Jan Odijk, and Stelios Piperidis, editors, *Proceedings of the Eight International Conference on Language Resources and Evaluation (LREC'12)*, Istanbul, Turkey, may. European Language Resources Association (ELRA).

Paul Rodrigues and Sandra Kübler. 2013. Part of speech tagging bilingual speech transcripts with intrasentential model switching. In *Analyzing Microtext, Papers from the 2013 AAAI Spring Symposium, Palo Alto, California, USA, March 25-27, 2013*.

Herbert Schendl and Laura Wright. 2012. *Code-Switching in Early English*. Topics in English Linguistics [TiEL]. De Gruyter.

Helmut Schmid. 1995. Improvements in part-of-speech tagging with an application to german. In *In Proceedings of the ACL SIGDAT-Workshop*, pages 47–50.

Thamar Solorio and Yang Liu. 2008a. Learning to predict code-switching points. In *Proceedings of the Conference on Empirical Methods in Natural Language Processing*, EMNLP '08, pages 973–981, Stroudsburg, PA, USA. Association for Computational Linguistics.

Thamar Solorio and Yang Liu. 2008b. Part-of-speech tagging for english-spanish code-switched text. In *Proceedings of the Conference on Empirical Methods in Natural Language Processing*, EMNLP '08, pages 1051–1060, Stroudsburg, PA, USA. Association for Computational Linguistics.

Tim vor der Brück and Alexander Mehler. 2016. TLT-CRF: A lexicon-supported morphological tagger for Latin based on conditional random fields. In *Proceedings of the 10th International Conference on Language Resources and Evaluation*, LREC 2016. Accepted.

S. Wenzel. 1994. *Macaronic sermons: bilingualism and preaching in late-medieval England*. Recentiores : Later Latin Texts and Contexts. University of Michigan Press.

Yin-Lai Yeong and Tien-Ping Tan. 2011. Applying grapheme, word, and syllable information for language identification in code switching sentences. In *International Conference on Asian Language Processing, IALP 2011, Penang, Malaysia, 15-17 November, 2011*, pages 111–114.

Dealing with word-internal modification and spelling variation in data-driven lemmatization

Fabian Barteld   Ingrid Schröder   Heike Zinsmeister

Institut für Germanistik
Universität Hamburg
`firstname.lastname@uni-hamburg.de`

Abstract

This paper describes our contribution to two challenges in data-driven lemmatization. We approach lemmatization in the framework of a two-stage process, where first lemma candidates are generated and afterwards a ranker chooses the most probable lemma from these candidates. The first challenge is that languages with rich morphology like Modern German can feature morphological changes of different kinds, in particular word-internal modification. This makes the generation of the correct lemma a harder task than just removing suffixes (stemming). The second challenge that we address is spelling variation as it appears in non-standard texts. We experiment with different generators that are specifically tailored to deal with these two challenges. We show in an oracle setting that there is a possible increase in lemmatization accuracy of 14% with our methods to generate lemma candidates on Middle Low German, a group of historical dialects of German (1200–1650 AD). Using a log-linear model to choose the correct lemma from the set, we obtain an actual increase of 5.56%.

1 Introduction

Lemmatization is the task of finding the lemma or base form for a given word token. It is used as a preprocessing step for information retrieval and other NLP applications for languages with rich morphology and has been shown to outperform stemming for some tasks (Korenius et al., 2004). Lemmatization can be formalized as a string transduction task where for an input sequence of tokens $t_1 \ldots t_n$ an output sequence of lemmas $l_1 \ldots l_n$ is produced. This task has been approached in a variety of ways, e.g. by combining morphological rules with dictionary lookups (Sennrich and Kunz, 2014). Chrupała (2006) introduced a sequence-labeling approach to lemmatization in which a token is labeled with a rule that transforms it to its lemma. The set of rules from which the labels are chosen are induced automatically from the training data. Müller and Schütze (2015) use a similar setting, but, instead of choosing a rule to apply, they apply all possible rules and afterwards use a ranker to select the lemma. Conceptually, this is a two-stage approach towards lemmatization – first generating lemma candidates for a given type, i.e. an inflected word form, and then choosing the best of these candidates for the token. We follow this approach and present generators that increase the number of correct lemma candidates that can be generated for out-of-vocabulary (OOV) words in the case of word-internal modification and spelling variation:

(i) Word-internal modifications like the *umlaut* (*Schläge - Schlag* "strikes - (the) strike") and infixation (*aufgegessen - aufessen* "eaten up - eat up") in Modern German (DEU)[1] pose special problems to lemma candidate generation. In order to improve the generalization capabilities of the rules induced from the training data, we substitute the edit trees (ET) (Chrupała, 2008) used by Müller and Schütze (2015) with lexical correspondences (LC) (Fulop and Neuvel, 2013).

(ii) Spelling variation as it appears in historical language or computer-mediated communication results in an increase in data sparsity and therefore a large number of OOV words. We add a generator that returns the lemma candidates for the most similar in-vocabulary (IV) word(s). Thereby, the lemmatization can be made more ro-

---

[1]Abbreviations for language names follow the ISO 639-3 codes.

Proceedings of the 10th SIGHUM Workshop on Language Technology for Cultural Heritage, Social Sciences, and Humanities (LaTeCH), pages 52–62,
Berlin, Germany, August 11, 2016. ©2016 Association for Computational Linguistics

bust against simple misspellings or spelling variations, since the correct lemma can be returned even in these cases.

We test our approach on Middle Low German (GML) texts. GML is a group of historical dialects of German (1200–1650 AD), which – like DEU – features word-internal modification. Also, as a historical language, GML exhibits spelling variation. In order to see how hard these features make the task of lemmatizing GML, we compare it with lemmatizing DEU newswire texts.

2 Related work

The methods presented here are general in nature and can be incorporated into different lemmatization approaches. We apply our methods with LEMMING (Müller and Schütze, 2015), a state-of-the-art lemmatizer which performs lemmatization with a log-linear model that combines candidate generation with a probabilistic ranker.[2] LEMMING can be used to do lemmatization independently from morphological tagging or to combine both tasks with a joint model. As we are interested in lemmatization, we only use the independent lemmatization model.[3] The generator used for lemma candidate generation can be of any kind. The original version of LEMMING uses a deterministic rule-based generator and learns the set of rules from the training data. Following Chrupała (2008), the standard generator in LEMMING uses edit trees (ET). In ETs – unlike in the shortest edit scripts on reversed strings that are used by Chrupała (2006) – the positions of edits are not all indexed from one end of the string but either from the beginning or the end. This is similar to prefix and suffix replacement rules (Gesmundo and Samardžić, 2012). Therefore prefixes and suffixes are handled independently from the length of the word. However, as Jongejan and Dalianis (2009) point out, languages like German and Dutch also allow word-internal modifications, which are not covered independently of the word length by rules which index the position of the change relative to either the beginning or the end of the word. This is illustrated with ETs in Figure (1a) and (1b). The numbers at the nodes of the ETs denote the position of the substring this node represents measured from the beginning and the end of the type. In the case of *Bäume* and *Baum* the longest common substring *um* starts after the second character in *Bäume* and ends before the last character. Therefore, the first node is indexed with 2 and 1. See Chrupała (2008) for a detailed description of edit trees.[4] As can be seen from Figure (1a) and (1b) the word-internal umlaut leads to different indices. Our contribution to this challenge is to test rules that model word-internal modifications independently of the word length. We use *lexical correspondences* that have been proposed in Whole Word Morphology by Fulop and Neuvel (2013) and have been used in morphological learning (Neuvel and Fulop, 2002).

Our second addition to the generator addresses spelling variation. Spelling variation is often dealt with in a preprocessing step called normalization before taggers or lemmatizers are applied to the data (Eisenstein, 2013). Formally, such a normalization is a string transduction task like lemmatization. Therefore, LEMMING directly deals with spelling variation by learning rules that generate the lemma, simultaneously removing inflection and normalizing variation. The rules inferred from the training data, however, will only deal with specific combinations of inflection and spelling variation.

A way of dealing with spelling variation independently of inflection is to identify possible spelling variants and use them for the lemmatization. In several approaches spelling variation patterns are learned from the training data exploiting the annotation (Kestemont et al., 2010; van Halteren and Rem, 2013; Logačev et al., 2014). Apart from using these patterns to expand the training data by creating probable spelling variants, Kestemont et al. (2010) produce IV words that have a high probability to be a spelling variants for OOV words and use their lemmatization to predict the lemma of OOV words. We adopt a similar approach for lemma candidate generation: We determine probable spelling variants for all OOV types in the set of IV types and generate lemma candidates based on these. We experiment with different similarity measures for detecting the probable spelling variants.

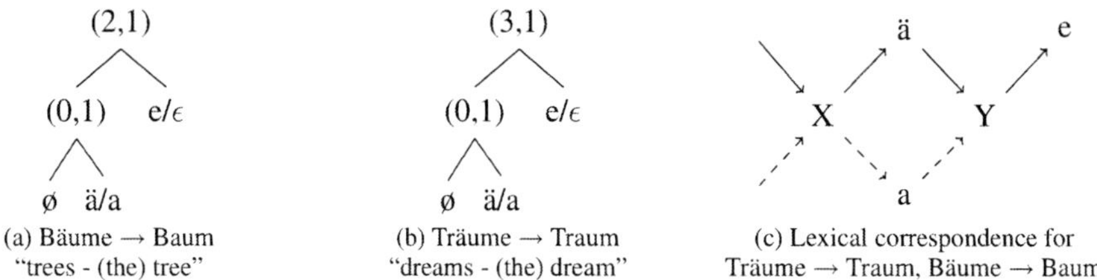

Figure 1: Edit trees and lexical correspondence for the a-umlaut + -e inflection pattern

3 Dealing with word internal modification

As mentioned above, edit trees (ET) do not generalize over word-internal modifications. An ET learned from the pair *Bäume, Baum* "trees – (the) tree" cannot predict the lemma *Traum* "(the) dream" for *Träume* "dreams". In order to allow for such generalizations, we use lexical correspondences for lemma candidate generation instead.

We define a *lexical correspondence* (LC) for two words over some alphabet $w_1, w_2 \in \Sigma^*$ as the tuple $\langle \mathcal{T}, \mathcal{L} \rangle$[5] where $\mathcal{T}$ and $\mathcal{L}$ are two sequences of constants and variables with the requirement that the same variables appear in both sequences.[6] Constants are elements of $\Sigma^* \backslash \{\epsilon\}$, i.e. the possible words over the alphabet Σ with the exception of the empty word ϵ. Variables are placeholders that can be replaced with constants. Note that we do not allow empty strings as constants. Therefore, a variable must be replaced with at least one letter. Figure (1c) depicts the LC for the ETs in Figures (1a) and (1b). This shows that LCs are able to generalize over pairs of type and lemma that ETs do not generalize over.

The solid arrows in Figure (1c) represent the sequence $\mathcal{T}$ (representing e.g. *Bäume*) and the dashed arrows the sequence $\mathcal{L}$ (representing e.g. *Baum*). The variables X and Y are depicted in the middle. By replacing the latter with the missing parts of the words, e.g. $\{X/\text{B}, Y/\text{um}\}$, type and lemma can be read off the sequences.

In order to create a lemma given a type and a LC, the constants in sequence $\mathcal{T}$ are matched with characters in the type and the variables are replaced with the remaining substrings. Then the lemma can be read off the second sequence $\mathcal{L}$. For instance, given the type *Träume* and the LC in Figure (1c) the constants match with *ä* and the final *e* in *Träume*, creating the replacements $\{X/\text{Tr}, Y/\text{um}\}$. Using these replacements in the second sequence creates the lemma *Traum*.

An ET can be unambiguously transformed into a LC. Hence, type-lemma pairs from which the same ET is induced lead to the same LC. This proves that LCs generalize over all cases over which ETs generalize.[7] On the other hand, as Fulop and Neuvel (2013) pointed out, lexical correspondences with more than one variable cannot always be unambiguously applied. One example is the type *Säbelschläge* "(the) blows with a saber" and the LC from Figure (1c). The *ä* can be matched with two positions in the type leading to two different replacements and corresponding lemma candidates: $\{X/\text{S}, Y/\text{belschläg}\}$ (lemma candidate: **Sabelschläg*) and $\{X/\text{Säbelschl}, Y/\text{g}\}$ (lemma candidate: *Säbelschlag*).

In the context of LEMMING, we can generate both variants and let the ranker decide. However, this leads to a trade-off between better generalization of the rules and possible indeterminacy, i.e. bigger candidate sets.[8] The latter increases the computational costs for training and applying the ranker. It also introduces new possible errors for the ranker. Consequently, we are looking for a way to restrict the overgeneralization. One source of overgeneralization are LCs of the form $\langle [X, Y], [X, \text{'constant'}, Y] \rangle$. An LC like this is applicable to all types. It creates a lemma candidate by inserting the constant and does this between all

---

[5] Note that the order of the sequences is fixed as we always use lexical correspondences between type and lemma in that order.

[6] Our definition of lexical correspondence is less strict than the original definition given by Fulop and Neuvel (2013). Their definition also takes syntactic categories and semantic relations into account.

[7] See Appendix A.2 for details.

[8] Note that the ET in Figure (1a) learned from *Bäume, Baum* will be applicable to *Säbelschläge* as well and creates the lemma candidate *Sabelschläg*. Therefore, in this case, it is unlikely that the LC generates more false lemma candidates than created with using ETs.

the letters. One example for a similar LC results from the German pair *sind, sein* "(they) are – (to) be" which leads to $\langle [X, Y, \text{'d'}], [X, \text{'e'}, Y] \rangle$. This LC is applicable to all types ending with d and allows the insertion of e at multiple positions.

In order to avoid this kind of overgeneration insertions are anchored by their character offset either from the beginning or the end of the type. This position can be read off directly from an ET.[9] Therefore, these lexical correspondences with anchored insertions (LC-AI) have a generalization capacity that is reduced in comparison to unanchored LCs but is still higher when compared to ETs.

4 Dealing with spelling variation

In this section, we present a method for allowing the lemmatizer to deal with spelling variation – namely generating lemma candidates from similar in-vocabulary (IV) types. Using this approach, the correct lemma candidate can be generated for out-of-vocabulary (OOV) types that are spelling variants of IV types. We restrict this additional generation of lemma candidates to OOV types to avoid overgeneration.

An upper bound for improving the coverage by this method is given by generating the lemma candidates for all of the training instances and add them to the lemma candidate set for OOV types. The problem with this approach is the large number of lemma candidates for OOV words. This makes it hard for the ranker to find the correct lemma. Therefore, our aim is to select an appropriate subset from the training data that contains possible spelling variants and only add the candidates generated on this subset to the lemma candidates. There are distance measures explicitly proposed for finding spelling variants (Kempken, 2005; Pilz, 2009; Bollmann, 2012) that could be used for this task. However, these measures need to be trained on pairs of spelling variant and standard spelling which are not available in our case. Consequently, we use string similarity measures that can be used without training data of this kind. Kestemont et al. (2010) use the Levenshtein distance (Levenshtein, 1966) and Dice's coefficient (Dice, 1945) to detect spelling variants in Middle Dutch texts. While they report a better performance of the Levenshtein distance, Jin (2015) achieves good results with the Jaccard

Index (Levandowsky and Winter, 1971) for candidate generation in normalizing English Twitter data and also proposes a weighted version.[10] This weighted version is given by Equation 1.

$$JaccardIndex_w(f(t_1), f(t_2)) = \frac{\displaystyle\sum_{\mathsf{f} \in f(t_1) \cap f(t_2)} w(\mathsf{f})}{\displaystyle\sum_{\mathsf{f} \in f(t_1) \cup f(t_2)} w(\mathsf{f})} \quad (1)$$

Here, $f(t) \subseteq F$ is the set of similarity features for a type t and $w : F \to \mathbb{R}$ is a weight function. Both can be chosen differently allowing to fine-tune the measure for specific data. For normalizing Twitter data, Jin uses bigrams, skip-1-bigrams and sets the weight for each feature to 1.

Barteld et al. (2015) use yet another similarity measure, Proxinette (Hathout, 2014), for spelling variant detection. Similar to the Jaccard Index, Proxinette uses similarity features to compute the similarity of two types. Differing from the Jaccard Index, in Proxinette the similarity score is obtained by the probability of a random walk in a bipartite graph with types and similarity features as vertices. This leads to a weight for the features of $\frac{1}{deg(f)}$, where $deg(f)$ is the degree of the vertex f, i.e. the number of types having this similarity feature. Since in this form, the weights are dependent on the corpus size, we use $1 - relFreq(f)$ as a weight function. Thereby we keep the general idea of giving more weight to infrequent similarity features while avoiding the dependency on the corpus size.[11] The relative frequency is estimated based on a training corpus (in our case the training corpus for the lemmatizer) leading to a weight of 0 for all features that appear in every type of the corpus, and 1 for features that did not appear in the corpus.

The similarity features used in Proxinette are not only character n-grams of given lengths, but all possible n-grams above a given length including the whole type. This is a way to prevent a similarity of 1 for two different types, a problem that

---

[9]See Appendix A.3 for a detailed description.

[10]As $Dice(x,y) = \frac{2*JaccardIndex(x,y)}{JaccardIndex(x,y)+1}$ (Egghe, 2010) Dice's coefficient and the Jaccard Index will give the same results in our threshold setting. Therefore, we restrict ourselves to the Jaccard Index.

[11]This weight is only dependent on the size of the corpus in the sense that bigger corpora lead to better estimates of the relative frequency.

has been noted by Jin (2015) for the Jaccard Index with character n-grams of fixed lengths.

Even when no training data for spelling variation in the form of variant and standard form is available, variation patterns can be learned approximately using data annotated with POS tags and/ or lemmas (Kestemont et al., 2010; van Halteren and Rem, 2013; Logačev et al., 2014). We follow Kestemont et al. (2010), who use word forms annotated with the same lemma that have a Levenshtein distance of 1 as proxies for pairs of spelling variants. They train a memory-based learner (MBL) on the typical differences between those spelling variants and use it to rerank Levenshtein neighbours according to these variation patterns. As using a MBL is slow at tagging time, we estimate the probability of two types being spelling variants directly, following an approach similar to Logačev et al. (2014). Given an edit operation e, we estimate its probability of leading to a spelling variant, $P(e)$, by

$$\sum_{(t_i, t_j) \in tr(e)} min(1, |l(t_i) \cap l(t_j)|) * \frac{1}{|tr(e)|} \quad (2)$$

where $tr(e) = \{(t_i, t_j) | t_i \xrightarrow{e} t_j\}$, i.e. the set of all pairs of types (t_i, t_j) from the training data, such that t_i can be transformed into t_j by applying e and $l(t)$ is the set of all lemmas type t appears with in the training data. The $P(e)$ for an edit operation e that does not appear in the training data is set to $1 -$ thereby the probabilities capture negative evidence against the assumption that an edit operation leads to a spelling variant.

Given a pair of two types (t_1, t_2) we estimate the probability of (t_1, t_2) being spelling variants by the product of the probabilities of all the atomic edit operations that transform t_1 into t_2. Using the null hypothesis that the pairs are spelling variants, any set of possible spelling variants can be reduced by removing those for which the probability is below a given threshold.

We will apply these different similarity measures to extract types more similar to a given OOV type than a threshold from the IV types. These extracted types will then be used to generate lemma candidates for the OOV type. All possible generators are usable for this. We only use the lemmas that occured with the selected IV types in the training data and combine these with the lemma candidates generated by a rule-based generator (using LCs or ETs) from the OOV type.

5 Experiments

In this section we evaluate the effects of using lexical correspondences and the generation of lemma candidates from similar IV types. We test our approach on Middle Low German (GML). The data comes from the 'Reference Corpus Middle Low German/ Low Rhenish (1200-1650)' (ReN) (Peters and Nagel, 2014).[12] We use two texts: Johannes (19,641 tokens) as training data and Griseldis (9,057 tokens), that we split into two nearly equal parts, as development set (4,505 tokens) and test set (4,552 tokens). Full bibliographical information is given in the bibliography.[13] To assess the difficulty of lemmatizing GML, we compare our results with the accuracy on Modern German (DEU) newswire texts. For this, we use the TIGER corpus (Release 2.2) (Brants et al., 2004) with the same splits as Müller and Schütze (2015). In order to make the tasks on GML and DEU more comparable, we limit the training data to roughly 20,000 tokens and lowercase all types and lemmas in both datasets.

Examples for word-internal modification in DEU have been given in Figure (1). An example for spelling variation in GML is the pair of types *vigenbome* and *vighenbome* "(the) fig tree.SG.DAT" (Johannes). The corresponding lemma *vîgenbôm* also illustrates a special convention in the lemmatization of the GML texts: diacritics are added. In this case they denote the length of the vowels. These diacritics have the same effect as word-internal modification for the lemmatization.[14]

We evaluated the effects of different parameter settings on the development set.[15] The numbers in this section report the performance of selected settings on the test set measured on tokens.

[12]Note that the corpus is still under construction. The tokenization and the annotations used are prefinal. Therefore, the size of the texts might deviate from the numbers given elsewhere.

[13]We do not train and evaluate the lemmatization accuracy on splits of the same text as we are interested in the performance of the lemmatization in the situation were a set of lemmatized texts exists for training and the obtained model is applied to a new text.

[14]The lemmas also contain numbers to disambiguate meanings. Since this adds a word-sense-disambiguation task to the lemmatization, they have been removed for the experiments.

[15]The results can be found in Appendix B.

5.1 Coverage experiments

First, we look at the coverage of the different generators described in the previous sections, i.e. the number of tokens for which the generated set of lemma candidates contains the correct lemma, in other words, the accuracy given an oracle that chooses the correct lemma. We train the generators on the training set. In addition to the lemma candidates generated by the rules induced from the training data, we always extend the set of lemma candidates by all the lemmas that an IV type appears with in the training data.

Coverage should be increased because it sets an upper bound to the lemmatization accuracy. At the same time, the average size of the candidate sets should be kept as small as possible, to make the task of the ranker easier, i.e. choosing the correct lemma in real-life settings without an oracle.

We experimented with using only rules that appear at least n times with type-lemma pairs in the training data. In addition, we tested whether a POS-tag dependent application of the rules would limit the amount of overgeneration. We found that using all rules POS-tag dependently gave the best trade-off between coverage and average candidate set size on the development set.[16]

Table 1 and 2 give the results from the experiments on the test data. Table 1 contains a comparison between DEU and GML. The results show that lemmatizing GML is harder than lemmatizing DEU. Given a similar amount of training data (about 20,000 tokens), there is a difference of about 24.5% in the coverage between the two languages – using ETs the coverage drops from 98.92% for DEU to 74.3% for GML. While for DEU all of the generators reach a high coverage with a small average number of lemma candidates ($\emptyset$ cand.) the coverage for GML is significantly lower with an average size of the candidate sets that is more than three times larger than for DEU. The reason for the drop in coverage and the increase in the average number of lemma candidates might be more word internal modifications and the existence of spelling variation in GML. Following, we present the improvements coming from the methods we introduced to deal with word-internal modification and spelling variation.

Word-internal modification. Next to the results for ETs, Table 1 gives the coverage results for lexical correspondences (LC) and lexical correspondences with anchored insertions (LC-AI, see section 3) on the test data. The improvements in coverage coming from the better modeling of word-internal modifications are the same for LCs and LC-AIs for both languages while LC-AIs effectively reduce the number of wrongly generated lemma candidates compared with pure LCs. This is especially visible for GML.

For DEU, using LC(-AI)s leads to a small improvement for OOV words of 0.41% which is an error reduction of about 10%. Given the homogeneity of data in the TIGER corpus, this only leads to an overall improvement of the coverage of 0.12%. These numbers decrease further when more training material is used. Using about 100,000 tokens from the TIGER corpus for training, the coverage goes up to 99.50% (OOV: 97.84%) with ETs and 99.54% (OOV: 98%) with LC-AIs. However, the numbers indicate that even languages with moderate word-internal modification can benefit from the usage of LCs, especially when the amount of training data is limited and the lemmatizer has to deal with a large number of OOV types. As has been expected, the effect of using LC(-AI)s is bigger for GML, leading to an overall increase of 1.25% points. However, the gap in performance between DEU and GML remains huge.

Spelling Variation. The additional complexity of the task on GML is at least partially due to spelling variation. To deal with this, we carried out experiments with a regularized[17] version of the data and compare it with the generation of lemma candidates from similar IV types described in Section 4. The regularized version of the data is created using a rule-based approach with 26 handcrafted rewrite rules (in the form of regular expressions and substitutions), which was created by experts on GML for the purpose of reducing the spelling variation.[18] Like before, lemma candi-

---

[16]We used gold tags for the training and evaluation. When using predicted POS tags, the performance of POS-tag dependent candidate generation depends on the quality of the predictions.

[17]We follow Barteld et al. (2015) by using the term regularization, as normalization is usually used to describe a mapping to a standardized or modern variety of the language which is not the case here.

[18]The script has been created by Melissa Farasyn in the project 'Corpus of Historical Low German' (CHLG; `http://www.chlg.ac.uk/index.html`) and contains rules by Melissa Farasyn with additions by Sarah Ihden and Katharina Dreessen both from the project 'Reference Corpus Middle Low German/ Low Rhenish (1200-1650)'.

Data	Generator	all		oov	
		Coverage (%)	∅ cand.	Coverage (%)	∅ cand.
DEU	ET	98.92	2.79	96.65	3.69
	LC-AI	99.04	3.20	97.06	4.64
	LC	99.04	4.20	97.06	7.04
GML	ET	74.30	10.73	24.06	14.78
	LC-AI	75.55	14.12	27.60	22.45
	LC	75.55	25.17	27.60	47.53

Table 1: Coverage statistics
Coverage (%): number of tokens for which the candidate set contains the correct lemma; ∅ cand.: the average size of the candidate sets.

dates are generated using all LC-AIs learned from the training data POS-tag dependently. For IV types, all their lemmas from the training data are added as well.

Firstly, we determined an upper bound by adding all lemmas that appeared in the training data to the candidate sets. Table 2 shows that the coverage increases from 74.3% to 88.31% using our method. This is a potential gain of about 14% – 7.58% more than with regularization (80.73%). However, using all lemma candidates for OOV types increases the average candidate set size to 302.46.

Secondly, we tested the trade-off between coverage and set size for our method of generating lemma candidates only from similar IV types (cf. Section 4). Table 2 gives examplary results on the test set.

We explored the effects of different paramater settings on the development set. For the Levenshtein distance, we used the maximal distance as parameter and Levenshtein automata (Schulz and Mihov, 2002) for finding candidates efficiently.[19] For the Jaccard Index, we varied the minimal similarity (between 0 and 0.7 in steps of 0.1, adding 0.25 and a smaller step size of 0.11 between 0.1 and 0.2), the minimal size of character n-grams ($\{1, 2, 3, 4\}$), the maximal size of n-grams ($\{2, 3, 4, \infty\}$) and the maximal size of skips ($\{0, 1, 2, 3, 4\}$). Furthermore, we optionally applied the frequency-based weighting on the similarity features.

To improve the precision, we calculated the probability of the possible spelling variants returned by the best parameter set-

tings for different thresholds on the set size ($\{15, 16, 17, 18, 19, 20\}$), using the product of the $P(e)$ estimated by Equation 2. We tested different thresholds on the probability below which the pair was excluded (between 0.5 and 0.2, decreasing by 0.1 and decreasing by 0.025 between 0.2 and 0).

The Levenshtein distance is an easy to use method, leading to good results with a distance of 1 or 2. Using a distance of 1 already leads to a better coverage than the regularization with only a small increase in the average set size. The Jaccard Index has more parameters. With tuning them, it is possible to reach better coverage for any given upper bound on the average set size than with Levenshtein. In sum, we get best results by using the Jaccard Index with a small similarity threshold, n-grams up to the length of the type, allowing skips in the n-grams, and weighting the features by their inverse frequency. In addition, using the probabilities for edit operations to exclude unlikely pairs helped to improve precision.

5.2 Lemmatization accuracy

In contrast to the oracle setting in the previous section, we present the actual accuracy gain for lemmatization in this section. For evaluation we use the log-linear model described in Müller and Schütze (2015) to select the best lemma candidates from the sets. The authors report state-of-the-art results for a couple of languages among them DEU with this model. We use all the features described there.[20] The only exception is Wikipedia data for GML as this does not exist. We train the

---

[19]We used the implementation from `https://github.com/universal-automata/liblevenshtein-java`.

[20]We also include morphological tags as we train and lemmatize using gold tags. When using predicted tags, using this feature might hurt the performance as described by Müller and Schütze (2015). For Wikipedia, we use the dump available at `http://cistern.cis.lmu.de/marmot/naacl2015/` (Müller et al., 2015).

Spelling variation handling	all		oov	
	Coverage (%)	∅ cand.	Coverage (%)	∅ cand.
None (ET)	74.30	10.73	24.06	14.78
None (LC-AI)	75.55	14.12	27.60	22.45
Regularization	80.73	13.92	29.58	24.45
Upper	88.31	302.46	68.72	951.33
Levenshtein(1)	83.79	14.52	54.14	23.73
Levenshtein(2)	86.27	17.83	62.14	34.41
Jaccard(0.25,2-∞,0)	81.00	14.46	45.15	23.55
Jaccard(0.25,2-∞,3)	84.73	15.09	57.18	25.59
Jaccard-weighted(0.25,2-∞,3)	84.29	14.75	55.77	24.47
Jaccard-weighted(0.25,2-∞,3), $P \geq 0.05$	84.14	14.58	55.27	23.94

Table 2: Coverage for lemma generation with handling of spelling variation on GML Parameter for Levenshtein: maximal distance; Parameters for Jaccard: minimal similarity, minimal and maximal size of character n-grams, maximal size of skips; P denotes the product of the P(e).

model using the implementation of L-BFGS (Liu and Nocedal, 1989) from MALLET (McCallum, 2002).

For the rule-based generators we compare ETs as they are used in the original version of LEM-MING and our LC-AIs both with all rules induced from the training data. In contrast to the experiments in Müller and Schütze (2015), we apply the rules POS-tag dependently.

For the variation handling we tested the generators with the best coverage below different thresholds in candidate set size (increasing by 0.1) on the development set. The accuracy first increases but starts to decrease when the average set size becomes larger than 14.6. This shows that this specific log-linear model cannot exploit the potential of our generators, because it is tailored to the usage of ETs as generators. We selected the generator that led to the best results on the development set.

Table 3 shows the results of the best models. For spelling variation handling, we compare our approach with the rule-based regularization. The oracle experiment has shown that the rule-based regularization does not remove all of the spelling variation. Therefore, we applied our approach to spelling variation handling to the regularized data as well, again choosing the best parameters settings on the development set.

The results show that using LCs to generate candidates leads to better results. As expected from the coverage data (Section 5.1), the DEU data shows only a small but statistically significant in-

crease in accuracy ($\chi_1^2 = 11.40$, $p < 0.001$).[21] GML profits more from using LCs (1.23%; $\chi_1^2 = 52.16$, $p < 0.001$). The handling of spelling variation has a bigger impact than modeling word-internal modification. The ranker cannot exploit the full potential of the generator and performs best with parameter settings that lead to a small increase of the average set size. The best performing model used LC-AIs to generate lemma candidates. The total increase in accuracy with this method is 5.56% ($\chi_1^2 = 34.88$, $p < 0.001$) above the baseline model, i.e. generating lemma candidates using ETs without handling spelling variation. This is comparable to the increase obtained by regularizing the texts before applying the lemmatization with LCs as generator (5.87%). The difference between both methods for handling the spelling variation is not significant ($\chi_1^2 = 0.2$, $p = 0.66$). Combining regularization and handling of spelling variation during lemmatization results in an additional increase of 1.6% ($\chi_1^2 = 21.87$, $p < 0.001$) over the model using LC-AIs with regularized texts, leading to a total improvement of 7.38% over the baseline.

6 Conclusion

We presented two methods for dealing with word-internal modification and spelling variation in lemma candidate generation. Both were implemented and tested in the context of data-driven lemmatization with the program LEMMING.

The experiments showed that a better modeling

---

[21] Significance has been tested using McNemar's test (Mc-Nemar, 1947) with continuity correction (Edwards, 1948).

Data	Generator	Spelling variation handling	correct (%) all	oov
DEU	ET	-	97.76	93.35
	LC-AI	-	97.83	93.57
GML	ET	-	71.86	23.78
	LC-AI	-	73.09	27.25
	ET	Regularization	76.58	36.16
	LC-AI	Regularization	77.64	39.35
	LC-AI	Generator	77.42	41.19
	LC-AI	Regularization+Generator	79.24	44.52

Table 3: Lemmatization accuracy

of word-internal modification leads to small improvements for a language like Modern German that features a moderate amount of word-internal modification (0.22% on OOV types). On a homogenous resource like the TIGER corpus, the overall effect of better coverage of OOV types on the lemmatization accuracy is small (0.07%). However, for languages with more word-internal modification and data with more OOV types the gain is higher. This was shown with a Middle Low German corpus. Here, using lexical correspondences (LC) leads to an increase in accuracy of 1.23%.

For the historical Middle Low German texts handling spelling variation is another important factor in lemma candidate generation. Our language-independent approach to generate lemma candidates from potential IV spelling variants for OOV types leads to an increase of 5.56% in accuracy. In comparison, limiting the spelling variation by preprocessing the data with rewrite rules created manually by language experts leads to an improvement of 5.87%. Combining both methods lead to a total increase of 7.38%.

While these are good improvements of the accuracy, the potential accuracy in terms of coverage is even higher for our data-driven method. However, the actual ranker used in our experiments was not able to exploit this potential. Consequently, there are two possible ways for further research: Firstly, adapting the ranker to our modified generators, or, secondly, to improve the precision of the generators. We plan to concentrate on the second strand for further research.

An alternative solution for the problem of restricting the generative capacity of LCs (see Section 3) might be an anchoring by lexicalization, i.e., adding letters before or/and after insertion as a constant. For instance German *sind*, *sein* "(they) are – (to) be" would lead to the less permissive LC $\langle[\text{'s'}, Y, \text{'d'}], [\text{'se'}, Y]\rangle$. This strategy is similar to adding context to lemmatization rules used by Loponen and Järvelin (2010).

The distance measures for detecting possible spelling variants used in this paper only use string similarities of the types ignoring their distribution in the texts. Barteld et al. (2015) also took context similarity into account by filtering the subset obtained from the string similarity with Brown clusters (Brown et al., 1992), keeping only those IV types which are in the same cluster as the OOV type. This – or other methods to include contextual similarity in the selection of potential spelling variants – is a promising way to improve the precision of the measures.

7 Resources

The paper is created reproducibly using org-mode (http://orgmode.org). The org-file and the scripts that where used to run the experiments are available at github (https://github.com/fab-bar/paper-LaTeCH2016). This version also includes the appendices.

With this paper, we also release our additions to LEMMING including the generators described in this paper. They are available at github as well (https://github.com/fab-bar/cistern).

Acknowledgements

The work of the first and second authors has been funded by the DFG. We would like to thank the anonymous reviewers for their helpful remarks and Andrew Fassett for improving our English. All remaining errors are ours.

Primary data

Johannes *Buxtehuder Evangeliar.* GML manuscript from about 1480. Transcribed in the DFG-funded project "Referenzkorpus Mittelniederdeutsch / Niederrheinisch (1200-1650)".

Griseldis *Griseldis / Sigismunda und Guiscardus.* GML print of two tales from 1502. Transcribed in the DFG-funded project "Referenzkorpus Mittelniederdeutsch / Niederrheinisch (1200-1650)".

References

Fabian Barteld, Ingrid Schröder, and Heike Zinsmeister. 2015. Unsupervised regularization of historical texts for POS tagging. *Proceedings of the Workshop on Corpus-Based Research in the Humanities (CRH)*, pages 3–12.

Marcel Bollmann. 2012. (Semi-)automatic normalization of historical texts using distance measures and the Norma tool. In Francesco Mambrini, Marco Passarotti, and Caroline Sporleder, editors, *Proceedings of the Second Workshop on Annotation of Corpora for Research in the Humanities (ACRH-2)*, pages 3–14.

Sabine Brants, Stefanie Dipper, Peter Eisenberg, Silvia Hansen-Schirra, Esther König, Wolfgang Lezius, Christian Rohrer, George Smith, and Hans Uszkoreit. 2004. TIGER: Linguistic interpretation of a German corpus. *Research on Language and Computation*, 2(4):597–620.

Peter F. Brown, Peter V. deSouza, Robert L. Mercer, Vincent J. Della Pietra, and Jenifer C. Lai. 1992. Class-based N-gram models of natural language. *Computational Linguistics*, 18(4):467–479.

Grzegorz Chrupała. 2006. Simple data-driven contextsensitive lemmatization. *Procesamiento del Lenguaje Natural*, 37:121–127.

Grzegorz Chrupała. 2008. *Towards a machine-learning architecture for lexical functional grammar parsing*. Ph.D. thesis, Dublin City University.

Lee R. Dice. 1945. Measures of the amount of ecologic association between species. *Ecology*, 26(3):297–302.

Allen L. Edwards. 1948. Note on the "correction for continuity" in testing the significance of the difference between correlated proportions. *Psychometrika*, 13(3):185–187.

Leo Egghe. 2010. Good properties of similarity measures and their complementarity. *Journal of the American Society for Information Science and Technology*, 61(10):2151–2160.

Jacob Eisenstein. 2013. What to do about bad language on the internet. In *Proceedings of the North American Chapter of the Association for Computational Linguistics (NAACL)*, pages 359–369.

Sean A. Fulop and Sylvain Neuvel. 2013. Networks of morphological relations. In *Proceedings of the International Symposium on Artificial Intelligence and Mathematics (ISAIM-2014)*.

Andrea Gesmundo and Tanja Samardžić. 2012. Lemmatisation as a tagging task. In *Proceedings of the 50th Annual Meeting of the Association for Computational Linguistics: Short Papers-Volume 2*, pages 368–372.

Nabil Hathout. 2014. Phonotactics in morphological similarity metrics. *Language Sciences*, 46, Part A:71–83.

Ning Jin. 2015. NCSU-SAS-Ning: Candidate generation and feature engineering for supervised lexical normalization. In *Proceedings of the Workshop on Noisy User-generated Text*, pages 87–92.

Bart Jongejan and Hercules Dalianis. 2009. Automatic training of lemmatization rules that handle morphological changes in pre-, in- and suffixes alike. In *Proceedings of the Joint Conference of the 47th Annual Meeting of the ACL and the 4th International Joint Conference on Natural Language Processing of the AFNLP: Volume 1*, pages 145–153.

Sebastian Kempken. 2005. *Bewertung historischer und regionaler Schreibvarianten mit Hilfe von Abstandsmaßen*. Ph.D. thesis, Universität Duisburg-Essen.

Mike Kestemont, Walter Daelemans, and Guy De Pauw. 2010. Weigh your words—memory-based lemmatization for Middle Dutch. *Literary and Linguistic Computing*, 25(3):287–301.

Tuomo Korenius, Jorma Laurikkala, Kalervo Järvelin, and Martti Juhola. 2004. Stemming and lemmatization in the clustering of Finnish text documents. In *Proceedings of the Thirteenth ACM International Conference on Information and Knowledge Management*.

Michael Levandowsky and David Winter. 1971. Distance between sets. *Nature*, 234(5323):34–35.

Vladimir Levenshtein. 1966. Binary codes capable of correcting deletions, insertions, and reversals. *Soviet Physics Doklady*, 10:707–710.

Dong C. Liu and Jorge Nocedal. 1989. On the limited memory BFGS method for large scale optimization. *Mathematical Programming*, 45(1-3):503–528.

Pavel Logačev, Katrin Goldschmidt, and Ulrike Demske. 2014. POS-tagging historical corpora: The case of Early New High German. In *Proceedings of the Thirteenth International Workshop on Treebanks and Linguistic Theories (TLT-13)*, pages 103–112.

Aki Loponen and Kalervo Järvelin. 2010. A dictionary-and corpus-independent statistical lemmatizer for information retrieval in low resource languages. In Maristella Agosti, Nicola Ferro, Carol Peters, Maarten de Rijke, and Alan Smeaton, editors, *Multilingual and Multimodal Information Access Evaluation*, pages 3–14. Springer, Berlin and Heidelberg.

Andrew K. McCallum. 2002. MALLET: A machine learning for language toolkit. (http://mallet.cs.umass.edu).

Quinn McNemar. 1947. Note on the sampling error of the difference between correlated proportions or percentages. *Psychometrika*, 12(2):153–157.

Thomas Müller and Hinrich Schütze. 2015. Robust morphological tagging with word representations. In *Proceedings of the North American Chapter of the Association for Computational Linguistics: Human Language Technologies (NAACL: HLT)*, pages 526–536.

Thomas Müller, Ryan Cotterell, Alexander Fraser, and Hinrich Schütze. 2015. Joint lemmatization and morphological tagging with Lemming. In *Proceedings of the 2015 Conference on Empirical Methods in Natural Language Processing (EMNLP)*, pages 2268–2274.

Sylvain Neuvel and Sean A. Fulop. 2002. Unsupervised learning of morphology without morphemes. In *Proceedings of the ACL-02 workshop on Morphological and phonological learning-Volume 6*, pages 31–40.

Robert Peters and Norbert Nagel. 2014. Das digitale ‚Referenzkorpus Mittelniederdeutsch / Niederrheinisch (ReN)'. *Jahrbuch für Germanistische Sprachgeschichte*, 5(1):165–175.

Thomas Pilz. 2009. *Nichtstandardisierte Rechtschreibung - Variationsmodellierung und rechnergestützte Variationsverarbeitung*. Ph.D. thesis, Universität Duisburg-Essen.

Klaus Schulz and Stoyan Mihov. 2002. Fast string correction with Levenshtein-automata. *International Journal of Document Analysis and Recognition*, 5:67–85.

Rico Sennrich and Beat Kunz. 2014. Zmorge: A German morphological lexicon extracted from Wiktionary. In *Proceedings of the 9th International Conference on Language Resources and Evaluation (LREC 2014)*, pages 1063–1067.

Hans van Halteren and Margit Rem. 2013. Dealing with orthographic variation in a tagger-lemmatizer for fourteenth century Dutch charters. *Language Resources and Evaluation*, 47(4):1233–1259.

You Shall Know People by the Company They Keep:
Person Name Disambiguation for Social Network Construction

Mariona Coll Ardanuy
Göttingen University
Göttingen Centre for
Digital Humanities
mcollar@uni-goettingen.de

Maarten van den Bos
Utrecht University
Dept. of History and
Art History
M.J.A.vandenBos@uu.nl

Caroline Sporleder
Göttingen University
Göttingen Centre for
Digital Humanities
csporled@uni-goettingen.de

Abstract

The growth of digitization in the cultural
heritage domain offers great possibilities
to broaden the boundaries of historical research. With the ultimate aim of creating social networks of person names from
news articles, we introduce a person name
disambiguation method that exploits the
relation between the ambiguity of a person
name and the number of entities referred
to by it. Modeled as a clustering problem
with a strong focus on social relations, our
system dynamically adapts its clustering
strategy to the most suitable configuration
for each name depending on how common
this name is. Our method's performance
is on par with the state-of-the-art reported
for the CRIPCO dataset, while using less
specific resources.

1 Introduction

Resolving person names across documents is an
open problem of unquestionable importance in
natural language processing. Person names represent 30% of the overall number of queries in the
web domain (Artiles et al., 2005), and have an
equally significant presence in the news domain,
where people are often at the core of the events
reported in articles. This is particularly interesting in historical research. As more and more historical newspapers are digitized, new potentialities
arise to explore history in a way that was infeasible
until recent years. People are drivers and carriers
of change, and newspapers have traditionally been
the platform for someone to become a public figure. High-quality entity mining, though, is at the
moment difficult to achieve, partly because of the
high ambiguity which is often associated with person names.

Cross-document coreference resolution (from
now on CDCR) is the task of grouping mentions
of the same person entities together.[1] Person
names are not uniformly ambiguous. Very uncommon names (such as 'Edward Schillebeeckx') are
virtually non-ambiguous, whereas very common
names (such as 'John Smith') are highly ambiguous. CDCR is closely related to word sense disambiguation, from which it differs greatly in one
aspect: contrary to word senses, the set of entities referred to by a person name is *a priori* unknown. The approach we propose assumes a correlation between the commonness of a name and
the number of entities referred to by it. Our disambiguation strategy relies on the social circle of
the query name. We bring the maxim "you shall
know a word by the company it keeps" back to the
social realm. Can the social network of a person
be an indicator of who that person is? We intend
to bring CDCR to the social dimension, with the
assumption that the social circle around our target
entity can be a source of evidence for disambiguation. Partially-supervised, our approach is competitive with state-of-the-art methods, without relying on a knowledge base (KB) nor other expensive resources. It is easily portable and adaptable
to different datasets and different languages without the need of learning new parameters.

2 Formal definition of the task

Given a query name qn and a set of documents
in which it appears $\{d_1, d_2, ..., d_j\}$, CDCR aims
at grouping together documents containing references to the same entity e. The expected output for each query name is a set of clusters
$\{c_1, c_2, ..., c_k\}$, each corresponding to a different

---

[1] Unlike traditional coreference resolution, CDCR does
not usually attempt to resolve definite NPs and pronouns.
Following this tradition, we focus only on linking person
names.

Proceedings of the 10th SIGHUM Workshop on Language Technology for Cultural Heritage, Social Sciences, and Humanities (LaTeCH), pages 63–73,
Berlin, Germany, August 11, 2016. ©2016 Association for Computational Linguistics

entity $\{e_1, e_2, ..., e_k\}$ and each containing the documents referring to it.

For clarity, we describe the terminology used in this paper, which we illustrate with an example:

(1)   The character of **John Smith** expresses some of the confusion in **Alexie**'s own upbringing. He was raised in **Wellpinit**, the only town on the **Spokane Indian Reservation**.

A *person name* is any named entity expression in a text referring to a person. An *entity* is the real-world referent that is referred to by a person name. In example 1, 'John Smith' and 'Alexie' are person names, and the real persons behind these names are entities. The *query name* is the target person name to disambiguate, in this case 'John Smith', which is mentioned at least once per document. We assume all mentions of the query name to refer always to the same entity within a document, hence person name clustering amounts to grouping together the documents in which a specific person name refers to a given entity. A *mention name* is any person name that is mentioned in a document, except for the query name, i.e. 'Alexie' in our example. We call a *full name* any person name with at least two tokens (first name and last name), whereas a *namepart* is each of the tokens that form a full name. 'John Smith' is the only full name in our example, and 'John' and 'Smith' are its nameparts. Finally, by *non-person mention* we mean any named entity expression that does not refer to a person ('Wellpinit' and 'Spokane Indian Reservation' in our example).

3   Related work

The idea of using social networks to find information from historical texts is not a new one. One of the first and more influential works is Padgett and Ansell (1993), in which its authors use networks of marriages between the most eminent Florentine families in the 1430s to illustrate the dramatic political changes in the Florence of the time. There exist several recent studies advocating for the use of social networks in historical research (see Jackson (2014), Rochat et al. (2014), i. a.). Most studies relying on social networks concern pre-modern history, where sources are much more limited in number and thus the networks are created either manually or from structured data, thus avoiding one of the greatest challenges in network creation,

namely person name disambiguation. One of the few fully automatic approaches is Coll Ardanuy et al. (2015), which does not so much focus on the problem of person name disambiguation, however.

Resolving and disambiguating person names across documents is an open problem in natural language processing, its difficulty stemming from the high ambiguity which is often associated with person names.[2] Sentences 2, 3, and 4 provide three examples of cases in which the same name (in this case 'John Smith') refers to three different persons: the CEO of General Motors, the Labour Party leader, and a coach.

(2)   UAW President Stephen Yokich then met separately for at least an hour with chief executives Robert Eaton of Chrysler Corp., Alex Trotman of Ford Motor Co. and finally with John Smith Jr. of General Motors Corp.

(3)   Blair became Labour leader after the sudden death of his successor John Smith in 1994 and since then has steadily purged the party of its high-spend and high-tax policies and its commitment to national ownership of industrial assets.

(4)   Two years ago, Powell switched coaches from Randy Huntington to John Smith, who is renowned for his work with sprinters from 100 to 400 meters.

These examples are drawn from *The John Smith Corpus*, the first reference set for CDCR, which was introduced by Bagga and Baldwin (1998). The authors also proposed a new scoring algorithm, B-Cubed, in order to evaluate the task, which was modeled as a document clustering problem. To solve the problem, the authors applied the standard vector space model based on context similarity. Several subsequent studies adapted and extended the approach (Ravin and Kazi (1999), Gooi and Allan (2004)). More recent methods apply LDA and other topic models (Song et al. (2007), Kozareva and Ravi (2011)).

Yoshida et al. (2010) distinguish between weak and strong features. Weak features are the context words of the document, as opposed to strong features such as named entities, biographical information, key phrases, or temporal expres-

---

[2]According to the U.S. Census Bureau, only 90,000 different names are shared by up to 100 million people (Artiles et al., 2009a).

sions (see Mann and Yarowsky (2003), Niu et al. (2004), Al-Kamha and Embley (2004), Bollegala et al. (2006)). The most exploited source of evidence for clustering is named entities (Blume (2005), Chen and Martin (2007), Popescu and Magnini (2007), Kalashnikov et al. (2007)). Artiles et al. (2009a) thoroughly study the role of named entities in the task and conclude that they often increase precision at the expense of recall, even though they leave the door open to more sophisticated approaches using named entities, such as in combination with other levels of features (Yoshida et al., 2010) or in graph-based approaches (Kalashnikov et al. (2008), Jiang et al. (2009), Chen et al. (2012)). Over the last years, the trend has moved towards using resource-based approaches, such as a knowledge base (KB) (Dutta and Weikum, 2015) or Wikipedia, and the person name disambiguation task has been in most cases subsumed by entity linking. Bunescu and Pasca (2006), Cucerzan (2007) and Han and Zhao (2009) are only some of the many approaches that exploit the wide coverage of Wikipedia by linking entity mentions to the referring Wikipedia articles.

An evaluation campaign was organized in 2007 to tackle the problem of name ambiguity on the WWW and the interest of this task moved largely to the web domain (Artiles et al., 2007). However, web pages and news articles differ greatly in their form. Even though more heterogeneous, web pages tend to be more structured and provide additional features that can be exploited (url, e-mail addresses, phone numbers, etc.). In 2011 a similar evaluation campaign was proposed at EVALITA 2011 in order to evaluate CDCR in Italian in the news domain (Bentivogli et al., 2013).

Pairwise clustering has been the most popular clustering method: two documents are grouped together if their similarity is higher than a certain threshold. To date, most approaches have used a fixed similarity threshold. Very few approaches (Popescu (2009), Bentivogli et al. (2013)) have warned of the importance of determining the ambiguity degree of a person name in order to be able to estimate the number of output clusters. In Zanoli et al. (2013), a dynamic threshold similarity is introduced by estimating the ambiguity of the query name. This work, which in this aspect is the most similar to ours, differs greatly from ours with respect to the clustering strategy, since they rely on a KB, whereas we exploit only the context.

Our method aims at providing a solution for the problem of person name disambiguation in the task of automatically constructing social networks from historical newspapers. The articles that constitute our corpus are likely to be populated by many people that are absent from historical accounts and, therefore, also from KBs. We intentionally refrain from linking entities to a knowledge base to avoid the bias towards entities which are present in it. Ter Braake and Fokkens (2015) discuss the problem of biases in historiography and the importance of rescuing long-neglected individuals from the oblivion of history.

4   The model

Given the assumption that a person name always refers to the same entity in a given document,[3] person name clustering amounts to document clustering. In order to cluster documents, a similarity measure is needed. The core idea is that two documents should be clustered together if they are similar enough, i.e. if there exists enough evidence that they belong together. The evidence needed, though, may vary greatly depending on the query name. If the query name is not ambiguous at all, very low similarity between documents suffices to group them into one cluster. Conversely, if the query name is very ambiguous, a higher similarity is required to ensure that only documents that refer to the same entity are clustered together. In section 4.1, we describe how we assess person name ambiguity. Our model relies heavily on the social dimension of news, so we model document similarity based on social network similarity. Thus, for each query name we represent documents as social networks in which the nodes are the people mentioned in them. To determine network similarity (see section 4.2.1), we take two types of information into account: the amount of node overlap (for which we learn a threshold from a small manually labeled data set) and the ambiguity of the overlapping nodes (for which we manually set a penalty function). Network overlap is not always a sufficient source of information (in particular, small overlap does not mean that the documents involved should not be clustered together), and we additionally make use of further features in those cases where networks do not provide sufficient ev-

---

[3]This is an assumption made by previous approaches and reminiscent of the 'one sense per discourse' assumption in word sense disambiguation.

idence: BoW representations of the content, the dominant topic according to a topic modeling algorithm, and the overlap in other named entity expressions (see 4.2.2). These additional features model document content.

4.1 Assessing name ambiguity

Person names are usually combinations of a first name, a last name, and occasionally one or more middle names. Only with the list of all the people in the world would it be possible to assess the true ambiguity of each person name. Since this is an unavailable resource, alternative ways of approximating person name ambiguity need to be found.

4.1.1 Building the resource

Zanoli et al. (2013) use an Italian specific resource, the phonebook *Pagine Bianche*. It has wide coverage, but it could be argued that its use leads to a gender-biased calculation of name ambiguity, since only one person per household is included in its pages, usually its male head. We extract person names from a large corpus of text using a named entity recognizer. To optimize precision, we consider only names consisting of at least two tokens, since single tokens are often misidentified or misclassified by the recognizer. The identified person names are then used to build three lists — one for first names, one for last names, and one for middle names — in which each distinct name is associated with its occurrence frequency in the corpus.

4.1.2 Name ambiguity calculation

We propose an ambiguity scale that spans from 0 to 1, in which very ambiguous names would occupy the highest range and very non-ambiguous names would take the lowest range. Formally, we distinguish three types of names that we can encounter in texts: **(1) Single-token names** are the most ambiguous. In order to calculate the ambiguity of a given single-token name, we merge the first, middle, and last names lists into one and estimate the relative frequency of the target name in the resulting list. We place them within the range 0.8 (the rarest) to 1.0 (the most common). **(2) Two-token names** (usually first and last name) are the most common combination to be expected. Thus, they occupy the central and largest part of the spectrum, the range between 0.2 and 0.8; the most ambiguous name being 0.8, the least ambiguous starting from 0.2. We calculate the weighted

average of the two nameparts according to our observation that first names are 15 times more ambiguous than last names. The frequency of the most common two-token name ('Giovanni Rossi' for Italian, 'John Smith' for English) is taken as the maximum value against which we calculate the ambiguity value of any other two-token name. **(3) Multiple-token names** consist of three parts or more (usually first name, middle name(s), and last name) and are given the lowest ambiguity range, from 0.0 to 0.2. The most common multiple-token combination will have an ambiguity of 0.2, while the ambiguity of the least common name will start from 0.0. Multiple-token names are weighted in the same fashion as two-part names, distributing the weight of the first and the middle names equally.

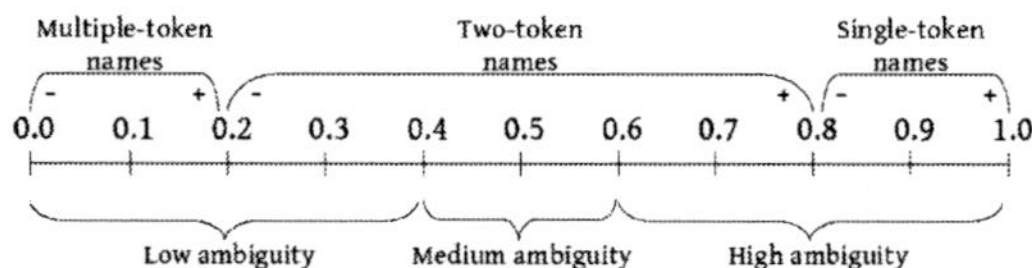

Figure 1: Person name ambiguity range.

We distinguish three degrees of ambiguity. **Low-ambiguity** consists of the multiple-token names and the least ambiguous two-token names. **High-ambiguity** consists of the single-token names and the most ambiguous two-token names. **Middle-ambiguity** contains the names that fall into the middle spectrum (see Figure 1). Table 1 shows examples of English names that fall into each range.

AmbR	Examples
0.0-0.1	Lena Mary Atkinson, Edward William Elgar
0.1-0.2	Mary Anne Smith, John Douglas Williams
0.2-0.3	Douglas Morris, Anne Atkinson
0.3-0.4	Donald Taylor, Emma White
0.4-0.5	Mary Johnson, George Williams
0.5-0.6	Thomas Jones, James Williams
0.6-0.7	John Williams, Mary Smith
0.7-0.8	John Smith, William Smith
0.8-0.9	Atkinson, Terrence
0.9-1.0	John, William

Table 1: On the left, the ambiguity range; on the right, some examples of names from each range.

4.2 Clustering scheme

Fixed similarity thresholds have been the most used for this task: two documents are clustered together if their similarity surpasses a predefined threshold. Such algorithms do not take the ambiguity of the query name into account. Ideally, ambiguous names should have high thresholds, allowing fewer documents to be clustered together, whereas non-ambiguous names should have low thresholds, therefore yielding less clusters.

Our method's first step is to represent each document containing the query name as a social network of the people mentioned in it. To identify the names we used a named entity recognizer. We perform naive within-document coreference resolution of mention names based on their matching surface forms and construct undirected social networks weighted by the coocurrence of entities within a text window. We initiate our clustering algorithm by taking the social network with the highest number of nodes, and sort the remaining networks by decreasing number of nodes overlapping with the largest network. If the similarity between both social networks is bigger than a certain threshold (this is discussed more thoroughly in the next section), we cluster both documents together and merge the two social networks, re-rank the list of overlapping networks and take again the top one from the list. We repeat this process until no partially-overlapped network is found. In this case, we repeat the whole procedure of finding the largest remaining network and finding its fully- or partially-overlapping networks. We continue until all the networks/documents have been considered. This is a greedy algorithm, and it is thus of prime importance that two documents are only clustered together if there exists enough evidence that this should be the case.

Each query name is assigned an ambiguity range, which falls into one of the three ambiguity degrees: low, medium or high. The clustering strategy varies according to the range and degree of ambiguity of each query name, so that non-ambiguous names allow low-similarity documents to be clustered together, whereas ambiguous names require high document similarity.

4.2.1 Social network similarity

The core idea behind our approach is that the social circle of people tells us who they are: it is their social context. A very naive version of our approach would consist in joining together under the same entity all documents with at least one shared person name (apart from the query name). This is obviously dangerous, as using this method in a large enough dataset would eventually cluster all documents together. In order to understand how reliable it is to cluster networks together when sharing a certain number of nodes, we decided to learn clustering probabilities from a development set. For each ambiguity range, we learn the probabilities of two documents being clustered together when they have one, two or three nodes in common. A pair of networks with no overlapping nodes gives us no information about the social context. We observed in the development set that, with more than four overlapping nodes, two documents are unequivocally clustered together.

Node overlapping quality. We have so far talked about overlapping nodes as a synonymous expression for overlapping entities, assuming that a mention name that appears in two documents refers to the same entity. This is of course not necessarily the case. Mention names can range from single tokens to multiple tokens, and correspond to names that can be both very ambiguous (such as 'John') or very unambiguous (such as 'Edward Cornelis Florentius Alfonsus Schillebeeckx'). The confidence that we are talking about the very same person varies greatly from the first case to the second case. The likelihood that two documents belong to the same cluster given a certain overlap of person names will therefore depend on the 'quality' of these overlaps. An overlapping name that provides greater evidence that we are dealing with one only entity (i.e. a low-ambiguity name) is considered of higher quality than an overlapping name that provides little evidence that it corresponds to one only entity (i.e. a high-ambiguity name).

Node ambiguity penalty. We compute the ambiguity of each mention name and assign it an ambiguity degree: high, medium, or low. A penalty function is defined to lower the learned probabilities when applied to networks with low-quality overlapping nodes:

$$penalty = \frac{Pr(n[i]) - Pr(n[i-1])}{i+1} \quad (1)$$

where i is the number of overlapping nodes between two documents, n the set of networks sharing a certain number i of nodes, and thus $Pr(n[i])$ the probability that two networks belong together if they have i nodes in common. Table 2 shows how probabilities are recalculated.

4.2.2 Other similarity metrics

Even though the skeleton architecture of our clustering scheme is based on the social circle of peo-

ONE OVERLAPPING NODE	
$penalty = \frac{Pr(n[1])-Pr(n[0])}{2}$	
Amb	**Probability recalculated**
$\uparrow$	$Pr(n[1]) - 2 \cdot penalty = Pr(n[0])$
$\rightarrow$	$Pr(n[1]) - penalty$
$\downarrow$	$Pr(n[1]) - 0 \cdot penalty = Pr(n[1])$
TWO OVERLAPPING NODES	
$penalty = \frac{Pr(n[2])-Pr(n[1])}{3}$	
Amb	**Probability recalculated**
$\uparrow\uparrow$	$Pr(n[2]) - 4 \cdot penalty$
$\uparrow\rightarrow$	$Pr(n[2]) - 3 \cdot penalty = Pr(n[1])$
$\rightarrow\rightarrow$	$Pr(n[2]) - 2 \cdot penalty$
$\uparrow\downarrow$	$Pr(n[2]) - 2 \cdot penalty$
$\rightarrow\downarrow$	$Pr(n[2]) - 1 \cdot penalty$
$\downarrow\downarrow$	$Pr(n[2]) - 0 \cdot penalty = Pr(n[2])$
THREE OVERLAPPING NODES	
$penalty = \frac{Pr(n[3])-Pr(n[2])}{4}$	
Amb	**Probability recalculated**
$\uparrow\uparrow\uparrow$	$Pr(n[3]) - 6 \cdot penalty$
$\uparrow\uparrow\rightarrow$	$Pr(n[3]) - 5 \cdot penalty$
$\uparrow\uparrow\downarrow$	$Pr(n[3]) - 4 \cdot penalty = Pr(n[2])$
$\uparrow\rightarrow\rightarrow$	$Pr(n[3]) - 4 \cdot penalty = Pr(n[2])$
$\uparrow\rightarrow\downarrow$	$Pr(n[3]) - 3 \cdot penalty$
$\rightarrow\rightarrow\rightarrow$	$Pr(n[3]) - 3 \cdot penalty$
$\downarrow\rightarrow\rightarrow$	$Pr(n[3]) - 2 \cdot penalty$
$\downarrow\downarrow\uparrow$	$Pr(n[3]) - 2 \cdot penalty$
$\downarrow\downarrow\rightarrow$	$Pr(n[3]) - 1 \cdot penalty$
$\downarrow\downarrow\downarrow$	$Pr(n[3]) - 0 \cdot penalty = Pr(n[3])$

Table 2: Recalculation of probabilities. The left column shows the combination of nodes according to their ambiguity degree. Each arrow represents one node: $\uparrow$ a high-ambiguity name, $\rightarrow$ a medium-ambiguity name, and $\downarrow$ a low-ambiguity name. In the right column, the probability of two networks being clustered together based on the number of nodes they share is lowered according to the quality of their overlapping nodes.

ple, the evidence social network similarity provides is limited. As discussed in Artiles et al. (2009a), approaches that focus on named entities achieve high precision at the cost of recall. Our method is especially vulnerable when two networks share zero or one overlapping nodes, since the evidence that the two networks should be clustered together is in these cases non-existent or very small. In order to address this problem, each social network stores the set of named entity expressions that were not used for the network creation (e.g. locations and organizations) and three bag-of-words representations of the document: with tf-idf weightings, with simple counts, and with non-person mentions. For each ambiguity range and for each feature, we learn the probabilities that two networks sharing one or no overlapping nodes still belong together. Finally, we applied LDA using collapsed Gibbs sampling to our datasets to produce a lower dimensional representation of our dataset, and assign the most relevant latent topic to each network.

4.3 Clustering decisions

We have so far discussed the general clustering architecture, but not how the actual decision of whether to group a pair of documents together is made. We base this decision on a set of seven features which can be extracted for each document pair: **(1)** number of person overlaps; **(2)** number of non-person mention overlaps; **(3)** probability that, given an ambiguity range (that of the query name), two networks are clustered together if they share one, two, or three nodes; **(4)** probability that, given an ambiguity range, two documents are clustered together in terms of a BoW vector representation of word counts; **(5)** probability that, given an ambiguity range, two documents are clustered together in terms of a BoW vector representation with tf-idf weightings; **(6)** probability that, given an ambiguity range, two documents are clustered together if they have a certain number of non-person mentions in common; **(7)** and the most relevant topic for the document.

Since a less ambiguous name tends to correspond to fewer entities than a more ambiguous one, the clustering decision threshold for a low-ambiguity query name should be more permeable than the threshold for an ambiguous name. Each query name is assigned an ambiguity value that corresponds to one of three ambiguity degrees: low, medium, or high. Since a **low-ambiguity** query name is likely to refer to very few entities, if any of the extracted features is true, we consider this evidence enough to cluster the two documents together. On the other side of the spectrum, **high-ambiguity** names are likely to correspond to several entities, so the amount of evidence needed in order to cluster documents is bigger. We assume that an overlap of five entities (be them person names, locations, or organizations) should be enough evidence that we are talking about the same person. The smaller the named entity overlap is, the more evidence will be required and thus the more features will have to be true. **Medium-ambiguity** names will have a middle stance between low-ambiguity and high-ambiguity names when it comes to permeability.

5 Experiments

5.1 Data

To our knowledge, no datasets are available for assessing the value of our method in historical newspaper texts. Therefore, we evaluate our model on three existing datasets from the contemporary press (with articles starting from the year 1987). The **Cross-document Italian People Coreference corpus (CRIPCO)** (Bentivogli et al., 2008) comes with a development and test set, in Italian, of 105 and 103 query names respectively, with an average of 3.45 entities per query name and a total of 20,754 documents. The **NYTAC Pseudo-name Corpus** is an artificial corpus created by conflating dissimilar person names together. With a total of 19,360 documents, this dataset consists of 100 pairs of conflated person names (i.e. 200 entities), matching in gender and 50 of which being topically similar, such as Robert Redford and Clint Eastwood (actors) or Plácido Domingo and Luciano Pavarotti (opera singers). Finally, the **John Smith Corpus** consists of only one query name, 'John Smith', the most common name of the English language. It consists of 197 documents containing at least one instance of 'John Smith', representing 35 entities. The documents are not equally distributed among the different entities: 24 entities appear mentioned only in one document, whereas one entity is mentioned in 88 documents.

In addition to the quantitative evaluation on contemporary data, we also provide a qualitative evaluation on historical data in section 6.

5.2 Baselines

We compare our method **SNcomplete** with two baseline methods: (1) **SNsimple** is the base case, the most naive representation of our method, in which two documents are grouped together if their network representations share at least one node; and (2) **TopicModel** clusters together the documents that share the most relevant topic. We also provide the state-of-the-art results for the *CRIPCO* dataset (Zanoli et al., 2013) and for the *NYTAC pseudo-name corpus* (Rao et al., 2010), who also presented results on the *John Smith Corpus*.

5.3 Settings

We use the Stanford NER (Finkel et al., 2005) and TextPro (Pianta et al., 2008) to identify NEs in En-

glish[4] and Italian[5], respectively. We make use of an unannotated Italian corpus, PAISÀ,[6] consisting of 1.5GB of raw text at the moment of download (March 2015), from which we extract person name lists to compute ambiguity ranges for Italian. The extracted list of 718,568 person names is not a census of the Italian population, but a list of people mentioned in news, webpages or blogs. For the English experiment, we used the Persondata information from the DBPedia[7] project (only available for English and German at the moment), which was built by collecting all the Wikipedia articles about people. The Persondata database had 7,889,574 entries at the moment of download (December 2014).

Our method does not require a big amount of training data, but just a representative selection spreading over the ambiguity range is enough to set the appropriate parameters. The CRIPCO corpus provides a development set of documents corresponding to 103 different query names, but a small fraction of it (15 query names, about 15% of the set) is already sufficient to set the appropriate parameters (using the whole dataset makes no significant difference in the performance). We randomly selected the query names, making sure we would, when possible, have a query name for each of the ten ambiguity ranges.[8] Our training dataset does not have a query name for all of the ambiguity ranges: we lack training examples from the range 0.1-0.2, as well as for the three upper ranges (0.7-0.8, 0.8-0.9, and 0.9-1.0). In our experiment, if a query name from the testing dataset falls into one of these ranges, it would take the probability of its immediately precedent ambiguous range. The mentioned fifteen instances from the development set have also been used to find the optimal combination of features. The learned probabilities and feature combination strategy have been applied directly, without further learning nor tuning, to the other two datasets.

---

[4] http://nlp.stanford.edu/software/CRF-NER.shtml
[5] http://textpro.fbk.eu/
[6] http://www.corpusitaliano.it/
[7] http://wiki.dbpedia.org/Downloads
[8] The fifteen training instances for each range are: 'Isabella Bossi Fedrigotti' *(0.0-0.1)*; 'Marta Sala', 'Alberto Sighele', 'Roberto Baggio', 'Bruno Degasperi', 'Ombretta Colli', and 'Leonardo da Vinci' *(0.2-0.3)*; 'Luisa Costa', 'Mario Monti', and 'Andrea Barbieri' *(0.3-0.4)*; 'Antonio Conte', 'Antonio de Luca', and 'Antonio Russo' *(0.4-0.5)*; 'Paolo Rossi' *(0.5-0.6)*; and 'Giuseppe Rossi' *(0.6-0.7)*.

Approach	cripco			nytac_sel			johnsmith		
	P	**R**	**F**	**P**	**R**	**F**	**P**	**R**	**F**
SNsimple	0.94	0.67	0.78	0.65	0.74	0.67	0.65	0.6	0.62
TopicModel	0.91	0.44	0.55	0.76	0.27	0.37	0.71	0.51	0.59
Zanoli et al. 2013	0.89	0.97	**0.93**	–	–	–	–	–	–
Rao et al. 2010 [1]	–	–	–	0.61	0.78	**0.68**	0.60	0.63	0.61
Rao et al. 2010 [2]	–	–	–	0.82	0.24	0.37	0.85	0.59	**0.70**
SNcomplete	0.87	0.95	**0.91**	0.63	0.75	**0.68**	0.79	0.60	0.68

Table 3: Evaluation results.

5.4 Results and discussion

Table 3 shows the results of applying our model to the three datasets. We use the evaluation metrics provided for the WePS task (Artiles et al., 2009b). While our results are slightly lower than Zanoli et al. (2013), this difference is not statistically significant (Wilcoxon test, p=0.054). An advantage of our method is that it can easily be adapted to any other dataset without requiring expensive resources, such as a knowledge base.

The only work we are aware of that has reported results for the *NYTAC pseudo-name corpus* is by the creators of the dataset (Rao et al., 2010), who also report results for the *John Smith Corpus*. The NYTAC dataset was artificially created, and some of our assumptions do not hold: in this dataset, ambiguity of the query name does not play a role because there are invariably two clusters for each query name, one for each conflated name. Besides, half the entity pairs of the dataset are very closely related (e.g. Luciano Pavarotti and Plácido Domingo, two names that very often appear mentioned in the same text). Therefore, their social networks have much less predictive power than in natural data, where we assume that two people with the exact same name have low probability to share a big portion of their social networks. That would explain why we report low precision for this dataset, and yet the results obtained are comparable to those from the best of the two models introduced by Rao et al. (2010).

The result reported for *John Smith Corpus* improves upon recent models, such as Singh et al. (2011), who obtained 0.664, but is far from the most recent approach (Rahimian et al., 2014), who obtained around 0.80. This might be well due to the fact that there was only one query name in our development set that had high ambiguity, which was, still, far from being as ambiguous as 'John Smith'. Our method works overall better than any of the two methods from Rao et al. (2010) when we average the results for both English datasets.

Using the ambiguity of the query name to dynamically decide on a clustering strategy is crucial for the success of our method. Failing to choose an adequate ambiguity range for query names can lead to considerably lower results. Our F-Score for the *John Smith Corpus* drops to 0.37 if we consider 'John Smith' a low-ambiguity name, and to 0.52 if we consider it of medium-ambiguity. The F-Score for the *CRIPCO* dataset drops to 0.77 when the ambiguity range of the query names of this dataset is randomly assigned.

6 Impact in the social sciences: a case study on Dutch religious history

To assess the impact of this approach in the social sciences, we introduce here a case study that analyzes its performance and proves its contribution. Due to lack of annotated data from the historical news domain, we can only offer a qualitative analysis. As a use case, we focus on two actors who played a pivotal role in the religious transformations of the postwar years in the Netherlands: Willem Banning and Edward Schillebeeckx. The first was a leading intellectual in the movement responsible for a major transformation within the Reformed Church; the latter was a prominent member of an international network of progressive theologians who deeply influenced discourse on the future of the Catholic Church.

Our data consist of all the articles from the newspaper collection of the Dutch National Library containing the query words 'Banning' and 'Schillebeeckx'. In order to remove obvious outliers, we applied some heuristics to disregard those articles in which the query name was preceeded by any capitalized word not coinciding with their first and middle names, their initials, or with any title. We restricted the data to the years in which we are interested, namely between 1930 and 1970 in the case of Banning, and 1950 and 1990 in the case of Schillebeeckx. We ended up with 26,984 documents for Banning (137 MB) and 2,796 documents for Schillebeeckx (8.5 MB). The name 'Banning' is much more common in Dutch than the name 'Schillebeeckx', which is probably the reason behind the large difference in the number of articles between the two. Whereas all mentions of 'Schillebeeckx' in the collection seem to refer to the person in which we were interested, a quick search at the beginning of the experiment revealed that there were several different persons with the name 'Banning' in the collection, among which at least a shopkeeper, a swimming champion, a man on trial, and an amateur fisherman.

Our method returns one network for each disambiguated entity. Figure 2 shows an example of social network created with our method.[9] As mentioned, each edge is a container of information (context words and non-person mentions weighted with tf-idf) that can be found in the articles where the two nodes connected by the edge are present. This information is encoded for each pair of nodes that can be found in the network. Each edge also stores the list of documents in which both nodes appear, in order to grant access to the original sources to the historian.

Figure 2: Fragment of the resulting social network for Willem Banning for the year 1963.

The amount of noise that can be found in the networks created from historic newspapers is clearly higher than in the standard benchmarks, mostly due to OCR. As a result, the named entity recognizer, trained on modern Dutch,[10] performs worse, but the final networks do not suffer much from this, since noisy nodes are pushed to the periphery of the networks. The historian in our team was able to find only expected names in the center of the networks, with very few exceptions. By

thoroughly looking at the connections between the nodes of the networks and the context information stored in the edges, several points and episodes of the lives of the two politicians could be confirmed: the importance of Schillebeeckx as an advisor of the Dutch episcopacy and his triple heavy scrutiny by the Vatican, and a higher number of international relations than in the case of Banning. Expected information in the networks is interesting because it proves the validity of the approach. Even more interesting is the presence of unexpected results in the network, since they can lead to potential hypotheses that may challenge the dominant narratives of history. Our networks suggest, contrary to what is believed, that Schillebeeckx was a popular theologian not only because of his conflict with Rome, but also because of his theological ideas, and that Banning's work in politics was not separated from his ideas on the role of the church in society. Given these promising findings, we intend to pursue research in this direction.

The network approach provides historians with a quick but thorough overview of the role of someone in the public eye: with whom was he or she connected, which topics were central and in which debates he or she participated. By navigating through the networks, one can explore the collection at ease, validating well-known historical reports, developing new ideas, and even rediscovering new actors who may have had a bigger role in the past than that which History granted them, always from the perspective of a certain newspaper collection. It is then the task of the historian to verify, by looking at the pieces of news selected by our method, whether there is some truth in the information yielded by the network.

7   Conclusions

We have presented a new method for constructing social networks of disambiguated person entities from news articles. Our method explores the relationship between name ambiguity and the amount of different entities that can be referred to by the same name. Our approach is partially supervised and has proved to be competitive in different languages and throughout very different collections without need to retrain it. The method outputs a set of social networks, one for each distinct entity, which can be of great assistance in the exploration of historical collections.

---

[9] We used Gephi (`https://gephi.org/`) for visualizing it, the size and position of the nodes depend on the weights of their edges.

[10] We use the training data from CoNLL-2002: `http://www.cnts.ua.ac.be/conll2002/ner/`

References

Reema Al-Kamha and David W. Embley. 2004. Grouping search-engine returned citations for person-name queries. In *Proceedings of the 6th ACM WIDM Workshop*, pages 96–103.

Mariona Coll Ardanuy, Maarten van den Bos, and Caroline Sporleder. 2015. Laboratories of community: How digital humanities can further new European integration history. In *Histoinformatics 2014*, pages 284–293, Barcelona.

Javier Artiles, Julio Gonzalo, and Felisa Verdejo. 2005. A testbed for people searching strategies in the WWW. In *Proceedings of SIGIR*, pages 569–570.

Javier Artiles, Julio Gonzalo, and Satoshi Sekine. 2007. The SemEval-2007 WePS Evaluation: Establishing a benchmark for the Web People Search Task. In *Proceedings of SemEval*, pages 64–49.

Javier Artiles, Enrique Amigó, and Julio Gonzalo. 2009a. The role of named entities in Web People Search. In *Proceedings of EMNLP'09*, pages 534–542.

Javier Artiles, Julio Gonzalo, and Satoshi Sekine. 2009b. WePS-2 evaluation campaign: Overview of the web people search clustering task. In *Proceedings of the 2nd WePS Workshop*.

Amit Bagga and Breck Baldwin. 1998. Entity-based cross-document coreferencing using the vector space model. In *Proceedings of Coling*, pages 79–85.

Luisa Bentivogli, Alessandro Marchetti, and Emanuele Pianta. 2008. Creating a gold standard for person cross-document coreference resolution in Italian news. In *Proceedings of LREC Workshop on Resources and Evaluation for Identity Matching, Entity Resolution and Entity Management*, pages 19–26.

Luisa Bentivogli, Alessandro Marchetti, and Emanuele Pianta. 2013. The news people search task at EVALITA 2011: Evaluating cross-document coreference resolution of named person entities in Italian news. In *Proceedings of EVALITA 2012*, pages 126–134.

Matthias Blume. 2005. Automatic entity disambiguation: benefits to NER, relation extraction, link analysis, and inference. In *Proceedings of the Intl Conference on Intelligence Analysis*.

Danushka Bollegala, Yutaka Matsuo, and Mitsuru Ishizuka. 2006. Extracting key phrases to disambiguate personal name queries in web search. In *Proceedings of the ACL Workshop on How Can Computational Linguistics Improve Information Retrieval?*

Razvan Bunescu and Marius Pasca. 2006. Using encyclopedic knowledge for named entity disambiguation. In *Proceedings of EACL*, pages 9–16.

Ying Chen and James Martin. 2007. Towards robust unsupervised personal name disambiguation. In *Proceedings of EMNLP-CoNLL*, pages 190–198.

Liwei Chen, Yansong Feng, Lei Zhou, and Dongyan Zhao. 2012. Explore person specific evidence in web person name disambiguation. In *Proceedings of EMNLP-CoNLL*, pages 832–842.

Silviu Cucerzan. 2007. Large-scale named entity disambiguation based on Wikipedia data. In *Proceedings of EMNLP-CoNLL*, pages 708–716.

Sourav Dutta and Gerhard Weikum. 2015. Cross-document co-reference resolution using sample-based clustering with knowledge enrichment. In *Transactions of the Association for Computational Linguistics (TACL)*, volume 3, pages 15–28.

Jenny Rose Finkel, Trond Grenager, and Christopher Manning. 2005. Incorporating non-local information into information extraction systems by Gibbs sampling. In *Proceedings of ACL*, pages 363–370.

Chung Heong Gooi and James Allan. 2004. Cross-document coreference on a large scale corpus. In *Proceedings of HLT-NAACL*, pages 9–16.

Xianpei Han and Jun Zhao. 2009. Named entity disambiguation by leveraging Wikipedia semantic knowledge. In *Proceedings of CIKM*, pages 215–224.

Cornell Jackson. 2014. Using social network analysis to reveal unseen relationships in Medieval Scotland. In *Digital Humanities Conference*, Lausanne.

Lili Jiang, Jianyong Wang, Ning An, Shengyuan Wang, Jian Zhan, and Lian Li. 2009. Grape: A graph-based framework for disambiguating people appearances in web search. In *Proceedings of IEEE International Conference on Data Mining*, pages 199–208.

Dmitri V. Kalashnikov, Stella Chen, Rabia Nuray, Sharad Mehrotra, and Naveen Ashish. 2007. Disambiguation algorithm for people search on the web. In *Proceedings of IEEE International Conference on Data Engineering*, pages 1258–1260.

Dmitri V. Kalashnikov, Rabia Nuray-Turan, and Sharad Mehrotra. 2008. Towards breaking the quality curse. a web-querying approach to web people search. In *Proceedings of SIGIR*, pages 27–34.

Zornitsa Kozareva and Sujith Ravi. 2011. Unsupervised name ambiguity resolution using a generative model. In *Proceedings of EMNLP*, pages 105–112.

Gideon S. Mann and David Yarowsky. 2003. Unsupervised personal name disambiguation. In *Proceedings of the 7th Conference on Natural Language Learning at HLT-NAACL*, pages 33–40.

Cheng Niu, Wei Li, and Rohini K. Srihari. 2004. Weakly supervised learning for cross-document person name disambiguation supported by information extraction. In *Proceedings of ACL*, pages 598–605.

John F. Padgett and Christopher K. Ansell. 1993. Robust action and the rise of the Medici, 1400–1434. *American Journal of Sociology*, pages 1259–1319.

Emanuele Pianta, Christian Girardi, and Roberto Zanoli. 2008. The TextPro tool suite. In *Proceedings of LREC*, pages 2603–2607.

Octavian Popescu and Bernardo Magnini. 2007. IRST-BP: Web people search using name entities. In *Proceedings of SemEval*, pages 195–198.

Octavian Popescu. 2009. Person cross document coreference with name perplexity estimates. In *Proceedings of EMNLP*, pages 997–1006.

Fatemeh Rahimian, Sarunas Girdzijauskas, and Seif Haridi. 2014. Parallel community detection for cross-document coreference. In *Proceedings of IEEE/WIC/ACM International Joint Conferences on Web Intelligence and Intelligent Agent Technologies*, pages 46–53.

Delip Rao, Paul McNamee, and Mark Dredze. 2010. Streaming cross document entity coreference resolution. In *Proceedings of Coling*, pages 1050–1058.

Yael Ravin and Zunaid Kazi. 1999. Is Hillary Rodham Clinton the President? Disambiguating names across documents. In *Processinds of the Workshop on Coreference and its Applications*, pages 9–16.

Yannick Rochat, Melanie Fournier, Andrea Mazzei, and Frédéric Kaplan. 2014. A network analysis approach of the Venetian Incanto system. In *Digital Humanities Conference*, Lausanne.

Sameer Singh, Amarnag Subramanya, Fernando Pereira, and Andrew McCallum. 2011. Large-scale cross-document coreference using distributed inference and hierarchical models. In *Proceedings of ACL-HLT*, pages 793–803.

Yang Song, Jian Huang, Isaac G. Councill, Jia Li, and C. Lee Giles. 2007. Efficient topic-based unsupervised name disambiguation. In *Proceedings of Joint Conference on Digital Libraries*, pages 342–351.

Serge ter Braake and Antske Fokkens. 2015. How to make it in History. working towards a methodology of canon research with digital methods. In *Biographical Data in a Digital World*, pages 85–93.

Minoru Yoshida, Masaki Ikeda, Shingo Ono, Issei Sato, and Hiroshi Nakagawa. 2010. Person name disambiguation by bootstrapping. In *Proceedings of SIGIR*, pages 10–17.

Roberto Zanoli, Francesco Corcoglioniti, and Christian Girardi. 2013. Exploiting background knowledge for clustering person names. In *Proceedings of EVALITA'2012*, pages 135–145.

Deriving Players & Themes in the Regesta Imperii using SVMs and Neural Networks

Juri Opitz and **Anette Frank**

Department of Computational Linguistics

69120 Heidelberg, Germany

{opitz|frank}@cl.uni-heidelberg.de

Abstract

The Regesta Imperii (RI) are an important source for research in European-medieval history. Sources spread over many centuries of medieval history – mainly charters of German-Roman Emperors – are summarized as "Regests" and pooled in the RI. Interesting medieval demographic groups and players are i.a. *cities, citizens* or *spiritual institutions* (e.g. bishops or monasteries). Themes of historical interest are i.a. *peace and war* or the endowment of *new privileges*. We investigate the RI for important *players and themes*, applying state-of-the-art text classification methods from computational linguistics. We examine the performance of different classification methods in view of the linguistically very heterogeneous RI, including a Neural Network approach that is designed to capture complex interactions between players and themes.

1 Introduction

The Regesta Imperii (RI)[1] are considered a fundamental, autonomous source for German and European history. It extends over many centuries, from the Karolinger dynasty to Maximilian I, from around 800 to 1500 AD. The RI have their roots in the 19th century, when the German librarian Johann Friedrich Böhmer started to collect and document the charters (including known and possibly unknown fakes) of the German-Roman emperors, in terms of so-called *Regests*. The Regests contain relevant judicial content of the referenced charters (cf. Zimmermann (2000), Niederkorn (2005), Rübsamen and Kuczera (2006)). A royal charter

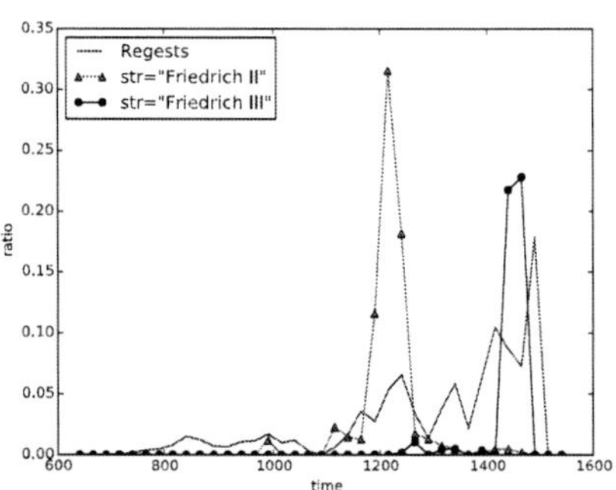

Figure 1: Blue line: distribution of the 129,504 Regests across time. Others: ratios of Regests, in which the terms "Friedrich II." (triangles) and "Friedrich III." (circle) occur. The names of these German-Roman kings are examples for concepts which are rather confined in time in the RI.

was created, for example, when an emperor decided to give a land grant, or privileges such as new rights to one of his landlords or cities.

Covering about 13 million tokens, the RI constitutes a large-scale resource that is still growing today[2]. The 129,504 Regests we have access to can be treated as a collection of corpora (e.g., one corpus for each Roman-German emperor dynasty), or as a single corpus covering all collected materials. Our work treats the RI as a single corpus. The RI comprises texts written in different German varieties, as well as Latin. Often we find up to three different languages or varieties within a single Regest.

As seen in Figure 1, the Regests are not evenly distributed over time but have the greatest mass from about 1200 to 1500 AD. Many terms and concepts only occur in certain times. An overview

---

[1] http://www.regesta-imperii.de/cei

[2] We retrieved a "snapshot" of the RI via the public REST interface http://www.regesta-imperii.de/cei/ on 26.4.2015.

Proceedings of the 10th SIGHUM Workshop on Language Technology for Cultural Heritage, Social Sciences, and Humanities (LaTeCH), pages 74–83,
Berlin, Germany, August 11, 2016. ©2016 Association for Computational Linguistics

# Regests	129,504
# types	$\approx 407,000$
# tokens	$\approx 13,000,000$
mean length (in tokens)	≈ 85
median length (in tokens)	≈ 52
ttr_{log}	≈ 0.79
ttr_{log} SDeWaC	≈ 0.68

Table 1: Corpus statistics for the RI at the time we used it. $ttr_{log} = \frac{log(\#types)}{log(\#tokens)}$ is the logarithmic type-token ratio. Taking the logarithm allows better comparison with corpora of different sizes. SDeWaC is a German Corpus comprising 44 million sentences crawled from the internet.

abbreviation	groups and themes traced in RI
b0	nobility, nobles
b1	spiritual Institutions
b2	lesser nobles
b3	city, citizens
b4	Jews
b5	women
b6	new privileges
b7	confirmation of privileges
b8	land grants, land bestowal
b9	finances
b10	justice
b11	war and peace

Table 2: Traced demographic groups and themes.

of corpus statistics is given in Table 1. The high logarithmic type-token ratio (ttr_{log}) supports the observation that the language of the RI is highly heterogeneous: although the domain of the RI is rather focused (abstracts of medieval charters), it is notably higher than what we find in the contemporary German SDeWaC corpus[3].

A Regest itself is a very unique form of a document, and some of them are not easy to comprehend even for humans. Consider

Example 1 *A Regest from 1332, issued in Parma by Karl IV. (*1316, †1378).*[4]

> bekennt dem Johann de Landulphis, iudici et auditori curie paterne et sue, achtzig goldgulden für besoldung und sechzig goldgulden wegen versendungen desselben schuldig zu sein. Registr. priv. von Pavia hs. (fol. pap. sec. 15 vel 16) zu Pavia bl. 5.

The Regest describes an action of King Karl IV. in 1332, in Parma, Italy. Karl IV. acknowledges that he owes "Johann de Landulphis", "achtzig goldgulden" (eighty gold coins) for wages and "sechzig goldgulden" (sixty gold coins) for reasons which are rather difficult to interpret: "(...) wegen versendungen desselben schuldig zu sein" (interpretable as wages and travel expenses). Beyond that, the Regest contains information in Latin ("iudici et auditori curie paterne et sue"), plus references and meta information (last sentence).

It is easy for humans to infer that the theme of the above Regest is about *finances* (indicated by mentions of "goldgulden" (gold coins) and "besoldung" (wages)). Further, a specific group of persons plays a role, namely *nobles*. This is indicated

by "de" in the name of "Johann de Landulphi", who is promised money by the king. The Latin "de" in the middle of a name generally suggests that the person belongs to the class of nobles, as in "Elizabeth of (=de) England". So, one may conclude that in the above Regest, the players are *nobles*, acting under the theme *finances*.

Our aim is to trace within the RI interesting *demographic groups* joint with the *themes of their interactions*. We aim to identify which Regest is about which theme(s) and group(s), to perform interesting data analysis, e.g. visualizing the importance of different groups and themes not only in relation to time but also in relation to other factors such as issuer, location, and possibly more.

With the support of a domain expert we determined interesting demographic groups (players) and themes which play a role in the Regests. All players and themes can be treated as individual binary classification problems. An overview is given in Table 2. It can be interesting, e.g., to relate the occurrence of *city* or *citizens* with occurrences of *privileges* with respect to time, thus approximately tracing the development of *privileges* for cities.[5]

A Regest can be labeled with zero to all of the 12 selected labels. Thus, there exist many possible combinations.[6] We cast the labeling problem as a multi-label document classification task, allowing several labels (i.e. groups and themes) to be assigned for a single document (i.e. Regest).

For automatic pattern recognition on this historic data, we deploy four state-of-the text classification methods, (i.) Support Vector Machines (SVM) (binary classification); (ii.) Semi-

---

[3]http://www.ims.uni-stuttgart.de/forschung/ressourcen/korpora/sdewac.html

[4]cf.: RI VIII n. 1, in: Regesta Imperii Online, URI: http://www.regesta-imperii.de/id/1332-09-22_1_0_8_0_0_7_1(29.04.2016).

[5]This is an important field of historic research because rights of European cities originated in the Middle Ages.

[6]Since each group and theme represents a binary variable, there are 2^{12} possible combinations.

Supervised SVMs (S^{3}VMs), to exploit the large amount of unlabeled data; (iii.) a Neural Network as a meta-learner applied to the SVM outputs (do the groups and themes influence each other?) and (iv.). a Convolutional Neural Network (CNN) classifier with pre-trained word vectors as input, which operates directly on the input documents.

We evaluate all methods on a manually labeled test set and perform data analyses on the full RI to illustrate its usage in Digital Humanities research.

2   Related Work

To the best of our knowledge, no (published) research has yet been conducted in the Digital Humanities community about NLP of the RI. Kuczera (2015) experimentally transfers attributes and relations between entities from the times of Friedrich III. (i.e. a subset of the RI) into a graph database and shows how historians could profit from the possibilities offered by such structured data repositories.

Ruotsalo et al. (2009) suggests that knowledge- and machine learning based NLP methods can help with complex annotation tasks in the cultural heritage domain. Their experiments demonstrate that automatic annotation of certain roles in artwork descriptions closely matches the performance of human annotators.

Piotrowski (2012) gives an overview of the manifold challenges in applying NLP to historical documents. He reports that the effectiveness of normalization strongly depends on text type and language, and satisfying results are achieved mainly on more recent texts. Piotrowski concludes that "the highly variable spelling found in many historical texts has remained one of the most troublesome issues for NLP". Thus we chose our procedure to not depend on normalized texts.

Massad et al. (2013) give an overview of the processing of recorded history texts. They examined a graph-based approach and an approach based on NLP. In their NLP experiments they analyzed the Wikipedia corpus with respect to time, relating specific strings and n-grams to time and page edits. The authors suggest that future research should focus on data analysis, trends and, most importantly, the access to historic corpora spanning a larger time span compared to the corpus employed in their experiments. We think that our research covers these aspects.

Meroño-Peñuela et al. (2014) in their survey on *History and Computing* propose NLP methods for dealing with raw corpora, yet do not propose specific tools due to manifold decisions to be taken, that strongly depend on the nature of the data.

3   Approach

The aims of our work are two-fold. On the application side, we aim to discover structures involving players and themes over times in the RI. On the methods side, we investigate to what extent Neural Networks (NN) are capable of learning complex relationships between players and themes, beyond the capacity of ordinary SVM classifiers that treat each classification label independently. E.g., if *nobles* play a role in a given Regest, it seems more likely that it is about *bestowal of land*, rather than e.g. justice, which presumably concerns other groups equally. We compare two architectures: a NN that builds on the output of *independent* binary SVM classifiers, in addition to other information, such as document vectors, in contrast to a full-fledged Convolutional Neural Network (CNN).

3.1   Preprocessing

Given the heterogeneous nature of the RI, we do not perform major pre-processing of the data. The Regests are only tokenized and converted to lower case. Thereafter they are mapped to boolean and tf-idf vectors of dimensions 2,000 and 10,000. The value at index i of a boolean vector representing document d encodes whether the term represented by i appears in d (1) or not (0). Tf-idf is similar but assumes that words that appear in many documents are less informative, and hence their respective vector-value is decreased[7].

3.2   Using SVMs and S^{3}VMs

SVMs are binary maximum-margin classifiers that can be extended to the multi-label case by training one SVM for each label. Semi-supervised SVMs (S^{3}VMs) work by forcing the hyperplane separating the labeled data with margin also through low density regions of space, making use of the cluster hypothesis (Chapelle et al., 2008). S^{3}VMs have been shown to be very successful especially when few labeled training data is available (Sindhwani and Keerthi, 2006). The downside is that

---

[7]More precisely, it is weighted by term frequency and the logarithm of $\frac{|D|}{|D_w|}$, where $|D|$ is the number of all documents and $|D_w|$ the number of documents in which w appears.

the S^3VM's optimization problem loses the global optimality of the standard SVM problem.

In both approaches – SVM and S^3VM – the assumption is that labels do not influence each other. I.e., if *women* play a role in a given Regest, it is *not* less likely that it is also about *war and peace*.

3.3 Combining SVMs and NNs

To enable our classifiers to capture possible dependencies between players and themes, we extend the SVM classifiers with a Neural Network, realizing a meta-learning architecture. The NN may learn that if groups x and y participate in a Regest, some theme z is unlikely to occur, even if predicted so by an independent binary classifier.

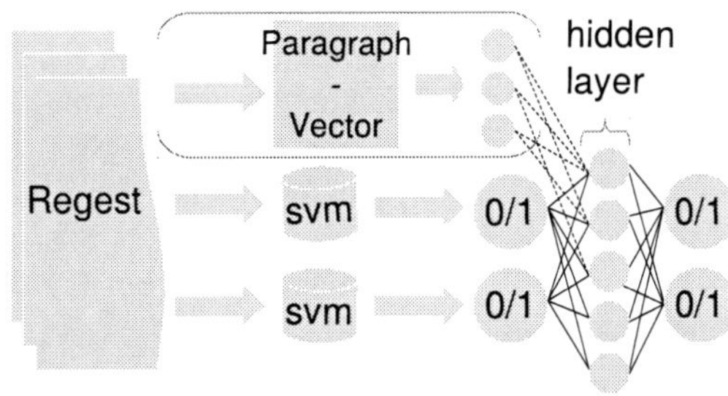

Figure 2: A Neural Network as a meta learner over multiple binary classifier's outputs, supplemented with a paragraph vector over the document. The figure is simplified to a multi-labeling task with only 2 classifiers (in reality there are 12 SVMs).

After choosing the "best" SVMs for each label, the outputs of the SVMs are fed into a Deep Neural Network (cf. Figure 2). We employ three input settings: (a.) using SVM output labels only, (b.) using SVM output labels and the document vectors (the boolean variant), and (c.) the SVM output labels jointly with *Paragraph Vectors*. Paragraph Vectors are learned similar to word embeddings but represent sentences or documents. They have been shown to yield strong performance in classifying sentences, IMDB opinions and also in Information Retrieval. As the Regests are short documents, they are suitable for being represented by these dense vectors, which are learned in an unsupervised manner (Le and Mikolov, 2014).

3.4 Using Convolutional NNs

Recently, CNNs have been successfully applied to various text and semantic sentence classification tasks, and often achieved very good performance (Kim, 2014; Zhang et al., 2015). Since CNNs usually require large numbers (thousands or more) of training samples to achieve very good performance, it would come rather as a surprise if trained on some few hundred samples, they would generalize better on unseen data compared to a mix of binary maximum-margin classifiers. We included this setting to serve as a baseline on the Neural NLP side and generated pre-trained word-embeddings of two sizes using all Regests.

4 Experiments and Results

4.1 Experimental Setup

Training and Test Data. We manually labeled 500 Regests, randomly drawn from the corpus to prevent bias.[8][9] The data was split into a training and test section of 400 and 100 Regests. The first two lines in Table 4 display the distribution of players and themes in the annotated data. Some of them occur rarely in both training and test data (e.g. Jewish people (b4) with only 3% and 2% of the respective data sets). On the other hand, *nobles* play a role in over 70% of annotated Regests. For estimation of model parameters we apply cross validation (CV) on the training set. We proceed as follows: (i) *Parameter tuning of SVMs*. For each different vector size and representation scheme, we tune the inner parameters of an SVM with CV on the training data. (ii) *Testing of SVMs*. We retrain each SVM on the full training data using the chosen hyperparameters, and evaluate the model on the test data set. (iii) *Determining an independent multi-label system*. As input to the NN models as meta learners over SVM outputs, we determine an IMC ("Independent Margin Classifiers"), a set of independent margin classifiers, consisting of the 12 SVMs that achieve maximum training CV score for each problem. (iv) *Training NN models*. For different NN models we again determine hyperparameters with CV on the IMC-outputs for the training section, and retrain the final NN models on the full training data, before (v), *Testing of the NNs* is again done on the final test set.

Evaluation Metrics. Our evaluation needs to take into account that many labels underlie a skewed distribution (cf. Table 4). For example,

---

[8]One of the authors, with experience in history sciences, annotated the data. In future work we plan to obtain comparable annotations possibly with help of experts in online history forums.

[9]Our data set and further details of experimental settings are available at https://cl.uni-heidelberg.de/~opitz/ri/

consider that one label only is positive among 100 test samples. A classifier that labels all instances as negative yields a deceivingly high score of 0.99 accuracy. Hence we employ *Balanced Accuracy*, the mean of Recall (Sensitivity) and inverse Recall (Specificity[10]), defined as $Acc_{bal} = \frac{Sensitivity+Specificity}{2}$.

In the above example, where Accuracy yields a biased score of almost one, balanced Accuracy yields a more realistic value of 0.5. Given the unbalanced distribution of our test data set, we report balanced accuracy for each of the 12 binary problems. We also report their arithmetic mean $\overline{Acc_{bal}}$ to provide a global measure of performance.

Baselines. As Baselines we choose, besides a simple majority voter, a Multinomial Naive Bayes algorithm, which is commonly used in text classification tasks (both in an independent binary manner for each label). Table 3 shows that Naive Bayes improves over the majority baseline for all problems and yields a solid 0.67 $\overline{Acc_{bal}}$, 0.17 pp. above the majority voter.

IMC achieves 0.795 $\overline{Acc_{bal}}$ and significantly outperforms both the majority baseline (+0.3 $\overline{Acc_{bal}}$) and Naive Bayes (+0.13). For each problem the score is better with up to +0.47 Acc_{bal} for recognizing *women* (b5) in a Regest. For *lesser nobles* (b2) and *war and peace* (b11), the independent classifiers combination baseline yields the overall best results (0.62 and 0.79 Acc_{bal}).

4.2 Evaluation Results: In Depth Analysis

SVMs/S³VMs combined into the multi-labeler ("IMC", Table 3) achieve good performance (0.795 $\overline{Acc_{bal}}$). Based on the training CV scores, IMC consists of six supervised SVMs and four S³VMs. S³VMs in the IMC were chosen for problems b0, b1, b8 and b10. With respect to b2 and b11, IMC outperforms all NN approaches (b2: +0.04, b11: +0.01). The Naive Bayes Baseline is outperformed with +0.128 $\overline{Acc_{bal}}$. This strong improvement could be due to the generalization capacity of the maximum margin, which might be especially useful with small training set sizes.

With regard to representation schemes such as boolean or tfidf and 2,000 words or 10,000 words, we observe no clear patterns whether one works generally better than the other on the RI. 5 classifiers of IMC are trained on 10,000 words and 10 classifiers use boolean word-features.

CNNs fed with 128 dimensional embeddings outperform majority vote (+0.06 $\overline{Acc_{bal}}$) but not Naive Bayes (-0.11), most likely due to the low amount of training data. Another explanation is that the 129,504 Regests were not sufficient to pre-train useful word-vectors (possibly also negatively influenced by the word variety). As the vector size increases (512 dimensions), the performance drops further (+0.01 over the majority voter).

The remaining classifier models are intended to detect dependencies between players and themes and had access to the outputs of IMC. Specifically, the question is whether NNs are suitable for detecting such dependencies. As baselines we considered SVM and Decision Tree models, trained on the outputs of the independent learners (in Table 3: +Decision Tree, +SVMs). Neither copes specifically well with this input information (-0.045 $\overline{Acc_{bal}}$ for +Decision Tree and -0.007 for +SVMs). Even when supplied with more information using various sizes of Paragraph Vectors (omitted in Table 3), both systems do not improve their previous scores.

Neural Networks employed as meta learners, by contrast, are able to improve results for specific problems, especially when supplied with Paragraph Vectors, resulting in the overall best system on test, a NN with 2048 hidden nodes and Paragraph Vectors of dimension 512 (+NN$_{2048}$+PV$_{512}$, Table 3). Still, the overall performance gain is small with only +0.004 $\overline{Acc_{bal}}$. When omitting b3 (*lesser nobles*) from the result calculation (it was the most controversial class in the annotation), the gain over IMC increases to +0.006. Notable individual performance gains are achieved for b0 (*nobles*, +0.02), b6 (*new privileges*, +0.05) and *bestowal of land* (+0.02). We conclude that there are dependencies between *nobles*, *bestowal of land* and *privileges* which cannot be captured by considering these classes independently.

To analyze on which groups and themes the neural network meta-learner offers *significantly* differing predictions ("it disagrees with its input"), we calculate mid-p-values with McNemars test (Fagerland et al., 2013) between different systems outputs (cf. Table 3). Comparing the best three NNs among each other, the 1,200 single predictions each system made do not differ significantly (min. $p = 0.065$), however the opposite is true when comparing the best three NNs to IMC (all p-values < 0.05). This indicates that there is more

---

[10] $Specificity = \frac{TN}{TN+FP}$

classifier types	b0	b1	b2	b3	b4	b5	b6	b7	b8	b9	b10	b11	$\overline{Acc_{bal}}$
majority baseline	0.5	0.5	0.5	0.5	0.5	0.5	0.5	0.5	0.5	0.5	0.5	0.5	0.5
Naive Bayes	0.52	0.78	0.62	0.53	0.72	0.51	0.62	0.68	0.71	0.74	0.67	0.69	0.667
SVMs + PV_{128}	0.5	0.51	0.5	0.5	0.5	0.5	0.5	0.5	0.5	0.5	0.5	0.5	0.501
IMC	0.72	**0.82**	**0.62**	**0.76**	**1.0**	**0.98**	0.66	**0.94**	0.8	**0.76**	**0.7**	**0.79**	0.795
+Decision Tree	0.68	**0.82**	0.58	**0.76**	0.75	**0.98**	0.63	0.86	0.71	0.75	**0.7**	0.77	0.75
+SVMs	0.72	**0.82**	0.58	**0.76**	**1.0**	**0.98**	0.67	0.94	0.76	**0.76**	**0.7**	0.77	0.788
+NN_{2048}	0.72	**0.82**	0.58	**0.76**	**1.0**	**0.98**	0.68	**0.94**	<u>0.84</u>	**0.76**	**0.7**	0.76	0.796
+NN_{2048}+PV_{512}	**0.74**	**0.82**	0.58	**0.76**	**1.0**	**0.98**	**0.7**	**0.94**	0.82	**0.76**	**0.7**	0.77	**0.797**
+NN_{2048}+BV	0.71	**0.82**	0.56	**0.76**	0.5	0.97	**0.7**	0.91	0.55	**0.76**	**0.7**	0.78	0.727
CNN_{128}	0.56	0.49	0.52	0.5	0.5	0.55	0.53	0.61	0.5	0.6	0.64	0.67	0.557

Table 3: Performance of different systems on the test set, measured with balanced accuracy (Acc_{bal}). Majority vote and Naive Bayes represent first-order baselines, IMC can be viewed as a second-order baseline. Systems marked with + have access to individual classifier outputs (IMC) and optionally paragraph (PV) and bag-of-words (BV) vectors. Best scores for each group are bolded. Underscores mark an improvement ≥ 0.03 (3%) Acc_{bal} for a specific group by NN classifiers over the IMC baseline or vice versa. NN_n: Neural Network with n hidden units, PV_n: Paragraph Vectors of dimension n, BV: boolean bag-of-words, CNN_n: Convolutional Neural Network with pre-trained vectors of dimension n.

binary problem	b0	b1	b2	b3	b4	b5	b6	b7	b8	b9	b10	b11
prevalence RI Train	0.56	0.33	0.1	0.23	0.03	0.1	0.15	0.13	0.07	0.18	0.1	0.19
prevalence RI Test	0.53	0.43	0.12	0.15	0.02	0.05	0.2	0.13	0.09	0.2	0.07	0.16
prevalence RI IMC	0.77	0.39	0.17	0.15	0.01	0.07	0.23	0.13	0.16	0.13	0.09	0.26
prevalence RI NN	0.7	0.39	0.07	0.15	0.01	0.07	0.19	0.13	0.06	0.13	0.09	0.18

Table 4: Prevalence of groups and themes: humanly labelled data vs. full automatically labelled RI.

consensus about the label-predictions between different NN architectures than between the NNs and IMC. On the binary problem level, the p-value for theme 6, new privileges, lies below 0.05 for all NN architectures with more than 512 hidden units. For b8, land grants, all p-values are < 0.05 for architectures with more than 128 hidden units. Observation of the predictions further suggests that the NNs feel the most need to correct the SVMs with b6 and b8 (with these the correction ends up in better predictions) and b0, nobles. However, in predicting nobles the difference is never significant. For example, NN2048+PV512, the best NN on the test set disagrees with the SVM on the nobles-label in 11 of 100 cases. Here the NN is correct only in 6 cases, making the difference non-significant with p=0.77. With b8 on the other hand there are 14 disagreements and 13 accurate corrections, resulting in a p-value of 0.001 (b6: 6 corrections, 6 accurate, p=0.016). Taking predictions over all groups again (1,200 predictions), this NN differs in 46 cases from the IMC choice and is correct 39 times ($p < 0.0005$). Why is the resulting perfomance increase in $\overline{Acc_{bal}}$ only 0.2%? This is due to the fact that the NN is more restrictive in assigning labels than the independent learner

model: in all 129,504 Regests, it predicts 50,968 less positive labels than IMC. As positive labels are strongly under-represented in the manually labeled data, the (non-weighted) Acc_{bal} measure is much more influenced by an additional True Positive than a True Negative for a rare group or theme.

Paragraph Vectors (PV) used as input to the NNs apparently contain more information than standard (boolean) bag-of-word (BoW) vectors. When the best NN is fed with BoW vectors instead of PVs it achieves lower performance (-0.07 $\overline{Acc_{bal}}$). To test whether Paragraph Vectors work better simply in general, we trained 12 independent SVM classifiers on PVs only, to predict players and themes. The result, for several dimensions of Paragraph Vectors (between 64 and 2048) fed into an SVM (best result: SVMs+PV_{128} in Table 3), did not exceed the Naive Bayes baseline, indicating strongly that PVs alone are inferior to BoW vectors for standard textual classification of the RI. Our explanation is as follows: While Quoc Le (2014) achieved good results in classifying sentiment of movie reviews with Paragraph Vectors, he hypotheses that movie reviews are tailor-cut for learning the vectors for this problem, because *compositionality plays an important* *role in deciding whether the review is positive or negative.* The RI are a more complex source and it is debatable whether compositionality plays a role with regard to co-occurring groups and themes. Also, while movie reviews often contain similar (sentiment) vocabulary, each Regest presents its content in rather unique ways. The NN that learns Paragraph Vectors is thus presented with very diverse information, most likely generating vectors containing every and thus little information. We conclude that using standard BoW vectors as first-order information was the correct choice, while PVs prove more suitable as higher-order information for the NN acting as a meta-classifier (as they add little but additional information).[11]

Players and themes that can be predicted with great success by many systems on the test set are *confirmation of privileges* (b7: 0.94), *Jews* (b4: 1.00) and *women* (b5: 0.98). By contrast, all systems fail to reliably predict class b2 (*lesser nobles*), which yields a maximum of 0.12 points beyond majority and no gains beyond Naive Bayes. One explanation for this low performance is that it was really hard (if not sometimes impossible) to distinguish between non-nobles and nobles in the annotation process. All other groups and themes can be predicted with solid accuracy scores ($\geq$ 0.20 above majority, $\geq$ 0.02 above Naive Bayes, and $\geq$ 0.62 Acc_{bal} per category in general).

The system $+NN_{2048}+PV_{512}$ perfoms best in $\overline{Acc_{bal}}$. We also analyze two additional criteria of performance: (i) the Kullback-Leibler (KL) divergence between distributions of labels in the manually annotated data to the distributions of labels automatically assigned to the full RI and (ii), the KL divergence between the distributions of amounts of labels (0-12 labels can be assigned to a Regest). For (i), the KL divergences are $KL_{train,test} = 0.033$ and $KL_{train,RI_{NN}} = 0.036$, $KL_{train,RI_{IMC}} = 0.058$ indicating only a small divergence between human and automatic labeling by the NN w.r.t. the distributions of the twelve groups and themes (cf. Table 4). In fact, all of the best three NNs appear to have smaller KL-divergencies than IMC. Also (ii), number of group and theme labels that are assigned by human vs. automatic labeling, shows similar tendencies: $KL_{train,test} = 0.02$, $KL_{train,RI_{NN}} = 0.01$,

$KL_{train,RI_{IMC}} = 0.07$. On average, two labels were assigned to a Regest by all labeling systems. The human assigned 43% of the Regests two labels, IMC 27% and the NN 34%.

In sum, our results indicate that NNs can learn dependencies of labels from independent classifier predictions. NNs are thus suitable to detect structures in the data that are intuitive for humans.

5 Deriving Structures of European Medieval Times

We labeled all Regests with $+NN_{2048} + PV_{512}$. We eye-balled several annotations and found many of the predicted classes to be correctly inferred[12].

5.1 Feature Analysis

The learned weight vectors of the SVMs offer interpretation of the terms w.r.t. the classified groups and themes. Table 5 displays, for selected classes, the phrases which were assigned the highest weights. Many of these intuitively make sense. Indicator terms for War and Peace are "truppen" (troops), "friedensverhandlungen" (peace talks) and the preposition "gegen" (against), other terms point geographically to the East: türken (turkish) or konstantinopel (today: Istanbul).

From the analysis we conclude that the decision to not normalize the texts was reasonable, given that we find many high-weighted terms that are abbreviations, e.g., "urkk" (charter), "kgin" (queen) or latin expressions: 'ecclesia" (christian community), "abbati" (father), "monasterii" (locative of monastery) are indicators for spiritual institutions.

5.2 Investigating the Regesta Imperii

Using the automatically assigned labels for *players* and *themes* in the full set of 129,504 Regests, we are able to investigate structures that emerge between specific players and themes, with respect to time or certain locations. In Figure 3 we trace the development of the ratio of Regests which were both about *cities* and *privileges* w.r.t. time. Given that in some years no Regests are available, the ratios are "smoothed" by calculating them over bins of 25 years. The occurrence ratio is determined by $Ratio(gt, b) = \frac{|Regests_{b,gt}|}{|Regests_b|}$, where gt is the set of groups and themes we want to "trace" and b is one of the bins of 25 years. $|Regests_{b,gt}|$

---

[11]Note that this applies only to NNs as meta-learners: the SVM-based meta-learner baseline performed below majority baseline when supplied also with Paragraph Vectors ($\overline{acc_{bal}}$ with additional Paragraph Vectors: 0.786, without: 0.788).

[12]The automatic annotations (for the full RI) can be obtained from `https://cl.uni-heidelberg.de/~opitz/ri/`

Group/Theme	highest (positively) weighted terms
Spiritual Institutions	ecclesia, reims, lucius, erzbischof, abbati, imperatoris, abt, nonnenkloster, mönch, bischfliche
	vice, konvent, intervention, monasterii, episcopi, kloster, besitz, besitzungen, bischof, papst, kirche
Jews	haupt, angesichts, anspruch, aufnehmen, freyburg, niemals, christen, vidimus, heilbronn ungelt
	frevel, judenschaft, stifter, quittieren, kost, verstoßen, christliche, gebrechen, einnehmer, judensteuer
City/Citizens	docum, beglaubigung, landfriede, weltlich, reichssteuern, cons, gemeinde, breslau, schffen, urkk
	gelnhausen, laden, verhören, einwohner, rathe, städte, bürgern, brgermeister, bürger, stad, stadt
War and Peace	friedensverhandlung, entschdigung, kräften, schiedsspruch, hoffe, umso, castilien, klar, sehr, türken
	pabstes, belagerung, dienen, konstantinopel, sagt, friede, truppen, kriege, krieg, gegen
Justice	verhngt, einwohnern, schiedsrichter, aberacht, lichtenberg, gewhrte, theile, bestraft, begangen, stand
	fremdes, landgerichte, verlorene, landgericht, einerseits, andererseits, wiedergutmachung, urteil

Table 5: Highly weighted terms for groups and themes found in SVM classifiers. Some terms are difficult to translate, but most terms intuitively make sense. For example: many terms for *Jews* relate to financial taxes ("quittieren"–to receipt; "einnehmer"–collector). Other terms for this group are negatively connotated: "frevel"–sacrilege, "verstoßen"–outcast. Jews in medieval times often were at most tolerated and had to pay special taxes (above: "judensteuer"). For all themes and groups a large amount of the heigh-weighted terms is in Latin, suggesting that it was a correct decision not to filter out Latin words.

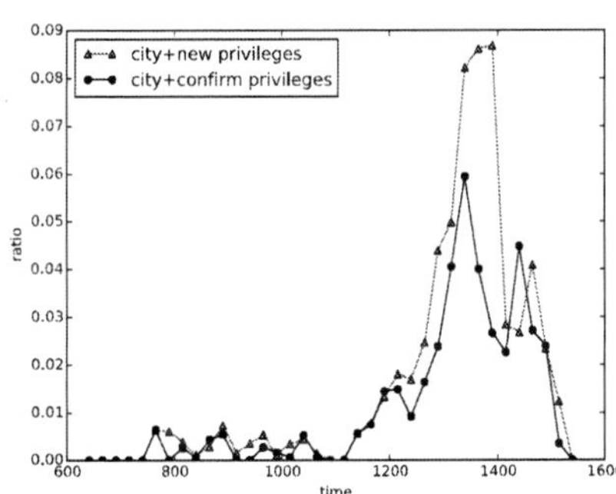

Figure 3: Functions from times to ratios of occurrence for *city* and *new privileges* (triangles) and *city* and *confirmation of privileges* (circles) in the RI. High concentration of *cities* and *privileges* are found from the 12th century onwards, with a peak in the 14th century. *new privileges* outweigh *confirmation of privileges* around the 14th century.

is the number of Regests from time bin b which are about *all* groups and themes contained in gt.

Not only can groups and themes be traced with regard to time, but also to locations or/and to certain emperors. This is exemplified in Fig. 6 and 4 where we count the occurrences of all 12 themes and groups with respect to these parameters and normalize by the sum of all 12 occurrence counts.

6   Conclusions

We solved a multi-label text classification problem to derive interesting demographic groups (e.g. *citizens*) and themes of interactions (i.a. *bestowal of privileges* or *justice*) in the Regesta Imperii.

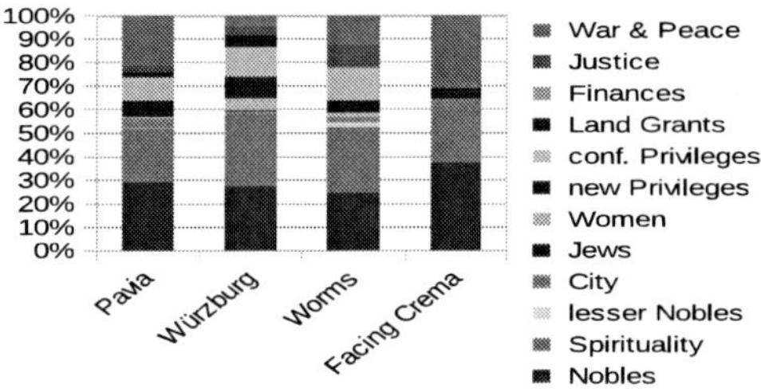

Figure 6: Players and themes in Regests submitted under the name of the German-Roman emperor Friedrich I. (*1122, †1190) in different locations. *War and Peace* played the greatest role in the Italian city Crema, which indeed was involved in war during Friedrich's regency and subjected 1160.

Evaluation on a held out test set suggests that most groups and themes can be predicted with good reliability: 9 out of 12 classes can be predicted with a (balanced) Accuracy score ≥ 0.75. The arithmetic mean of all 12 scores – our global performance measure – is 0.797 for the system that was finally chosen to label the entire RI.

A Neural Network acting as a meta learner over the outputs of independent maximum margin classifiers and Paragraph Vectors (document embeddings learned by neural networks) led to a minor improvement of 0.2% mean score. However, for the group *nobles* and the themes *bestowal of land* and *new privileges* the scores were improved by up to 3%, 4% and 5%, indicating dependencies between these classes that cannot be captured by classifiers working under the label-independence assumption. We conclude that NNs can give ad-

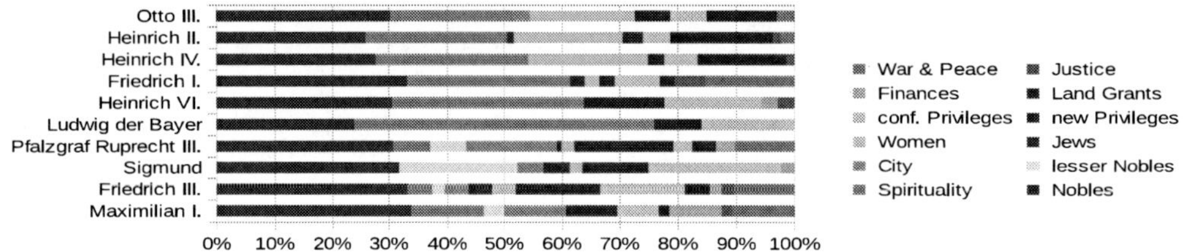

Figure 4: Impact of groups and themes in the German city of Mainz with respect to emperors and time: From Otto III. (crowned German-Roman King in 983) to Maximilan I. (crowned in 1486). The impact of *spiritual institutions* (from Ruprecht III onwards) and *women* and *land bestowals* (both from Friedrich I. onwards) seems to decrease. Finances seem to play a more important role in the later Middle Ages.

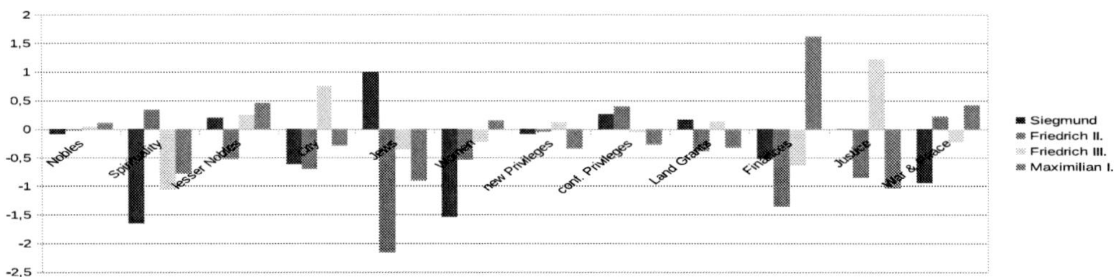

Figure 5: Logistic Regression weights when we force themes and groups to predict the issuing emperor. Negative Weights suggest negative correlation, positive weights suggest positive correlation. Observably *finances* and *war and peace* are associated with Maximilian I. He was notoriously famous for his flamboyant lifestyle and led many wars. Two components leading to great debts, which he mostly owed to Jakob Fugger, banker from the famous Fugger family.

ditional information on possible dependencies between classes in a multi-label classification task.

Conceptually the approach is straightforward, but a complicating factor is the exploding parameter space: Besides the "inner parameters" of the Learners, regularization control or the number of neurons in the Neural Network, there are numerous "outer parameters", e.g., possible ways of document representation or pre-processing.

As best-performing system we determined a NN model with additional Paragraph Vector information. It obtained the best results on the test set and also yields the minimum KL divergence for the label distribution over manually labeled training data compared to system predictions. This model was chosen to label all 129,504 Regests.

For the project *Regesta Imperii* and Digital Humanities in general, our work offers the possibility to trace demographic groups (players) and themes through almost one thousand years of medieval history across different European locations. We showcased data analyses and visualizations. Manifold other possibilities may be explored in future work.

The Regesta Imperii in our opinion is a most challenging and linguistically interesting corpus. For historians, the RI is important as a fundamental source for medieval European studies. For linguists the RI may be very interesting due to its linguistic "uniqueness": syntactic constructions range from simple to most complex, the languages range from more modern German to different forms of medieval German to Latin. Great varieties in word forms exist. Semantically, the referenced objects and concepts are often confined to short periods of time. Thus, the RI presents challenges for researchers from many research fields. The challenging language, the considerable amount of data and the many interesting questions of humanities regarding the medieval times of Europe make the RI a great corpus for NLP researchers with special interest in Humanities.

Acknowledgments

We are grateful to the anonymous reviewers for their valuable comments.

References

Olivier Chapelle, Vikas Sindhwani, and Sathiya S. Keerthi. 2008. Optimization Techniques for Semi-Supervised Support Vector Machines. *J. Mach. Learn. Res.*, 9:203–233, June.

Morten W. Fagerland, Stian Lydersen, and Petter Laake. 2013. The McNemar test for binary matched-pairs data: mid-p and asymptotic are better than exact conditional. *BMC Medical Research Methodology*, 13(1):1–8.

Yoon Kim. 2014. Convolutional Neural Networks for Sentence Classification. *CoRR*, abs/1408.5882.

Andreas Kuczera. 2015. Graphdatenbanken für Historiker. Netzwerke in den Registern der Regesten Kaiser Friedrichs III. mit neo4j und Gephi. *Mittelalter. Interdisziplinre Forschung und Rezeptionsgeschichte*.

Quoc V. Le and Tomas Mikolov. 2014. Distributed Representations of Sentences and Documents. In *ICML*, volume 32 of *JMLR Proceedings*, pages 1188–1196. JMLR.org.

D. Massad, E. Omodei, C. Strohecker, Y. Xu, J. Garland, M. Zhang, and L.F. Seoane. 2013. Unfolding History: Classification and analysis of written history as a complex system. Complex Systems Summer School Proceedings, Santa Fe Institute.

Albert Meroño Peñuela, Ashkan Ashkpour, Marieke van Erp, Kees Mandemakers, Leen Breure, Andrea Scharnhorst, Stefan Schlobach, and Frank van Harmelen. 2014. Semantic Technologies for Historical Research: A Survey. *Semantic Web Journal*.

Jan Paul Niederkorn. 2005. Julius von Ficker und die Fortführung der Regesta Imperii vom Tod Böhmers (1863) bis zu ihrer Übernahme durch die Kaiserliche Akademie der Wissenschaften in Wien (1906). In *Wege zur Urkunde, Wege der Urkunde, Wege der Forschung. Beiträge zur europäischen Diplomatik des Mittelalters (= Forschungen zur Kaiser- und Papstgeschichte des Mittelalters. Volume 24)*, Forschungen zur Kaiser- und Papstgeschichte des Mittelalters., pages 293–302, Köln, Weimar, Wien. Böhlau.

Michael Piotrowski. 2012. *Natural Language Processing for Historical Texts*. Synthesis Lectures on Human Language Technologies. Morgan & Claypool Publishers.

Dieter Rübsamen and Andreas Kuczera. 2006. Verborgen, vergessen, verloren? Perspektiven der Quellenerschlieung durch die digitalen Regesta Imperii. In *Forschung in der digitalen Welt. Sicherung, Erschließung und Aufbereitung von Wissensbeständen. Tagung des Staatsarchivs Hamburg und des Zentrums Geisteswissenschaften in der digitalen Welt an der Universitt Hamburg am 10. und 11. April 2006*, Forschungen zur Kaiser- und Papstgeschichte des Mittelalters, pages 109–123, Hamburg. Rainer Hering, Jürgen Sarnowsky, Christoph Schäfer und Udo Schäfer.

Tuukka Ruotsalo, Lora Aroyo, and Guus Schreiber. 2009. Knowledge-Based Linguistic Annotation of Digital Cultural Heritage Collections. *IEEE Intelligent Systems*, 24(2):64–75.

Vikas Sindhwani and S. Sathiya Keerthi. 2006. Large Scale Semi-supervised Linear SVMs. In *Proceedings of the 29th Annual International ACM SIGIR Conference on Research and Development in Information Retrieval*, SIGIR '06, pages 477–484, New York, NY, USA. ACM.

Xiang Zhang, Junbo Zhao, and Yann LeCun. 2015. Character-level Convolutional Networks for Text Classification. *CoRR*, abs/1509.01626.

Harald Zimmermann. 2000. *Die Regesta imperii im Fortschreiten und Fortschritt*, volume 20 of *Forschungen zur Kaiser- und Papstgeschichte des Mittelalters*. Böhlau, Köln, Weimar, Wien.

Semi-automated annotation of page-based documents within the *Genre and Multimodality* framework

Tuomo Hiippala
Centre for Applied Language Studies
University of Jyväskylä
P.O. Box 35, 40014 Finland
`tuomo.hiippala@iki.fi`

Abstract

This paper describes ongoing work on a tool developed for annotating document images for their multimodal features and compiling this information into a corpus. The tool leverages open source computer vision and natural language processing libraries to describe the content and structure of multimodal documents and to generate multiple layers of XML annotation. The paper introduces the annotation schema, describes the document processing pipeline and concludes with a brief description of future work.

1 Introduction

Multimodality – or how multiple modes of communication interact and co-operate – has become a concern within many fields that fall under the umbrella of digital humanities (Svensson, 2010; O'Halloran et al., 2014). Whereas gestures, gaze and postures accompany spoken language in face-to-face conversation, written language works together with photographs, diagrams, typography and other communicative resources in documents. Given the inherent complexity of multimodal phenomena, combined with the variation arising from contextual factors, corpus-based approaches have been suggested as necessary for bringing multimodality under increased analytical control (Allwood, 2008; Bateman, 2014b).

This paper contributes to the empirical study of multimodality in page-based documents by presenting a prototype tool for creating multimodal corpora from document images that were not born digital. The tool generates stand-off XML annotation following the *Genre and Multimodality* (GeM) model, which provides an annotation schema with multiple layers of description that at-tend to the content, layout, appearance and discourse relations in page-based documents (Bateman, 2008).

The GeM annotation schema, which is intended to "function as a tool for isolating significant patterns against the mass of detail that multimodal documents naturally present" (Bateman, 2014a, 33), has proven useful for comparing the multimodality of documents across cultures (Thomas, 2009; Kong, 2013) and describing their change over time (Hiippala, 2015b). Yet the GeM model has not been adopted widely, because applying the multi-layered annotation schema requires ample time and resources. This requirement arises from the aforementioned mass of detail that occurs in multimodal documents.

The tool presented in this paper attacks the bottleneck issues of time and resources by leveraging several open source computer vision and optical character recognition libraries for the semi-automatic annotation of multimodal documents. To support this task, the paper proposes a variant of the GeM annotation schema named *auto-GeM*. This variant of the annotation schema is geared towards generating machine-readable annotation, which may be studied using tools developed for the purpose (Hiippala, 2015a), while also providing ground truths for specific document genres, whose availability is considered a prerequisite for automating other parts of the annotation process.

The paper begins with a brief introduction to the GeM model and its annotation schema, relating the work on the prototype tool to previous attempts at automating parts of the annotation process. The document processing pipeline and the proposed *auto-GeM* annotation schema are then described in greater detail. Finally, the conclusion outlines current challenges and sketches future work on the tool.

Proceedings of the 10th SIGHUM Workshop on Language Technology for Cultural Heritage, Social Sciences, and Humanities (LaTeCH), pages 84–89,
Berlin, Germany, August 11, 2016. ©2016 Association for Computational Linguistics

2 The Genre and Multimodality model

The GeM model provides a multi-layered XML schema for stand-off annotation of multimodal documents (Henschel, 2003; Bateman, 2008).

The model has four layers of annotation: any document described using the GeM model is first segmented into *base* units. These units constitute the base layer. Recognized base units include, among others, sentences, headers, photographs, captions and illustrations (Bateman, 2008, 111). The base units are then picked up for description in the *layout* layer, which features three components that describe their grouping and logical organization (layout structure), determine their typographic and graphic features (realization information), and establish their position in the document layout (area model).

The *rhetorical* layer, in turn, describes the discourse relations holding between the content, extending Rhetorical Structure Theory to cover both verbal and visual base units (Mann and Thompson, 1988; Taboada and Mann, 2006). Finally, the *navigation* layer describes how documents support their use with pointers such as "see page 5" and their corresponding entries, such as page and section numbers.

Each document is thus described from four different perspectives, and the annotation for each layer is cross-referenced using unique identifiers. These identifiers help to track how content elements relate to each other across the layout, rhetorical and navigation layers. Unlike other frameworks developed for describing documents, such as the Text Encoding Initiative (TEI), which is slowly beginning to pay attention to layout, typography and materiality, but continues to be primarily concerned with the representation of documents built around linear written language (Muñoz and Viglianti, 2015), the GeM model is inherently geared towards describing all kinds of multimodal documents, whether they organize their content linearly or make extensive use of the two-dimensional layout space.

Moreover, the GeM model was designed for corpus-driven research from the outset, and several tools have been developed to support the analysis of corpora annotated using its schema. Thomas (2007) describes a concordancer for querying GeM annotation, while Hiippala (2015a) uses Python to parse GeM corpora, transforming the annotation into GraphViz DOT graphs (Gansner and North, 2000) to visualize descriptions of document structure stored in the layout, rhetorical and navigation layers.

Certain attempts have also been made to address the bottleneck issues of time and resources required for producing GeM-annotated corpora. Thomas (2009) explores the use of commercial optical character recognition (OCR) software for automatically producing GeM annotation by using XSLT and Perl to transform and enrich the OCR output. Using XML output from *ABBYY FineReader 8.0 SDK* for generating annotation for the base and layout layers, Thomas observes that OCR output proves useful for the time-consuming task of describing typographic features, but nevertheless requires extensive manual post-processing.

Thomas (2009, 245) concludes that producing GeM annotation for the layout areas missed by the OCR engine constitutes the most time-consuming post-processing task. Thomas et al. (2010) attempt to reduce the time spent on post-processing by using XSLT to transform the OCR output into the OpenDocument format, in which the output could be manually tweaked and improved. Despite integrating well into the document processing pipeline, the OpenDocument format loses most of the information pertaining to the document layout, which multimodal documents frequently exploit to provide cues about their use and organization (Waller, 2012).

Building on the previous work, this paper proposes several improvements to annotating multimodal documents semi-automatically within the framework proposed by the GeM model. Firstly, preferring open source libraries over commercial software enables a top-down approach, that is, attending to the key features of the layout first. Secondly, controlling the design of the entire document processing pipeline removes the need for interim formats, generating the annotation only after major corrections have been applied, propagating these modifications across all annotation layers. These improvements have been implemented in the prototype annotator, which is introduced in the following section.

3 The prototype annotator

3.1 System design

The prototype annotator is provided as an interactive Jupyter/IPython notebook to help novice users to deploy and use the tool (Pérez and Granger,

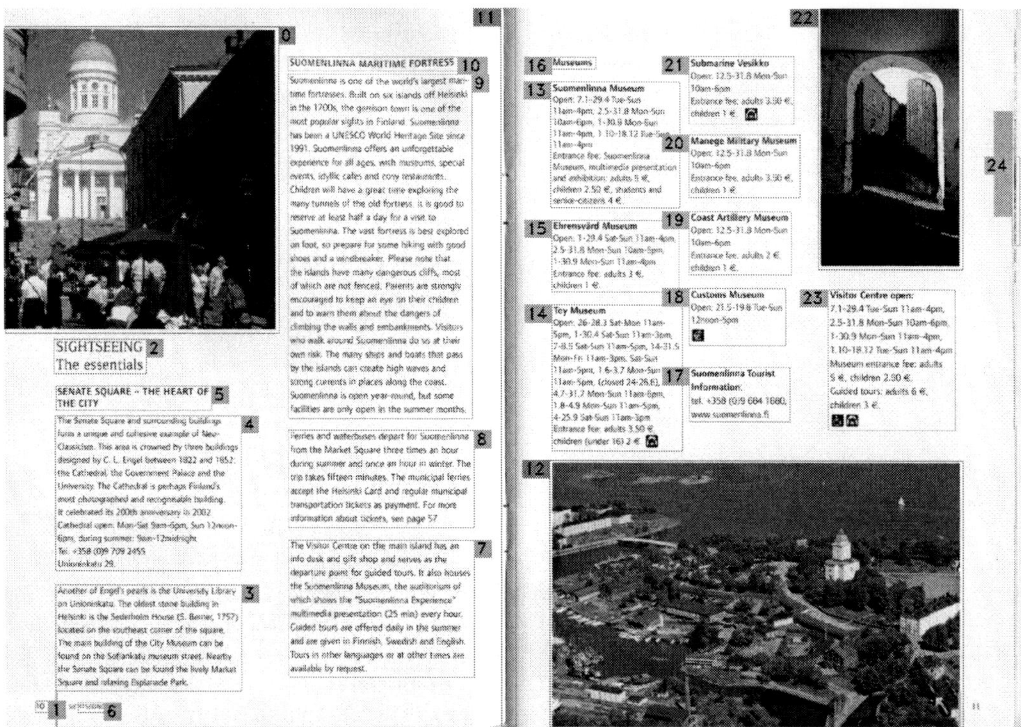

Figure 1: Detected and classified bounding boxes on a document image, labelled with identifiers.

2007). The notebook calls its functions from an external module, *generator*, which contains the main functions for processing and annotating document images. The annotator is available at www.github.com/thiippal/gem-tools.

To process the documents and to generate a description using the *auto-GeM* annotation schema, the annotator relies on several open source libraries: OpenCV[1] for computer vision, Tesseract[2] for OCR and NLTK[3] for natural language processing. The integration of these libraries into the document processing pipeline is described in the following section.

3.2 Document processing pipeline

The high-resolution document image, preferably of 300 DPI resolution, is first resized into a canonical width of 1200 pixels, while naturally maintaining the original aspect ratio of the document. A smaller size allows more efficient processing in OpenCV, which is first used to convert the document image from colour to grayscale. Next, bilateral filtering is applied to the grayscale image to reduce noise while preserving the edges of document elements. The filtered image is converted into a binary image, calculating the threshold using Otsu's method.

At this stage, the user is required to define a kernel size for performing a series of morphological operations on the thresholded image. The kernel height should correspond roughly to the x-height of the font used for body text in the document image, which is a prerequisite for detecting text paragraphs correctly. The following morphological operations involve applying a morphological gradient to establish the outlines of document elements, followed by an erosion to separate the elements clearly from each other. The user can set the number of iterations performed for the erosion in the notebook.

To help the user to fine-tune the annotator parameters, such as kernel size and erosion iterations, each step involving image processing is documented in an HTML-file using the *visual-logging*[4] module. This log is provided with the output.

[1] www.opencv.org

[2] www.github.com/tesseract-ocr

[3] www.nltk.org

[4] www.github.com/dchaplinsky/visual-logging

Next, connected-components labelling is performed to filter out remaining noise, before detecting contours using OpenCV. Contour detection is performed twice: during the first pass, each detected contour is filled with solid colour. The second pass retrieves the contours of filled elements: this procedure suppresses unwanted contours nested within photographs and other graphical elements. In initial testing, this procedure provided better results for grid-based layouts than applying a Non-Maximum Suppression algorithm. This, however, is likely to be largely dependent on the kind of document genre described.

The annotator then sorts the detected contours and feeds them to a Random Forest classifier, which classifies the regions of interest defined by the contours into two categories: text or graphics. The model, trained using Haralick textures and colour statistics extracted from 400 photographs and 400 text blocks, achieves on a high precision (1.00) and recall (0.99) on the testing data.

Finally, the classified contours are drawn on the resized image and displayed to the user in the notebook, as shown in Figure 1. The user is then asked to enter the identifiers of any false positives among the detected regions of interest. In Figure 1, these include regions labelled 11 and 24. The regions marked by the user are removed from the list of contours. At this stage, the user can also manually draw any regions of interest that evaded detection, such as the page number on the lower right-hand corner of Figure 1. For this purpose, the annotator uses the OpenCV HighGUI module.

When the user is finished, the contours are projected on the original high-resolution image to extract regions of interest, which are assumed to correspond roughly to layout units defined within the GeM model, that is, to text paragraphs, images, headers, captions and the like. Regions classified as text are then thresholded, resized to double their original size and fed to Tesseract for OCR. NLTK's Punkt tokenizer (Kiss and Strunk, 2006) is subsequently used for segmenting the layout units into sentences.

Three kinds of description are then created for each layout unit: basic layout segmentation, position in the document layout, and visual appearance. The base layer annotation is generated simultaneously using the segmentation produced by the Punkt tokenizer. Each region of interest is also extracted from the original high-resolution image

and stored into the corpus, anticipating their use as training data for machine learning algorithms and for visualizing parts of the original document image in concordancer output (Thomas, 2007).

3.3 The auto-GeM annotation schema

The annotator generates *auto-GeM* annotation for the base and layout layers as described below. The base layer is first extracted from the layout layer, generating annotation for the minimal units of analysis defined within the GeM model. Within the base layer, each base unit is stored within a `unit` element and provided with a unique identifier in the `id` attribute to handle cross-references across annotation layers.

```
<unit id="u-1.4">Another of En-
gel's pearls is the University
Library on Unioninkatu.</unit>
```

The base units are picked up for description in the layout layer, in which they are combined into larger layout units, such as text paragraphs. In the layout layer annotation, the layout units are stored under the parent element `segmentation`. The following example shows the annotation for one child element, `layout-unit`, which represents a text paragraph consisting of multiple base units:

```
<layout-unit id="lay-1.4" src=
"lay-1.4.png" location="sa-1.4"
xref="u-1.4 u-1.5 u-1.6 u-1.7"/>
```

The `src` attribute refers to the image that contains the region of interest described by the layout unit, whereas the `location` attribute designates the position of the layout unit by referring to the `sub-area` element. The `xref` attribute refers to the base units that constitute the layout unit in question.

The `sub-area` element, positioned under the parent element `area-model`, contains a bounding box with relational coordinates, which can be projected on images of different sizes or used to render an abstract representation of the physical layout.

```
<sub-area id="sa-1.4" bbox=
"0.0490168139071 0.800747198007
0.231689940154 0.946865919469"/>
```

Finally, under the `realization` element, the `text` element characterizes the layout unit in terms of realization information, identifying the layout unit as consisting of written language.

```
<text xref="lay-1.4"/>
```

For graphic elements, the corresponding element `graphics` features additional attributes, `width` and `height`, which store relational values indicating the size of the graphic element in relation to the entire layout.

In comparison to the original GeM schema proposed in Bateman (2008), the coverage of the document structure in the *auto-GeM* schema is currently limited. Whereas the original GeM annotation schema can provide a rich description of the document layout and its appearance, but requires investing a considerable amount of time and resources in the annotation process, the tool described in this paper can be used to generate the base layer and parts of the layout layer much more efficiently. Given this trade-off and the current state of development, the prototype tool is likely to be most effective for generating a baseline for manual annotation. Future work will seek to bridge the gap between the original GeM schema and its proposed *auto-GeM* variant.

4   Conclusions and future work

This paper described the ongoing development of an annotation tool for describing the multimodal content and structure of page-based documents that were not born digital. The tool is intended to speed up the process of creating multimodal corpora for empirical research and generating rich descriptions to be used as ground truths for machine learning tasks.

Future work on the tool will involve covering the entire scope of the original GeM model in the *auto-GeM* variant, while taking the automation process further. This includes:

- enriching the realization information with a description of typographic properties, such as font size and family, while also describing the types of graphic elements more accurately,

- determining and suggesting optimal kernel size and iteration parameters to the user,

- enhancing the classification of graphical document elements using emerging multimodal resources such as Elliott and Kleppe (2016),

- captioning photographs using the method proposed in Karpathy and Fei-Fei (2015),

- representing the logical organization of the content by constructing a hierarchical XY-tree from the detected bounding boxes,

- creating an interface for annotating the rhetorical structure, which will undoubtedly require the most manual input from the user,

- detecting and annotating pointers and entries in the document image to provide a representation of the navigation structure.

Additional user-configured parameters will also be included in future versions, in order to ensure that the tool can meet the demands of different document genres. To tackle the problem of variation, test corpora representing various different document genres are also being planned at the moment.

References

Jens Allwood. 2008. Multimodal corpora. In Anke Lüdeling and Merja Kytö, editors, *Corpus Linguistics: An International Handbook*, pages 207–225. Mouton de Gruyter, Berlin.

John A. Bateman. 2008. *Multimodality and Genre: A Foundation for the Systematic Analysis of Multimodal Documents*. Palgrave Macmillan, London.

John A. Bateman. 2014a. Developing a GeM (Genre and Multimodality) model. In Sigrid Norris and Carmen D. Maier, editors, *Interactions, Images and Texts: A Reader in Multimodality*, pages 25–36. De Gruyter Mouton, Berlin and New York.

John A. Bateman. 2014b. Using multimodal corpora for empirical research. In Carey Jewitt, editor, *The Routledge Handbook of Multimodal Analysis*, pages 238–252. Routledge, London and New York, second edition.

Desmond Elliott and Martijn Kleppe. 2016. 1 million captioned Dutch newspaper images. In *Proceedings of the 10th International Conference on Language Resources and Evaluation (LREC 2016)*. May 23–28, Portorož, Slovenia.

Emden R. Gansner and Stephen C. North. 2000. An open graph visualization system and its applications to software engineering. *Software - Practice and Experience*, 30(11):1203–1233.

Renate Henschel, 2003. *GeM Annotation Manual*. University of Bremen, University of Stirling, second edition.

Tuomo Hiippala. 2015a. *gem-tools*: Tools for working with multimodal corpora annotated using the Genre and Multimodality model. DOI: 10.5281/zenodo.33775

Tuomo Hiippala. 2015b. *The Structure of Multimodal Documents: An Empirical Approach*. Routledge, New York and London.

Andrej Karpathy and Li Fei-Fei. 2015. Deep visual-semantic alignments for generating image descriptions. In *Proceedings of the IEEE Conference on Computer Vision and Pattern Recognition (CVPR 2015)*. June 7–12, Boston, MA.

Tibor Kiss and Jan Strunk. 2006. Unsupervised multilingual sentence boundary detection. *Computational Linguistics*, 32(4):485–525.

Kenneth C. C. Kong. 2013. A corpus-based study in comparing the multimodality of Chinese- and English-language newspapers. *Visual Communication*, 12(2):173–196.

William C. Mann and Sandra A. Thompson. 1988. Rhetorical Structure Theory: Toward a functional theory of text organization. *Text*, 8(3):243–281.

Trevor Muñoz and Raffaele Viglianti. 2015. Texts and documents: New challenges for TEI interchange and lessons from the Shelley-Godwin archive. *Journal of the Text Encoding Initiative*, 8. DOI: 10.4000/jtei.1270

Kay L. O'Halloran, Alvin Chua, and Alexey Podlasov. 2014. The role of images in social media analytics: A multimodal digital humanities approach. In David Machin, editor, *Visual Communication*, pages 565–588. De Gruyter Mouton, Berlin.

Fernando Pérez and Brian E. Granger. 2007. IPython: A system for interactive scientific computing. *Computing in Science and Engineering*, 9(3):21–29.

Patrick Svensson. 2010. The landscape of digital humanities. *Digital Humanities Quarterly*, 4(1).

Maite Taboada and William C. Mann. 2006. Rhetorical structure theory: looking back and moving ahead. *Discourse Studies*, 8(3):423–459.

Martin Thomas, Judy Delin, and Robert H. W. Waller. 2010. A framework for corpus-based analysis of the graphic signalling of discourse structure. In *Proceedings of Multidisciplinary Approaches to Discourse (MAD 2010)*, Moissac, France, March 17-20.

Martin Thomas. 2007. Querying multimodal annotation: A concordancer for GeM. In *Proceedings of the Linguistic Annotation Workshop*, pages 57–60, Prague, Czech Republic, June 28–29. Association for Computational Linguistics.

Martin Thomas. 2009. *Localizing pack messages: A framework for corpus-based cross-cultural multimodal analysis*. Ph.D. thesis, University of Leeds.

Robert H. W. Waller. 2012. Graphic literacies for a digital age: The survival of layout. *The Information Society*, 28(4):236–252.

Nomen Omen. Enhancing the Latin Morphological Analyser Lemlat with an Onomasticon

Marco Budassi
Università di Pavia
Corso Strada Nuova, 65
27100 Pavia - Italy
marcobudassi@hotmail.it

Marco Passarotti
Università Cattolica del Sacro Cuore
Largo Gemelli, 1
20123 Milan - Italy
marco.passarotti@unicatt.it

Abstract

Lemlat is a morphological analyser for Latin, which shows a remarkably wide coverage of the Latin lexicon. However, the performance of the tool is limited by the absence of proper names in its lexical basis. In this paper we present the extension of Lemlat with a large Onomasticon for Latin. First, we describe and motivate the automatic and manual procedures for including the proper names in Lemlat. Then, we compare the new version of Lemlat with the previous one, by evaluating their lexical coverage of four Latin texts of different era and genre.

1 Introduction

Since the time of the *Index Thomisticus* by father Roberto Busa (Busa, 1974-1980), which is usually mentioned among the first electronic (nowadays called "digital") annotated corpora available, NLP tools for automatic morphological analysis and lemmatisation of a richly inflected language like Latin were needed. Over the last decades, this need was fulfilled by a number of morphological analysers for Latin. Among the most widespread ones are *Morpheus* (Crane, 1991), Whitaker's *Words* (http://archives.nd.edu/words.html) and Lemlat (Passarotti, 2004). Over the past ten years, such tools have become essential, in light of a number of projects aimed at developing advanced language resources for Latin, like treebanks.[1]

The most recent advances in linguistic annotation of Latin treebanks are moving beyond the level of syntax, by performing semantic-based tasks like semantic role labelling and anaphora and ellipsis resolution (Passarotti, 2014). In particular, in the area of Digital Humanities there is growing interest in Named Entity Recognition (NER), especially for purposes of geographical-based analysis of texts.

NER is a sub-branch of Information Extraction, whose inception goes back to the Sixth Message Understanding Conference (MUC-6) (Grishman and Sundheim, 1996). NER aims at recognising and labelling (multi)words, as names of people, things, places, etc. Since MUC-6, NER has largely expanded, with several applications also on ancient languages (see, for example, Depauw and Van Beek, 2009).

Although Lemlat provides quite a large coverage of the Latin lexicon, its performance is limited by the absence of an Onomasticon in its lexical basis, which would be helpful for tasks like NER. Given that in Latin proper names undergo morphological inflection, in this paper we describe our work of enhancing Lemlat with an Onomasticon. The paper is organised as follows. Section 2 presents the basic features of Lemlat. Section 3 describes our method to enhance Lemlat with an Onomasticon, by detailing the rules for the automatic enhancement and discussing the most problematic kinds of words. Section 4 evaluates the rules and presents one experiment run on four Latin texts. Section 5 is a short conclusion and sketches the future work.

2 Lemlat

The lexical basis of Lemlat results from the collation of three Latin dictionaries (Georges and Georges, 1913-1918; Glare, 1982; Gradenwitz, 1904). It counts 40,014 lexical entries and 43,432 lemmas, as more than one lemma can be included into the same lexical entry.

---

[1] Three dependency treebanks are currently available for Latin: the Latin Dependency Treebank (Bamman and Crane, 2006), the *Index Thomisticus* Treebank (Passarotti, 2009) and the Latin portion of the PROIEL corpus (Haug and Jøndal, 2008).

Proceedings of the 10th SIGHUM Workshop on Language Technology for Cultural Heritage, Social Sciences, and Humanities (LaTeCH), pages 90–94,
Berlin, Germany, August 11, 2016. ©2016 Association for Computational Linguistics

Given an input wordform that is recognised by Lemlat, the tool produces in output the corresponding lemma(s) and a number of tags conveying (a) the inflectional paradigm of the lemma(s) (e.g. first declension noun) and (b) the morphological features of the input wordform (e.g. singular nominative), as well as the identification number (ID) of the lemma(s) in the lexical basis of Lemlat. No contextual disambiguation is performed.

For instance, receiving in input the wordform *abamitae* ("great-aunt"), Lemlat outputs the corresponding lemma (*abamita*, ID: A0019), the tags for its inflectional paradigm (N1: first declension noun) and those for the morphological features of the input wordform (feminine singular genitive and dative; feminine plural nominative and vocative).

The basic component of the lexical look-up table used by Lemlat to analyse input wordforms is the so-called LES ("LExical Segment"). The LES is defined as the invariable part of the inflected form (e.g. *abamit* for *abamit-ae*). In other words, the LES is the sequence (or one of the sequences) of characters that remains the same in the inflectional paradigm of a lemma (hence, the LES does not necessarily correspond to the word stem).

Lemlat includes a LES archive, in which LES are assigned an ID and a number of inflectional features among which are a tag for the gender of the lemma (for nouns only) and a code (called CODLES) for its inflectional category. According to the CODLES, the LES is compatible with the endings of its inflectional paradigm. For instance, the CODLES for the LES *abamit* is N1 (first declension nouns) and its gender is F (feminine). The wordform *abamitae* is thus analysed as belonging to the LES *abamit* because the segment *-ae* is recognised as an ending compatible with a LES with CODLES N1.

3   Enhancing Lemlat. Method

The bedrock of our work is Busa's (1988) *Totius Latinitatis Lemmata*, which contains the list of the lemmas (92,052) from the 5th edition of *Lexicon Totius Latinitatis* (Forcellini, 1940). In Busa (1988), three kinds of metadata are assigned to each lemma: (a) a code for the section of the dictionary in which the lemma occurs (e.g. ON: the lemma occurs in the *Onomasticon*), (b) a code for the inflectional paradigm the lemma belongs to and its gender (e.g. BM: second declension masculine nouns) and (c) the number of lines of the lexical entry for the lemma in Forcellini.

In order to enhance Lemlat with Forcellini's Onomasticon, we first extracted from Busa (1988) the list of those lemmas that occur in the ON section. This list counts 28,178 lemmas. Then, we built a number of rules to automatically include the lemmas of the Onomasticon into the lexical basis of Lemlat.

3.1   Types of Rules

Including the Onomasticon of Forcellini into Lemlat means converting the list of proper names provided by Busa (1988) into the same format of the LES archive. In order to perform this task as automatically as possible, we built a number of rules to extract the relevant information for each lemma in the list, namely its LES, CODLES and gender. By exploiting the morphological tagging of Busa (1988), which groups sets of lemmas showing common inflectional features, our rules treat automatically such inflectionally regular groups. In total, we wrote 122 rules, which fall into four types.

The first type (60 rules) builds the LES by removing one or more characters from the right side of the lemma. Such a removal is constrained by the code for the inflectional paradigm of the lemma, which is then used to create both the CODLES and the tag for the gender. For instance, the lemma *marcus* ("Mark") is assigned the inflectional paradigm BM in Busa (1988). One rule states that the LES for BM lemmas ending in *-us* is built by removing the last two characters from the lemma (*marcus* > *marc*) The inflectional code BM stands for second declension (B) masculine (M) nouns: this is converted into the CODLES of Lemlat for second declension nouns (B > N2) and into the tag for masculine gender (M > m).

The second type of rules (19) adds one or more characters on the right side of the lemma to build the LES. Again, this is done according both to the inflectional paradigm and to the ending of the lemma in Busa (1988). For instance, the LES for lemmas with inflectional code CM (third declension masculine nouns) and ending in *-o* is built by adding an *-n* after the last character. One example is the lemma *bappo* ("Bappo"), whose LES is *bappon*, as third declension imparisyllable nouns are analysed by Lemlat by using the basis for their singular genitive (*bappon-is*).

The third type of rules (19) replaces one or more characters on the right side of the lemma with others. For instance, the LES of *clemens* ("Clement", third declension masculine noun ending in *-s*, with singular genitive *clement-is*) is built by replacing the final *-s* with a *-t* (*clement*).

The last type of rules (24) deals with those lemmas that are equal to their LES (no change is needed). These are uninflected nouns, (like *hamilcar* - "Hamilcar"), which can be easily retrieved because they are assigned a specific inflectional code in Busa (1988).

3.2 Problematic Cases

Not all inflectional paradigms are as much regular as to allow for a fully automatic rule-based treatment.

For instance, third declension feminine nouns represent an entangled class. The lemma *charybdis, -is* ("Charybdis") is a third declension parisyllable feminine noun ending in *-is*. Instead, *phegis, -gidis* ("daughter of Phegeus") is a third declension imparisyllable feminine noun ending in *-is*. One common rule cannot be used for these two kinds of words. We overcome such problem by building two more specific rules: one accounting for third declension feminine nouns ending in *-dis* and one for third declension feminine nouns ending in *-gis*. However, there are sub-groups of nouns for which such a solution does not work, like third declension feminine nouns ending in *-mis*, which can be both imparisyllable nouns (e.g. *salamis, -minis*, "Salamis") and parisyllable nouns (e.g. *tomis, -is*, "Tomis"). For these lemmas we checked manually their inflection in Forcellini and assigned LES and CODLES accordingly.

Another group of tricky words includes those lemmas that show two (or even more) different inflectional paradigms. For instance, *apollonides* ("Apollonides") shows both a singular genitive of the second declension (in *-i*) and one of the first declension (in *-ae*). We treated these cases manually by checking their lexical entries in Forcellini.

A further problem is represented by graphical variants, which are managed by Lemlat through so-called "exceptional forms". These are word-forms that are hard-coded in the LES archive and are assigned the same ID of the LES used to build their base lemma. For instance, the nominative singular of the lemma *jesus* ("Jesus") is attested also as *hiesus, ihesus* and *zesus*. Beside the LES *jes* (used for the base lemma *jesus*), in the LES archive also the wordforms *hiesus, ihesus* and *zesus* are recorded and assigned the same ID of the LES *jes*.

4 Evaluating the Enhancement

We evaluated the enhancement of Lemlat with the Onomasticon of Forcellini in two steps. First, we focused on the accuracy of the rules for automatic enhancement. Then, we compared the new version of Lemlat with the previous one by the lexical coverage they provide for four Latin texts.

4.1 Rules

We evaluated the quality of the rules for automatic enhancement by precision and recall (Van Rijsbergen, 1979).

Measuring the precision of our rules is straightforward. As said, while writing the rules, we focused on inflectionally regular groups of lemmas. As a consequence, we never had to modify the output of rules neither in terms of removal of results (i.e. wrong results due to overproduction) nor in terms of completion of results (i.e. wrong results due to underproduction). Thus, the precision of our rules is always 100%.

To calculate recall, we grouped all those rules that treat lemmas of the same inflectional class (e.g. all rules for nouns of the first declension). We measured the recall of such groups of rules by comparing the number of lemmas automatically inserted into Lemlat by one group of rules with the total number of lemmas in the Onomasticon of Forcellini belonging to the inflectional class addressed by that group of rules. Table 1 shows the results.

Inflectional Class	Lemmas per Class	Lemmas per Rules	Recall
1st decl.	6,597	6,597	100%
2nd decl.	12,968	12,961	99.946%
3rd decl.	5,397	3,923	72.688%
4th decl.	50	11	22%
5th decl.	6	6	100%
Uninflected	1,166	11,66	100%
	26,184	**24,664**	**94.194%**

Table 1: The recall of rules.

The most problematic inflectional class is that of third declension nouns.[2] As mentioned above, this is motivated by the fact that it is not always

---

[2] The rules for fourth declension nouns show an even lower recall than those for third declension, but the results for such class must be evaluated carefully as the lemmas of the fourth declension in the Onomasticon are just a few (50).

possible to match regularly an inflectional paradigm (e.g. third declension imparisyllable nouns) with one specific ending. Hence, given such a low recall, the amount of manual work required for enhancing Lemlat with third declension proper names was quite considerable. To provide an example, the number of third declension feminine nouns in the Onomasticon is 1,200. Our rules covered only 542 out of them. Thus, 658 nouns had to be inserted into Lemlat manually (54.833% of the total for that class).

There are also entire inflectional classes for which writing a rule was not possible, like for instance Busa's class of irregularly inflected nouns (146 wordforms). All these lemmas were inserted into the LES archive manually.

In total, the number of lemmas transferred manually into Lemlat is 1,752 (6.632% of all the lemmas of the Onomasticon).

4.2 Coverage

We evaluated the enhancement of Lemlat with the Onomasticon of Forcellini by comparing the lexical coverage provided by the two versions of the tool for four Latin texts of similar size and different genre (prose and poetry) and era (Classical and Late Latin).[3] Table 2 presents the number of distinct words (types) analysed by the original version of Lemlat and by the one enhanced with the Onomasticon (LemlatON).

Text	Types	Lemlat	LemlatON	Improv.
(1)	3,092	2,888 (93.4%)	3,039 (98.1%)	+4.7%
(2)	5,057	4,717 (93.27%)	5,005 (98.97%)	+5.7%
(3)	3,542	3,357 (94.78%)	3,487 (98.45%)	+3.67%
(4)	4,589	4,292 (93.53%)	4,537 (98.87%)	+5.34%
Avg	**4,070**	**93.74%**	**98.6%**	**+4.86%**

Table 2: Type-based evaluation.

The coverage of Lemlat on the four test texts improved of 4.86% on average after the enhancement with Forcellini's Onomasticon. The highest improvement is on Virgil (+5.7%).

Most of the words not analysed by LemlatON are graphical variants (e.g. *creüsa* for *creusa* - "Creusa") or part of the inflectional paradigm of lemmas not available in its lexical basis. Beside these words, there are Roman numbers (e.g. *XV*, "fifteen"), abbreviations (e.g. *kal* for *kalendae*, "calends") and foreign words (e.g. μητέρα, "mother").[4] Table 3 shows the results by category of unknown words (types).

Text	**Unk**	RN	FW	Abb	Misc.
(1)	**53**	19	0	2	32
(2)	**51**	0	1	0	52
(3)	**55**	0	5	0	50
(4)	**52**	0	1	3	48

Table 3: Categories of unknown words.[5]

Roman numbers are frequent in Caesar's text (1). The fact that Lemlat does not analyse Roman numbers is not a major concern, as their form is regular, easily predictable and interpretable. Only a few of them can raise ambiguity when written lowercase. For instance, *vi* ("six") is homograph with the singular ablative of the third declension noun *vis* ("power").

Homography can hold also between items of of the Onomasticon and the original lexical basis of Lemlat. For instance, the lemma *augustus* occurs both in the original Lemlat (a first class adjective, "solemn") and in the Onomasticon (a proper name, "Augustus").

If we look at tokens instead of types, coverage rates remain quite similar, as it is shown by Table 4.

Text	Tokens	Lemlat	LemlatON	Improv.
(1)	8,171	7,558 (92.49%)	8,100 (99.13%)	+6.64%
(2)	10,045	9,478 (94.36%)	9,971 (99.26%)	+4.9%
(3)	7,317	7,059 (96.47%)	7,260 (99.22%)	+2.75%
(4)	6,991	6,604 (94.46%)	6,931 (99.14%)	+4.68%
Avg	**8,131**	**94.39%**	**99.19%**	**+4.8%**

Table 4: Token-based evaluation.

---

[3] (1) Caesar, *De Bello Gallico*, lib. 1 (Classical Lat., prose); (2) Virgil, *Aeneid*, lib. 1 & 2 (Classical Lat., poetry); (3) Tertullian, *Apologeticum* (Late Lat., prose); (4) Claudian, *De Raptu Proserpinae* (Late Lat., poetry). All the texts were downloaded from the Perseus Digital Library (www.perseus.tufts.edu).

[4] We do not consider as foreign words Greek proper names transliterated into Latin characters (e.g. *cytherea*).
[5] "Unk": total number of words per text not analysed by LemlatON. "RN": Roman numbers. "FW": foreign words. "Abb": abbreviations. "Misc": graphical variants and missing lemmas.

It is worth noting that, while the text of Virgil shows the highest improvement in type-based evaluation (+5.7%), Caesar's *De Bello Gallico* is the one that mostly benefits from the extension of Lemlat with the Onomasticon in token-based evaluation (+6.64%). This is due to the higher number of occurrences of proper names in Caesar than in Virgil. Indeed, although the number of new word types analysed by LemlatON in comparison to Lemlat is lower for Caesar than for Virgil, the opposite holds when tokens are concerned.[6] In more detail, the average number of occurrences (tokens) of the new word types analysed by LemlatON for Caesar is 3.59 (542/151), while it is 1.71 for Virgil (493/288).

5 Conclusion and Future Work

In this paper we described the enhancing of the morphological analyser for Latin Lemlat with a large Onomasticon provided by a reference dictionary for Latin (Forcellini).

Although we have included most of the words of the Onomasticon into Lemlat, the work is far from being complete. Indeed, we have just started to enhance the analyser with graphical variants. Furthermore, around 2,000 words of the Onomasticon belonging to minor and irregular inflectional classes still have to be included into Lemlat. Although this promises to be a largely manual and time-consuming work, it is worth doing for achieving the lexicographically motivated completeness of the tool's lexical basis.

Once completed, the lexical look-up table of the Onomasticon will become part of the overall Lemlat suite, which will be shortly made available for free download and on-line use.

References

David Bamman and Gregory Crane. 2006. The Design and Use of a Latin Dependency Treebank. *TLT 2006: Proceedings of the Fifth International Treebanks and Linguistic Theories Conference,* 67–78.

Roberto Busa. 1974-1980. *Index Thomisticus: sancti Thomae Aquinatis operum omnium indices et concordantiae, in quibus verborum omnium et singulorum formae et lemmata cum suis frequentiis et contextibus variis modis referuntur quaeque / consociata plurium opera atque electronico IBM automato usus digessit Robertus Busa SJ.* Frommann-Holzboog, Stuttgart-Bad Cannstatt.

Roberto Busa. 1988. *Totius Latinitatis lemmata quae ex Aeg. Forcellini Patavina editione 1940 a fronte, a tergo atque morphologice opera IBM automati ordinaverat Robertus Busa SJ.* Istituto Lombardo, Accademia di scienze e lettere, Milano.

Gregory Crane. 1991. Generating and Parsing Classical Greek. *Literary and Linguistic Computing,* 6(4): 243–245.

Mark Depauw and Bart Van Beek. 2009. People in Greek Documentary Papyri: First Results of a Research Project. *JJurP,* 39: 31–47.

Egidio Forcellini. 1940. *Lexicon Totius Latinitatis / ad Aeg. Forcellini lucubratum, dein a Jos. Furlanetto emendatum et auctum; nunc demum Fr. Corradini et Jos. Perin curantibus emendatius et auctius meloremque in formam redactum adjecto altera quasi parte Onomastico totius latinitatis opera et studio ejusdem Jos. Perin.* Typis Seminarii, Padova.

Karl E. Georges and Heinrich Georges. 1913-1918. *Ausführliches Lateinisch-Deutsches Handwörterbuch.* Hahn, Hannover.

Peter G. W. Glare. 1982. *Oxford Latin Dictionary.* Oxford University Press, Oxford.

Otto Gradenwitz. 1904. *Laterculi Vocum Latinarum.* Hirzel, Leipzig.

Ralph Grishman and Beth Sundheim. 1996. Message Understanding Conference-6. A Brief History. *COLING,* 96: 466–471.

Dag T. T. Haug and Marius L. Jøhndal. 2008. Creating a Parallel Treebank of the Old Indo-European Bible Translations. *Proceedings of the Second Workshop on Language Technology for Cultural Heritage Data (LaTeCH 2008),* 27–34.

Marco Passarotti. 2004. Development and perspectives of the Latin morphological analyser LEMLAT. *Linguistica Computazionale,* XX-XXI: 397–414.

Marco Passarotti. 2014. From Syntax to Semantics. First Steps Towards Tectogrammatical Annotation of Latin. *Proceedings of the 8th Workshop on Language Technology for Cultural Heritage, Social Sciences and Humanities (LaTeCH 2014),* 100–109.

Marco Passarotti. 2009. Theory and Practice of Corpus Annotation in the *Index Thomisticus* Treebank. *Lexis,* 27: 5–23.

Cornelis J. Van Rijsbergen. 1979. *Information Retrieval.* Butterworths, London.

---

[6] Caesar: 151 types (3,039–2,888) and 542 tokens (8,100–7,558). Virgil: 288 types (5,005–4,717) and 493 tokens (9,971–9,478).

How Do Cultural Differences Impact the Quality of Sarcasm Annotation?: A Case Study of Indian Annotators and American Text

Aditya Joshi[1,2,3]   **Pushpak Bhattacharyya**[1]   **Mark Carman**[2]
Jaya Saraswati[1]   **Rajita Shukla**[1]

[1]IIT Bombay, India
[2]Monash University, Australia
[3]IITB-Monash Research Academy, India
{adityaj, pb}@cse.iitb.ac.in, mark.carman@monash.edu

Abstract

Sarcasm annotation extends beyond linguistic expertise, and often involves cultural context. This paper presents our first-of-its-kind study that deals with impact of cultural differences on the quality of sarcasm annotation. For this study, we consider the case of American text and Indian annotators. For two sarcasm-labeled datasets of American tweets and discussion forum posts that have been annotated by American annotators, we obtain annotations from Indian annotators. Our Indian annotators agree with each other more than their American counterparts, and face difficulties in case of unfamiliar situations and named entities. However, these difficulties in sarcasm annotation result in **statistically insignificant degradation** in sarcasm classification. We also show that these disagreements between annotators can be predicted using textual properties. Although the current study is limited to two annotators and one culture pair, our paper opens up a novel direction in evaluation of the quality of sarcasm annotation, and the impact of this quality on sarcasm classification. This study forms a stepping stone towards systematic evaluation of quality of these datasets annotated by non-native annotators, and can be extended to other culture combinations.

1 Introduction

Sarcasm is a linguistic expression where literal sentiment of a text is different from the implied sentiment, with the intention of ridicule (Schwoebel et al., 2000). Several data-driven approaches have been reported for computational detection of sarcasm (Tsur et al., 2010; Davidov et al., 2010; Joshi et al., 2015). As is typical of supervised approaches, they rely on datasets labeled with sarcasm. We refer to the process of creating such sarcasm-labeled datasets as sarcasm annotation.

Linguistic studies concerning cross-cultural dependencies of sarcasm have been reported (Boers, 2003; Thomas, 1983; Tannen, 1984; Rockwell and Theriot, 2001; Bouton, 1988; Haiman, 1998; Dress et al., 2008).

However, these studies do not look at the notion of cross-cultural sarcasm *annotation* of text. This paper reports the first set of findings from our ongoing line of research: evaluation of quality of sarcasm annotation when obtained from annotators of non-native cultures.

We consider the case of annotators of Indian origin annotating datasets (consisting of discussion forums/tweets from the US) that were earlier annotated by American annotators. It may be argued that since crowd-sourcing is prevalent now, a large pool of annotators makes up for cultural differences among few annotators. However, a fundamental study like ours that performs a micro-analysis of culture combinations is likely to be useful for a variety of reasons such as judging the quality of new datasets, or deciding among annotators. Balancing the linguistic and computational perspectives, we present our findings in two ways: (a) degradation in quality of sarcasm annotation by non-native annotators, and (b) impact of this quality on sarcasm classification.

The motivation behind our study is described in Section 2, while our annotation experiments are in Section 3. We present our analysis in terms of four questions: (a) Are there peculiar difficulties that non-native annotators face during sarcasm annotation? (Section 4.1), (b) How do these difficulties impact the quality of sarcasm annotation? (Section 4.2), (c) How do cultural differences affect sarcasm classification that uses such annotation? (Section 4.3), and (c) Can these difficulties be predicted using features of text? (Section 4.4). All labeled datasets are available on request for future work. For every textual unit, they contain multiple annotations, by native (as given in past works), and non-native annotators.

2 Why is such an evaluation of quality important?

To build NLP systems, creation of annotated corpora is common. When annotators are hired, factors such as language competence are considered. However, while tasks like sense annotation or part-of-speech labeling require linguistic expertise, sarcasm annotation extends beyond linguistic expertise, and often involves cultural context. Tannen (1984) describe how a guest thanking

95

Proceedings of the 10th SIGHUM Workshop on Language Technology for Cultural Heritage, Social Sciences, and Humanities (LaTeCH), pages 95–99,
Berlin, Germany, August 11, 2016. ©2016 Association for Computational Linguistics

the host for a meal may be perceived as polite in some cultures, but sarcastic in some others.

Due to popularity of crowd-sourcing, cultural background of annotators may not be known at all. Keeping these constraints in mind, a study of non-native annotation, and its effect on the corresponding NLP task assumes importance. Our work is the first-of-its-kind study related to sarcasm annotation. Similar studies have been reported for related tasks. Hupont et al. (2014) deal with result of cultural differences on annotation of images with emotions. Das and Bandyopadhyay (2011) describe multi-cultural observations during creation of an emotion lexicon. For example, they state that the word 'blue' may be correlated to sadness in some cultures but to evil in others. Similar studies to understand annotator biases have been performed for subjectivity annotation (Wiebe et al., 1999) and machine translation (Cohn and Specia, 2013). Wiebe et al. (1999) show how some annotators may have individual biases towards a certain subjective label, and devise a method to obtain bias-corrected tags. Cohn and Specia (2013) consider annotator biases for the task of assigning quality scores to machine translation output.

3 Our Annotation Experiments

In this section, we describe our annotation experiments in terms of datasets, annotators and experiment details.

3.1 Datasets

We use two sarcasm-labeled datasets that have been reported in past work. The first dataset is **Tweet-A**. This dataset, introduced by Riloff et al. (2013), consists of 2278 manually labeled tweets, out of which 506 are sarcastic. We call these annotations American1. An example of a sarcastic tweet in this dataset is '*Back to the oral surgeon #yay*'. The second dataset is **Discussion-A**: This dataset, introduced by Walker et al. (2012), consists of 5854 discussion forum posts, out of which 742 are sarcastic. This dataset was created using Amazon Mechanical Turk. IP addresses of Turk workers were limited to USA during the experiment[1]. We call these annotations American2. An example post here is: '*A master baiter like you should present your thesis to be taken seriously. You haven't and you aren't.*'.

3.2 Our Annotators

Our annotators are two female professional linguists of Indian origin with more than 8K hours of experience in annotating English documents for tasks such as sentiment analysis, word sense disambiguation, etc. [2]. They are both 50+ years old and follow only international news that would expose them to American culture. We refer to these annotators as Indian1 and Indian2. The

___

[1] We acknowledge the possibility that some of these annotators where not physically located within USA, despite IP, due to VPN or similar infrastructure

[2] This description highlights that they have strong linguistic expertise.

choice of 'Indian' annotators was made bearing in mind the difference between American and Indian cultures. Our two-annotator configuration is reasonable due to explanation provided in Section 1. Also, it is similar to Riloff et al. (2013) where three annotators create a sarcasm-labeled dataset.

3.3 Experiments

The annotation experiment is conducted as follows. Our annotators read a unit of text, and determine whether it is sarcastic or not. The experiment is conducted in sessions of 50 textual units, and the annotators can pause anywhere through a session. This results in datasets where each textual unit has three annotations as follows: (A) Tweet-A annotated by American1, Indian1, Indian2, (B) Discussion-A annotated by American2, Indian1, Indian2. The American annotations are from past work. (A) and (B) differ in domain (tweets v/s discussion forum posts). These annotated datasets are available on request.

4 Analysis

We now analyze these datasets from three perspectives: (a) difficulties during creation and impact on quality, (b) degradation in annotation quality, (c) impact of quality degradation on sarcasm classification, and (c) prediction of disagreement.

4.1 What difficulties do our Indian annotators face?

Table 1 shows examples where our Indian annotators face difficulty in annotation. We describe experiences from the experiments in two parts:

1. **Situations in which they were unsure of the label**: These include sources of confusion for our annotators, but may or may not have led to incorrect labels.

   Data bias: There are more non-sarcastic texts in the dataset than sarcastic ones. Despite that, the annotators experienced suspicion about every sentence that they had to mark as sarcastic or non-sarcastic. This resulted in confusion as in the case of example *1* in Table 1.

   Unfamiliar words: The annotators consult a dictionary for jargon like 'abiogenesis' or 'happenstance'. For urban slang, they look up the urban dictionary website[3]. Hashtags and emoticons were key clues that the annotators used to detect sarcasm. For example, '*No my roommate play out of tune Zeppelin songs right outside my door isnt annoying. Not at all #sigh*'. They also stated that they could understand the meaning after few occurrences. They had to verify the annotation that they had assigned in the previous instances. Thus, it is helpful *if annotation tools*

___

[3] http://www.urbandictionary.com/

	Example	Remarks
	Situations in which they were unsure of the label	
1	I have the worlds best neighbors!	The annotators were not sure if this was intended to be sarcastic. Additional context would have been helpful.
	Situations in which their label did not match that by American annotators	
2	@twitter_handle West Ham with Carlton Cole and Carroll up front. Going to be some free flowing football this season then	Annotators were not familiar with these players. Hence, they were unable to determine the underlying sentiment.
3	And, I'm sure that Terri Schiavo was fully aware of all that Bush and radical right-wing religionists did for her and appreciates what they did.	Indian annotators did not know about Terri Schiavo, and had to look up her story on the internet.
4	Love going to work and being sent home after two hours	The Indian annotators were unaware of the context of the long commute and the possibility that 'being sent home' meant being fired from job. Hence, they could not detect the sarcasm.
5	@twitter_handle Suns out and I'm working,#yay	The annotators were not sure if a sunny day is pleasant - considering temperatures in India.
6	'So how are those gun free zones working out for you?'	With inadequate knowledge about gun free zones, the annotators were doubtful about sarcasm in the target sentence.

Table 1: Examples of sentences that the Indian annotators found difficult to annotate; 'twitter_handle' are twitter handles suppressed for anonymity

Annotator Pair	κ	Agreement (%)
Avg. American1	0.81	-
Indian1 & Indian2	**0.686**	85.82
Indian1 & American1	0.524	80.05
Indian2 & American1	0.508	79.98

Table 2: Inter-annotator agreement statistics for Tweet-A; Avg. American1 is as reported in the original paper

allow correction of a previously annotated text, since annotators may understand such words during the course of annotation.

2. **Situations in which their labels did not match their American counterparts**:

Unknown context about named entities Consider examples *2* and *3* in Table 1. In case of named entities in domains such as sports or politics, annotators were unfamiliar with popular figures and their associated sentiment. **Unknown context about situations**: Example *4* is a case of Indian annotators marking a text as non-sarcastic, while their American counterparts marked it as sarcastic. **Unclear understanding of socio-political situations**: The tweet in example *5* was labeled as non-sarcastic by Indian annotators. Similarly, example *6* appears to be a non-sarcastic question. However, based on their perception about gun shooting incidents in USA, they were unsure if this statement was indeed non-sarcastic.

4.2 How do cross-cultural difficulties affect quality of annotation?

We now compare quality of non-native annotation using inter-annotator agreement metrics. Table 2 shows statistics for Tweet-A dataset. Kappa coefficient as re-ported in the original paper is 0.81. The corresponding value between Indian1 and Indian2 is 0.686. The values for discussion forum dataset Discussion-A are shown in Table 4. For Discussion-A, Kappa coefficient between the two Indian annotators is 0.700, while that between Indian1/2 and American annotators is 0.569 and 0.288 respectively. Average values for American annotators are not available in the original paper, and hence not mentioned. This shows that inter-annotator agreement between our annotators is higher than their individual agreement with the American annotators. Kappa values are lower in case of tweets than discussion forum posts. Agreement (%) indicates the percent-

Annotator Pair	κ	Agreement (%)
Indian1 & Indian2	**0.700**	92.58
Indian1 & American2	0.569	89.81
Indian2 & American2	0.288	83.33

Table 4: Inter-annotator agreement statistics for Discussion-A

age overlap between a pair of labels. This agreement is high between Indian annotators in case of Tweet-A (85.82%), and Discussion-A (92.58%), and comparable with American annotators.

Table 5 shows the percentage agreement separately for the two classes, with American labels as reference labels. In case of Tweet-A, our annotators agree more with American annotators on sarcastic than non-sarcastic tweets. This means that in case of short text such as tweets, it is the non-sarcastic tweets that cause disagreement. This highlights the fuzziness of sarcastic expressions. On the contrary, in case of long text such as discussion forum posts, sarcastic tweets cause disagreement for our annotators because sarcasm may be in a short portion of a long discussion forum post.

Training Label Source	Test Label Source	Accuracy (%)	Precision (%)	Recall (%)	F-Score (%)	AUC
Tweet-A						
American	American	80.5	71.5	69.2	70.27	0.816
Indian	American	74.14	65.78	68.61	65.28	0.771
Discussion-A						
American	American	83.9	61.5	59.05	59.97	0.734
Indian	American	79.42	58.28	56.77	56.36	0.669

Table 3: Impact of non-native annotation on sarcasm classification; Values for Indian-American are averaged over Indian annotators

Annotator Pair	Sarcastic	Non-sarc
Tweet-A		
Indian1 & American1	**84.78**	77.71
Indian2 & American1	79.24	**80.24**
Discussion-A		
Indian1 & American2	67.24	**93**
Indian2 & American2	40.91	**89.5**

Table 5: Class-wise agreement (%) for pairs of annotators, for both datasets

4.3 How do these difficulties affect sarcasm classification?

We now evaluate if difficulties in sarcasm annotation have an impact on sarcasm classification. To do so, we use LibSVM by Chang and Lin (2011) with a linear kernel to train a sarcasm classifier that predicts a given text as sarcastic or not. We use unigrams as features, and report five-fold cross-validation performance. Table 3 shows performance values for Discussion-A and Tweet-A, specifically, Accuracy, Precision, Recall, F-score and Area Under Curve (AUC). These values are averaged over both Indian annotators, for the respective configuration of training labels[4]. For Tweet-A, using the dataset annotated by American annotators as training labels, leads to an AUC of 0.816. The corresponding value when annotation by Indian annotators is used, is 0.771. Similar trends are observed in case of other metrics, and also for Discussion-A. However, *degradations for both Tweet-A and Discussion-A are not statistically significant for the 95% confidence interval.* Thus, although our Indian annotators face difficulties during annotation resulting in partial agreement in labels, it seems that annotations from these annotators did not lead to significant degradation to what the sarcasm annotation will eventually be used for, *i.e.*, sarcasm classification. The two-tailed p-values for Tweet-A and Discussion-A are 0.221 and 0.480 respectively.

[4]This means that the experiment in case of Indian annotators as training labels consisted of two runs, one for each annotator.

4.4 Can disagreements be predicted?

We now explore if we can predict, solely using properties of text, whether our Indian annotators will disagree with their American counterparts. This goal is helpful so as to choose between annotators for a given piece of text. For example, if it can be known beforehand (as we do in our case) that a text is likely to result in a disagreement between native and non-native annotators, its annotation can be obtained from native annotator alone. With this goal, we train a SVM-based classifier that predicts (dis)agreement. In the training dataset, the agreement label is assigned using our datasets with multiple annotations. We use three sets of features: (a) POS, (b) Named entities, (c) Unigrams (a & b are obtained from NLTK (Bird, 2006)). Table 6 shows performance for 3-fold cross-validation, averaged over the two annotators as in the previous case. We obtain an AUC of 0.56 for Tweet-A, and 0.59 for Discussion-A. The high accuracy and AUC values show that words and lexical features (such as named entities and part-of-speech tags) can effectively predict disagreements.

Dataset	Accuracy (%)	AUC
Tweet-A	67.10	**0.56**
Discussion-A	75.71	**0.59**

Table 6: Predicting annotator agreement using textual features; Values are averaged over Indian annotators

5 Conclusion & Future Work

Concerns about annotation quality may be raised if nature of the task is dependent on cultural background of annotators. In this paper, we presented a first-of-its-kind annotation study that evaluates quality of sarcasm annotation due to cultural differences. We used two datasets annotated by American annotators: one consisting of tweets, and another consisting of discussion forum posts. We obtained another set of sarcasm labels from two annotators of Indian origin, similar to past work where three annotators annotate a dataset with sarcasm labels. We discussed our findings in three steps. The key insights from each of these steps are as follows: (1) Our Indian annotators agree with each other more than they agree with their American counterparts. Also, in case of short text (tweets), the agreement is higher in sarcastic text while for long text (discussion forum posts), it is higher in non-sarcastic text. Our annotators face difficulties due to unfamiliar situations, named entities, etc. (2) Our sarcasm classifiers trained on labels by Indian annotators show a statistically insignificant (as desired) degradation as compared to trained on labels by American annotators, for Tweet-A (AUC: 0.816 v/s 0.771), and for Discussion-A (AUC: 0.734 v/s 0.669). (3) Finally, using textual features, the disagreement/difficulty in annotation can be predicted, with an AUC of 0.56.

Sarcasm detection is an active research area, and sarcasm-labeled datasets are being introduced. Our study forms a stepping stone towards systematic evaluation of quality of these datasets annotated by non-native annotators, and can be extended to other culture combinations.

References

Steven Bird. 2006. Nltk: the natural language toolkit. In *Proceedings of the Annual Meeting of the Association for Computational Linguistics on Computational Linguistics 2006: Systems Demonstrations*, pages 69–72.

Frank Boers. 2003. Applied linguistics perspectives on cross-cultural variation in conceptual metaphor. *Metaphor and Symbol*, 18(4):231–238.

Lawrence F Bouton. 1988. A cross-cultural study of ability to interpret implicatures in english. *World Englishes*, 7(2):183–196.

Chih-Chung Chang and Chih-Jen Lin. 2011. Libsvm: A library for support vector machines. *ACM Transactions on Intelligent Systems and Technology (TIST)*, 2(3):27.

Trevor Cohn and Lucia Specia. 2013. Modelling annotator bias with multi-task gaussian processes: An application to machine translation quality estimation. In *Proceedings of the Annual Meeting of the Association for Computational Linguistics on Computational Linguistics 2013*, pages 32–42.

Amitava Das and Sivaji Bandyopadhyay. 2011. Dr sentiment knows everything! In *Proceedings of the Annual Meeting of the Association for Computational Linguistics/Human Language Technologies 2011: Systems Demonstrations*, pages 50–55.

Dmitry Davidov, Oren Tsur, and Ari Rappoport. 2010. Semi-supervised recognition of sarcastic sentences in twitter and amazon. In *Proceedings of the Fourteenth Conference on Computational Natural Language Learning 2010*, pages 107–116.

Megan L Dress, Roger J Kreuz, Kristen E Link, and Gina M Caucci. 2008. Regional variation in the use of sarcasm. *Journal of Language and Social Psychology*, 27(1):71–85.

John Haiman. 1998. Talk is cheap: Sarcasm, alienation, and the evolution of language. *Oxford University Press*.

Isabelle Hupont, Pierre Lebreton, Toni Maki, Evangelos Skodras, and Matthias Hirth. 2014. Is affective crowdsourcing reliable? In *IEEE Fifth International Conference on Communications and Electronics (ICCE) 2014*, pages 516–521.

Aditya Joshi, Vinita Sharma, and Pushpak Bhattacharyya. 2015. Harnessing context incongruity for sarcasm detection. *Proceedings of the Conference on Empirical Methods in Natural Language Processing 2015*, page 757.

Ellen Riloff, Ashequl Qadir, Prafulla Surve, Lalindra De Silva, Nathan Gilbert, and Ruihong Huang. 2013. Sarcasm as contrast between a positive sentiment and negative situation. In *Proceedings of the Conference on Empirical Methods in Natural Language Processing 2013*, pages 704–714.

Patricia Rockwell and Evelyn M Theriot. 2001. Culture, gender, and gender mix in encoders of sarcasm: A self-assessment analysis. *Communication Research Reports*, 18(1):44–52.

John Schwoebel, Shelly Dews, Ellen Winner, and Kavitha Srinivas. 2000. Obligatory processing of the literal meaning of ironic utterances: Further evidence. *Metaphor and Symbol*, 15(1-2):47–61.

Deborah Tannen. 1984. The pragmatics of cross-cultural communication. *Applied Linguistics*, 5(3):189–195.

Jenny Thomas. 1983. Cross-cultural pragmatic failure.

Oren Tsur, Dmitry Davidov, and Ari Rappoport. 2010. Icwsm-a great catchy name: Semi-supervised recognition of sarcastic sentences in online product reviews. In *International AAAI Conference on Web and Social Media 2010*.

Marilyn A Walker, Jean E Fox Tree, Pranav Anand, Rob Abbott, and Joseph King. 2012. A corpus for research on deliberation and debate. In *Language Resources and Evaluation Conference 2014*, pages 812–817.

Janyce M Wiebe, Rebecca F Bruce, and Thomas P O'Hara. 1999. Development and use of a gold-standard data set for subjectivity classifications. In *Proceedings of the Annual Meeting of the Association for Computational Linguistics on Computational Linguistics 1999*, pages 246–253.

Combining Phonology and Morphology for the Normalization of Historical Texts

Izaskun Etxeberria, Iñaki Alegria, Larraitz Uria
IXA taldea, UPV-EHU
{izaskun.etxeberria,i.alegria,larraitz.uria}@ehu.es

Mans Hulden
Department of Linguistics
University of Colorado
mans.hulden@colorado.edu

Abstract

This paper presents a proposal for the normalization of word-forms in historical texts. To perform this task, we extend our previous research on induction of phonology and adapt it to the task of normalization. In particular, we combine our earlier models with models for learning morphology (without additional supervision). The results are mixed: induction of the segmentation of morphemes fails to directly offer significant improvements while including known morpheme boundaries in standard texts do improve results.

1 Introduction and scenario

1.1 Normalization of historical documents

Historical documents are usually written in ancient languages which exhibit a number of differences in comparison with modern text, all of which have a significant impact on Natural Language Processing (NLP) (Piotrowski, 2012).

Carrying out a form of normalization before indexing historical texts makes it possible to perform queries against the text using standard (modern-day) words or lemmas and find their historical variants. This offers a method to make ancient documents more accessible to non-expert users. In addition, NLP tools developed for working with standard word forms perform better after normalization, in turn allowing for deeper processing such as information extraction for the identification of historical events.

1.2 The scenario

In this paper, we propose an approach for the normalization of historical texts. It is assumed that the corpus operated upon is digitized and that optical character recognition (OCR) has been carried out.

A unique book—or a collection of them in case they are available from the same historical period or dialect—will be the processing unit. Under this scenario, long parallel texts are not available and statistical machine translation (SMT) approaches are therefore excluded.

For the normalization of historical texts, we develop an approach based on the induction of phonology and morphology. It is a lightly supervised model motivated by the need to achieve reasonable performance without requiring unrealistic amounts of manual annotation effort. In our previous work (Etxeberria et al., 2016) we have obtained good results using only induced phonological weighted finite state transducers (WFSTs). However, we have conjectured that additional lexicon and morphological paradigm information could serve to complement the phonological model (Beesley and Karttunen, 2003), and so we have sought to combine the two types of information in the normalization task. In this paper we present our work and results trying to demonstrate that additional lexical/morphological information can be advantageous in the normalization task.

In our setting the type of supervised data available is restricted to a limited number of annotated pairs of non-standard and standard (modern) word forms in a short piece of text. Availability of such annotations presumes an annotator with expertise in historical texts, but not necessarily in NLP.

2 Related work

Techniques for normalization can be roughly divided into two groups that take advantage of either. (1) hand-written morphophonological grammars and (2) machine-learning based techniques

Unsupervised techniques are also often used as a baseline for addressing the problem of normalization. Using edit-distance (Levenshtein dis-

Proceedings of the 10th SIGHUM Workshop on Language Technology for Cultural Heritage, Social Sciences, and Humanities (LaTeCH), pages 100–105,
Berlin, Germany, August 11, 2016. ©2016 Association for Computational Linguistics

tance) or a measure of phonetic distance (e.g. Soundex) are some of the more popular simple solutions.

In the realm of rule-based methods, Jurish (2010) compares a linguistically motivated context-sensitive rewrite rule-system with several unsupervised solutions in an information retrieval task in a corpus of historical German verse, reducing errors by over 60%.

Porta et al. (2013) presents a system for the analysis of Old Spanish word forms using weighted finite-state transducers.

Using machine learning techniques, Kestemont et al. (2010) documents a system that carries out lemmatization in a Middle Dutch literary corpus and presents a language-independent system that can 'learn' intra-lemma spelling variation.

Mann and Yarowsky (2001) presents a method for inducing translation lexicons based on transduction models of cognate pairs via bridge languages. Bilingual lexicons within language families are learned using probabilistic string edit distance models.

More recently, Scherrer and Erjavec (2015) presents a language-independent word normalization method which is tested on the problem of modernizing historical Slovene words. The method relies on supervised data and employs a model of character-level statistical machine translation (CSMT). Pettersson et al. (2014) also proposes a similar method and applies it to several languages.

As we want to obtain a morphological segmentation of variants, we have studied the state-of-the-art on unsupervised and semi-supervised morphology learning. Paradigms or morphological segmentations can be inferred from historical texts without supervision. Hammarström and Borin (2011) presents an interesting survey on unsupervised methods in morphology induction. *Morfessor* (Creutz and Lagus, 2002) is probably the most popular out-of-the-box tool for this task. (Bernhard, 2006) proposes an alternative solution to *Morfessor*.

In our previous work (Etxeberria et al., 2016) we have mainly used the *Phonetisaurus* tool,[1] a WFST-driven phonology tool (Novak et al., 2012) which is commonly used to map grapheme sequences to phoneme sequences under a noisy

channel model. It is a solution that relies on some amount of supervision in order to achieve adequate performance, without however, requiring large amounts of manual development. We evaluated the system on the same corpus used in this paper using the usual parameters: precision, recall and F_1-score.

In the same paper we showed that the method works language-independently as we employed the same setup for both Spanish and Slovene and obtained similar or stronger results than that of previous systems reported by Porta et al. (2013) and Scherrer and Erjavec (2015). For Spanish our results are comparatively high, even with a small training set. For Slovene our method, without tuning, improves or equals the performance of the rest of the methods.

3 Corpus

As in our prior experiments, our main corpus is a 17th century literary work in Basque (*Gero*, written by Pedro Agerre "Axular" and published in 1643).

After a very simple process to clean up the noise in the corpus, 10% and 5% of the text was randomly selected for training and testing. Table 1 elaborates on the details of each slice.

Corpus	Tokens	OOVs	Types	OOVs
Training	8,223	1,931	3,025	1,032
Test	4,386	1,105	1,902	636

Table 1: Training and test corpora for Basque.

The training and test parts of the corpus were analyzed by a morphological analyzer of standard Basque. This way, words to be set aside for manual checking—e.g. out-of-vocabulary (OOV) items—were detected and after annotating these, a small parallel corpus was built.

The *BRAT* annotation tool (Stenetorp et al., 2012) was used for manual revision and annotation of the OOV words. Each OOV item was annotated as either "variation", "correct", or "other". For words in the first class, the corresponding standard word form was provided.

Finally, two lists of pairs (variant-standard) were obtained, one for training/tuning and the second one for testing. The test was carried out on the set of OOVs from the list.

---

[1] `https://github.com/AdolfVonKleist/Phonetisaurus`

4 Methods

4.1 Basic WFSTs

In order to learn the changes that occur within the selected word pairs, the previously mentioned *Phonetisaurus* tool was used. This tool is a WFST-driven grapheme-to-phoneme (g2p) framework suitable for rapid development of high quality g2p or p2g systems. It is a new alternative for such tasks; it is open-source, easy-to-use, and its authors report promising results (Novak et al., 2012). As the results obtained with this tool were the best ones in our previous research, we decided to focus only on using and improving our *Phonetisaurus*-based model for this task. In essence, we are leveraging a grapheme-to-phoneme tool in order to address the more general problem of word-form to word-form mappings.

After training a model with *Phonetisaurus*, a WFST is obtained which can be used to generate correspondences between previously unseen words and their matching standard forms. It is possible to change the number of transductions that the WFST returns for each input word and we have carried out a tuning process to choose the best value for this parameter.

Whenever we obtain multiple answers for a corresponding historical variant, some filtering becomes necessary. In our case, the answers that do not correspond to any accepted standard words are eliminated immediately. From among the rest of the words, the most probable answer (according to *Phonetisaurus*) is then selected.

To test if adding information about morpheme-boundaries helps in the task, our previous experiments in learning from word-pairs was complemented with a method of using word/morpheme-sequence pairs.

In our earlier approach, the tool was given complete plain word-form pairings to learn from. For example:

bekhaturik → bekaturik

emaiteak → emateak

In the augmented experiment, we use a different dictionary for generating training data. That is, we provide the morphological segmentation of the standard word instead of simply using the word itself. The result is the concatenation of the morphemes in their canonical forms:

bekhaturik → bekatu+rik

emaiteak → eman+te+ak

4.2 First extension: getting unsupervised morphological segmentation

Our hypothesis is that providing such morphological segmentations as given above together with morphological paradigms generated automatically from the original and annotated corpora could improve the previous results.

At this point, a problem is how to obtain the morpheme sequence of the corresponding historical forms as our morphological analyzer does not recognize historical variants found in the corpus. To address this, we have performed an automatic segmentation of the data using the *Morfessor* tool (Creutz and Lagus, 2005).

Morfessor is a program that takes as input a corpus of unannotated text and produces a segmentation of the word forms observed in the text. It is a state-of-the-art tool, language independent, and the number of segments per word is not restricted as in other existing morphology learning models.

After the tuning phase (using standard Basque) we input the entire historical corpus to *Morfessor*. Using this text, *Morfessor* creates a model which is then used to obtain the segmentation of any word forms annotated in the corpus. This way, we can produce a new dictionary for *Phonetisaurus* consisting of segmented pairs of historical/standard forms. Following the previous example, the output would be:

bekha+turik → bekatu+rik

emai+te+ak → eman+te+ak

4.3 Second extension: morphological inference from the parallel corpus

Another alternative approach to expanding the training data is to identify new lemmas and affixes among the historical forms by taking advantage of the (limited) parallel entries. For example, from the entries

bertzetik → beste+tik

dadukanak → dauka+n+ak

beranduraiño → berandu+raino

it can be inferred that *bertze/beste* and *daduka/dauka* are equivalent lemmas and *raiño/raino* equivalent suffixes.

With such equivalences, we built, using the finite-state tool *foma* (Hulden, 2009), an enhanced morphological analyzer that recognizes, in addition to the standard Basque, historical variants, including the identified new morphemes and also links the variants to the corresponding standard word-forms. With such an enhanced analyzer previously unseen historical words can be identified and linked to the corresponding standard word-form. Considering the previous example *bertzeraiño* and *dadukanetik* (non-standard forms); these can now be analyzed because the non-standard lemmas (*bertze* and *daduka*) and non-standard suffixes (*raiño*) are recognized by the new analyzer.

Because of possible noise in the data we use a threshold of two for the minimum number of times a morpheme/affix needs to be seen before it is included in the new analyzer.[2] As the resulting analyzer is strong on precision (98.17%) but weak on recall (37.99%), we combine it with the first WFST in a hierarchical way: by first applying the enhanced analyzer, and that failing to give results, passing the word on to the WFST from the first experiment.

5 Evaluation

We evaluated the quality of the different approaches using the standard measures of precision, recall and F_1-score. We have also analyzed how the different options in each approach affect the results.

The baseline for our experiments is a simple method based on using a dictionary of equivalent words with the list of word pairs learned. This approach involves simply memorizing all the distinct word pairs of historical and the standard forms, and subsequently applying this knowledge during the evaluation task.

5.1 Results

The first three different runs corresponding to the three possible representations were tuned using cross-validation and increasing the number of retrieved answers (5, 10, 20 or 30). Retrieving more answers yields a better F_1-score in the WFST model until an upper limit is reached. 20 answers were selected for the last two experiments and 5 for the first. After tuning, a new evaluation was carried out using the test corpus (shown in Table 2).

The results for the model that uses the morphological segmentation are slightly worse than

System	Prec.	Recall	F-score
Baseline	**94.87**	39.22	55.50
Word/word	91.53	78.27	84.34
Word/morph	91.08	77.56	83.78
Morph/morph	90.68	75.62	82.47
Supervis. morph & and word/word	91.94	**78.62**	**84.76**

Table 2: Results on the test corpus for the baseline and the four proposed systems

the ones obtained using only the phonological induction (full word-form pairs) from the parallel corpus, but they are quite close. When the enhanced morphological analyzer is applied before the word/word WFST a slight improvement is seen. We believe that if we were able to improve the quality of the inferred morphological segmentation the overall results could also be improved.

5.2 Combination and Oracle

In order to detect if the behaviors of the two systems are complementary we looked for words that were well normalized in only one system, as in the following words: *arintkiago(arinkiago)*, *autsikizetik(ausikitzetik)*, *baillezakete(bailezakete)*, *bereganik(beregandik)*, *dathorrenean(datorrenean)*, *etzedilla(ez_zedila)*, *fintkiago(finkiago)*, *lothu(lotu)*, *zeikan(zitzaion)* and *zuetzaz(zuetaz)* are correctly normalized by the first system (word/word); *baiteraku(baitigu)*, *erraxten(errazten)*, *fariseoek(fariseuek)*, *hilzaileak(hiltzaileak)* and *lekhukok(lekukok)* only by the second (word/morph); and *ezterauet(ez_diet)*, *konsideratzeak(kontsideratzeak)* and *malizia(malezia)* by the third (morph/morph).[3]

Due to this complementarity we decided to combine the first three systems. In a first (simple) attempt we applied a voting system: if two systems offer the same proposed output, we choose that, else we choose the output of the first system. This yields a slight improvement.

We also calculated an oracle score using the same three systems—i.e. hypothetically always picking the best output. While we observe that a simple voting system improves slightly over the single-answer methods, examining the oracle re-

---

[2]Better single results were obtained using the threshold only for the suffixes, but the best combination is obtained using the threshold for both suffixes and lemmas

[3]It may also be observed that some non-phonological cases of variation (i.e. zeikan/zitzaion) can be solved by the first system which does not use morphological information

sults (table 3), we conclude that there is indeed room for improvement.

System	Prec.	Recall	F-score
Voting	91.94	78.62	84.76
Oracle	95.48	82.16	88.32

Table 3: Results on the test corpus.

6 Conclusions and future work

We have extended previous work on normalization of historical texts and tested the new methods against 17th century literary work in Basque.

Some extensions for taking advantage of morphological information have been proposed; this includes using morphological segmentation as a source of information as well as expanding a morphological analyzer. The results are somewhat limited because segmentation of morphemes only improves the results slightly over a purely phonological model.

We expect to further develop and test these techniques on more languages and corpora (additional historical texts in Basque and Spanish in a first step).

In the near future, our aim is to improve the results by taking advantage of a more precise and wider morphological segmentation and to attempt to combine the various models in a more effective way. Based on the oracle results we surmise that there is much opportunity for improvement.

Acknowledgments

The research leading to these results was carried out as part of the TADEEP project (Spanish Ministry of Economy and Competitiveness, TIN2015-70214-P, with FEDER funding) and the ELKA-ROLA project (Basque Government funding).

References

Kenneth R Beesley and Lauri Karttunen. 2003. Finite-state morphology: Xerox tools and techniques. *CSLI, Stanford.*

Delphine Bernhard. 2006. Unsupervised morphological segmentation based on segment predictability and word segments alignment. In *Proceedings of the Pascal Challenges Workshop on the Unsupervised Segmentation of Words into Morphemes*, pages 19–23.

Mathias Creutz and Krista Lagus. 2002. Unsupervised discovery of morphemes. In *Proceedings of the ACL-02 workshop on Morphological and phonological learning-Volume 6*, pages 21–30. Association for Computational Linguistics.

Mathias Creutz and Krista Lagus. 2005. *Unsupervised morpheme segmentation and morphology induction from text corpora using Morfessor 1.0.* Helsinki University of Technology.

Izaskun Etxeberria, Iñaki Alegria, Larraitz Uria, and Mans Hulden. 2016. Evaluating the noisy channel model for the normalization of historical texts: Basque, spanish and slovene. In *Proceedings of the Tenth International Conference on Language Resources and Evaluation (LREC 2016)*, Paris, France, may. European Language Resources Association (ELRA).

Harald Hammarström and Lars Borin. 2011. Unsupervised learning of morphology. *Computational Linguistics*, 37(2):309–350.

Mans Hulden. 2009. Foma: a finite-state compiler and library. In *Proceedings of the 12th Conference of the European Chapter of the Association for Computational Linguistics: Demonstrations Session*, pages 29–32, Athens, Greece. Association for Computational Linguistics.

Bryan Jurish. 2010. Comparing canonicalizations of historical German text. In *Proceedings of the 11th Meeting of the ACL Special Interest Group on Computational Morphology and Phonology*, pages 72–77. Association for Computational Linguistics.

M. Kestemont, W. Daelemans, and G. De Pauw. 2010. Weigh your words—memory-based lemmatization for Middle Dutch. *Literary and Linguistic Computing*, 25(3):287–301.

Gideon S Mann and David Yarowsky. 2001. Multipath translation lexicon induction via bridge languages. In *Proceedings of the second meeting of the North American Chapter of the Association for Computational Linguistics on Language technologies*, NAACL '01, pages 1–8. Association for Computational Linguistics.

Josef R. Novak, Nobuaki Minematsu, and Keikichi Hirose. 2012. WFST-based grapheme-to-phoneme conversion: Open source tools for alignment, model-building and decoding. In *Proceedings of the 10th International Workshop on Finite State Methods and Natural Language Processing*, pages 45–49, Donostia–San Sebastian, July. Association for Computational Linguistics.

Eva Pettersson, Beáta Megyesi, and Joakim Nivre. 2014. A multilingual evaluation of three spelling normalisation methods for historical text. *Proceedings of LaTeCH*, pages 32–41.

Michael Piotrowski. 2012. Natural language processing for historical texts. *Synthesis Lectures on Human Language Technologies*, 5(2):1–157.

Jordi Porta, José-Luis Sancho, and Javier Gómez. 2013. Edit transducers for spelling variation in old Spanish. In *Proc. of the workshop on computational historical linguistics at NODALIDA 2013. NEALT Proc. Series*, volume 18, pages 70–79.

Yves Scherrer and Tomaž Erjavec. 2015. Modernising historical Slovene words. *Natural Language Engineering*, pages 1–25.

Pontus Stenetorp, Sampo Pyysalo, Goran Topić, Tomoko Ohta, Sophia Ananiadou, and Jun'ichi Tsujii. 2012. BRAT: a web-based tool for NLP-assisted text annotation. In *Proceedings of the Demonstrations at the 13th Conference of the European Chapter of the Association for Computational Linguistics*, pages 102–107. Association for Computational Linguistics.

Towards Building a Political Protest Database to Explain Changes in the Welfare State

Çağıl Sönmez
Department of Computer
Engineering
Boğaziçi University
Istanbul, Turkey
cagil.ulusahin
@boun.edu.tr

Arzucan Özgür
Department of Computer
Engineering
Boğaziçi University
Istanbul, Turkey
arzucan.ozgur
@boun.edu.tr

Erdem Yörük
Department of Sociology
Koç University
Istanbul, Turkey
eryoruk@ku.edu.tr

Abstract

Despite considerable theoretical work in social sciences, ready to use resources are very limited compared to digitally available mass media resources. Thus, this project creates a political protest database from online news resources in Brazil that will be used to explain Brazilian welfare state policy changes. In this paper we present the preliminary results of a system that automatically crawls digital resources and produces a protest database, which includes events such as strikes, rallies, boycotts, protests, and riots, as well as their attributes such as location, participants, and ideology.

1 Introduction

Social assistance programs in Brazil have largely expanded during the last two decades. The work presented in this paper is part of a project, which hypothesizes that this social assistance expansion in Brazil is a political response of the Brazilian state to the changes in social movements, particularly to the growing political radicalism of the poor and ethnic/racial minorities. Demonstrating a causal chain between social movements and social welfare outcomes in a systematic way has often been a difficult task. This is partly because of the lack of quantitative data on social movements beyond labour strike statistics and the field is marked by more or less informed speculation (Hutter, 2014). Using computational linguistics based methods and online newspaper archives, this study will create a holistic protest event database for Brazil for the period since the mid-1980s, when new social assistance programs began to emerge. This database will be used in pooled cross-sectional time-series regression analysis to explain welfare policy changes.

The protest database will count the number of events such as strikes, rallies, boycotts, protests, riots, and demonstrations, i.e. the "repertoire of contention" (Tarrow, 1994; Tilly, 1984). It will also indicate the location, city, neighbourhood of the event, ethnicity, religion, political identity of participants and organizers, the number of participants, death and casualty if occurred. We will collect data on all protest events and operationalize protest events of the poor by including (i) spontaneous or organized protests that take place in poor urban and rural areas, (ii) protests led by organizations (political, ethnic, religious or criminal) that work among the poor, independently of the location of the protest event.

The research does not intend to produce an exhaustive count for all, or for even most incidences of political events, since newspapers report on a fraction of the events that occurred (Davenport, 2009; Earl et al., 2004; Ortiz et al., 2005). The assumption is that during times of strong social movements, newspapers report social events more than usual (Silver, 2003). Therefore, the database will count each time that an event is reported in order to differentiate events in terms of their importance. It intends to create a measure of the changing levels of grassroots politics events over time and space during the welfare transformation. It is interested in the waves of contentious political activities with a comparison between the poor and other social groups.

Newspaper archives are the most reliable source from which to create protest databases, i.e. to

Proceedings of the 10th SIGHUM Workshop on Language Technology for Cultural Heritage, Social Sciences, and Humanities (LaTeCH), pages 106–110,
Berlin, Germany, August 11, 2016. ©2016 Association for Computational Linguistics

transform "words to numbers" as they provide access, selectivity, reliability, continuity over time and ease of coding (Hutter, 2014; Franzosi, 2004). International news wires and newspapers are not the best source in cross-national research because of the low level of incidence reported on each country, undermining the representativeness of each case (Imig, 2001). Yoruk (2012) has already created a protest database for Turkey that records and classifies protest activities spanning the whole period from 1970 on by leading a research team that manually surveyed microfilm archives. This database shows that grassroots politics in Turkey has shifted from the formal working class to the informal working class and from Turks to Kurds, which explains the shift in Turkish welfare policies from social insurance to social assistance and the disproportional targeting of the Kurdish poor in social assistance provision.

The protest database, the initial phase of which is introduced in this paper, will be the first comparable protest event database on emerging markets, created using local news sources and, ambitiously, using computational methods of natural language processing and machine learning.

The protest database includes events and event properties (Table 1).

Event type	protest, strike, armed struggle, occupation, rebellion
Participants	workers, teachers, poor, peasant, favelado, student, women, youth, environmentalist
Organizer	labor Union, political party, illegal party, student organization, NGO, religious organization, occupational organizations, drug traffic, peasant organization
Neighbourhood or District	centro, burantan, zona norte, zona sul, Jardim Educandário, Liberdade, etc.
Place	factory, street, university, neighborhood, courthouse, political party, public office, theatre, association, workplace, square, building, fazenda
City	Sao Paulo, Ribeirão Preto, São José, Araçagi, etc.
Participants ethnicity	mix, white, black, Indigenous, Asian
Participants ideology	left-wing, right-wing, religious, feminist, environmentalist, uncertain

Table 1: Event Attributes

In this paper, we present the article classification and entity tagging results of a system that targets producing a protest database automatically, using newspaper articles/archives from previous decades. We develop a classification module that classifies newspaper articles as reporting or not reporting a protest event. The articles that are classified as reporting a protest event are further processed and the entity mentions are extracted using our supervised maximum entropy tagger. The classification and entity tagging methods are evaluated using a manually annotated data set. In addition, the results of running the classification method on 200k newspaper articles are reported.

2 Methodology

First, we compile a newswire data set that includes daily news articles in textual form from a local newspaper. Next, we develop a classification system that filters out news articles that do not include any protest events. Lastly, we build an entity extraction system that identifies entity mentions such as the location or participants of an event.

2.1 Newswire Data Set

In the manually produced Turkish protest database (Yoruk, 2012), an average of three protest events per day for 365 days during the last 30 years, yielded a 30 thousand entry database.

We collected publicly available news articles that had been digitized and are available at the newspaper archives from Brazilian daily Folha de São Paulo[1]. The Folha Digital News Archives are available beginning from early 1920s. However, only after 1994 articles are available in text format, older archives are only available in pdf (of image) format.

We collected 200 thousand news articles in Portuguese, published between 2004 and 2015 at Folha de São Paulo. The number of articles between the years 2007 and 2011 are shown in Table 2. We only collected the articles from specific categories such as daily and politics. Our Portuguese Newswire data set is publicly available[2].

Year	2007	2008	2009	2010	2011
News count	18579	19281	16337	24062	22372

Table 2: Number of news articles per year between 2007 and 2011

---

[1] www.folha.uol.com.br/
[2] mann.cmpe.boun.edu.tr/folha_data/

2.2 Classification

Classification is an important step in our system. Newspaper archives include several news articles, and keyword based search yields thousands of irrelevant articles besides the few relevant ones. Given the news articles, we trained a binary classifier to differentiate protest-related news articles from others.

We converted the data into feature vectors using Weka "StringToWordVector" function and selected top 50 words for each class using tf and idf transformations on word count[3].

We compared different classifiers using our manually annotated newswire data set, namely, Random Forest (RF), Support Vector Machines (LIBSVM) (Chang and Lin, 2011), John Platt's sequential minimal optimization algorithm for training a support vector machine classifier (SMO) (Platt, 1999), Multilayer Perceptron (MLP), C4.5 decision tree (DT), Voted Perceptron (VP), Naive Bayes (NB), and Naive Bayes with kernel estimator (NB-K). The performance results of each classifier are available in Section 3.

2.3 Data Set Annotation

The system first classifies protest related news and secondly extracts components of protest information (participants, place, ethnicity etc.) via entity tagging.

For news article classification, 1000 news articles (500 reporting protest events, 500 not reporting protest events) are manually annotated and used for training and evaluation.

For entity tagging, 500 news articles are manually annotated following the ACE 2005 annotation guideline (Consortium and others, 2005). ACE is a comprehensive annotation standard that aims to annotate entities, events, and relations within a variety of documents in a consistent manner (Aguilar et al., 2014). We used the BRAT annotation tool (Stenetorp et al., 2012) for annotating the corpus (See Figure 1). Brat[4] is based on a visualizer and was initially developed to visualize BioNLP'11 Shared Task data.

---

[3]Configuration used to compute feature vectors: *weka.filters.unsupervised.attribute.StringToWordVector -R first-last -W 50 -prune-rate -1.0 -C -T -I -N 0 -L -M 1*
[4]`brat.nlplab.org/`

2.4 Entity Tagging

For entity tagging we used a maximum entropy model (Berger et al., 1996). We used the maxent[5] (Maximum Entropy Modeling Toolkit) library to built our entity tagger with BIO scheme and textual features.

3 Preliminary Results

The results of each article classifier computed using the Weka tool (Hall et al., 2009) are shown in Table 3. These results are obtained using 10-fold cross-validation over the 1000 manually annotated news articles described in Section 2.3. The best performance with an F-measure of 95.4% is achieved by the Random Forest model.

Classifier	Precision	Recall	F-Measure	TP	FN
RF	95.4	95.4	95.4	461	19
SMO	95.4	95.2	95.2	450	10
MLP	94.2	94.2	94.2	455	25
DT	93.8	93.7	93.7	448	23
VP	92.4	92.4	92.4	449	37
LIBSVM	92.4	92.4	92.4	440	37
NB	91.6	91.4	91.4	461	59
NB-K	91.5	91.1	91.1	465	66

Table 3: Comparison of different classifiers on the news article classification data set

We ran the Random Forest classifier over the 200 thousand news articles that we compiled from Brazilian daily Folha de São Paulo. The classifier identified 20 thousand articles as reporting protest events. Figure 2 shows the first tentative results of our analysis, indicating the changes in the number of total monthly protest events in Brazil between 2004 and 2011.

We used 10-fold cross-validation over the 500 news articles manually annotated for events to evaluate our entity tagger. The accuracy obtained is 76.25%.

4 Discussion and Future Work

The focus in this paper is Brazil and Brazillian Portuguese newswire text. However, our ultimate goal is to build our system in a way that will produce protest databases for other emerging countries using local newspaper archives.

The future work will be a further modification, where we will form a language independent

---

[5]`http://homepages.inf.ed.ac.uk/ lzhang10/maxent_toolkit.html`

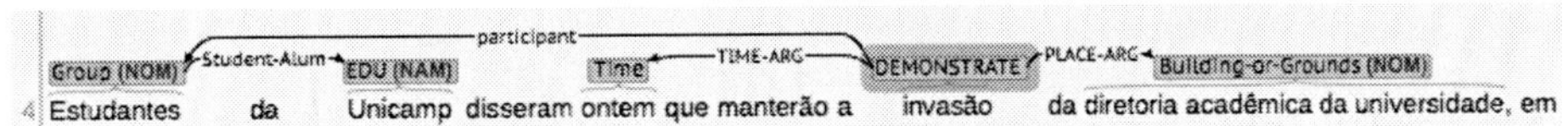

Figure 1: Annotation of a sentence in Brat

Figure 2: Changes in the number of total monthly protest events in Brazil between 2004 and 2011

tool. Then, we will use the language independent tool on news sources in English and Spanish languages, for which state-of-the-art in language processing and language resources is much more developed than for Portuguese. A tool for Turkish will also be produced by utilizing the manually created protest database in (Yoruk, 2012) for training and evaluation.

A comparative analysis of protest behaviour using quantified indicators from newspaper archives from each country will be a novelty in the literature. The collected data will be analyzed both as time-series indicator and independent variable in a pooled cross-sectional time-series multivariate regression analysis to establish causal relations between protest waves and welfare policy changes.

Acknowledgments

This research was supported by Marie Curie FP7-Reintegration-Grants within the 7th European Community Framework Programme. We would like to thank Duru Ors and Atılberk Çelebi for their contributions during the data set corpus collection and annotation process. We would also like to thank Deniz Yuret who provided insight and expertise that greatly assisted the research.

References

Jacqueline Aguilar, Charley Beller, Paul McNamee, and Benjamin Van Durme. 2014. A comparison of the events and relations across ACE, ERE, TAC-KBP, and FrameNet annotation standards. *ACL 2014*, page 45.

Adam L Berger, Vincent J Della Pietra, and Stephen A Della Pietra. 1996. A maximum entropy approach to natural language processing. *Computational linguistics*, 22(1):39–71.

Chih-Chung Chang and Chih-Jen Lin. 2011. LIB-SVM: a library for support vector machines. *ACM Transactions on Intelligent Systems and Technology (TIST)*, 2(3):27.

Linguistic Data Consortium et al. 2005. ACE (automatic content extraction) english annotation guidelines for events.

Christian Davenport. 2009. Regimes, Repertoires and State Repression. *Swiss Political Science Review*, 15(2):377–385, June.

Jennifer Earl, Andrew Martin, John D. McCarthy, and Sarah A. Soule. 2004. The Use of Newspaper Data in the Study of Collective Action. *Annual Review of Sociology*, 30:65–80.

Roberto Franzosi. 2004. *From words to numbers: Narrative, data, and social science*, volume 22. Cambridge University Press.

Mark Hall, Eibe Frank, Geoffrey Holmes, Bernhard Pfahringer, Peter Reutemann, and Ian H Witten. 2009. The WEKA data mining software: an update. *ACM SIGKDD explorations newsletter*, 11(1):10–18.

Swen Hutter, 2014. *Methodological Practices in Social Movement Research*, chapter Protest Event Analysis and Its Offspring, pages 335–367. Oxford University Press, Oxford.

Douglas R. Imig. 2001. *Contentious Europeans: Protest and Politics in an Emerging Polity*. Rowman & Littlefield, Lanham - Boulder - New York - Oxford, January.

David Ortiz, Daniel Myers, Eugene Walls, and Maria-Elena Diaz. 2005. Where Do We Stand with Newspaper Data? *Mobilization: An International Quarterly*, 10(3):397–419.

John C. Platt, 1999. *Advances in Kernel Methods*, chapter Fast Training of Support Vector Machines Using Sequential Minimal Optimization, pages 185–208. MIT Press, Cambridge, MA, USA.

Beverly J. Silver. 2003. *Forces of Labor: Workers' Movements and Globalization Since 1870.* Cambridge University Press, April.

Pontus Stenetorp, Sampo Pyysalo, Goran Topić, Tomoko Ohta, Sophia Ananiadou, and Jun'ichi Tsujii. 2012. BRAT: a web-based tool for NLP-assisted text annotation. In *Proceedings of the Demonstrations Session at EACL 2012*, Avignon, France, April. Association for Computational Linguistics.

Sidney Tarrow. 1994. *Power in Movement: Social Movements, Collective Action and Politics.* Cambridge University Press, Cambridge, UK, July.

Charles Tilly. 1984. *Big Structures, Large Processes, Huge Comparisons.* Russell Sage Foundation, New York, December.

Erdem Yoruk. 2012. *The Politics of the Turkish Welfare System Transformation in the Neoliberal Era: Welfare as Mobilization and Containment.* Ph.D. Dissertation, The Johns Hopkins University, Baltimore, Maryland.

An Assessment of Experimental Protocols for Tracing Changes in Word Semantics Relative to Accuracy and Reliability

Johannes Hellrich
Research Training Group "The Romantic
Model. Variation - Scope - Relevance"
Friedrich-Schiller-Universität Jena
Jena, Germany
johannes.hellrich@uni-jena.de

Udo Hahn
Jena University Language & Information
Engineering (JULIE) Lab
Friedrich-Schiller-Universität Jena
Jena, Germany
http://www.julielab.de

Abstract

Our research aims at tracking the semantic
evolution of the lexicon over time. For
this purpose, we investigated two well-
known training protocols for neural language models in a synchronic experiment
and encountered several problems relating
to accuracy and reliability. We were able to
identify critical parameters for improving
the underlying protocols in order to generate more adequate diachronic language
models.

1 Introduction

The lexicon can be considered the most dynamic
part of all linguistic knowledge sources over time.
There are two innovative change strategies typical
for lexical systems: the creation of entirely new
lexical items, commonly reflecting the emergence
of novel ideas, technologies or artifacts, on the
one hand, and, on the other hand, shifts in the
meaning of already existing lexical items, a process
which usually takes place over larger periods of
time. Tracing semantic changes of the latter type is
the main focus of our research.

Meaning shift has recently been investigated
with emphasis on neural language models (Kim
et al., 2014; Kulkarni et al., 2015). This work is
based on the assumption that the measurement of
semantic change patterns can be reduced to the
measurement of lexical similarity between lexical
items. Neural language models, originating from
the word2vec algorithm (Mikolov et al., 2013a;
Mikolov et al., 2013b; Mikolov et al., 2013c), are
currently considered as state-of-the-art solutions
for implementing this assumption (Schnabel et
al., 2015). Within this approach, changes in
similarity relations between lexical items at two
different points of time are interpreted as a signal

for meaning shift. Accordingly, lexical items which
are very similar to the lexical item under scrutiny
can be considered as approximating its meaning
at a given point in time. Both techniques were
already combined in prior work to show, e.g., the
increasing association of the lexical item *"gay"*
with the meaning dimension of "homosexuality"
(Kim et al., 2014; Kulkarni et al., 2015).

We here investigate the accuracy and reliability
of such similarity judgments derived from different
training protocols dependent on word frequency,
word ambiguity and the number of training epochs
(i.e., iterations over all training material). *Accuracy*
renders a judgment of the overall model quality,
whereas *reliability* between repeated experiments
ensures that qualitative judgments can indeed be
transferred between experiments. Based on the
identification of critical conditions in the experimental set-up of previously employed protocols,
we recommend improved training strategies for
more adequate neural language models dealing
with diachronic lexical change patterns. Our results
concerning reliability also cast doubt on the repro-
ducibility of experiments where semantic similarity
between lexical items is taken as a computationally valid indicator for properly capturing lexical
meaning (and, consequently, meaning shifts) under
a diachronic perspective.

2 Related Work

Neural language models for tracking semantic
changes over time typically distinguish between
two different training protocols—*continuous training* of models (Kim et al., 2014) where the
model for each time span is initialized with the
embeddings of its predecessor, and, alternatively,
independent training with a mapping between
models for different points in time (Kulkarni et al.,
2015). A comparison between these two protocols,

111

Proceedings of the 10th SIGHUM Workshop on Language Technology for Cultural Heritage, Social Sciences, and Humanities (LaTeCH), pages 111–117,
Berlin, Germany, August 11, 2016. ©2016 Association for Computational Linguistics

such as the one proposed in this paper, has not been carried out before. Also, the application of such protocols to non-English corpora is lacking, with the exception of our own work relating to German data (Hellrich and Hahn, 2016b; Hellrich and Hahn, 2016a).

The `word2vec` algorithm is a heavily trimmed version of an artificial neural network used to generate low-dimensional vector space representations of a lexicon. We focus on its skip-gram variant, trained to predict plausible contexts for a given word that was shown to be superior over other settings for modeling semantic information (Mikolov et al., 2013a). There are several parameters to choose for training—learning rate, downsampling factor for frequent words, number of training epochs and choice between two strategies for managing the huge number of potential contexts. One strategy, *hierarchical softmax*, uses a binary tree to efficiently represent the vocabulary, while the other, *negative sampling*, works by updating only a limited number of word vectors during each training step.

Furthermore, artificial neural networks, in general, are known for a large number of local optima encountered during optimization. While these commonly lead to very similar performance (LeCun et al., 2015), they cause different representations in the course of repeated experiments.

Approaches to modelling changes of lexical semantics not using neural language models, e.g., Wijaya and Yeniterzi (2011), Gulordava and Baroni (2011), Mihalcea and Nastase (2012), Riedl et al. (2014) or Jatowt and Duh (2014) are, intentionally, out of the scope of this paper. In the same way, we here refrain from comparison with computational studies dealing with literary discussions related to the Romantic period (e.g., Aggarwal et al. (2014)).

3   Experimental Set-up

For comparability with earlier studies (Kim et al., 2014; Kulkarni et al., 2015), we use the fiction part of the GOOGLE BOOKS NGRAM corpus (Michel et al., 2011; Lin et al., 2012). This part of the corpus is also less affected by sampling irregularities than other parts (Pechenick et al., 2015). Due to the opaque nature of GOOGLE's corpus acquisition strategy, the influence of OCR errors on our results cannot be reasonably estimated, yet we assume that they will affect all experiments in an equal manner.

The wide range of experimental parameters described in Section 2 makes it virtually impossible to test all their possible combinations, especially as repeated experiments are necessary to probe a method's reliability. We thus concentrate on two experimental protocols—the one described by Kim et al. (2014) (referred to as *Kim protocol*) and the one from Kulkarni et al. (2015) (referred to as *Kulkarni protocol*), including close variations thereof. Kulkarni's protocol operates on all 5-grams occurring during five consecutive years (e.g., 1900–1904) and trains models independently of each other. Kim's protocol operates on uniformly sized samples of 10M 5-grams for each year from 1850 onwards in a continuous fashion (years before 1900 are used for initialization only). Its constant sampling sizes result in both oversampling and undersampling as is evident from Figure 1.

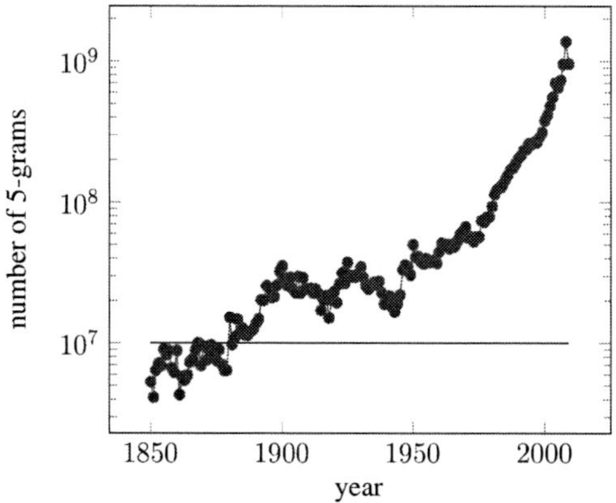

Figure 1: Number of 5-grams per year (on the logarithmic y-axis) contained in the English fiction part of the GOOGLE BOOKS NGRAM corpus. The horizontal line indicates a constant sampling size of 10M 5-grams according to the Kim protocol.

We use the PYTHON-based GENSIM[1] implementation of `word2vec` for our experiments; the relevant code is made available via GITHUB.[2] Due to the 5-gram nature of the corpus, a context window covering four neighboring words is used for all experiments. Only words with at least 10 occurrences in a sample are modeled. Training for each sample is repeated until convergence[3] is achieved or 10 epochs have passed. Following both protocols, we use word vectors with 200

---

[1] https://radimrehurek.com/gensim/
[2] github.com/hellrich/latech2016
[3] Defined as averaged cosine similarity of 0.9999 or higher between word representations before and after an epoch (see Kulkarni et al. (2015)).

Table 1: Accuracy and reliability among top n words for threefold application of different training protocols. Reliability is given as fraction of the maximum for n. Standard deviation for accuracy ± 0, if not noted otherwise; reliability is based on the evaluation of all lexical items, thus no standard deviation.

Description of training protocol			top-n Reliability					Accuracy
			1	2	3	4	5	
independent	negative	in all texts	0.40	0.41	0.41	0.40	0.40	0.38
		in 10M sample	0.45	0.48	0.50	0.51	0.52	0.25
		between 10M samples	0.09	0.10	0.10	0.10	0.10	0.26
	hierarchical	in all texts	0.33	0.34	0.34	0.34	0.34	0.28
		in 10M sample	0.38	0.40	0.42	0.42	0.43	0.22
		between 10M samples	0.09	0.09	0.10	0.10	0.10	0.22 ± 0.01
continuous	negative	in 10M sample	0.54	0.55	0.56	0.56	0.57	0.25
		between 10M samples	0.21	0.21	0.22	0.22	0.22	0.25
	hierarchical	in 10M sample	0.31	0.32	0.32	0.32	0.33	0.22
		between 10M samples	0.12	0.13	0.13	0.13	0.13	0.23

dimensions for all experiments, as well as an initial learning rate of 0.01 for experiments based on 10M samples, and one of 0.025 for systems trained on unsampled texts; the threshold for downsampling frequent words was 10^{-3} for sample-based experiments and 10^{-5} for unsampled ones. We tested both negative sampling and hierarchical softmax training strategies, the latter being canonical for Kulkarni's protocol, whereas Kim's protocol is underspecified in this regard.

We evaluate *accuracy* by using the test set developed by Mikolov et al. (2013a). This test set is based on present-day English language and world knowledge, yet we assume it to be a viable proxy for overall model quality. It contains groups of four words connected via the analogy relation '::' and the similarity relation '~', as exemplified by the expression *king* ~ *queen* :: *man* ~ *woman*.

We evaluate *reliability* by training three identically parametrized models for each experiment. We then compare the top n similar words (by cosine distance) for each word modeled by the experiments with a variant of the Jaccard coefficient (Manning et al., 2008, p.61). We limit our analysis to values of n between 1 and 5, in accordance with data on `word2vec` accuracy (Schnabel et al., 2015). The 3-dimensional array $W_{i,j,k}$ contains words ordered by similarity (i) for a word in question (j) according to an experiment (k). If a word in question is not modeled by an experiment, as can be the case for comparisons over different samples, $\emptyset$ is the corresponding entry. The reliability r for a specific value of n ($r@n$) is defined as the magnitude of the intersection of similar words produced by all three experiments with a rank of n or lower, averaged over all t words modeled by any of these experiments and normalized by n, the maximally achievable score for this value of n:

$$r@n := \frac{1}{t*n} \sum_{j=1}^{t} \| \bigcap_{k=1}^{3} \{W_{1 \leq i \leq n, j, k}\} \|$$

4 Results

We focus our analysis on the representations generated for the initial period, i.e., 1900 for sample-based experiments and 1900–1904 for unsampled ones. This choice was made since researchers can be assumed to be aware of current word meanings, thus making correct judgments on initial word semantics more important. As a beneficial side effect, we get a marked reduction of computational demands, saving several CPU years compared to an evaluation based on the most recent period.

4.1 Training Protocols

Table 1 depicts the assessments for different training protocols. Four results seem relevant for future experiments. First, reliability at different top-n cut-offs is rather uniform, so that evaluations could be performed on top-1 reliability only without real losses. Second, both accuracy and reliability are often far higher for negative sampling than for hierarchical softmax under direct comparison of the evaluated conditions; under no condition hierarchical softmax outperforms negative sampling. Third, continuous training improves reliability, yet not accuracy, for systems trained on samples. Fourth, reliability for experiments between samples heavily degrades compared to reliability for repeated experiments on the same sample.

4.2 Detailed Investigation

As variations of Kulkarni's protocol yield more consistent results, we further explore its performance considering word frequency, word ambiguity and the number of training epochs. All experiments described in this section are based on the complete 1900–1904 corpus. Figure 2 shows the influence of word frequency, negative sampling being overall more reliable, especially for words with low or medium frequency. The 21 words reported to have undergone traceable semantic changes[4] are all frequent with percentiles between 89 and 99. For such high-frequency words hierarchical softmax performs similar or slightly better.

Entries in the lexical database WORDNET (Fellbaum, 1998) can be employed to measure the effect of word ambiguity on reliability.[5] The number of WORDNET synsets a word belongs to (i.e., the number of its senses) seems to have little effect on top-1 reliability for negative sampling, while hierarchical softmax underperforms for words with a low number of senses, as shown in Figure 3.

Model reliability and accuracy depend on the number of training epochs, as shown in Figure 4. There are diminishing returns for hierarchical softmax, reliability staying constant after 5 epochs, while negative sampling increases in reliability with each epoch. Yet, both methods achieve maximal accuracy after only 2 epochs; additional epochs lead to a small decrease from 0.4 down to 0.38 for negative sampling. This could indicate overfitting, but accuracy is based on a test set for modern-day language, and can thus not be considered a fully valid yardstick.

5 Discussion

Our investigation in the performance of two common protocols for training neural language models on historical text data led to several hitherto unknown results. We could show that negative sampling outperforms hierarchical softmax both in terms of accuracy and reliability, especially

---

[4]Kulkarni et al. (2015) compiled the following list based on prior work (Wijaya and Yeniterzi, 2011; Gulordava and Baroni, 2011; Jatowt and Duh, 2014; Kim et al., 2014): *card, sleep, parent, address, gay, mouse, king, checked, check, actually, supposed, guess, cell, headed, ass, mail, toilet, cock, bloody, nice* and *guy*.

[5]We used WORDNET 3.0 and the API provided by the Natural Language Toolkit (NLTK): www.nltk.org

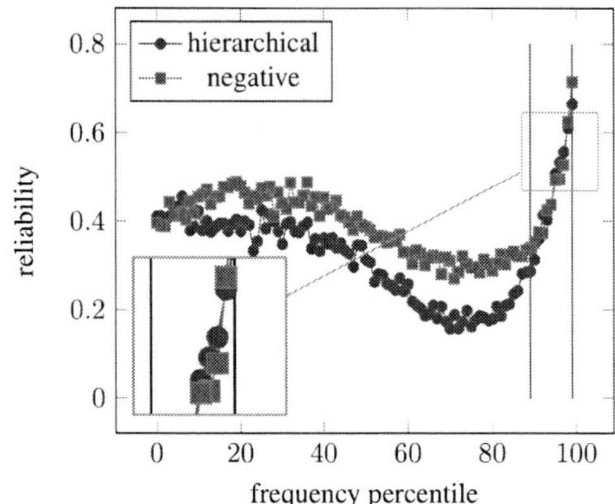

Figure 2: Influence of percentile frequency rank on reliability for models trained for 10 epochs on 1900–1904 data. Words reported to have changed during the 20th century fall into the rank range marked by vertical lines.

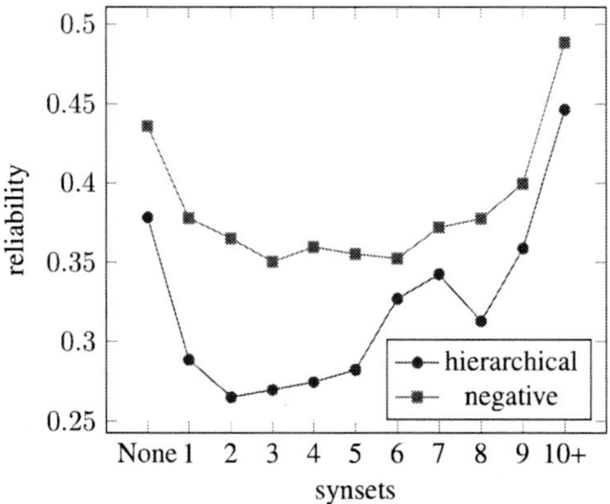

Figure 3: Influence of ambiguity (measured by the number of WORDNET synsets) on top-1 reliability for models trained for 10 epochs on 1900–1904 data.

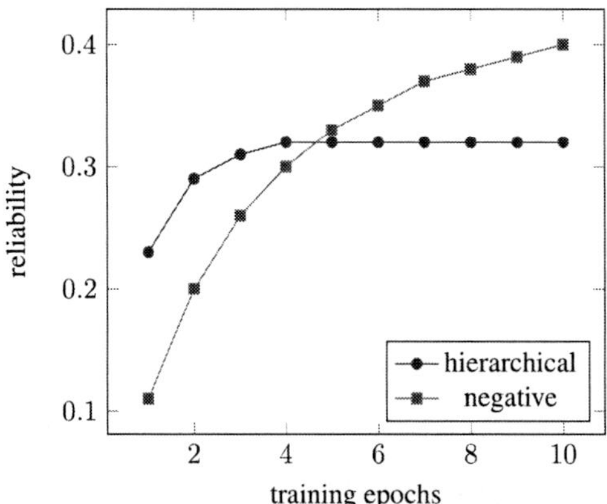

Figure 4: Top-1 reliability as influenced by the number of training epochs, for 1900–1904 data.

for infrequent and low-ambiguity words, if time for sufficient training epochs is available.[6] Our synchronic experiments provide evidence for the superiority of Kulkarni's over Kim's protocol, especially if modified to use negative sampling. Longer training time, due to unsampled corpora, can be mitigated by training models in parallel, which is impossible for Kim's protocol. We strongly suggest to train only on full corpora, and not on samples, due to very low reliability values for systems trained on different samples. If samples are necessary, continuous training can somewhat lower its negative effect on reliability between samples.

Even the most reliable system often identifies widely different words as most similar. This carries unwarranted potential for erroneous conclusions on a words' semantic evolution, e.g., *"romantic"* happens to be identified as most similar to *"lazzaroni"*[7], *"fanciful"* and *"melancholies"* by three systems trained with negative sampling on 1900–1904 texts. We are thus skeptical about using such similarity clouds to describe or visualize lexical semantics at a point in time.

In future work, we will explore the effects of continuous training based on complete corpora. The selection of a convergence criterion remains another open issue due to the threefold trade-off between training time, reliability and accuracy. It would also be interesting to replicate our experiments for other languages or points in time. Yet, the enormous corpus size for more recent years might require a reduced number of maximum epochs for these experiments. In order to improve the semantic modeling itself one could lemmatize the training material or utilize the part of speech annotations provided in the latest version of the GOOGLE corpus (Lin et al., 2012). Also, recently available neural language models with support for multiple word senses (Bartunov et al., 2016; Panchenko, 2016) could be helpful, since semantic changes can often be described as changes in the usage frequency of different word senses (Rissanen, 2008, pp.58–59). Finally, it is clearly important to test the effect of our proposed changes, based on synchronic experiments, on a system for tracking diachronic changes in word semantics.

---

[6]Using parallel 8 processes on an Intel Xeon E5649@2.53Ghz, completing a training epoch for 1900–1904 data takes about three hours, while 5 days are necessary for 2005–2009 data.

[7]A historical group of lower-class persons from Naples ("lazzarone, n", 2016).

Acknowledgments

This research was conducted within the Research Training Group *"The Romantic Model. Variation – Scope – Relevance"* (http://www.modellromantik.uni-jena.de/) supported by grant GRK 2041/1 from the *Deutsche Forschungsgemeinschaft (DFG)*. The first author (J.H.) wants to thank the members of the GRK for their collaborative efforts.

References

Nitish Aggarwal, Justin Tonra, and Paul Buitelaar. 2014. Using distributional semantics to trace influence and imitation in Romantic Orientalist poetry. In Alan Akbik and Larysa Visengeriyeva, editors, *Proceedings of the AHA! Workshop on Information Discovery in Text @ COLING 2014. Dublin, Ireland, August 23, 2014*, pages 43–47. Association for Computational Linguistics (ACL).

Sergey Bartunov, Dmitry Kondrashkin, Anton Osokin, and Dmitry P. Vetrov. 2016. Breaking sticks and ambiguities with adaptive skip-gram. In Arthur Gretton and Christian C. Robert, editors, *AISTATS 2016 — Proceedings of the 19th International Conference on Artificial Intelligence and Statistics. Cadiz, Spain, May 7-11, 2016*, number 51 in JMLR Workshop and Conference Proceedings, pages 130–138.

Christiane Fellbaum, editor. 1998. WORDNET: *An Electronic Lexical Database*. MIT Press, Cambridge/MA; London/England.

Kristina Gulordava and Marco Baroni. 2011. A distributional similarity approach to the detection of semantic change in the Google Books Ngram corpus. In Sebastian Padó and Yves Peirsman, editors, *GEMS 2011 — Proceedings of the Workshop on GEometrical Models of Natural Language Semantics @ EMNLP 2011. Edinburgh, UK, July 31, 2011*, pages 67–71, Stroudsburg/PA. Association for Computational Linguistics (ACL).

Johannes Hellrich and Udo Hahn. 2016a. Measuring the dynamics of lexico-semantic change since the German Romantic period. In *Digital Humanities 2016 – Proceedings of the 2016 Conference of the Alliance of Digital Humanities Organizations (ADHO). Digital Identities: The Past and the Future. Kraków, Poland, 11-16 July 2016*.

Johannes Hellrich and Udo Hahn. 2016b. Romantik im Wandel der Zeit – eine quantitative Untersuchung. In *DHd 2016 – 3. Jahrestagung des Verbandes der Digital Humanities im deutschsprachigen Raum. Modellierung-Venetzung-Visualisierung. Die Digital Humanities als fächerübergreifendes Forschungsparadigma. Leipzig, Germany, March 7-12, 2016*, pages 325–326.

Adam Jatowt and Kevin Duh. 2014. A framework for analyzing semantic change of words across time. In *JCDL '14 — Proceedings of the 14th ACM/IEEE-CS Joint Conference on Digital Libraries. London, U.K., September 8-12, 2014*, pages 229–238, Piscataway/NJ. IEEE Computer Society Press.

Yoon Kim, Yi-I Chiu, Kentaro Hanaki, Darshan Hegde, and Slav Petrov. 2014. Temporal analysis of language through neural language models. In Cristian Danescu-Niculescu-Mizil, Jacob Eisenstein, Kathleen R. McKeown, and Noah A. Smith, editors, *Proceedings of the Workshop on Language Technologies and Computational Social Science @ ACL 2014. Baltimore, Maryland, USA, June 26, 2014*, pages 61–65, Stroudsburg/PA. Association for Computational Linguistics (ACL).

Vivek Kulkarni, Rami Al-Rfou, Bryan Perozzi, and Steven Skiena. 2015. Statistically significant detection of linguistic change. In *WWW '15 — Proceedings of the 24th International Conference on World Wide Web. May 18-22, 2015, Florence, Italy*, pages 625–635, New York, N.Y. Association for Computing Machinery (ACM).

"lazzarone, n". 2016. In *OED Online*. Oxford University Press. `http://www.oed.com/view/Entry/106565` (accessed June 16, 2016).

Yann LeCun, Yoshua Bengio, and Geoffrey E. Hinton. 2015. Deep learning. *Nature*, 521(7553):436–444, May.

Yuri Lin, Jean-Baptiste Michel, Erez Lieberman Aiden, Jon Orwant, William Brockman, and Slav Petrov. 2012. Syntactic annotations for the Google Books Ngram corpus. In Min Zhang, editor, *Proceedings of the System Demonstrations @ 50th Annual Meeting of the Association for Computational Linguistics — ACL 2012. Jeju Island, Korea, 10 July 2012*, pages 169–174, Stroudsburg/PA. Association for Computational Linguistics (ACL).

Christopher D. Manning, Prabhakar Raghavan, and Hinrich Schütze. 2008. *Introduction to Information Retrieval*. Cambridge University Press, New York/NY, USA.

Jean-Baptiste Michel, Yuan Kui Shen, Aviva Presser Aiden, Adrian Veres, Matthew K. Gray, The Google Books Team, Joseph P. Pickett, Dale Hoiberg, Dan Clancy, Peter Norvig, Jon Orwant, Steven Pinker, Martin A. Nowak, and Erez Lieberman Aiden. 2011. Quantitative analysis of culture using millions of digitized books. *Science*, 331(6014):176–182, January.

Rada Mihalcea and Vivi Nastase. 2012. Word epoch disambiguation: Finding how words change over time. In *ACL 2012 — Proceedings of the 50th Annual Meeting of the Association for Computational Linguistics. Jeju Island, Korea, July 8-14, 2012*, volume 2: Short Papers, pages 259–263, Stroudsburg/PA. Association for Computational Linguistics (ACL).

Tomas Mikolov, Kai Chen, Gregory S. Corrado, and Jeffrey Dean. 2013a. Efficient estimation of word representations in vector space. In *ICLR 2013 — Workshop Proceedings of the International Conference on Learning Representations. Scottsdale, Arizona, USA, May 2-4, 2013*.

Tomas Mikolov, Ilya Sutskever, Kai Chen, Gregory S. Corrado, and Jeffrey Dean. 2013b. Distributed representations of words and phrases and their compositionality. In Christopher J. C. Burges, Léon Bottou, Max Welling, Zoubin Ghahramani, and Kilian Q. Weinberger, editors, *Advances in Neural Information Processing Systems 26 — NIPS 2013. Proceedings of the 27th Annual Conference on Neural Information Processing Systems. Lake Tahoe, Nevada, USA, December 5-10, 2013*, pages 3111–3119.

Tomas Mikolov, Wen-tau Yih, and Geoffrey Zweig. 2013c. Linguistic regularities in continuous space word representations. In Lucy Vanderwende, Hal Daumé, and Katrin Kirchhoff, editors, *NAACL-HLT 2013 — Proceedings of the 2013 Conference of the North American Chapter of the Association for Computational Linguistics: Human Language Technologies. Atlanta, GA, USA, 9-14 June 2013*, pages 746–751, Stroudsburg/PA. Association for Computational Linguistics (ACL).

Alexander Panchenko. 2016. Best of both worlds: Making word sense embeddings interpretable. In Nicoletta Calzolari, Khalid Choukri, Thierry Declerck, Sara Goggi, Marko Grobelnik, Bente Maegaard, Joseph Mariani, Helene Mazo, Asuncion Moreno, Jan Odijk, and Stelios Piperidis, editors, *LREC 2016 — Proceedings of the 10th International Conference on Language Resources and Evaluation. Portorož, Slovenia, 23-28 May 2016*, pages 2649–2655, Paris. European Language Resources Association (ELRA-ELDA).

Eitan Adam Pechenick, Christopher M. Danforth, and Peter Sheridan Dodds. 2015. Characterizing the Google Books Corpus: Strong limits to inferences of socio-cultural and linguistic evolution. *PLoS One*, 10(10):e0137041, October.

Martin Riedl, Richard Steuer, and Chris Biemann. 2014. Distributed distributional similarities of Google Books over the centuries. In Nicoletta Calzolari, Khalid Choukri, Thierry Declerck, Hrafn Loftsson, Bente Maegaard, Joseph Mariani, Asuncion Moreno, Jan Odijk, and Stelios Piperidis, editors, *LREC 2014 — Proceedings of the 9th International Conference on Language Resources and Evaluation. Reykjavik, Iceland, May 26-31, 2014*, pages 1401–1405, Paris. European Language Resources Association (ELRA).

Matti Rissanen. 2008. Corpus linguistics and historical linguistics. In Anke Lüdeling and Merja Kytö, editors, *Corpus Linguistics. An International Handbook*, number 29/1 in Handbücher zur Sprach- und

Kommunikationswissenschaft / Handbooks of Linguistics and Communication Science (HSK), chapter 4, pages 53–68. de Gruyter Mouton, Berlin, New York.

Tobias Schnabel, Igor Labutov, David Mimno, and Thorsten Joachims. 2015. Evaluation methods for unsupervised word embeddings. In *EMNLP 2015 — Proceedings of the 2015 Conference on Empirical Methods in Natural Language Processing. Lisbon, Portugal, 17-21 September 2015*, pages 298–307. Association for Computational Linguistics (ACL).

Derry Tanti Wijaya and Reyyan Yeniterzi. 2011. Understanding semantic change of words over centuries. In Sergej Sizov, Stefan Siersdorfer, Philipp Sorg, and Thomas Gottron, editors, *DETECT '11 — Proceedings of the 2011 International Workshop on DETecting and Exploiting Cultural diversiTy on the Social Web @ CIKM 2011. Glasgow, U.K., October 24, 2011*, pages 35–40, New York, N.Y. Association for Computing Machinery (ACM).

Universal Morphology for Old Hungarian

Eszter Simon
Research Institute for Linguistics,
Hungarian Academy of Sciences
Benczúr u. 33.
H-1068 Budapest, Hungary
simon.eszter@nytud.mta.hu

Veronika Vincze
MTA-SZTE Research Group
for Artificial Intelligence
Tisza Lajos krt. 103.
H-6720 Szeged, Hungary
vinczev@inf.u-szeged.hu

Abstract

This paper provides a description of the automatic conversion of the morphologically annotated part of the Old Hungarian Corpus. These texts are in the format of the Humor analyzer, which does not follow any international standards. Since standardization always facilitates future research, even for researchers who do not know the Old Hungarian language, we opted for mapping the Humor formalism to a widely used universal tagset, namely the Universal Dependencies framework. The benefits of using a shared tagset across languages enable interlingual comparisons from a theoretical point of view and also multilingual NLP applications can profit from a unified annotation scheme. In this paper, we report the adaptation of the Universal Dependencies morphological annotation scheme to Old Hungarian, and we discuss the most important theoretical linguistic issues that had to be resolved during the process. We focus on the linguistic phenomena typical of Old Hungarian that required special treatment and we offer solutions to them.

1 Introduction

There is a growing interest not only in the natural language processing (NLP) community, but even among theoretical and historical linguists for building and using databases of historical texts. High quality historical corpora enriched with some kinds of linguistic information and metadata can provide a fertile ground for theoretical investigations. Several databases of historical texts have recently been created for various Indo-European languages, such as the Penn-Helsinki Parsed Corpus of Middle English (Kroch and Taylor, 2000), the Tycho Brahe Parsed Corpus of Historical Portuguese (Galves and Britto, 2002), or the Welsh Prose corpus (Thomas et al., 2007) and for non-Indo-European languages as well, such as the Old Hungarian Corpus (Simon, 2014).

Historical corpora represent a rich source of data, but only if the relevant information is specified in a computationally interpretable and retrievable way. Moreover, following the current standardisation efforts allows for cross-lingual comparative studies, as well as for longitudinal investigations on language change. With the recent increase in the number of annotated corpora, it seems advisable to move towards a harmonized common framework and methodology. Standardization always facilitates future research – in this case even for researchers who do not know the Old Hungarian language.

Natural language processing activities in Hungary were not synchronized in the past, hence similar resources were developed in parallel at different locations. As a consequence, there are two morphological analyzers for Hungarian: Hunmorph (Trón et al., 2005) and Humor (Novák, 2003). The former one has not been maintained recently, while the latter one is not freely available. Moreover, they use different formalisms, which share only one common property: they do not follow any international standards. For the morphological annotation of Old Hungarian texts, the Humor analyzer was used, thus all of the morphologically annotated texts are in a special format, which is hard to be interpreted for a non-Hungarian researcher. That is the reason behind the need of mapping the Humor formalism to a widely used universal tagset, for which we chose the Universal Dependencies (UD) framework.

The UD tagset and annotation scheme have just been adapted to Modern Hungarian (Vincze et al.,

Proceedings of the 10th SIGHUM Workshop on Language Technology for Cultural Heritage, Social Sciences, and Humanities (LaTeCH), pages 118–127,
Berlin, Germany, August 11, 2016. ©2016 Association for Computational Linguistics

2016). In this paper, we report the adaptation of the morphological annotation scheme to Old Hungarian, and we discuss the most important theoretical linguistic issues that had to be resolved during the process. Section 2 briefly presents the international project Universal Dependencies and Morphology, then we summarize the part-of-speech (POS) tags and morphological features that are relevant for Old Hungarian. Section 3 gives a brief introduction of the Old Hungarian language and describes the morphologically annotated part of the Old Hungarian Corpus which has been converted into the UD tagset. Section 4 reports on our experiences in the conversion and discusses the specific linguistic issues concerning parts-of-speech and features. In Section 5, we contrast the annotation schemes developed for Old and Modern Hungarian. Conclusions and the planned future work end the paper in Section 6.

2 Universal Dependencies and Morphology

Universal Dependencies is an international project that aims at developing a unified annotation scheme for dependency syntax and morphology in a language-independent framework (Nivre, 2015). Currently (as of June 2016), there are annotated datasets available for 45 languages, including modern languages such as English, German, French, Hungarian and Irish, and old languages such as Ancient Greek, Coptic, Latin and Old Church Slavic, among others[1]. Datasets from all these languages apply the same tagsets at the morphological and syntactic levels and are annotated on the basis of the same linguistic principles, to the widest extent possible, however, in some cases, language-specific decisions had to be made. The benefits of using a shared tagset across languages enable interlingual comparisons from a theoretical point of view and also multilingual NLP applications can profit from a unified annotation scheme.

Standardized tagsets for both morphological and syntactic annotation have been constantly improved in the international NLP community. As for dependency syntax, Stanford dependencies is one of the most widely used tagsets (de Marneffe and Manning, 2008). For morphology, the MSD coding system was developed for a bunch of Eastern European languages including Hungarian (Erjavec, 2012). Interset functions as an in-

---

[1] http://universaldependencies.org

POS	description
ADJ	adjective
ADP	adposition
ADV	adverb
AUX	auxiliary
CONJ	coordinating conjunction
DET	determiner
INTJ	interjection
NOUN	noun
NUM	number
PART	particle
PRON	nominal pronoun
PROPN	proper noun
PUNCT	punctuation
SCONJ	subordinating conjunction
VERB	verb
X	other

Table 1: POS tags for Old Hungarian.

terlingua for different morphological tagsets and it enables the conversion of different tagsets to the same morphological representation (Zeman, 2008). Rambow et al. (2006) defined a multilingual tagset for POS tagging and parsing, while McDonald and Nivre (2007) identified eight POS tags based on data from the CoNLL-2007 Shared Task (Nivre et al., 2007). Petrov et al. (2012) offered a tagset of 12 POS tags and applied this tagset to 22 languages.

Now, Universal Dependencies is the latest standardized tagset that we are aware of. In its current form, morphological information is encoded in the form of POS tags and feature–value pairs. There is a fixed set of universal POS tags without the possibility of introducing new members, but features and values can have language-specific additions if needed. Features are divided into the categories lexical features and inflectional features. Lexical features are features that are characteristics of the lemmas rather than the word forms, whereas inflectional features are those that are characteristics of the word forms. Both lexical and inflectional features can have layered features: some features are marked more than once on the same word, e.g. a Hungarian noun may denote its possessor's number as well as its own number. In this case, the `Number` feature has an added layer, `Number[psor]`.

As mentioned above, Universal Morphology

annotates words with POS information and morphological features. Tables 1 and 2 summarize the POS tags and morphological features that are relevant for Old Hungarian, based on the annotation scheme created for Modern Hungarian, described at the UD website and in Vincze et al. (2016).

3 Old Hungarian

The Old Hungarian era lasted from 896 to 1526, the year of the occupation of the major part of the Hungarian Kingdom by the Ottoman Empire. The first part of this period (between 896–1350), documented by linguistic fragments and short coherent texts, is called the Early Old Hungarian period. The Late Old Hungarian period between 1350–1526 is the period of codices.

The Old Hungarian Corpus (Simon, 2014) contains all codices from the Late Old Hungarian period and several minor texts from the Early Old Hungarian period in their original orthographic form. Because of the heterogeneity of the Old Hungarian orthographic system, the original tokens had to be transcribed into their modernized form during a normalization step (for more details, see Oravecz et al. (2010)). Twelve of 47 codices have been normalized so far, and five of them have been morphologically analyzed and disambiguated.

The five codices are (in the order of the year of their writing/translation): Jókai Codex (after 1372/around 1448), Munich Codex (1466), Festetics Codex (before 1494), Guary Codex (before 1495) and Booklet on the Dignity of the Apostles (1521). These codices contain legends of saints, prayers, psalms, Bible translations and religious readings.

The Humor morphological analyzer was originally developed for Modern Hungarian and later it was extended to be capable of analyzing words containing morphological constructions, suffixes, paradigms and stems that were used in Old Hungarian but no longer exist in Modern Hungarian (Novák et al., 2013). Since the analyzer generates all potential morphological analyses for each token, a disambiguation step is required to select the most appropriate analysis. For this purpose, an HMM-based trigram tagger, PurePos (Orosz and Novák, 2012) was used, whose output was manually validated and corrected. This is the source data of the present conversion process, which contains 158,746 tokens altogether.

4 Language-specific extensions

Since the time interval of the Old Hungarian period is more than 600 years, several linguistic phenomena were in permanent change during this period. That is one of the reasons behind the heterogeneity of Old Hungarian texts. For instance, the progress in which postpositions became verbal particles or adverbs roots back to the Proto-Hungarian period and lasts even in the Modern Hungarian era, thus making a decision on their POS tag is far from trivial (discussed in more detail in Section 4.2). Such issues posed several problems during the conversion process, which are detailed in this section.

In examples, throughout the section, the relevant parts are emboldened. As a morphological description, we apply and follow the standard Leipzig Glossing Rules. The source of the example is provided in brackets after the translation. If the example is part of the Bible, the translation is copied from the King James Bible, and its biblical locus (book, chapter, verse) is also provided.

First, we discuss general issues of the conversion, then we illustrate specific cases that are relevant to only some or only one POS. Finally, challenges concerning morphological features are summed up.

4.1 General issues

Derivations changing part-of-speech

Hungarian has a great number of derivational suffixes, some of which change the POS of the word. These may derive – among others – verbs from nouns, e.g. *fül* ('ear') $\sim$ *fülel* ('listen carefully'); nouns from adjectives, e.g. *vad* ('wild') $\sim$ *vadság* ('wildness'); adjectives from nouns, e.g. *hold* ('moon') $\sim$ *holdbeli* ('located on the moon'); or adverbs from adjectives, e.g. *víg* ('merry') $\sim$ *vígan* ('merrily') (for more details, see Törkenczy (2005)). They are formed either with a non-harmonic suffix or with harmonic two- or more-form suffixes, which are added to the stem. The choice of the appropriate harmonic variant is determined by vowel harmony (see below).

Hungarian derivational suffixes are denoted by the Humor morphological analyzer, but the UD formalism takes into account only the POS of the derived form and does not note the root and the derivational steps during which the final word form was created. During the conversion, POSs of words containing derivational suffixes

Feature	Description	POS
PronType	type of pronouns	ADV, DET, PRON
NumType	type of numerals	ADJ, ADV, DET, NUM
Reflex	reflexivity	PRON
Poss	possessive pronouns	PRON
Number	number	ADJ, ADV, AUX, NOUN, NUM, PRON, PROPN, VERB
Number[psor]	number of possessor	ADJ, NOUN, NUM, PRON, PROPN
Number[psed]	number of possessed	ADJ, NOUN, NUM, PRON, PROPN
Person	person	ADJ, ADV, AUX, PRON, VERB
Person[psor]	person of possessor	ADJ, NOUN, NUM, PRON, PROPN
Case	case	ADJ, NOUN, NUM, PRON, PROPN
Definite	definiteness	DET, VERB
Degree	degree	ADJ, ADV, NUM
VerbForm	form of the verb	ADJ, ADV, VERB
Mood	mood	AUX, VERB
Tense	tense	AUX, VERB
Aspect	aspect	ADJ, VERB
Voice	voice	ADJ, VERB

Table 2: Morphological features for Old Hungarian.

which do not change the lexical category were left unchanged, while POS-changing suffixes caused several difficulties. In addition to changing the POS, the lemma had also to be changed.

In the case of POSs which cannot be inflected, the full normalized word form can stand for the lemma as well. However, in those cases when the derived form may be inflected (verbs, nouns, adjectives), the lemma and the normalized form are not interchangeable. Thus the new lemma has to be generated from the old lemma and the harmonized form of the derivational suffix. Moreover, there are several irregular stems which may be changed before the derivational suffix, thus the converter must be capable to deal with them. The irregular stems occurring in the current version of the corpus are fully covered by the rules of the converter, but new stems may appear when expanding the corpus with new sources. Lemmas coming from the Humor morphological analyzer can be preserved in the 10th column of the CoNLL-U format, which is dedicated to any other annotation.

Allomorphs

In Hungarian, most suffixes harmonize with the stem they are attached to, which means that most suffixes exist in two or three alternative forms differing in the suffix vowel, and the selection of the suffix alternant is determined by the stem vowel(s). This phenomenon is known as vowel harmony, whose roots probably go back to the Proto-Uralic language, thus it exists in the Old Hungarian language as well.

There are several alternants in the Old Hungarian language which do not exist in Modern Hungarian and which therefore have specific markings in the formalism of Humor. An example of this phenomenon is the allomorph *-i*. In many cases, it is difficult or even impossible to decide whether it is the 3rd person singular form of the possessive suffix, or whether it marks the plurality of the possessed noun. For instance, the form *ÿgeretÿth* can be normalized either as *ígéret-é-t* ('promise-POSS.3SG-ACC'), or as *ígéret-e-i-t* ('promise-POSS.3SG-PL-ACC'). These forms get the morphological code N.PxS3=i.Acc or N.PxS3.Pl=i.Acc in the Humor formalism. However, these phenomena cannot be marked in the framework of UD, therefore they have been converted into the same feature–value pair as the corresponding Modern Hungarian suffix, without marking the surface form of the suffix. Since the CoNLL-U format of UD allows us to keep the original language-specific POS tags and morphological features, these kinds of information will not be lost.

4.2 Issues concerning parts-of-speech

Pronouns

In UD, only pronouns that substitute nouns are assigned the POS tag PRON, all the other pronouns are tagged according to the POS they stand for in the context. However, in the Old Hungarian Corpus, all pronouns – even those substituting other parts-of-speech – are tagged as pronouns. While converting the data, we could exploit the fact that pronouns inflected for case can only substitute nouns, compare the examples below:

<table>
<tr><td>(1)</td><td>ilyetén
such
'such prayers' (Kazinczy C. 26r)</td><td>könyörgés-ek-et
prayer-PL-ACC</td></tr>
</table>

<table>
<tr><td>(2)</td><td>soha
never
'such thing never to do' (Jókai C. 107)</td><td>ilyetén-t
such-ACC</td><td>nem
not</td><td>ten-ni
do-INF</td></tr>
</table>

Thus, inflected pronouns were automatically tagged as PRON. Words that were originally tagged as pronouns and occurred in the nominative case (i.e. they were not inflected) were assigned their UD POS tags with the help of lexical support: we defined lists for those pronouns and determined their UD POS tag manually. For instance, in Example 1, *ilyetén* was tagged as ADJ. These lists were then used in the automatic conversion process.

Postpositions

Some of the prepositional meanings found in other languages such as English are expressed in Hungarian by postpositions (Example 3) and case endings (Example 4). Hegedűs (2014) claims that there is historical evidence that the only difference between postpositions and case suffixes is that suffixes are monosyllabic and most of them show vowel harmony with the stem they are attached to. Syntactically, the two groups behave largely identically in Modern Hungarian.

<table>
<tr><td>(3)</td><td>ház-a
house-POSS.3SG
'above his house' (Festetics C. 57)</td><td>fölött
above</td></tr>
</table>

<table>
<tr><td>(4)</td><td>ház-á-ba
house-POSS.3SG-ILL
'into his house' (Jókai C. 88)</td></tr>
</table>

Similarly to the forms of pronouns inflected for case (Example 5), some postpositions may form postpositional pronominal forms (Example 6). The former word forms can be regarded as a combination of a case marker and a marker for person and number, while the latter ones consist of a postposition plus the regular person/number endings.

<table>
<tr><td>(5)</td><td>nek-em
DAT-1SG
'to me' (Festetics C. 54)</td></tr>
</table>

<table>
<tr><td>(6)</td><td>ellen-em
against-1SG
'against me' (Jókai C. 103)</td></tr>
</table>

In the Old Hungarian Corpus, however, these suffixes are analyzed as possessive endings, which is also a valid approach. Some of the Old Hungarian postpositions can appear in a structure that is analogous to the possessive construction (for more details on possessive constructions, see Section 4.3). Similarly to how the possessor can appear in dative case, the complement of some postpositions can also be in dative case, while a possessedness marker may appear on the postposition (Hegedűs, 2014), compare the examples below:

<table>
<tr><td>(7)</td><td>halál-a
death-POSS.3SG
'after his death' (Vienna C. 4)</td><td>után
after</td></tr>
</table>

<table>
<tr><td>(8)</td><td>halál-od-nak
death-POSS.2SG-DAT
'after your death' (Bod C. 14r)</td><td>után-a
after-POSS</td></tr>
</table>

Since inflected pronouns and inflected postpositions behave in a similar way, it can be argued that these endings are only markers of person and number, without referring to possession. In the UD morphology, we analyze both of them as personal pronouns as they can substitute inflected nouns, and assign them the features Person and Number, without any reference to possession.

Complex verb forms

According to the description on the UD website, auxiliaries express grammatical distinctions not carried by the lexical verb, thus the lexical verb and the auxiliary together bear all suffixes. In this sense, there are four auxiliaries in Old Hungarian (*vala, volt, volna, legyen*), which are parts of the Old Hungarian complex verb forms. In Hungarian, a conjugated verb form consists of the stem plus two inflectional slots, i.e. positions where inflectional suffixes can occur. The first of these suffix positions is that of tense/mood and the second one is that of person/number. This is the reason behind the need for complex verb forms, thus there is insufficient place in one inflected word form for expressing tense and mood at the same time. Therefore, one of the tense and mood markers has to be 'out-sourced' to an auxiliary, while agreement and definiteness markers stay on the lexical verb.

There are four complex verb forms in Old Hungarian: past continuous, past perfect, past conditional, and past subjunctive. With the only exception of past conditional, all of them are extinct from the Modern Hungarian language.

The past continuous and the past conditional constructions have a version in which the auxiliary also bears an agreement marker, as in Examples 9 and 10:

(9)
tart-om   **val-ék**
keep-1SG.DEF   be-IPFV.1SG
'I was keeping (them)'
(Munich C. 103vb)

(10)
ír-t-am   **vol-nék**
write-PST-1SG   be-COND.1SG
'I would have written' (Bod C. 15r)

In these cases, Person and Number features of both the lexical verb and the auxiliary have the same value. In the cases where the auxiliary does not carry any grammatical distinctions, but the tense or mood suffixes, Person, Number, Voice and Definite features remain underspecified.

Verbal particles

Hungarian verbs often have particles, which appear pre-verbally in neutral Hungarian sentences. In these cases, they are attached to the beginning of the verb, thus they constitute one token with the verb (Example 11). However, there are several cases when particles become separated from the verb and actually appear after the verb. For example, if another word or group of words is the focus in the sentence, the particle obligatorily follows the verb (Example 12).

(11)
ki-tisztul-ok   nagy   vétés-ből
out-purge-1SG   big   sin-ELA
'I am purged from big sin'
(Festetics C. 11)

(12)
sok-ak-at   **hagy-t-am**   **el**
many-PL-ACC   leave-PST-1SG   away
'I left many' (Könyvecse 18v)

If the verbal particle immediately precedes the verb, its code is attached to that of the verb in the Humor formalism. Since the verbal particle + verb construction is treated as one unit, only one POS tag can be assigned to it, which is VERB.

In cases when the particle is separated from the verb, the particle itself must have its own POS tag. According to the UD description, however, not all function words that are traditionally called particles automatically qualify for the PART tag, but they may be adpositions or adverbs by origin, therefore should be tagged as ADP or ADV, respectively.

The state and origin of verbal particles are constantly disputed even in Modern Hungarian. For example, D. Mátai (1992) claims that they developed from spatial adverbs, while Hegedűs (2014) proposes that they all go back to spatial postpositions with a lative (mostly goal) meaning.

The oldest particles are *meg* 'back', *ki* 'out', *le* 'down', *el* 'away', *be* 'into', *fel* 'up'. They are telicizing elements with often little spatial meaning left due to semantic bleaching. However, since they have not been fully grammaticalized, they have preserved some spatial meaning, and as a result we cannot treat them as regular particles.

In addition to the oldest particles, several new ones were born during the Old Hungarian period. According to the theory of Hegedűs (2014), all of them go back to, and are grammaticalized from postpositions, therefore we tagged them as ADP.

Adverbial participles

Old Hungarian has three types of adverbial participles, which are formed with one of the harmonising two-form suffixes: *-ván/-vén*, *-va/-ve*, and *-atta/-ette*. In the UD formalism, they all have the VerbForm=Trans feature–value pair, since they are transgressives, i.e. non-finite verb forms that share properties of verbs and adverbs.

While *-ván/-vén* adverbial participles do not agree, participles with *-va/-ve* can optionally agree with their subject (Examples 13 and 14), and participles with *-atta/-ette* ending obligatorily agree with their subject, see Example 15.

(13)
hal-va   lel-ik   val-a
dead-PART   find-3PL.DEF   be-PST
'they found him dead' (Guary C. 103)

(14)
mi **alu-vánk**
we sleep-PART.1PL
'while we slept'
(Munich C. 35vb; Matthew 28,13)

(15)
míg ő **beszéll-ette**
while he speak-PART.3SG
'while he yet spake'
(Munich C. 81vb; Luke 22,47)

While some of the Old Hungarian non-finites do agree with their subject, none of them distinguish the definite and indefinite conjugation like finite clauses do. Moreover, they do not bear temporal, mood, and aspect suffixes, thus in this sense their agreement paradigm can be said to be defective. Therefore, they can optionally get the `Person` and `Number` features in UD besides the `VerbForm=Trans` feature–value pair.

4.3 Issues concerning features

Definiteness of the verb

As a special type of agreement, Hungarian verbs also mark the definiteness of their objects. In other words, the form of the verb changes when the definiteness of the object also changes (Törkenczy, 2005). Proper nouns and noun phrases with a definite article are prototypical examples of definite objects while bare nouns and noun phrases with an indefinite article are indefinite objects. Compare:

(16)
lát-á az ház-at
see-IPFV.3SG.DEF the house-ACC
'he saw the house' (Kazinczy C. 13r)

(17)
lát-a álm-ot
see-IPFV.3SG.INDEF dream-ACC
'he had a dream' (Vienna C. 73)

As can be seen in Examples 16 and 17, the two verb forms differ only in one accent, more precisely, in the definite form there is an accented *a*, but in the indefinite form, there is no accent on the last vowel. However, due to the lack of standardized orthography and spelling conventions in the Old Hungarian period, the very same words can be spelled completely differently on the one hand, and different words can be spelled in the same way on the other hand, especially when no diacritics are used. Thus, we could encounter cases when it was impossible to decide whether the definite or the indefinite form of the verb was meant to be used, e.g. *lata* could be *láta* (the indefinite form) as well as *látá* (the definite form). For these cases, it seemed necessary to add another possible value of the `Definite` feature: the value `Underspecified` denotes that the definiteness of the verb cannot be figured out and it leaves this feature under-specified.

Possessive constructions

The possessor in Hungarian possessive constructions can have two different surface forms both in Old and Modern Hungarian, without any difference in meaning (similar to the English constructions *the boy's dog* and *the dog of the boy*). That is, both of the following examples are widely used:

(18)
Jézus tanítvány-a
Jesus disciple-POSS.3SG
'Jesus's disciple'
(Munich C. 35rb; Matthew 27,57)

(19)
Jézus-nak nev-é-be
Jesus-DAT name-POSS.3SG-ILL
'in the name of Jesus' (Booklet 16r)

The first (unmarked) form coincides with the nominative case whereas the second (marked) form coincides with the dative form of the noun, cf.:

(20)
mond-á **Jézus-nak**
say-IPFV.3SG.DEF Jesus-DAT
'said unto Jesus'
(Munich C. 23rb; Matthew 17,4)

According to the UD guidelines for Modern Hungarian, the case of the unmarked possessor is nominative, that is, a nominative possessor is not distinguished from the subject. However, the marked possessor is labeled differently from the dative argument, bearing a genitive label. In the original version of the Old Hungarian Corpus, a distinction was made in all of the cases, and the labels Nom, Dat, Nom_Gen and Dat_Gen are used for the subject, indirect object, nominative possessor and dative possessor, respectively.

Here, we voted for not making a distinction of the surface cases at the level of morphology. Hence, we annotated the unmarked possessor with the nominative case and the marked possessor with the dative case. On the other hand, the syntactic annotations of these should differ from each other, that is, the distinction will be made at the level of syntax. Table 4.3 summarizes these distinctions.

Example	Translation	UD for MH	OH original	UD for OH
a fiú kutyája	the boy's dog	Nom	Nom_Gen	Nom
a fiú játszott	the boy was playing	Nom	Nom	Nom
a fiúnak a kutyája	the dog of the boy	Gen	Dat_Gen	Dat
a fiúnak adta a könyvet	he gave the book to the boy	Dat	Dat	Dat

Table 3: Morphological features for possessors (MH: Modern Hungarian, OH: Old Hungarian).

5 Differences between Old and Modern Hungarian

In this section, we briefly contrast the annotation schemes for Old and Modern Hungarian, and we highlight the most important differences.

In Old Hungarian, there were more tenses and verb forms in use than in Modern Hungarian (see Section 4.2). Hence, more feature combinations are possible in Old Hungarian. Certain forms of adverbial participles agreed with the subject in Old Hungarian, however, this phenomenon is extinct now (cf. Section 4.2). For this reason, adverbial participles can have the features `Number` and `Person` in Old Hungarian but not in Modern Hungarian.

The verbal particle *meg* originates from a postposition meaning 'behind'. However, in Modern Hungarian, *meg* totally lost this shade of meaning and now is only used as a particle that perfectivizes the meaning of the verb it is attached to. Due to this historical change, *meg* is tagged as `PART` in Modern Hungarian but as `ADP` in Old Hungarian.

In Old Hungarian, ordinal and fractal numbers are not distinguished from each other, that is, the word form *harm-ad* ('three-DERIV.SFX') can mean 'a third part of something' and 'the third one' as well. However, in Modern Hungarian, it can only have the first meaning, the latter one is expressed by the word form *harm-ad-ik* ('three-DERIV.SFX-DES'). As a consequence, fractal numbers occur only in Modern Hungarian but not in Old Hungarian.

There are also differences concerning the marking of possessors. As discussed above in Section 4.3, the Old Hungarian UD annotation scheme makes use of only the labels `Nom` and `Dat`, regardless of whether the noun is used as a possessor or not. However, the morphological annotation of the UD treebank for Modern Hungarian was converted from the Szeged Treebank (Csendes et al., 2005), which makes a distinction between dative possessors and indirect objects (both ending in a dative suffix), thus the distinction was kept in the UD treebank as well. It should be noted, however, that it is not historical changes that led to this distinction: the annotation principles of the two treebanks are responsible for this divergence.

Due to the orthographic features of codices, the value `Underspecified` had to be added to the `Definite` feature for verbs, which is not present in Modern Hungarian (cf. Section 4.3). Nevertheless, this feature value might be of use in Modern Hungarian too: for instance, social media users tend to write their posts without accents, which might also yield ambiguous word forms. Thus, should social media texts be included in the Modern Hungarian UD treebank in the future, this feature value might be exploited there as well.

As can be seen, in some cases, Old Hungarian had a richer set of morphological processes (for instance, verbal conjugation), but in other cases, Modern Hungarian has developed some more morphological distinctions (like that of ordinal and fractal numbers). Thus, both additions and losses occurred in Hungarian morphology from a historical perspective. Later on, we intend to investigate whether this is true for syntax as well: we would like to adapt the UD annotation guidelines to Old Hungarian and see the syntactic differences between Old and Modern Hungarian.

6 Conclusions and future work

In this paper, we reported the automatic conversion of the morphological annotation of the Old Hungarian Corpus to the international standard framework of Universal Dependencies and Morphology. We presented the linguistic phenomena typical of Old Hungarian that required special treatment and we offered solutions to them. The detailed description of the Old Hungarian morphology has been made publicly available, together with the converted corpus[2]. Later on, we intend to adapt the Modern Hungarian UD depen-

---

[2]http://oldhungariancorpus.nytud.hu/

dency tagset and annotation principles to Old Hungarian as well. After that, we are planning to add syntactic annotation to the corpus and publish it at the UD website[3], together with the adapted dependency labels and their detailed description.

Currently, additional texts from the Old Hungarian period are being digitized and normalized, also, morphological annotation is being added to them. These texts will then be standardized according to the UD morphology on the basis of the conversion rules developed in this paper and thus, the dataset of Old Hungarian texts with UD morphology will be expanded too.

Finally, it should be noted that the Hungarian NLP community is currently implementing a new morphological analyzer, which is planned to provide output in different formalisms, one of which will be the UD morphology. We are confident that our corpus and the above-mentioned morphological analyzer can contribute to the more effective and faster processing of Old Hungarian texts.

Acknowledgments

The research reported in the paper was conducted with the support of the Hungarian Scientific Research Fund (OTKA) grant #112057. We thank the anonymous reviewers for their comments.

References

Dóra Csendes, János Csirik, Tibor Gyimóthy, and András Kocsor. 2005. The Szeged TreeBank. In Václav Matousek, Pavel Mautner, and Tomás Pavelka, editors, *Proceedings of the 8th International Conference on Text, Speech and Dialogue, TSD 2005*, Lecture Notes in Computer Science, pages 123–132, Berlin / Heidelberg, September. Springer.

Mária D. Mátai. 1992. Az igekötők [Particles]. In Loránd Benkő, editor, *A magyar nyelv történeti nyelvtana II/1. A kései ómagyar kor. Morfematika [Historical grammar of the Hungarian language. The Late Old Hungarian period. Morphology]*, pages 662–695. Akadémiai Kiadó, Budapest.

Marie-Catherine de Marneffe and Christopher D. Manning. 2008. Stanford dependencies manual. Technical report, Stanford University.

Tomaž Erjavec. 2012. MULTEXT-East: morphosyntactic resources for Central and Eastern European languages. *Language Resources and Evaluation*, 46(1):131–142.

Charlotte Galves and Helena Britto. 2002. The Tycho Brahe Corpus of Historical Portuguese. Online publication.

Veronika Hegedűs. 2014. The cyclical development of Ps in Hungarian. In É. Kiss, Katalin, editor, *The Evolution of Functional Left Peripheries in Hungarian Syntax*, pages 122–147. Oxford University Press.

Anthony Kroch and Ann Taylor. 2000. The Penn-Helsinki Parsed Corpus of Middle English (PPCME2). CD-ROM.

Ryan McDonald and Joakim Nivre. 2007. Characterizing the errors of data-driven dependency parsing models. In *Proceedings of the 2007 Joint Conference on Empirical Methods in Natural Language Processing and Computational Natural Language Learning (EMNLP-CoNLL)*, pages 122–131.

Joakim Nivre, Johan Hall, Sandra Kübler, Ryan McDonald, Jens Nilsson, Sebastian Riedel, and Deniz Yuret. 2007. The CoNLL 2007 shared task on dependency parsing. In *Proceedings of the CoNLL Shared Task Session of EMNLP-CoNLL 2007*, pages 915–932.

Joakim Nivre. 2015. Towards a Universal Grammar for Natural Language Processing. In Alexander Gelbukh, editor, *Computational Linguistics and Intelligent Text Processing*, pages 3–16. Springer.

Attila Novák, György Orosz, and Nóra Wenszky. 2013. Morphological annotation of Old and Middle Hungarian corpora. In *Proceedings of the 7th Workshop on Language Technology for Cultural Heritage, Social Sciences, and Humanities*, pages 43–48, Sofia, Bulgaria, August. Association for Computational Linguistics.

Attila Novák. 2003. Milyen a jó Humor? [What is good Humor like?]. In *Proceedings of the 1st Hungarian Computational Linguistics Conference*, pages 138–144, Szeged. SZTE.

Csaba Oravecz, Bálint Sass, and Eszter Simon. 2010. Semi-automatic Normalization of Old Hungarian Codices. In *Proceedings of the ECAI 2010 Workshop on Language Technology for Cultural Heritage, Social Sciences, and Humanities (LaTeCH 2010)*, pages 55–60, Lisbon, Portugal. Faculty of Science, University of Lisbon.

György Orosz and Attila Novák. 2012. PurePos: An Open Source Morphological Disambiguator. In *Proceedings of the 9th International Workshop on Natural Language Processing and Cognitive Science*, pages 53–63.

Slav Petrov, Dipanjan Das, and Ryan McDonald. 2012. A universal part-of-speech tagset. In *Proceedings of LREC*, May.

Owen Rambow, Bonnie Dorr, David Farwell, Rebecca Green, Nizar Habash, Stephen Helmreich, Eduard Hovy, Lori Levin, Keith J. Miller, Teruko Mitamura,

---

[3]As currently there is no dependency annotation available for the Old Hungarian Corpus, it is not officially listed among the UD treebanks on the UD website.

Reeder, Florence, and Advaith Siddharthan. 2006. Parallel syntactic annotation of multiple languages. In *Proceedings of LREC*, May.

Eszter Simon. 2014. Corpus building from Old Hungarian codices. In É. Kiss, Katalin, editor, *The Evolution of Functional Left Peripheries in Hungarian Syntax*, pages 224–236. Oxford University Press.

Peter Wynn Thomas, D. Mark Smith, and Diana Luft. 2007. Rhyddiaith Gymraeg 1350-1425.

Miklós Törkenczy. 2005. *Practical Hungarian Grammar*. Corvina, Budapest.

Viktor Trón, György Gyepesi, Péter Halácsy, András Kornai, László Németh, and Dániel Varga. 2005. Hunmorph: Open source word analysis. In *Proceedings of the ACL Workshop on Software*, pages 77–85, Ann Arbor, Michigan, June. Association for Computational Linguistics.

Veronika Vincze, Richárd Farkas, Katalin Ilona Simkó, Zsolt Szántó, and Viktor Varga. 2016. Univerzális morfológia és dependencia magyar nyelvre [Universal Morphology and Dependencies for Hungarian]. In *XII. Magyar Számítógépes Nyelvészeti Konferencia*.

Daniel Zeman. 2008. Reusable tagset conversion using tagset drivers. In Nicoletta Calzolari, Khalid Choukri, Bente Maegaard, Joseph Mariani, Jan Odijk, Stelios Piperidis, and Daniel Tapias, editors, *Proceedings of the Sixth International Conference on Language Resources and Evaluation (LREC'08)*, Marrakech, Morocco, may. European Language Resources Association (ELRA). http://www.lrec-conf.org/proceedings/lrec2008/.

Automatic Identification of Suicide Notes from Linguistic and Sentiment Features

Annika Marie Schoene and Nina Dethlefs
University of Hull, UK
amschoene@googlemail.com

Abstract

Psychological studies have shown that our state of mind can manifest itself in the linguistic features we use to communicate. Recent statistics in suicide prevention show that young people are increasingly posting their last words online. In this paper, we investigate whether it is possible to automatically identify suicide notes and discern them from other types of online discourse based on analysis of sentiments and linguistic features. Using supervised learning, we show that our model achieves an accuracy of 86.6%, outperforming previous work on a similar task by over 4%.

1 Introduction

The World Health Organisation outline in a recent report that suicide is the second leading cause of death for people aged 15-29 worldwide (2014). The total number of suicides per year is around 800,000 people. In recent years, there has been a trend recognized that especially young people tend to publish their suicide notes or express their suicidal feelings online (Desmet and Hoste, 2013).

Research in psychology has long recognised that our drive or motivation can affect the way in which we communicate, leading to the assumption that our spoken and written language represents those shifting psychological states (Osgood, 1960). This argument was elaborated by Cummings and Renshaw (1979), who suggest that there is a shift in people's linguistic expression due to the aroused cognitive state suicidal individuals experience.

Facebook has recently developed an online feature which relies on users reporting other users if they feel that they are at risk of committing suicide (Morese, 2016). New features such as the Facebook feature are undoubtedly important in suicide prevention as suicide is not only a result of mental health issues, but of various sociocultural factors and especially individual crisis (Worldwide, 2016). Therefore it has been argued by Desmet and Hoste (2013) that there is a need for automatic procedures that can spot suicidal messages and allow stakeholders to quickly react to online suicidal behaviour or incitement. This paper aims to investigate the linguistic features in discourse that are representative of a suicidal state of mind and automatically identify them based on supervised classification.

2 Related Work

Traditionally, the linguistic analysis of suicide notes has been conducted in the field of forensic linguistics in order to provide evidence for the genuineness of suicide notes in settings such as police investigations, court cases or coroner inquiries, where expert evidence is given by professionals, such as forensic linguists (Coulthard and Johnson, 2007).

As argued above, there is great impact potential in the automatic identification of suicide notes, e.g. on social media sites, in order to prevent such cases. Previous work in this direction by Jones and Benell (2007) developed a supervised classification model based on linguistic features that can differentiate genuine from forged suicide notes. The authors found that structural features such as nouns, adjectives or average sentence length were reliable predictors of genuine notes and report an overall classification accuracy of 82%.

An alternative direction was taken in research by Pestian et al. (2010) and Pestian et al. (2012), who investigate the impact of sentiment features on the identification of suicide notes. The authors

Proceedings of the 10th SIGHUM Workshop on Language Technology for Cultural Heritage, Social Sciences, and Humanities (LaTeCH), pages 128–133,
Berlin, Germany, August 11, 2016. ©2016 Association for Computational Linguistics

focus particularly on those emotion features that have been shown to play a role in the clinical assessment of a person (Pestian et al., 2010).

Most work to date has focused on the identification of genuine suicide notes against forged ones. Also, different types of features have been shown to be useful in this task. In this paper, we explore the impact of combining these features into a model that can differentiate suicide notes from other types of discourse, such as depressive notes or love letters—which share several linguistic features with genuine suicide notes.

3 Data Collection and Annotation

3.1 Corpora

We use three datasets for our analysis: a corpus of genuine suicide notes and two corpora for comparison. The latter two were collected from public posts made to the Experience Project website.[1]

- **Genuine Suicide Notes (GSN)**: this corpus contains genuine suicide notes which we collected from various sources, including newspaper articles and already existing corpora from other academic resources, e.g. Shneidman and Farberow (1957), Leenaars (1988) and Etkind (1997). Only notes of which there was a full copy available were included.

- **Love / happiness (LH)**: this corpus comprises 142 posts from the Experience Project's public groups 'I Think Being In Love Is One Of The Best Feelings Ever' and 'I Smile When I Think Of You'. We chose this topic as it could have interesting linguistic similarities with suicide notes in its use of cognitive verbs. However, there are also important differences as emotions are expected to be largely positive. Posts were collected randomly with an equal number of men and women to a keep a demographic balance.

- **Depression / loneliness (DL)**: the DL corpus was collected as it may be close in the emotions and language usage to the GSN corpus and could therefore demonstrate clear differences in how depressed and suicidal people communicate. This corpus was collected randomly from the Experience Project's group 'I Fight Depression And Loneliness Everyday'.

All corpora were collected from the public domain, but nevertheless anonymised in order to protect the privacy of the author as well as the privacy of those referenced in the communication. The other two corpora were chosen as both differ significantly in topic, purpose and arguably emotions. Similar research in this area has been conducted by Bak et al. (2014), who investigated how self-disclosure is used in twitter conversations, where self-disclosure is used as a means of gathering social support as well as "to improve and maintain relationships". Although it could be argued that suicide notes are a form of self-disclosure the purpose of a suicide note is different to the one mentioned by Bak et al (2014). The purpose of a suicide note is manifold and can range from statements of their current feelings, apologies or instructions, but not all suicide notes are written in order to comfort the survivors (Wertheimer, 2001). Therefore the level or type of self- disclosure may be another interesting feature to be included into a further analysis.

3.2 Features

All three corpora were annotated manually and on clause level by one author including the following features based on previous work discussed in Section 2.

Sentiment Features In terms of sentiment features, we annotated the following 12 emotions on a clause level: *fear, guilt, hopelessness, sorrow, information, instruction, forgiveness (fg), happiness/peacefulness (hp), hopefulness, pride, love* and *thankfulness*. Feature values were the number of occurrences of each emotion in a note, e.g. `sorrow=2`. These emotions are based on the work of Pestian et al. (2012), who uses 'abuse', 'anger' and 'blame' in addition. However, there were too few examples of these in our data, so that we excluded them from our analysis. Furthermore Yang et al. (2012) showed that assigning the emotions to a positive, neutral and negative group can improve classification accuracy. We therefore include grouping of emotions as well, again representing them by their number of occurrence, e.g. `positive=4`. The concepts 'information' and 'instruction' were assigned to the neutral group.

Some clauses can contain more than one emotion, so annotation features were not always mutually exclusive. In such cases, we chose to annotate the most prominent emotion. For example, in the

Category	GSN	LH	DL
No. of tokens in corpus	20,534	10,051	17,161
No. of notes in corpus	142	142	142
Ave. no. of words in note	141	71	121
No. of clauses in corpus	1,305	787	1,135
Ave. clause length	15	12	15

Table 1: Quantitative comparison of corpora collected in terms of number of words of each corpus, number of documents notes, average number of words in each note, clauses in each corpus and average clause length.

clause "i know that i will die dont be mean with me please" [sic] both *instruction* and *forgiveness* are possible, but only the first emotion was annotated as it appeared to be the prominent one.

Linguistic Features   In terms of linguistic features, we used Python's Natural Language Toolkit (NLTK) (Loper and Bird, 2002) to extract POS tag information, the most frequent lexical items, 2-grams and 4-grams. In addition, we used the LIWC tool [2] to extract note length, cognitive processes, tenses (past, present, future), average sentence length, relativity, negation, signs (e.g. +, &), adverbs, adjectives, and verbs. Finally, we manually annotated the feature 'endearment', which referred to words such as 'Dear' at the beginning of a note or post. Work by Gregory (1999) previously established a significant influence of 'endearment'.

Corpora Statistics   Table 1 shows a quantitative comparison of our three corpora showing the number of words of each corpus, number of documents notes, average number of words in each note, clauses in each corpus and average clause length. We can see that while each corpus contained exactly the same number of documents/notes, other statistics such as the number of words or clauses vary substantially across corpora.

Previous work by Gregory (1999) can perhaps help shed some light on these differences. Gregory (1999) found that suicide notes are often greater in length due to the fact that the suicidal individual wants to convey as much information as possible. This is due to the note writer's feeling that they will not have time to convey this information at a later point (Gregory, 1999). In our corpora,

[2] http://liwc.wpengine.com/
compare-versions/

we can see this tendency clearly reflected in the overall lengths of notes. In addition, the corpora differ noticeably in the average length per note. The notes in the GSN corpus are almost double in length compared to the LH corpus.

It can be seen in Table 1 that more similarities are found between the suicidal GSN corpus and the depressive DL corpus that with the love corpus LH. A possible explanation for this is work by Alvarez (1971) who explains that it is known in a clinical setting that there is a similarity between the state of mind of a suicidal person, and a person who experiences depression. When comparing the LH corpus to the other two corpora it is clear that although the number of tokens in the corpus is smaller, the sentence length is almost as high as the one of the GSN and DL corpora. It could be argued that this phenomenon may be due to a higher amount of adjectives used in a sentence, which will be tested at a later point. In addition to this, it has been argued that people who communicate under stress tend to break their communication down into shorter units (Osgood, 1959), thus perhaps pointing to a higher stress level of the suicidal individuals. The research however suggested that there is no significant difference in the overall length per unit when comparing suicide notes to regular letters to friends and simulated suicide notes (Osgood, 1959).

4   Classification Experiments

We use the WEKA toolkit (Hall et al., 2009) for our supervised learning experiments. Table 2 shows an overview of the models compared: a logistic tree regressor (LMT), a J48 decision tree classifier, a Naive Bayes classifier, and a simple majority baseline (Zero-R). All models were trained using 10-fold cross-validation in order to minimize variability in results (Alpaydin, 2012). The results are shown in Table 2, with the first box in the table including both sentiment and linguistic features, the second box only including sentiment features and the last box including only linguistic features. As can be seen, the best performance is achieved by a combination of sentiment and linguistic features by an LMT tree regressor with an overall accuracy of 86.61%. The following regression equation was learnt for a suicide note:

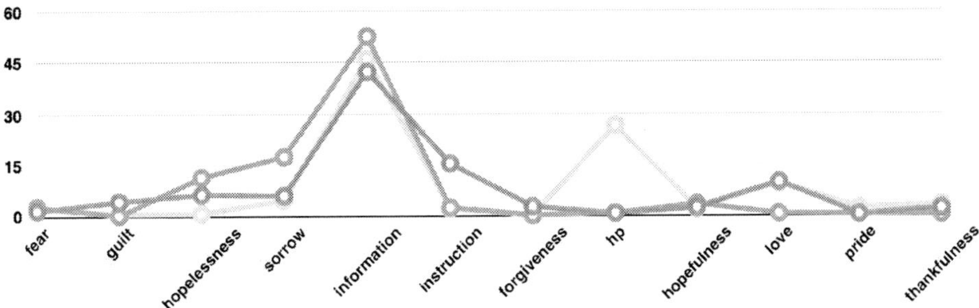

Figure 1: Different sentiments found in the GSN corpus (blue), the LH corpus (yellow) and the DL corpus (green). Emotions are in line with those expected by previous psychological studies. Emotion *hp* refers to happiness/peacefulness.

Classifier	ACC	PRE	REC	F-Score
LMT	**86.61**	**0.86**	**0.86**	**0.86**
J48	78.87	0.78	0.78	0.78
Naive Bayes	74.17	0.76	0.74	0.74
Zero-R	32.86	0.21	0.32	0.23
LMT	**78.63**	**0.79**	**0.78**	**0.78**
J48	71.36	0.71	0.71	0.71
Naive Bayes	69.01	0.72	0.69	0.68
Zero-R	32.86	0.21	0.32	0.23
LMT	**75.35**	**0.75**	**0.75**	**0.75**
J48	67.60	0.67	0.67	0.67
Naive Bayes	65.96	0.67	0.66	0.65
Zero-R	32.86	0.21	0.32	0.23

Table 2: Classification accuracy, precision, recall and F-Score metrics for different Weka classifiers. The first set of results includes *all features*, the second set is based on *sentiment features* only, and the last set of based on *linguistic features* only.

$$1.98 + [fear] * -0.55 + [guilt] * 0.76 +$$
$$[sorrow] * -0.13 + [instruction] * 0.66 +$$
$$[fg] * 2.28 + [endearment] * 2.95 +$$
$$[signs] * 1.51 + [cognitive] * -0.11 +$$
$$[relativity] * -0.05 + [negations] * -0.1 +$$
$$[adverb] * -0.11 + [noun] * 0.01$$

Our results exceed previously reported results on the (slightly different) task of classifying genuine suicide notes against forged ones by Jones and Benell (2007), who achieved 82%.

4.1 Discussion of Sentiment Features

Apart from the overall classification accuracy, we were interested in the contribution of the individual sentiment and linguistic feature sets. To this end, we conducted a sentiment analysis in order to identify which emotions are present in the three corpora and which proved to be most significant (Figure 1). 'Information' is the most frequent in all three corpora. This may be due to the fact that the clauses labelled as 'information' are mainly descriptive and inform the reader of things such as where a specific item is placed or give instructions (Yang et al., 2012). Examples are "I know it is going to hard with William and Sister." (information) or "Please see that Charles gets a Mickey Mouse Watch for his birthday." (instruction).

Furthermore, the results of the **GSN corpus** correspond to the findings of Lester and Leenaars (1988), who argue that there is a high likelihood that a person leaves instructions behind for the survivors. Also, Foster (2003) found that 60% of people convey their love for those who they leave behind in a suicide note, which would explain why the emotional concept of 'love' is so prominent. A further observation is that certain emotions occur with a higher percentage in the GSN corpus and less or not at all in the other two. This can be explained by the higher degree of confusion that Leenaars (1988) found in the emotions in suicide notes compared to other types of discourse. Our LMT model confirms this—5 different emotions are used in the regression equation, more than for the other two datasets (see below).

In relation to the **LH corpus**, Ben-Ze'ev (2004) argued that the emotions 'happiness' and 'love' are closely related to each other because sharing activities with a loved one can generate happiness on both sides. Therefore it is not surprising that besides the feature 'information', 'love' and 'happiness' are the two most predictive emotions in the LH corpus. Since people who wrote notes in the LH corpus are happily in love, the need for expressing negative emotions is reduced in this group. The LMT model identified the presence of 'happiness/peacefulness' and the absence of 'hopelessness' as the most important predictors.

Regarding the **DH corpus**, primary emotional concepts are 'hopelessness', 'sorrow' as well as 'anxiety'. These match the emotions that the Mental Health Foundation describe on their website[3] as typical feelings people experience when suffering from depression. We can argue that overall the emotions identified in the individual corpora match those that we expected based on previous research and psychological studies. Based on the LMT model, the presence of 'sorrow' was the most important predictor with 'hopelessness' and 'fear' also playing a role.

4.2 Discussion of Linguistic Features

Linguistic features which improved the classification accuracy substantially were the length of a note, number of verbs and nouns as well as the features endearment, and relativity.

Gregory (1999) argues that suicide notes are greater in length due to the fact that the author wants to convey as much information as possible, due to their feeling that they will not have time to convey this information at a later point. This proved to be true for the three corpora analysed as the average length of the GSN corpus (144.6 words) was substantially higher than the other two (LH= 70.78 words, DL= 120.85).

Gregory (1999) further found that suicidal individuals use more nouns and verbs in their notes. This was confirmed by Jones and Benell (2007), who explain that a person who is going to commit suicide is under a higher drive and therefore more likely to refer to a large amount of objects (nouns). Our LMT model identified the number of nouns and verbs as a significant predictor.

Previous work by Ogilvie et al. (1966) identified a high frequency of emotional endearment in genuine suicide notes, which was confirmed by our analysis. Interestingly, in our LMT model the feature 'endearment' is important both for suicide notes (in its presence) and for depressed notes (in

its absence), thereby representing one of the most important contrasts between these (in many ways similar) datasets.

A further predictor identified by our LMT model was 'signs', e.g. the use of '+' or '&' instead of 'and'. Previous research by Wang et al. (2012) also identified this tendency, but Wang et al. (2012) excluded the feature, applying automatic spelling correction to increase accuracy. We argue that the feature might be important in relation to Osgood and Walker's argument (1959) that spelling or punctuation errors can be a direct result of the drive that suicidal people experience. This is particularly noteworthy since the feature harldy occurs in the LH and DL corpora.

Finally, 'relativity' refers to references to space, motion and time in a note. Handelman and Lester (2007) found fewer references made to inclusive space made in suicide notes. Again, we confirm this with the lowest relativity in the GSN corpus and the higher in the LH corpus.

5 Conclusion and Future Work

The automatic identification of suicide notes is an important research direction due to its potential for suicide prevention. In this paper, we have demonstrated that using a combination of sentiment analysis and linguistic features, it is possible to learn a model of the emotions and linguistic features that are representative of suicide notes, and tell them apart from other types of discourse, such as depressive notes or love notes. Our study can be seen as an initial investigation, which comes with some limitations and could lead to a number of future research directions.

A potential limitation of our study is that the notes included in our GSN corpus were written at various points in time, which means that some of the notes are as old as 60 years. The posts collected from the Experience Project are all drawn from an online community, so that a comparison with online suicide notes would be appropriate to investigate whether language change affects the linguistic features characteristic of recent notes.

References

E. Alpaydin. 2012. *Introduction to Machine Learning*. MIT Press, Cambridge, Massachusetts, second edition.

A. Alvarez. 1971. *The savage God: A study of suicide*. Norton, New York.

J. Bak, C. Y. Lin, and A. H. Oh. 2014. Self-disclosure topic model for classifying and analyzing Twitter conversations. In *Proceedings of the Conference on Empirical Methods in Natural Language Processing (EMNLP)*, Doha, Qatar.

A. Ben-Ze'ev. 2004. *Love Online Emotions on the Internet*. Cambridge University Press, Cambridge.

M. Coulthard and A. Johnson. 2007. *An Introduction to FORENSIC LINGUISTICS: Language in Evidence*. Routledge, Abington.

H. Cummings and S. Renshaw. 1979. SLCA - 3: A meta theoretical approach to the study of language. *Human Communication Research*, 5:291–300.

B. Desmet and V. Hoste. 2013. Emotion detection in suicide notes. *Expert Systems with Applications*, 40:6351–6358.

M. Etkind. 1997. *A Collection of Suicide Notes*. The Berkeley Publishing Group, New York.

T. Foster. 2003. Suicide note themes and suicide prevention. *International Journal of Psychiatry in Medicine*, 33:323–331.

A. Gregory. 1999. The decision to die: The psychology of the suicide note. In D.Canter and L.Alison, editors, *Interviewing and deception*. Aldershot, Ashgate, UK.

Mark Hall, Eibe Frank, Geoffrey Holmes, Bernhard Pfahringer, Peter Reutemann, and Ian H. Witten. 2009. The weka data mining software: An update. *SIGKDD Explor. Newsl.*, 11(1):10–18, November.

L. Handelman and D. Lester. 2007. The content of suicide notes from attempters and completers. *Crisis*, 28:102–104.

N.J. Jones and C. Benell. 2007. The development and validation of statistical prediction rules for discriminating between genuine and simulated suicide notes. *Archives of Suicide Research*, 11:219–233.

A. Leenaars. 1988. *Suicide Notes*. Human Sciences Press, New York.

D. Lester and A.A. Leenaars. 1988. The moral justification of suicide in suicide notes. *Psychological Reports*, 63:106.

Edward Loper and Steven Bird. 2002. NLTK: The Natural Language Toolkit. In *Proceedings of the ACL-02 Workshop on Effective Tools and Methodologies for Teaching Natural Language Processing and Computational Linguistics - Volume 1*, ETMTNLP '02, pages 63–70.

F. Morese. 2016. Facebook adds new suicide prevention tool in the UK. http://www.bbc.co.uk/newsbeat/article/35608276/facebook-adds-new-suicide-prevention-tool-in-the-uk.

D. Ogilvie, P. Stone, and E. Shneidman. 1966. Some characteristics of genuine vs. simulated suicide notes. In D. C. Dunphy, D. M. Ogilvie, M. S. Smith, and P. J. Stone, editors, *The general inquirer: A computer approach to content analysis*. MIT Press, Cambridge, MA.

World Health Organisation. 2014. First WHO Suicide Report. http://www.who.int/mental_health/suicide-prevention/en/.

E.G. Osgood, C.E. and Walker. 1959. Motivation and language behaviour: A content analysis of suicide notes. *Journal of Abnormal Psychology*, 59:58–67.

C. Osgood. 1960. The cross-cultural generality of visual- verbal synesthetic tendencies. *Behavioural Sciences*, 5:146–169.

J. Pestian, H. Nasrallah, P. Matykiewicz, A. Bennet, and A. Leenaars. 2010. Suicide Note Classification Using Natural Language Processing: A Content Analysis. *Biomedical Informatics Insights*, 3:19–28.

J. Pestian, P. Matykiewicz, and M. Linn-Gust. 2012. What's in a note: Construction of a suicide note corpus. *Biomedical Informatics Insights*, 5:1–6.

E. Shneidman and N. Farberow. 1957. *Clues to suicide*. McGraw-Hill Book Company Inc., New York.

W. Wang, L. Chen, M. Tan, S. Wang, and A. Sheth. 2012. Discovering Fine- grained Sentiment in Suicide Notes. *Biomedical Informatics Insights*, 1:137–145.

A. Wertheimer. 2001. *A Special Scar: The Experiences of People Bereaved by Suicide*. Routledge, London, 2nd edition.

Befrienders Worldwide. 2016. Suicide statistics. http://www.befrienders.org/suicide-statistics.

H. Yang, A. Willis, A. De Roeck, and B. Nuesibeh. 2012. A hybrid model for automatic emotion recognition in suicide notes. *Biomedical Informatics Insights*, 5:17–30.

Towards a text analysis system for political debates

Dieu-Thu Le
IMS, Institute for NLP
University of Stuttgart
Germany

Ngoc Thang Vu
IMS, Institute for NLP
University of Stuttgart
Germany

Andre Blessing
IMS, Institute for NLP
University of Stuttgart
Germany

{dieu-thu.le,thang.vu,andre.blessing}@ims.uni-stuttgart.de

Abstract

Social scientists and journalists nowadays have to deal with an increasingly large amount of data. It usually requires expensive searching and annotation effort to find insight in a sea of information. Our goal is to build a discourse analysis system which can be applied to large text collections. This system can help social scientists and journalists to analyze data and validate their research theories by providing them with tailored machine learning methods to alleviate the annotation effort and exploratory facilities and visualization tools. We report initial experimental results in a case study related to discourse analysis in political debates.

1 Introduction

The overall goal of our project is to develop an interactive research environment for text collections that (a) puts state-of-the-art text analysis models from Computational Linguistics in the hands of social scientists or data journalists, allowing them to quickly tailor search facilities and filters to their research goal, i.e., finding and categorizing textual passages in the collection that instantiate a relevant position towards an issue under exploration. The environment furthermore (b) relates the categorized positions, or claims, to the uttering actors, capturing dates of utterance, the relation to relevant mentioned entities, and (c) provides exploratory facilities and visualization tools for performing time-series analysis and network analysis on aggregated text-analytical results, including differential analysis against trends observed in previous legislation processes. By keeping all backward links from aggregated results to the individual underlying text sources, the environment

readily supports (d) a critical assessment of the analysis and (e) a transparent presentation of the data basis of a news story.

A major side-effect of the project is to engage in an exchange among two different explorative points of view towards large heterogeneous data collections: social scientists and journalists on the one hand have certain intuitions and strategies how to proceed when they first approach a collection which they suspect to contain some newsworthy evidence. They cannot know however which substeps in their strategy can be supported or taken over by sufficiently reliable automatic means. Computational linguists on the other hand have a wide range of analytical tools at their disposal, they know how to adapt them to specifics of some application context, and they are able to combine tools to solve more complex structural questions about a text. However, ideas for completely novel types of complex analytical questions about a text collection have to come from outside of Computational Linguistics - so professional investigators of novel questions are highly interesting partners for developing explorative strategies.

In the next sections, we will report the first experimental results, which were carried out on an already annotated dataset to illustrate how the system could be used to assist social scientists and journalists to analyze data.

2 Approach

Argumentation mining is an arising research topic (Peldszus and Stede, 2013; Moens, 2013) which models argumentation in textual content. Most theories propose that each argumentation consists of two parts: i) the premise and ii) the conclusion/claim. For discourse network analysis only claims and the actor behind is relevant. Further-

Proceedings of the 10th SIGHUM Workshop on Language Technology for Cultural Heritage, Social Sciences, and Humanities (LaTeCH), pages 134–139,
Berlin, Germany, August 11, 2016. ©2016 Association for Computational Linguistics

more, our first analysis of existing labeled data showed that there are large divergences in the way claims are annotated in the different communities. Thus, we have chosen a task-driven approach, instead of a theory-driven approach, which is defined by actual questions of the journalists and social scientists on large text collections. Which means, that we follow a supervised approach since we use a seed of already annotated text segments. Nevertheless the annotation[1] process is also well-defined by complex codebooks (Koopmans, 2002).

3 Case Study: The debate of nuclear power phase-out

In March 2011, Japanese earthquake and tsunami caused a nuclear accident in Fukushima, which prompted a critical re-thinking of nuclear power. Germany witnessed a radical political change towards an accelerated phasing out of nuclear reactors as an immediate reaction to the disaster. The sudden changes in decisions could not be explained by traditional political science theories. A few months before the accident, an agreement related to prolonging of nuclear energy use had been made, but was quickly withdrawn after the energy debate and set the final exit date to the year 2022.

A political science group in Bremen (Haunss et al., 2013) has proposed using discourse network analysis to find a plausible explanation. They examined articles in two Germany newspapers published during this time. They argued that actor centrality, consistency and cohesion of discourse coalition could be used to explain the fast development in political changes.

4 Problem statement

The problems of identifying factors for text analysis of the political science group could be stated in machine learning tasks as follows (Figure 1):

Claim vs. Non-claim classification In our case study, claims are defined to be sentences related to political opinions and decisions of actors, while non-claims are general statements without content about political decision. In the first step, claims are extracted from articles. We train a claim classification that learns from some pre-annotated claims and help the annotators to automatically find other relevant claims.

---

[1]Social scientists use often the term *coding* instead of *annotation*.

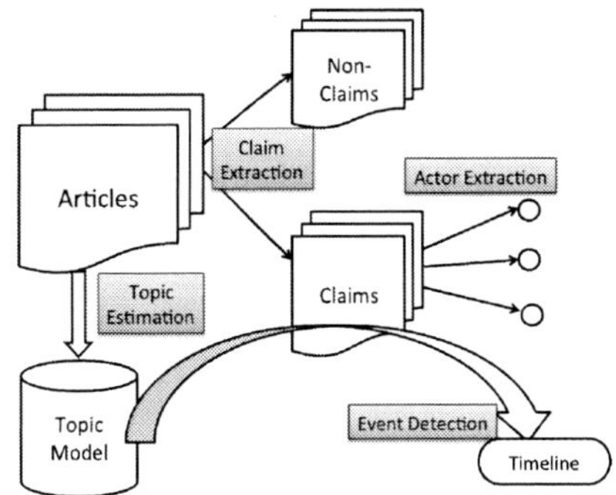

Figure 1: A computational linguistic pipeline for text analysis with main steps: Claim, actor extraction and event detection

Actor extraction One major part of the discourse analysis is to identify actors associated to each claim. We argue that using Named Entity recognition, the system can propose possible candidates for each claim and help annotators to select correct actors faster. The names of actors are usually mentioned within a claim itself or within the article where the claim is stated. By proposing a ranked list of named entities of type Person and Organization, the annotators can browse through the list of suggestions and select the correct one.

Topic estimation, trend and event detection In this pipeline, we use topic models (Blei et al., 2003) as a way to browse and summarize articles by dates and find out which topics/events are important. Firstly, a topic model is estimated from all articles. After that, we use this model to infer topics for claims grouped by dates. The topic distribution over time can be used to detect important events and to have an overview of what topics were discussed during which time.

5 Models and experiments

5.1 Term extraction

Figure 2 shows top terms that appear in claims and non-claims using term frequency (TF) and term extraction (TE). In term frequency, we counted how many times a term appears in all claims or non-claims. In term extraction, we compare how important a term is in the dataset in compared to the term appearing in a reference corpus, which is a collection of online German news articles.

The first glance at the top extracted terms from claims and non-claims suggests that terms in both categories are very similar. A traditional bag-of-

Claims		Non-claims	
TF	TE	TF	TE
Ausstieg	Salzstocks	Deutschland	Kernkraftwerke
Deutschland	designierte	Merkel	japanischen
Energien	Suchraum	Grünen	Kraftwerke
Kernenergie	Standortsuche	Japan	Teyssen
Merkel	unumkehrbaren	CDU	Reaktoren
Kernkraftwerke	geologische	Prozent	Atomkraftwerke
Atomausstieg	potenziellen	Bundesregierung	Moratoriums
Energiewende	gesetzliche	deutschen	Kernkraftwerken
deutschen	einzuspeisen	Jahr	Sicherheitsstandards
CDU	Endlagers	Ausstieg	Atomkraftwerken
Bundesregierung	Beeckens	FDP	warnte
Netz	Entsorgungskommission	Regierung	Fukushima
Meiler	inhaltlichen	Euro	nuklearen
müssen	erweitere	Atomausstieg	Huhne
Atomkraftwerke	Kaltreserve	Fukushima	bayerischen

Figure 2: Term extraction from claims and unlabeled data

word approach may not be sufficient to distinguish them to suggest appropriate claims for the annotators. Following, we present our claim classification method using deep learning to automatically detect important features for finding claims.

5.2 Claim classification

5.2.1 Settings

Claim classification can be considered as a sentence classification task. Hence, we applied convolutional neural networks (CNNs) - a state-of-the-art method (Kalchbrenner et al., 2014; Kim, 2014) for this task. CNNs perform a discrete convolution on an input matrix with a set of different filters. The input matrix represents a sentence, i.e. each column of the matrix stores the word embedding of the corresponding word. Word embedding can be randomly initialised or pre-trained with unsupervised training method. In both cases, we fine-tuned the embeddings during the network training. By applying a filter with a width of e.g. three columns, three neighbouring words (trigram) are convolved. Afterwards, the convolution results are pooled. In this work, our model used filters of width 3-5 with 100 filters each. Following (Collobert et al., 2011), we perform max-pooling which extracts the maximum value for each filter and, thus, the most informative n-gram for the following steps. Finally, the resulting values are concatenated and used for claim classification. To train the network we used stochastic gradient descent with a mini-batch size of 50 and AdaDelta (Zeiler, 2012) to adapt learning rate after each epoch. We pre-trained word embeddings with word2vec[2] using 99M German sentences collected from the news and Wikipedia. Motivated by the fact that claims are independent from person or

---

[2]https://code.google.com/archive/p/word2vec/

organization, we replaced all named entities with NE tags to improve the generalization of the network.

5.2.2 Results

In total, we have 1,837 sentences which are manually annotated as claims and 12,033 non-claim sentences. It is, however, not clear whether non-claim sentences are manually cross checked (if all non-claim sentences contain no claim at all). Furthermore to balance the claims:non-claim ratio, we randomly picked only 1,837 non-claim sentences. Table 1 summarized the average F1-scores on a 10-fold cross-validation with different experimental setups. Our results revealed that using pre-trained word embeddings and replacing all named entities with their corresponding tags are useful to improve the final performance.

Table 1: F1 score for claim classification

Systems	F1-score
using random initialized word embs	67.5%
+ replace NEs	68.5%
using pretrained word embs	70.3%
+ replace NEs	70.6%

5.3 Named Entities

We applied Named Entity recognition using Conditional Random Field explained in (Finkel et al., 2005) and the German model prepared by (Faruqui and Padó, 2010) to recognize entities in all claims. We used Person and Organization named entities to prepare a list of suggested actors for each claim.

We carried out two experiments: in the first one, only sentences where claims are annotated were used to extract named entities from; and in the second one, we further expanded to all sentences in articles that contain claims. The results are shown in Table 2, where 71.2% of actors could be found within the suggested named entity list extracted from articles where claims are annotated.

Table 2: Percentage of actors detected using NER in claims

using only sentences containing claims	51%
using articles containing claims	71.2%

5.4 Topic browsing - trend detection

Firstly, we estimated a topic model with 20 topics from all articles. Then we grouped claims by dates and inferred topics for these claims. We provide a visualization tool for social scientists to perform time-series analysis. Figures 3, 4, 5 show the topic distribution of claims over time. Figure

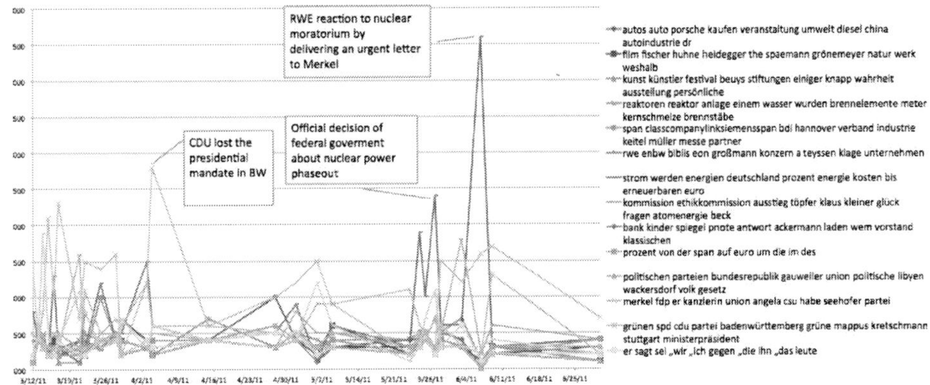

Figure 5: Topic timeline of claims related to CDU and Angela Merkel

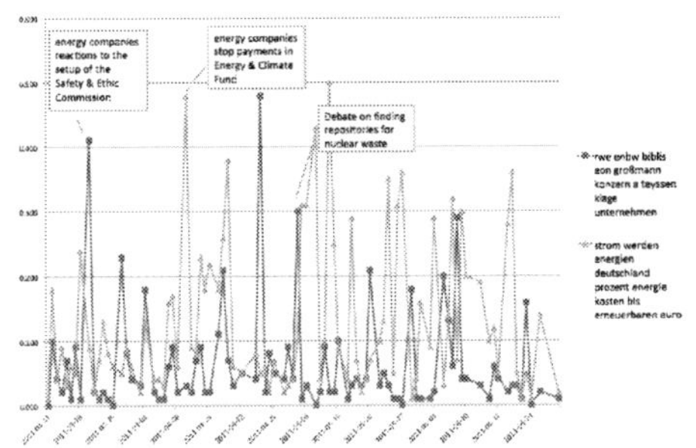

Figure 3: Discussion related to energy changing and energy companies

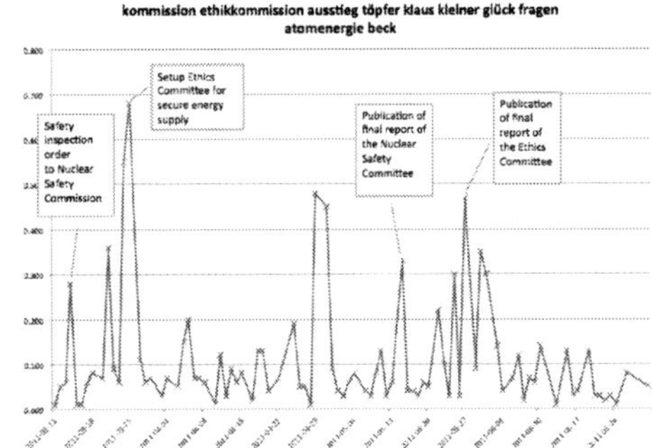

Figure 4: Timeline of discussion related to security and ethic commissions

3 shows that discussions related to the topic of energy changing heated up after the nuclear catastrophe in Japan, which involves statements of energy companies, their reactions and debates on problems such as payments in the energy and climate funds, finding repositories for nuclear waste. Important events related to the setup of security and ethic commissions to examine the safety of nuclear reactors can be spotted from Figure 4.

Finally, we grouped claims based on actors and do topic inference for these claims over time. Figure 5 shows an example of a topic timeline for the CDU party and Angela Merkel. Some events related to the election results and nuclear company reactions to the government can be spotted from the timeline (e.g., election in Baden-Württemberg (BW) - the first time CDU lost the presidential mandate, final decision of the federal state regarding nuclear phaseout, an energy company suing the government).

6 Related work

Textual content analysis in social science is still a handcrafted discipline which requires manual annotations (Baumgartner et al., 2008; Bruycker and Beyers, 2015; Koopmans and Statham, 1999). The main drawback besides the expensive manual work is that for each research questions the whole process has to be repeated. In contrast to other content analysis systems (Bamman and Smith, 2015; Qiu et al., 2015; Levy et al., 2014; Slonim et al., 2014) our approach can be seen as a bottom-up task-driven approach instead of a top-down approach based on the theory of argumentation (Moens, 2013).

7 Conclusions

In this paper, we have presented our first experimental results on building a tool to facilitate research in political and social science using discourse analysis. In particular, we focus on three tasks involving claim extraction, actor identification and timeline visualization for detecting important events and topics. In our case study, all data has been manually annotated. Our initial results show that this manual annotation process can be accelerated with the assistance of tailored state-of-the-art machine learning systems: for claim extraction, a fine-tuned word embedding system can achieve up to 70% F1-score when taking into account automatically tagged persons and organizations; for actor extraction, 71% of actors can be found using named entity recognition. Finally, we show how topic timelines could be used to spot important events related to the debate.

Acknowledgments

This research was supported by CRETA - Center for Reflected Text Analytics funded by the German Federal Ministry of Education and Research (BMBF) and by the project DebateExplorer funded by the VolkswagenStiftung.

References

David Bamman and Noah A. Smith. 2015. Open extraction of fine-grained political statements. In *Proceedings of the 2015 Conference on Empirical Methods in Natural Language Processing*, pages 76–85, Lisbon, Portugal, September. Association for Computational Linguistics.

Frank R Baumgartner, Suzanna L De Boef, and Amber E Boydstun. 2008. *The decline of the death penalty and the discovery of innocence.* Cambridge University Press.

David M. Blei, Andrew Y. Ng, and Michael I. Jordan. 2003. Latent dirichlet allocation. *J. Mach. Learn. Res.*, 3:993–1022, March.

Iskander De Bruycker and Jan Beyers. 2015. Balanced or biased? interest groups and legislative lobbying in the european news media. *Political Communication*, 32(3):453–474.

Ronan Collobert, Jason Weston, Léon Bottou, Michael Karlen, Koray Kavukcuoglu, and Pavel Kuksa. 2011. Natural language processing (almost) from scratch. *The Journal of Machine Learning Research*, 12:2493–2537.

Richard Eckart de Castilho, Chris Biemann, Iryna Gurevych, and Seid Muhie Yimam. 2014. Webanno: a flexible, web-based annotation tool for clarin. *Proceedings of the CLARIN Annual Conference (CAC) 2014*, October.

Manaal Faruqui and Sebastian Padó. 2010. Training and evaluating a german named entity recognizer with semantic generalization. In *Proceedings of KONVENS 2010*, Saarbrücken, Germany.

Jenny Rose Finkel, Trond Grenager, and Christopher Manning. 2005. Incorporating non-local information into information extraction systems by gibbs sampling. In *Proceedings of the 43rd Annual Meeting on Association for Computational Linguistics*, ACL '05, pages 363–370, Stroudsburg, PA, USA. Association for Computational Linguistics.

Sebastian Haunss, Matthias Dietz, and Frank Nullmeier. 2013. Der Ausstieg aus der Atomenergie. Diskursnetzwerkanalyse als Beitrag zur Erklärung einer radikalen Politikwende. *Zeitschrift für Diskursforschung*, 1(3):288–316.

Nal Kalchbrenner, Edward Grefenstette, and Phil Blunsom. 2014. A convolutional neural network for modelling sentences. *arXiv preprint arXiv:1404.2188*.

Yoon Kim. 2014. Convolutional neural networks for sentence classification. *arXiv preprint arXiv:1408.5882*.

Ruud Koopmans and Paul Statham. 1999. Political claims analysis: integrating protest event and political discourse approaches. *Mobilization: An International Quarterly*, 4(2):203–221.

Ruud Koopmans. 2002. Codebook for the analysis of political mobilisation and communication in european public spheres. http://europub.wzb.eu/Data/Codebooks

Ran Levy, Yonatan Bilu, Daniel Hershcovich, Ehud Aharoni, and Noam Slonim. 2014. Context dependent claim detection. In *COLING*, pages 1489–1500.

Marie-Francine Moens. 2013. Argumentation mining: Where are we now, where do we want to be and how do we get there? In *Proceedings of the 5th 2013 Forum on Information Retrieval Evaluation*, page 2. ACM.

Andreas Peldszus and Manfred Stede. 2013. From argument diagrams to argumentation mining in texts: A survey. *International Journal of Cognitive Informatics and Natural Intelligence (IJCINI)*, 7(1):1–31.

Minghui Qiu, Yanchuan Sim, Noah A. Smith, and Jing Jiang. 2015. Modeling user arguments, interactions, and attributes for stance prediction in online debate forums. In Suresh Venkatasubramanian and Jieping Ye, editors, *Proceedings of the 2015 SIAM International Conference on Data Mining, Vancouver, BC, Canada, April 30 - May 2, 2015*, pages 855–863. SIAM.

Srikrishna Raamadhurai, Oskar Kohonen, and Teemu Ruokolainen. 2014. Creating custom taggers by integrating web page annotation and machine learning. In *Proceedings of the Conference System Demonstrations , COLING*, pages 15–19.

Noam Slonim, Ehud Aharoni, Carlos Alzate Perez, Roy Bar-Haim, Yonatan Bilu, Lena Dankin, Iris Eiron, Daniel Hershcovich, Shay Hummel, Mitesh M. Khapra, Tamar Lavee, Ran Levy, Paul Matchen, Anatoly Polnarov, Vikas C. Raykar, Ruty Rinott, Amrita Saha, Naama Zwerdling, David Konopnicki, and Dan Gutfreund. 2014. Claims on demand - an initial demonstration of a system for automatic detection and polarity identification of context dependent claims in massive corpora. In Lamia Tounsi and Rafal Rak, editors, *COLING 2014, 25th International Conference on Computational Linguistics, Proceedings of the Conference System Demonstrations, August 23-29, 2014, Dublin, Ireland*, pages 6–9. ACL.

Matthew D Zeiler. 2012. Adadelta: an adaptive learning rate method. *arXiv preprint arXiv:1212.5701*.

Whodunit...and to Whom? Subjects, Objects, and Actions in Research Articles on American Labor Unions

Vilja Hulden
Department of History
University of Colorado
`vilja.hulden@colorado.edu`

Abstract

This paper investigates whether sentence structure analysis—examining who appears in subject versus object position—can illuminate who academic articles portray as having agency in labor relations. We extract subjects and objects from a corpus of 3,800 academic articles, and compare both the relative occurrence of different groups (workers, women, employers) in each position and the verbs that most commonly attach to each group. We conclude that agency, while elusive, can potentially be modeled by sentence structure analysis.

1 Introduction

In scholarship on grassroots movements and non-elite groups, the question of "agency" often looms large (Johnson, 2003). Who exactly do we, as scholars, portray as taking action, accomplishing historical change, doing rather than being done to?

With regard to scholarship on American labor unions, the main fault lines along which "doers" and "done-to" are split involve not only employers versus unions, but also the union leadership versus the rank and file, and unionized workers versus unaffiliated workers. This question has, indeed, informed some of the major shifts in the writing of labor history, as scholars have moved away from the "Wisconsin school" of John Commons, which focused on the institutional and organizational history of unions and toward a more inclusive and bottom-up social history of workers, affiliated or not (Isserman, 1976; Fink, 1988). More recently, perhaps spurred by the sorry state of American labor unions, interest in unions as institutions and organized movements has resurfaced (Currarino, 2011; Taillon, 2009). As many scholars have noted, however, there seems to often be an excess of attention to the articulate leadership and the actions of the union as an institution, even if the rank and file (let alone unaffiliated workers) may not share those views or endorse those actions (Pierce, 2010).

The question of who gets to speak for social movements is hardly limited to the history of organized labor. Similar questions about whose actions command attention (as well as about who does the hard work and who gets the credit) have been raised about the Civil Rights Movement as well (Hall, 2005; Ransby, 2003). More recently, the efforts of the Black Lives Matter movement to remain multipolar and avoid focusing attention on "leaders" have raised both the question of whether that is a useful strategy vis-à-vis the media or the public's perceptions of the significance or the message of the organization, and the question of the risks of one or a handful of "charismatic leaders" (Harris, 2015).

This paper investigates whether these problems of agency—fundamentally, who exercises some measure of power—can be perceived in scholarly writing using natural language processing (NLP) tools. A syntactic analysis has potential to go beyond bag-of-words models like topic modeling in illuminating power relations, as well as to capture more clearly who exactly is at the center of the analysis. Analysis of subjects and objects can also easily be combined with analysis of which actions are related to which subjects/objects, revealing interesting patterns about the ways different groups of actors are represented in the literature. In future work, we hope to expand the analysis by experimenting with Semantic Role Labeling in addition to syntactic analysis as well as with using FrameNet (Baker, 2008; Palmer, 2009) and VerbNet (Kipper et al., 2008) to discover patterns in the actions.

Proceedings of the 10th SIGHUM Workshop on Language Technology for Cultural Heritage, Social Sciences, and Humanities (LaTeCH), pages 140–145,
Berlin, Germany, August 11, 2016. ©2016 Association for Computational Linguistics

In what follows, we offer a preliminary analysis focusing on noun phrases (NP) that appear in either a subject (passive or active) or an object (indirect or direct) position, and of the actions they most commonly perform or are subjected to. Does this grammatical representation of the doers and the done-to reproduce the splits usually emphasized in scholarship? Who, in academic writing, appears as a doer, grammatically speaking? Do the actions associated with doers and done-to modify assumptions about who has agency in this corpus?

2 Dataset

The texts examined in this paper consist of the set of English-language research articles over 9 pages contained in the JSTOR article database answering the query ("american federation of labor"). The query was selected to weight attention toward "mainstream" organized labor rather than e.g. working-class culture or the Socialist movement, though naturally the dataset also contains articles on e.g. the radical Industrial Workers of the World (IWW).[1] This query produces a set of 4,183 articles, of which about 70 percent are published after 1945. The final set consists of a subset of 3,807 of these articles successfully processed using the Stanford CoreNLP parser (Manning et al., 2014).

3 Extracting subjects and objects

Extracting subjects and objects from the parsed articles was performed using the Stanford Tregex utility (Levy and Andrew, 2006).

The expressions used to extract subjects (active and passive) and objects (direct and indirect) are listed in table 1. The copula "to be" was excluded from consideration. As the main expressions capture rather long noun phrases (NPs), a constraining expression was used to further narrow those phrases down to more useful sub-NPs.

3.1 Most common entities

Disregarding for the moment whether an entity (NP) appears as subject, direct object, or indirect object, the list of most-frequent animate entities in the corpus reads like the cast of main characters

---


```
SUBJECT (ACTIVE):
 (NP [<<@/NN.?/])
    [$. (ADVP
       $. (VP < (@/VB.?/
          !< is|was|are|were
          !<< (be|been))))
    | $. (VP < (@/VB.?/
          !< is|was|are|were
          !<< (be|been)))]
SUBJECT (PASSIVE):
  NP  [<@/NN.?/]
    >> (PP < (IN < by))
       !> (PP < (IN < !by))
INDIRECT OBJECT:
  (NP [<<@/NN.?/])
    [> ((PP [< (IN < for)| < TO ]
          >> (VP  < (@/VB.?/
             !< is|was|are|were|
                have|had|has)))) ]
    | [ > VP $+ NP]
DIRECT OBJECT:
  NP << @/NN.?/
     > VP < @/VB.?/
          !< is|was|are|were
             |have|had|has
    !. NP
CONSTRAINT:
  NP [!>> PP & !>> VP]  [<@/NN.?/]
```

Table 1: Tregex expressions used

and issues of industrial relations, with e.g. *workers*, *employers*, and the *american federation* (of labor) as well as *legislation* and *wages* clearly represented (see table 2).[2]

Some trends can be extracted even from this basic count of subject/object NPs: for example, as figure 1 shows, women's involvement in the labor movement has been of shifting scholarly interest, with the first peak coinciding roughly with the suffrage movement and the second upward trend beginning around the rise of second wave feminism in the 1970s. Although the topic model[3] depicted in figure 2 finds a similar pattern in the data, the NP-based graph offers a much more fine-grained and more easily interpreted view.

3.2 Subjects and objects

But what about the question of agency? Is there any pattern in who appears as a subject and who appears as an object?

There is, though the results should be taken with some caution. Table 3 and figure 3 show selec-

---

[1] The American Federation of Labor was the dominant union umbrella group until the emergence of the Congress of Industrial Organizations (CIO) in the 1930s; the AFL and the CIO merged in 1955 to form the present-day AFL-CIO.

[2] The count is the sum of the times the NP appeared as indirect, object, direct object, passive subject, and active subject.

[3] Topic model created using MALLET (McCallum, 2002), 50 topics, 1000 iterations, optimize-interval 20.

NP	TOTAL COUNT
workers	13703
members	6537
labor	8148
people	6145
union	9625
work	6014
unions	8334
state	5509
men	5316
president	5465
government	4808
congress	5853
law	5485
employers	5522
organization	3340
united states	4492
employees	5427
power	3577
committee	4126
women	7399
majority	2893
attention	2735
wages	2937
american federation	1961
legislation	2678
example	3117
history	2492
study	2290
board	5774
court	9389

Table 2: Selections from the 50 most common subject/object NPs. Generic terms (e.g. purpose, example) excluded.

tions of the most frequent human or human-like entities according to the entity's degree of "subjectness." The table and figure were constructed by first selecting the 1,000 most frequent NPs in the data and then calculating for each the ratio of how many times it appeared as a subject (passive or active) versus as an object (indirect or direct). From this was then deducted the overall ratio of subjects to objects in the dataset, and the resulting figure was used as a proxy for "subjectness." Thus, negative ratios in table 3 indicate that the NP is found in object position more commonly than the average NP in the data (the count reflects the sum of mentions, each position being counted once per article). Of the 1,000 most frequent terms, few were of this "more-object-than-average" character; however, the spread of "subjectness" allows some preliminary conclusions.[4]

---

[4] We did not perform coreference resolution, and thus have no way of capturing repeated references to the same entity with different words. To mitigate this, we have used a count of how many *articles* an NP appears in as subject/object rather than allowing multiple counts per article. The order of the NPs in terms of subjectness if multiple instances per

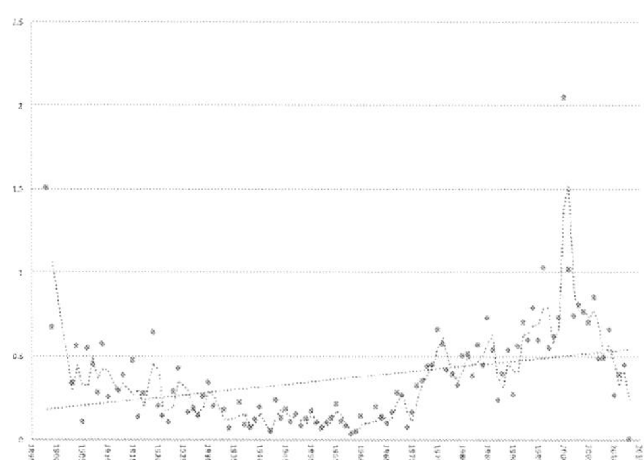

Figure 1: NP "women" (obj/subj) in the corpus

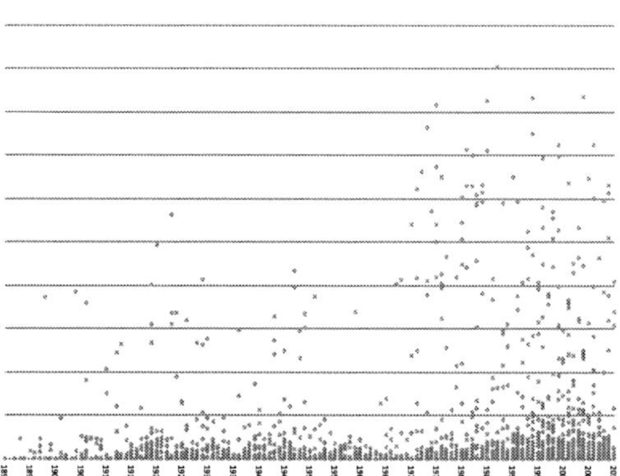

Figure 2: Topic "women" in the corpus (women women's work men woman female family male children gender working workers equal sexual sex suffrage)

On the whole, workers (even strikers) appear quite commonly in an object position, whereas the government, unions as organizations, and employers appear clearly more commonly than average in a subject position. Partly the results are explainable by specificity: the AFL-CIO and the well-known AFL leader Samuel Gompers are more likely to appear as subjects, whereas "workers" is only barely above average in its "subjectness." However, it is worth noting that "employers" and "manufacturers" are significantly above "workers" and variants thereof in subjectness. Even as "strikers," workers' subjectness is quite low—although as "unionists" their subjectness is slightly higher than that of manufacturers.

---

article are considered is very nearly the same as presented here.

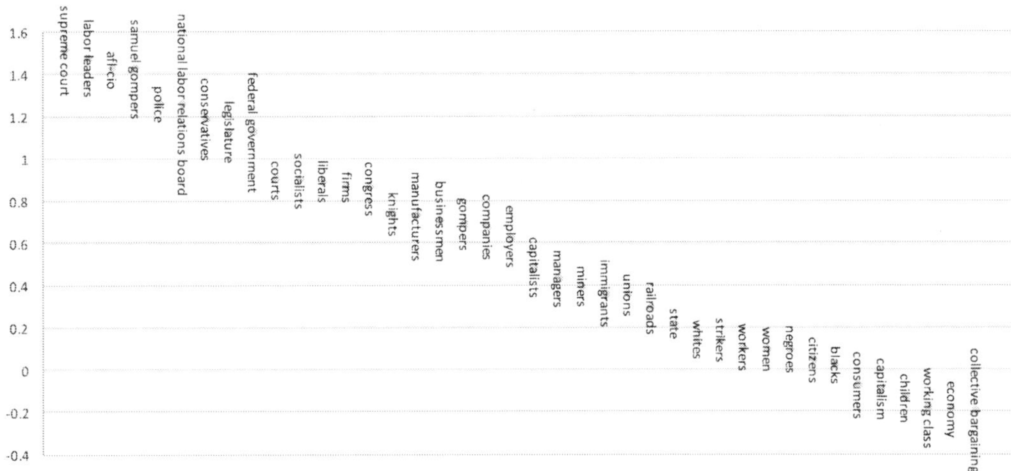

Figure 3: Selected NPs ordered from "subjectness" to "objectness."

4 The actions of doers and done-to

To further investigate the meaning of a word appearing in a subject versus object position, the most common verbs for each word and each category (object, indirect object, subject) were extracted. The indirect object category was mostly too ambiguous to draw conclusions from, involving verbs like *send*, *provide*, *give*, *distribute*; the analysis below therefore focuses on the subject versus indirect object categories.[5]

4.1 "Unions"

The verbs associated with unions as actors (subjects) are the bread and butter of union activity: they *affiliate*, *represent*, *organize*, *seek*, *agree*, *refuse*, *grow*, *demand* — and encouragingly, *win* rather more often than *lose*.

As acted-upon (direct objects), unions seem to mainly reflect worker activity: *join* is by far the most common verb, followed by verbs like *form*, *organize*, and *build*. The third most common verb here is *recognize*, i.e., achieving union recognition by the employer. However, high on the list are also *destroy*, *break*, and *prohibit*, reflecting the contested history of labor.

4.2 "Workers," "members," and "strikers"

High on the list of verbs associated with workers as actors are *organize* and *strike*; interestingly,

strike comes much higher on the list for "workers" than for "unions" (10th versus 73rd place).

"Members" as actors are clearly tied to the bureaucracy and process of union activity: they *appoint*, *vote*, *elect*, *represent*, and *participate*. Intriguingly, they also *grapple* and *adapt*.

As acted-upon, both members and workers are *organized*, *represented*, *recruited*, and *mobilized*, as well as *employed* and *hired*. However, workers are also *excluded* and *divided*, reflecting the divisions among workers and the not-always-inclusive nature of American labor unions. Meanwhile, members get *disciplined*, presumably reflecting conflicts between leadership and rank and file, and *forbidden*, possibly by police or courts. Both workers and members are the targets of someone's efforts to *educate*.

When they appear as "strikers," the main thing workers do is *return* (to work, presumably). They also *demand*, *remain* (on strike?), *refuse*, *vote*, and *win* or *lose*. As acted-upon, strikers most commonly get *replaced*. But they are also *supported*, *urged*, *aided*, *rehired*, and *reinstated* — as well as *restrained*, *arrested*, and *intimidated*.

4.3 "Employers"

Employers are not primarily the initiators of action in this corpus: rather, the two most common verbs for "employers" as actor are *refuse* and *agree*. In the top 25 are also *violate* (presumably agreements) and *resist* (presumably unions).

As acted-upon, employers in this corpus find

---

[5]Excessively generic verbs like *do* or *make* are ignored in the analysis.

NP	RATIO	COUNT
experts	2.137	250
president roosevelt	2.133	292
supreme court	1.511	1330
labor leaders	1.470	391
american federation	1.439	1656
afl-cio	1.421	338
samuel gompers	1.420	316
authorities	1.397	292
union leaders	1.307	386
police	1.259	460
national labor relations board	1.255	332
conservatives	1.184	243
legislature	1.123	555
federal government	1.120	945
republicans	0.954	426
courts	0.898	1306
socialists	0.896	461
liberals	0.887	244
congress	0.856	2524
politicians	0.787	342
unionists	0.753	320
manufacturers	0.723	411
legislators	0.721	260
businessmen	0.704	251
democrats	0.684	438
companies	0.673	698
employers	0.625	2441
americans	0.617	998
reformers	0.601	268
government	0.594	2543
cio	0.567	676
communists	0.537	521
organized labor	0.518	1080
lawyers	0.511	333
iww	0.491	286
capitalists	0.483	263
labor unions	0.438	728
managers	0.423	307
businesses	0.387	241
immigrants	0.355	487
unions	0.354	3033
railroads	0.286	403
socialist party	0.229	283
state	0.214	2900
democratic party	0.209	282
communist party	0.176	328
whites	0.137	456
strikers	0.134	765
skilled workers	0.114	237
african americans	0.107	287
workmen	0.104	435
industry	0.102	1505
workers	0.099	4627
women	0.090	1781
negroes	0.090	518
black workers	0.074	287
laborers	0.068	414
citizens	0.044	857
blacks	0.018	589
industrial workers	-0.030	314
consumers	-0.075	330
capitalism	-0.096	313
children	-0.140	1147
working class	-0.187	376
economy	-0.191	513
collective bargaining	-0.199	856

Table 3: NPs and "subjectness."

See section 3.2 for discussion.

themselves the target of efforts to *require*, *force*, *compel*, *prevent*, *prohibit*, and *coerce*, though also to *allow*, *permit*, and *induce*.

4.4 "Women"

The main thing that women do in this corpus is *work*; it seems that the main news about women as workers is that they exist. High on the list is also *enter*, probably from a phrase like "enter the workforce." However, women also *participate*, *want*, *organize* and *negotiate*.

As acted-upon, women are *given*, *organized*, *employed*, and bafflingly, *ordained*. They are also *encouraged* and *excluded* (7th and 8th position).

5 Discussion

As the above analysis demonstrates, grammatical subjects and objects function as a rough proxy for examining agency, illuminating who tends to be the doer and who the done-to: the broad lines of which NPs have high "subjectness" coincide with one's intuition of the prevailing power relations. At least as interesting, however, is that the verbs attached to each further demonstrate their different roles. Juxtaposing the subjectness and the common verbs is particularly interesting: for instance, it is intriguing that in a corpus where employers appear in a not-so-favorable light (as *resisting*, *refusing*, and *violating*, among other things), they are nevertheless as a group more likely than workers to occupy a position of agency as subjects. On the other hand, the tensions between union leadership and rank-and-file are also revealed in, for example, the fact that "members" find themselves the object of verbs like *discipline*.

6 Future research

In the future, we hope to investigate whether SRL analysis would offer greater clarity in distinguishing agents from non-agents. We also hope to refine the preliminary verb analysis presented here by using verb categories as defined in VerbNet and FrameNet. In addition, we plan to combine the type of analysis presented here with an analysis of named entities; this might allow us to investigate not only the prominence of well-known figures, but possibly also questions like whether the rise of bottom-up approaches in the 1970s or the cultural turn of the 1990s resulted in a greater variety of named entities.

References

Collin Baker. 2008. FrameNet, present and future. In *The First International Conference on Global Interoperability for Language Resources*, pages 12–17.

Roseanne Currarino. 2011. *The Labor Question in America: Economic Democracy in the Gilded Age*. University of Illinois Press, Urbana.

Leon Fink. 1988. The new labor history and the powers of historical pessimism: Consensus, hegemony and the case of the Knights of Labor. *Journal of American History*, 75:115–136, June.

Jacquelyn Dowd Hall. 2005. The long Civil Rights Movement and the political uses of the past. *Journal of American History*, 91(4):1233–1263.

Fredrick C. Harris. 2015. The next Civil Rights Movement? *Dissent*, 63(3):34–40, Summer.

Maurice Isserman. 1976. 'God bless our American institutions': The labor history of John R. Commons. *Labor History*, 17:309–328.

Walter Johnson. 2003. On agency. *Journal of Social History*, 37(1):9–21.

Karin Kipper, Anna Korhonen, Neville Ryant, and Martha Palmer. 2008. A large-scale classification of English verbs. *Language Resources and Evaluation*, 42(1):21–40.

Roger Levy and Galen Andrew. 2006. Tregex and Tsurgeon: tools for querying and manipulating tree data structures. *5th International Conference on Language Resources and Evaluation (LREC 2006)*.

Christopher D. Manning, Mihai Surdeanu, John Bauer, Jenny Finkel, Steven J. Bethard, and David McClosky. 2014. The Stanford CoreNLP natural language processing toolkit. In *Proceedings of 52nd Annual Meeting of the Association for Computational Linguistics: System Demonstrations*, pages 55–60.

Andrew Kachites McCallum. 2002. MALLET: A machine learning for language toolkit. http://mallet.cs.umass.edu.

Martha Palmer. 2009. Semlink: Linking PropBank, VerbNet and FrameNet. In *Proceedings of the Generative Lexicon Conference*, pages 9–15.

Michael Pierce. 2010. *Striking with the Ballot: Ohio Labor and the Populist Party*. Northern Illinois University Press, DeKalb.

Barbara Ransby. 2003. *Ella Baker and the Black Freedom Movement: A Radical Democratic Vision*. University of North Carolina Press.

Paul Michel Taillon. 2009. *Good, Reliable, White Men: Railroad Brotherhoods, 1877–1917*. University of Illinois Press, Urbana.

An NLP Pipeline for Coptic

Amir Zeldes
Department of Linguistics
Georgetown University
amir.zeldes@georgetown.edu

Caroline T. Schroeder
Department of Religious Studies
University of the Pacific
cschroeder@pacific.edu

Abstract

The Coptic language of Hellenistic era Egypt in the first millennium C.E. is a treasure trove of information for History, Religious Studies, Classics, Linguistics and many other Humanities disciplines. Despite the existence of large amounts of text in the language, comparatively few digital resources have been available, and almost no tools for Natural Language Processing. This paper presents an end-to-end, freely available open source tool chain starting with Unicode plain text or XML transcriptions of Coptic manuscript data, which adds fully automatic word and morpheme segmentation, normalization, language of origin recognition, part of speech tagging, lemmatization, and dependency parsing at the click of a button. We evaluate each component of the pipeline, which is accessible as a Web interface and machine readable API online.

1 Introduction

Coptic emerged as a written language during the Roman era of Egypt's history, a period of significant transformation in literacy, religion, and culture (Cribiore 2001, Bagnall 2009, Frankfurter 1998). As the last phase of the Egyptian language family, it evolved from Demotic (which was widely attested in the Greek period) and ultimately the language of the ancient hieroglyphs. Although no longer in use as a living, spoken language, Coptic remains a liturgical language for the Coptic Orthodox Church. Additionally, American Copts have attempted to revive knowledge of Coptic as a mechanism for preserving cultural heritage in Egypt and the diaspo-ra. Text corpora in this language thus hold significance for the identity formation for a current religious minority in the Middle East and U.S. as well as for research into a variety of Humanities fields, including History, Religious Studies, Classics and Linguistics, among many others.

The text corpora analyzed in this study illustrate the importance of access to original Coptic data. They originate from the formative or "classical" period of written Coptic, the fourth-fifth centuries, in the Sahidic dialect. New genres of writing emerge in this period: hagiography (saints' lives), monastic rules, Christian sermons and homilies. Coptic authors also transform and translate existing literary forms: formal epistles, gnomic sayings, and treatises. Finally, documentary sources (wills, receipts, contracts, transactional letters) as well as school exercises, prayers, magical texts, and literary fragments survive on scraps of papyri, potsherds (known as ostraca), or inscriptions and graffiti on monuments.

Our earliest witness to biblical passages in Coptic also survive as fragmentary documents or as quotations of scriptural passages within the classical Coptic texts. A fundamental, outstanding question for both biblical studies and the history of Christianity is whether our earliest known Coptic authors quoted from existing written translations of biblical books, or whether they translated scripture "on the fly" as they wrote and spoke. Coptologists have observed the influence of the Bible on Coptic composition patterns, describing some authors as writing in a biblical style (Goehring 1999:226, Schroeder 2006).

Coptic texts provide an important resource for the study of gender and language in premodern societies, as well. During a time when few texts about women were composed, and even fewer documents were written by women, Coptic letters by and about women have nonetheless sur-

Proceedings of the 10th SIGHUM Workshop on Language Technology for Cultural Heritage, Social Sciences, and Humanities (LaTeCH), pages 146–155,
Berlin, Germany, August 11, 2016. ©2016 Association for Computational Linguistics

vived, shedding light on otherwise obscure facts (Bagnall and Cribiore 2006, Wilfong 2002).

Investigations of questions like the above benefit directly from a digitized corpus with linguistic, lexical and syntactic annotations, which are quite complex. Moreover, the structure of the language and the dearth of existing digital resources for Coptic mean that the creation of NLP tools for this 'low-resource language' is more challenging than for other Classical languages, such as Greek and Latin. As we will show below, in order to study texts in the Coptic language, substantial pre-processing must be accomplished: Coptic word forms can contain multiple lexical items of interest, manuscript spelling must be normalized to allow searchability, foreign words (mostly Greek) need to be recognized, and tagging, lemmatization and parsing can allow much more detailed searches for both Linguistics and other Humanities research questions (grammatical patterns, identifying proper names, and more). The need to make these resources available to a broader audience outside of Computational Linguistics motivates the creation of an easy to use interface, which starts with transcribed text and proceeds automatically through the needed levels of analysis. The ideal architecture for such an interface is an NLP pipeline with modular components and an online API (cf. WebLicht, Hinrichs et al. 2010). This paper therefore presents and evaluates the necessary components for a new online API for Coptic NLP.

2 NLP Components

The NLP pipeline presented below offers an end-to-end solution for processing Coptic text from UTF-8 plain text or XML to segmented, machine readable data. In the following sections we describe and evaluate the different NLP tools applied to input data, including bound-group segmentation, normalization, morphological analysis, POS tagging, lemmatization, language of origin detection for loanwords, and syntactic dependency parsing.

2.1 Segmentation

Like many other languages of the Near East, Coptic 'words' in the sense of space delimited units contain multiple subunits that need to be made actionable. Similarly to Arabic or Hebrew, prepositions, conjunctions and enclitic pronouns are spelled together with lexical units in what is known as 'bound groups' (Layton 2011: 12-20),

as illustrated in (1).[1] Unlike Hebrew and Arabic, bound groups also contain verbal auxiliaries, such as the past tense base <a> in (1), and subject pronouns, such as <f> 'he'. We separate bound group elements with a '-', and smaller morphemes (e.g. affixes) with a '.'.

(1) <a-f-bōk mṇ-p-rōme>
     PAST-he-go with-the-man
     'he went with the man'

The situation in Coptic is further complicated, compared to some Semitic languages, since compounds are also spelled together (unlike Semitic construct states), and derivational prefixes may be added to lexical stems as well, as shown in (2) and (3). These must be handled, among other reasons, because we want to carry out language of origin detection later on: it is possible for only part of such a complex word to be a Greek stem, as in (3).

(2) <pe-ʃbṛ.ṛ.hōb>
     the-friend.do.act
     'the accomplice' (lit. 'act-do-friend')

(3) <t-mṇt.ref.hetḇ.psyxē>
     the-ness.er.kill.soul
     'the soul-killing'

In (3), only the incorporated object of the nominalized verb 'to soul kill' is of Greek origin (cf. 'psyche'). The agentive and abstract affixes corresponding to English *-er* and *-ness* demonstrate the incorporation (lit. 'soul-kill-erness'). For this paper, we will refer to the space delimited units such as <a-f-bōk> 'he went' and <mṇ-p-rōme> 'with the man' as 'bound groups' – these appear without spaces or hyphens in Coptic. Their constituents, such as <p> 'the' or <rōme> 'man' will be referred to as 'word units', while smaller parts (affixes, compound constituents) will be called morphs.

The first level of segmentation is separation into bound groups. Although early Coptic manuscripts were written without spaces entirely, scholars making use of our pipeline generally introduce spaces between bound groups as they transcribe. We therefore do not attempt to solve

---

[1] Throughout this paper, we will use angle brackets to denote Coptic graphemes (<b> the letter 'b' or Beta in Coptic), slashes for phonemes (the phoneme /b/), and square brackets for reconstructed pronunciations leading to spelling variation (e.g. /b/ may have been pronounced [p] and occasionally spelled as non-standard <p> by some). Syllabic consonants are marked with a vertical line below, and long vowels carry a macron.

the problem of segmenting continuous text into bound groups beyond the trivial whitespace and punctuation-based splitting.

The second level of splitting bound groups internally is the main challenge. In order to recognize the constituents of a bound group, we rely on an initial normalization, which amounts to stripping diacritics and expanding some contractions (see next section). These are harvested from our manually annotated training corpus of just over 50,000 word units. Of these, about 28,000 tokens come from Biblical texts translated from Greek, while the remainder comes from native literary Coptic texts, including sermons and letters by two abbots of the White Monastery, St. Shenoute of Atripe and Besa, as well as narrative texts from the Sayings of the Desert Fathers.[2]

Sequences known from our training corpus are immediately analyzed via majority vote, favoring the most frequent analysis in the training data.[3] For novel sequences, we rely on the assumption that each bound group contains only one open-class word unit (e.g. a noun or verb), notwithstanding compounds. Since compounds are considered single word units with multiple morphs, we can still rely on there being only one such word unit in the bound group.

We proceed to subject the bound group to a cascade of some 180 prioritized segmentation rules describing possible Coptic bound groups, which can be filled with open class items from our lexicon. The lexicon was constructed using items from the training corpus, over 4,000 items from the CMCL project (Orlandi 2004) and a further 1,700 Greek loan words from the Database and Dictionary of Greek Loanwords in Coptic[4], for a total of over 7,500 items.

Since Coptic bound group formation is non-recursive (no recursive compounding), we generate the finite set of possible derived forms using the lexicon, which accounts for compound nouns and denominal verbs. Open class items, whether listed in the lexicon or dynamically generated by this procedure, are subjected to morphological analysis. This allows us to output the final seg-

mented form with all three levels: bound group, word units and morphs.

As an example, consider the following bound group, which is decorated with several over-dots in a manuscript:

(4) <ji-nt-a-ï-eṙ.monaxos>
    since-REL-PAST-I-do.monk
    'since I became a monk'.

The original Coptic form has a spelling variant <er> for normalized <r> 'do' and dots, partly decorative and partly indicating syllabicity on the <r>. After the dots are stripped, we look for a segmentation based on rule priorities. Since this is a rather long, complicated sequence, it is not matched until rule #156, which matches the structure:

conjunction+relative+aux+subject+verb

Since the subject is pronominal the only open class element in this constellation is the verb, which is however a complex, denominal verb, derived from <monaxos> 'monk': <r.monaxos> 'being a monk' can roughly be rendered as 'do-monk' or 'monk-ify'. While <er> is non-standard orthography, the common variant <er> for <r> is listed in our lexicon. The unlisted normalized verb form <r.monaxos> can be generated from the lists of verbs and nouns, allowing the analysis to go through, as well as the subsequent morphological analysis, which attempts to find the longest possible constituent first, and only matches the option of <r>+<monaxos>: 'do'+'monk'.

Table 1 gives the current accuracy of our results using 10-fold cross-validation: some 14,000 bound groups, from the dataset described above, are shuffled and sliced into 10 equal blocks, each of which is used as test data again the remaining 90% training data. The baseline represents accuracy when no segmentation is carried out – nearly 40% of bound groups require no segmentation. Rules and training data used together achieve just over 90% accuracy, with less than 1% standard deviation.

(n=14,410)	Ø % correct	sd
baseline	39.85	1.21
training	69.42	0.99
rules	87.28	1.01
rules+training	**90.21**	0.70

Table 1: Segmentation accuracy in 10-fold cross validation.

---

[2] For a complete list of corpora used in this paper with version information and stable URNs, see the corpus references at the end.

[3] Unlike in the Semitic languages, multiple valid segmentations of the same string are very rare, largely owing to the fact that Coptic spelling includes vowels – see more below on the comparison with Semitic languages.

[4] http://research.uni-leipzig.de/ddglc/

These results are somewhat behind the state of the art in similar tasks for languages with larger data resources, such as Hebrew (92.32%, Adler & Elhadad 2006), and Arabic (between 97.61 and 98.23 on Standard Arabic news text, or 92.1% on Egyptian Arabic, Monroe et al. 2014). However, it must be kept in mind that the amount of training data available for those languages is orders of magnitude larger than the 14K bound groups used here, and that the nature of our texts is less standardized or redacted than modern newswire data. On the other hand, the relatively good results are probably due to availability of vowel information in Coptic, which is missing in most Hebrew and Arabic data.[5]

2.2 Normalization

For historical texts, normalization is an essential component for ensuring machine-actionability of data (see Piotrowski 2012: 69-84). In Coptic, at least three kinds of normalization issues must be resolved for subsequent processing: 1. diacritics, 2. spelling variation and 3. abbreviations.

Coptic diacritics are used to express non-linguistic decorations, abbreviations, or reading pause signs in manuscripts (5), linguistic properties such as diphthongs marked with diaresis or syllabic consonants marked with superlinear strokes or dots (6), as well as paleographic information introduced by transcribers to indicate damage to the manuscript (7).

(5) ⲛⲛⲉⲯⲩⲭⲏ` <n-ne[n]-psyxē> 'of our soul' (with pausal apostrophe sign at the end and raised tilde for an abbreviated /n/)
(6) ⲛⲁⲓ ⲙⲛ <nai mn̥> 'these and…'
(7) ϣⲱⲡⲉ <ʃōpe> 'become' (with underdot indicating damage to the /e/)

Although the variations in (6), which is shown in the original in Figure 1, are linguistically meaningful (consonant syllabicity can occasionally distinguish homographs), their presence is not reliable in many manuscripts, so that complete removal of diacritics is the safer strategy for input to subsequent stages in the pipeline.

Other spelling variations primarily affect vowels for which post-classical Greek pronunciation allows for confusion of similar sounds. Unlike the situation for older stages of English or

Figure 1: Diacritics in manuscript for (6). Image: Österreichische Nationalbibliothek, http://data.onb.ac.at/rec/RZ00002466

other European languages (Reynaert et al. 2012, Archer et al. 2015), spelling is relatively stable in Coptic, partly due to the phonetic nature of the script system. Most frequently we see variation between ⲉⲓ and ⲓ for the vowel /i/ (8), and various Greek letters representing /i/, such as ⲏ or ⲩ (9) (similar issues occasionally affect /u/).

(8) ⲉⲣⲟⲉⲓ <eroei> 'to me'; var. of ⲉⲣⲟⲓ <eroi>
(9) ⲥⲭⲩⲙⲁ <sxyma> 'habit', error for ⲥⲭⲏⲙⲁ <sxēma>, both pronounced [skʰi:ma]

In non-Greek words, most texts adhere to a convention where semivowels /j/ and /w/ are spelled by a simple 'i' or 'u' after another vowel, and otherwise with a preceding 'e' or 'o' (Layton 2011: 17-18). For Greek words and violations of these conventions in non-Greek words, the only recourse is to look up the word with the expected spelling of i/u in a lexicon and retrieve the normalized counterpart.

Finally, for abbreviations, such as sacred names (10), a list of common cases is maintained, which is consulted during normalization. Additionally, for some common abbreviations, such as an isolated stroke representing line-final /n/, the lexicon can be consulted.

(10) ⲓⲥ <is> 'Jesus' (for ⲓⲏⲥⲟⲩⲥ <iēsous>)

To evaluate our normalization component, we use only literary Coptic manuscript data, since the Bible data is partly edited (less than 2% of training data required normalization for the Bible dataset). Table 2 gives the results for 10-fold cross-validation.

normalization	% correct (sd)	tokens
baseline (ident)	61.12 (0)	21,400
training	89.76 (3.86)	21,400
deterministic	97.24 (1.19)	21,400
both	**98.01 (1.11)**	21,400

Table 2: Normalization accuracy.

As the table shows, the baseline of assuming the actual manuscript form is already correct is fairly high, at 61%, since very many of the most

---

⁵ At the same time, vowels introduce a possible locus for false segmentations, meaning their availability, and the resulting longer words, are not always an advantage.

frequent function words show virtually no variation (e.g. past auxiliary <a>, words like <auō> 'and'). Consulting 90% of the data to predict the correct form in each 10% of test data is also fairly successful, at 89% accuracy, since most common abbreviations will already be attested elsewhere in the corpus. However, consulting the deterministic list of most frequent variants and spelling adjustments (about 20 rules), as well as automatic handling of diacritics and capitalization variation already gives us almost optimal performance at 97%, while combining both strategies reaches 98%. It therefore appears that normalization of literary manuscripts on (gold segmented) data works well, with only about 2 words in 100 showing an unpredictable, aberrant spelling.

It should be noted, however, that our corpus focuses on prestigious, carefully copied works: a toy evaluation on 3 documentary papyri (personal contracts and letters) with only 281 word units taken from papyri.info (see Sosin 2010) resulted in 85.97% accuracy, improving on a baseline of 63.28% for this much harder dataset.

2.3 Tagging and lemmatization

Part of speech tagging and lemmatization are crucial, both in order to investigate grammatical patterns and to find different senses of the same word (e.g. as a noun or a verb, often having the same form in Coptic) or to generalize across inflected forms of the same word for non-linguistic research. Additionally, if special tags are given to items such as proper nouns, we can use a tagger to find mentions of people and places in texts, which ultimately contributes to named entity recognition (an NER component is planned for future work, see Section 5).

Previous work on tagging low resource languages has focused on annotation projection (see Yarowsky et al. 2001) from similar languages with larger training data that is available in translation in the target language. Most often, this has been the Bible, which is also available in Coptic. However, Coptic is structurally rather different from the typical 'large coverage' languages, and annotation projection approaches have typically produced results for comparatively 'general', not very language specific tag sets, with accuracies in the 70-90% range (Agić et al. 2015, Kim et al. 2015).[6] Additionally, since many native texts

beyond the Bible are available for Coptic, we decided to annotate and train a tagger on a larger variety of texts.[7]

For part of speech tagging, we use a set of 46 tags, most of which correspond to closed classes of auxiliary conjugation bases (15), pronouns (6), or complementizers (also known as 'converters' in Coptic grammar, 4). The main lexically open categories are verbs (4 classes) and nouns (common and proper), as well as some adverbs (Coptic has no open class of adjectives). The tagger's two main challenges are therefore guessing the tag for open class items that are either unfamiliar, or can be both a noun and a verb, and disambiguating closed class items. The latter can be highly ambiguous: for example, the most common functional elements in the language, <e> and <n>, can each carry 8 different tags (e.g. <e> is the prepsotion 'to', an adverbial complementizer, a form of 2nd person feminine pronoun, etc.).

In order to speed up manual tagging, and also for higher performance on noisy data, we also tested a more coarse grained tag set, collapsing several categories for a total of 24 tags. The main differences in the smaller tag set are not distinguishing each of the auxiliaries (which usually have distinct forms) and complementizers (which often do not), and collapsing all verbs to one tag (V), as well as common and proper nouns (N).

For tagging we use the TreeTagger (Schmid 1994), a fast, robust and trainable, language independent tagger based on decision trees. TreeTagger also has the advantage of carrying out lemmatization concurrently with lemma selection based on the induced tag sequence. Table 3 gives results for different subsets of the data described in Section 2.1, using 10-fold-cross validation (this time using randomly shuffled sentences instead of individual words, to maintain n-gram integrity).

tagging	% fine (sd)	% coarse (sd)	tokens
baseline (N)	14.21 (0)	15.32 (0)	50,300
all data	94.48 (1.95	95.12 (1.43)	50,300
no fragments	**94.99 (0.50)**	**95.65 (0.40)**	49,400
Bible only	95.89 (0.99)	96.14 (0.87)	28,600
documentary	87.54 (0)	92.52 (0)	281

Table 3: Tagging accuracy.

---

[6] The higher end of the spectrum contains some European languages, such as Lithuanian, while Afroasiatic

languages such as Hebrew are at more modest, near 70% performance using only annotation projection.

[7] This contrasts with Agić et al.'s titular situation 'when all you have is a bit of the Bible'.

The baseline figure is obtained by assigning the most frequent tag, N (common noun) to all items. Despite the relatively modest amount of data, performance on the entire data set is over 94%, which is above annotation projection results in previous work on other languages. Removing fragmentary sentences (under 1000 tokens) from the corpus, which contain lacunae in the original manuscripts, increases accuracy by 0.5%, though realistically such sentences are expected to occur in the Coptic data. Reducing the dataset to include only Biblical material, which is linguistically simpler than untranslated, native Coptic literature, sees a gain of almost 1%.

Switching to the coarse tag set offers a surprisingly modest gain, especially in the cleaner text of the Bible. However, we also ran a tentative test on the 281 words of non-literary papyri mentioned above: when tagging based on training data from the literary material, the coarse tag set is nearly 5% more accurate.

Lemmatization, which was also carried out via TreeTagger, is a considerably easier task for Coptic, since most words are uninflected (only about 5% of nouns and 17% of verbs in our data differ in form from their lemma). As a result, the baseline of assuming that a word has its own form as the lemma is fairly high (63%). Additionally, our lexical resources from CMCL and the Greek lemma list from DDGLC provide excellent coverage for literary Coptic, resulting in the tagger primarily having to disambiguate the correct tag to find the right lemma (under 97% accuracy). If we then assume that unknown forms have themselves as a lemma, we arrive at over 97% accuracy. Table 4 summarizes our results based on the subset of data which has been lemmatized so far, using 10-fold cross-validation.[8]

lemmas	% correct (sd)	tokens
baseline (=word)	63.01	37,800
stochastic lookup	96.78 (1.14)	37,800
no unknown	**97.23 (1.13)**	37,800

Table 4: Lemmatization accuracy.

2.4 Language of origin detection

Recognizing words of Greek and other origins is of great interest to a variety of humanities disciplines (Torallas-Tovar 2010), including religious studies, cultural history and contact linguistics. The influence of the Greek lexicon on the Coptic stage of the Egyptian language was substantial (Grossman 2013); in our data set we find about 8% word units of Greek origin in Bible data, and about 6% in native literary Coptic.

However, not all 'Greek' words in Coptic are of ultimately Greek origin: many words that are of Biblical Hebrew origin, as well as Latin words (especially official and legal terms) are well attested in Coptic. Although arguably all such words were loaned into Coptic from Greek, it is often difficult to tell – is the word <komes> 'governer, count' the Latin word *comes* or its Greek counterpart, *komes*? We therefore follow the guideline of assigning each word its earliest identifiable donor language, with the understanding that a total count of 'Greek' words may be extracted by considering all loans of this type.

Our language of origin recognizer component is fed the same normalized word units given to the tagger, which are outputted by the tokenizer and normalizer chain. They are matched against a list of items taken from DDGLC and our manually tagged data, amounting to a lexicon of over 2,700 loanword types. Additionally, we match some highly probable patterns, such as words ending in the typically Greek endings <os> or <ēs>, if they are not known to the recognizer (currently we have 8 such affix rules).

To evaluate language of origin tagging we used double-checked 7,200 word units from the Sayings of the Desert Fathers, which were translated from Greek, and three open letters by Archmandrite Shenoute and his successor Besa, abbots of the White Monastery in upper Egypt, which were originally composed in Coptic. The total accuracy for this subset (including correct negatives for all Coptic words) was 99.47%. However the entire dataset contained only 476 loanwords, meaning that a 'negative' baseline (guessing all words are native) gives 93.39% accuracy. Nevertheless, precision and recall within the data flagged by either annotators or the language recognizer was high, with 99.54% precision (almost no false positives) and 92.43% recall, for an F1 score of 95.85. Our results show that the DDGLC lemma list is very comprehensive for our data. Recall failures were largely due to (often Biblical Hebrew) proper names or their variant spellings which were not on the list.

2.5 Parsing

Syntactic parsing is an essential component in enabling information extraction (e.g. finding out

---

[8] This is the same data set evaluated above, but excluding two of Shenoute's sermons and some of the Bible data which have not been checked yet.

all predicates associated with the subject lemma 'angel' in a text), subsequent entity recognition (providing nominal phrase spans, identifying appositions) and of course the study of syntax itself. Recent approaches to parsing for low-resource languages have harnessed fully unsupervised, and semi-supervised methods, learning parsing models via simulations based on smaller datasets (Sun et al. 2014) or by analogy to larger data in similar languages (Duong et al. 2015). These approaches excel at requiring little to no manual annotation, but deliver parsing accuracy below 80%. As with tagging, we therefore opted to develop training data manually, which we complement with rule-based post-processing.

Because the construction of manually annotated treebank data is difficult and time consuming, especially for full constituent parses resembling the Penn Treebank scheme (Bies et al. 1995), we have chosen to focus on dependency parsing with a relatively simple scheme, following the Universal Dependencies project (de Marneffe et al. 2014), as used also in Duong et al.'s work. Universal Dependencies (UD) are a 'lexico-centric' formalism focused on marking relations between lexical heads, such as verbs and their arguments, while assigning functional elements such as prepositions and auxiliaries a dependent status. For example, prepositions are seen as 'case markers', dependent on nouns. Figure 2 illustrates a UD tree for Coptic.

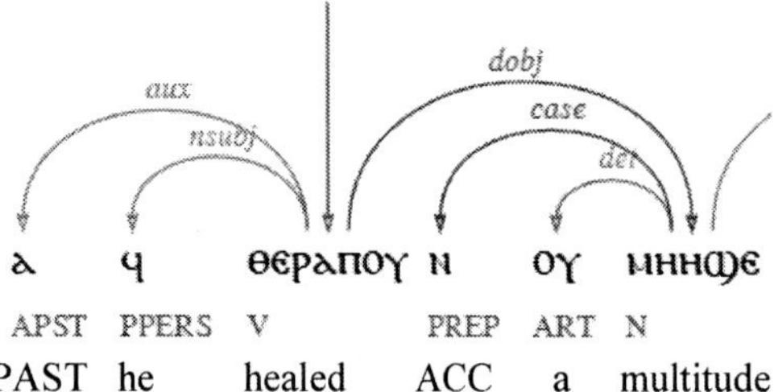

Figure 2: Coptic Universal Dependency tree from Mark 1:34: *He healed a multitude.*

Our inventory of labels follows the latest tag set at `http://universaldependencies.org/`, which includes as many as 40 labels (some rare labels, such as *reparandum* and *remnant* are not yet attested in our annotated data). Common labels include subject and object tags for nominals and clauses (*nsubj, dobj, csubj, ccomp*), case markers as seen in Figure 2, and nominal modifiers (*nmod*), among others (see de Marneffe et al. 2014 for a full discussion).

Our training data set is still very small, currently only 4,361 word units, coming from the sermons, Biblical material, and the Sayings of the Desert Fathers. The data is annotated with the fine-grained tags[9] described in section 2.3, as well as the university dependency labels and automatically generated universal POS tags as defined by the UD project. The data set is freely available for download under a CC-BY license from the UD website.

As a result of the small amount of data, only a rudimentary parsing model could be trained for the pipeline. As a baseline for parser performance we take the most frequent label for all items and assume each token attaches to its predecessor. We then test two approaches to parsing the data: using a rule based parser called DepEdit, which can apply attachment and labeling rules based on POS tag sequences, and MaltParser (Nivre 2009), a freely available trainable dependency parser implementing a variety of algorithms. Since DepEdit is not trainable, we evaluate it against the entire dataset; for MaltParser we use 10-fold cross-validation with random sentence ordering.

	attach (sd)	label (sd)	both (sd)
baseline	34.41 (0)	11.78 (0)	0.29 (0)
depedit	80.04 (0)	84.72 (0)	79.29 (0)
malt	85.72 (2.1)	85.83 (2.0)	80.09 (2.1)
malt+depedit	**85.85 (2.3)**	86.74 (2.1)	80.08 (2.1)
malt+morph+depedit	85.36 (2.4)	**87.51 (2.3)**	**81.06 (2.7)**

Table 5: Parser performance on 4,361 word units.

The rule-based DepEdit parser uses some 80 attachment and labeling heuristics, which achieve 80% attachment accuracy, almost always with correct labels (accuracy on both = 79%). These rules correspond more or less to the possible bound group configurations (e.g. connecting a verb to its subject and auxiliary with correct labels), plus some heuristics for clause juncture (attaching relative and adverbial clauses).

---

[9] An anonymous reviewer has suggested trying to train the parser on the coarse tag set and then using features from the parse to disambiguate coarse tags into fine ones. Although we were unable to test this idea before the deadline, it is an interesting prospect to go back from parses to the tagger or attempt joint inferences (cf. Bohnet & Nivre 2012). It should however be noted that Coptic subject and object pronouns are only distinguished in the fine-grained subset, which is therefore likely to be helpful for the parser.

The first Malt model[10] in the table beats DepEdit's attachment, by over 5%, with similar labeling accuracy. However, since DepEdit can apply rules to already parsed data, we tested a combined approach, in which Malt output is passed through a set of the most reliable DepEdit heuristics (60 rules) to correct very certain cases for which the small training data does not ensure correct parses. This approach maximizes attachment accuracy (85.85%). Finally, we tested automatic addition of morphological features for definiteness, gender, finiteness and subordination using adjacent articles (for nouns) or subordinators and infinitive markers (for verbs). Giving these to MaltParser produced the last model, with best labeling (87.51%) and labeled attachment accuracy (81.06%), at the cost of a small drop in attachment-only accuracy (85.36%).

3 Pipeline architecture and merging

The components outlined above are freely available as standalone command line tools, and as a pipeline wrapped inside a Python controller script. The pipeline can be accessed using a web interface, or also addressed programmatically, using a RESTful API (cf. Fielding 2000).

Communication between components uses the vertical SGML markup format used by the TreeTagger and codified by the IMS Corpus Workbench (CWB or CQP vertical format, see Hardie 2012: 390). In this format, minimal tokens of the running text are presented in a one token per line format, while XML opening and closing tags, each occupying their own line, designate span annotations encompassing multiple tokens. Spans of bound groups, morphemes, normalization, tagging and lemmatization are all expressed in this format, illustrated below.

```
<norm_group norm_group="ⲦⲘⲚⲦⲘⲞⲚⲀⲬⲞⲤ">
<norm xml:id="u5" pos="ART" lemma="ⲡ" norm="ⲧ" func="det"
head="#u6" >
ⲧ
</norm>
<norm xml:id="u6" pos="N" lemma="ⲘⲚⲦⲘⲞⲚⲀⲬⲞⲤ"
norm="ⲘⲚⲦⲘⲞⲚⲀⲬⲞⲤ" func="dobj" head="#u3">
<morph morph="ⲘⲚⲦ">
ⲘⲚⲦ
</morph>
<morph morph="ⲘⲞⲚⲀⲬⲞⲤ" xml:lang="grc">
ⲘⲞⲚⲀⲬⲞⲤ
</morph>
</norm>
</norm_group>
```

---

[10] We used the stackeager parsing algorithm and liblinear classifier throughout, as these achieved the best results.

In this example, which analyzes the bound group *t-mnt.monaxos* 'the monkhood', the entire group is encompassed by a `<norm_group>` tag and normalized by removing diacritics from 'mnt'. The feminine article 't' is recognized, split off by the tokenizer, tagged 'ART' and lemmatized by the tagger. The subsequent complex noun is also morphologically analyzed and assigned a Greek language of origin in the second morpheme. Finally the first 'norm' unit is assigned the syntactic function 'det(erminer)' and its syntactic head is set to the noun's xml:id. These pieces of information are added sequentially, as each component reads input from the tags it expects (usually the 'norm' tag) and injects its analysis as a further tag or attribute where appropriate (morphological analysis injects `<morph>` tags, tagging injects `pos` attributes in `<norm>` tags, etc.).

The format used above is also tolerant of hierarchy conflicts (hence SGML and not XML), which may arise if other span annotations exist in the input data, if it has been marked up for other properties, such as document structure using TEI XML (Burnard & Bauman 2008). Since pipeline components only look for and interact with specific tag names, any other markup in the data is simply preserved. Most frequently, such markup includes pages, columns and line break information from the manuscripts.

Individual components may be switched off, so that partial processing is possible. In practice, users may want to stop the pipeline early, e.g. after tokenization, in order to correct partial output and obtain better results on subsequent tasks. Correcting tokenization will prevent inevitable tagging errors, both on mistokenized words and their immediate neighbors. Subsequently, users can continue processing using the corrected data. Our ultimate goal is to integrate the NLP tools into an editing environment for transcribing Coptic manuscripts, so that annotators can consult the tools and get improved analyses of their data.

4 Access

All of the tools and data created within this project are open source and freely available: corpus data under Creative Commons licenses and tools under the Apache 2.0 license. An online interface and a REST API for the pipeline are available at: `https://corpling.uis.georgetown.edu/coptic-nlp/`.

Source code for both the pipeline wrapper controller script and the individual command line tools can be freely downloaded from

http://github.com/CopticScriptorium.
For more information on the NLP tools and for access to the corpus data sets, see http://copticscriptorium.org/ and the URLs in the references.

5   Conclusion and outlook

The NLP pipeline presented here is a first solution for largely automatic handling of Coptic text for Humanities research. By offering a pipeline that begins with raw, unsegmented, non-normalized text and automatically applying segmentation, normalization, tagging, lemmatization, language of origin detection and parsing, users only need to provide a transcription of the text they are working on, and receive a good approximation of a linguistic analysis of their data.

Beyond improving the existing components, and especially the tokenizer and parser, which leave substantial room for improvement, we plan to extend the pipeline to named entity recognition next, by developing lexical resources for contemporary entities (lists of people and places in 1st millennium Egypt) and harnessing nominal phrase boundary detection using the POS tagger and parser. This will enable us to approach quantitative questions spanning multiple annotation layers, such as who is mentioned where and how often, who does what to whom, what are typical sequences of events involving certain types of participants, where these differ, and more.

Acknowledgments

The research and corpus development for this paper was supported by grants from the National Endowment for the Humanities (HD-51907, PW-51672-14, HG-229371) and the German Federal Ministry of Education and Research (BMBF, 01UG1406). We thank the editors and annotators of the digital corpora used in this study: Rebecca Krawiec, Paul Lufter, Christine Luckritz Marquis, So Miyagawa, Tobias Paul, Elizabeth Platte, Janet Timbie, David Sriboonreuang, Lauren McDermott, Elizabeth Davidson, Alexander Turtureanu. Lexical resources were provided by the Corpus dei Manoscritti Copti Letterari (CMCL, http://www.cmcl.it/) and the Database and Dictionary of Greek Loanwords in Coptic (DDGLC, http://research.uni-leipzig.de/ddglc/). We would also like to thank three anonymous reviewers for their valuable comments on an earlier version of this paper. The usual disclaimers apply.

References

Meni Adler and Michael Elhadad. 2006. An Unsupervised Morpheme-Based HMM for Hebrew Morphological Disambiguation. In *Proceedings of the 21st International Conference on Computational Linguistics and 44th Annual Meeting of the ACL.* Sydney, 665–672.

Zeljko Agić, Dirk Hovy and Anders Søgaard. 2015. If All You have is a Bit of the Bible: Learning POS Taggers for Truly Low-resource Languages. In *Proceedings of the 53rd Annual Meeting of the Association for Computational Linguistics and the 7th International Joint Conference on Natural Language Processing.* Beijing, 268–272.

Dawn Archer, Merja Kytö, Alistair Baron and Paul Rayson. 2015. Guidelines for Normalising Early Modern English Corpora: Decisions and Justifications. *ICAME Journal* 39:5–24.

Roger S. Bagnall.. 2009. *Early Christian Books in Egypt.* Princeton, NJ: Princeton University Press.

Roger S. Bagnall and Raffaella Cribiore. 2006. *Women's Letters from Ancient Egypt, 300 BC-AD 800.* Ann Arbor: University of Michigan Press.

Ann Bies, Mark Ferguson, Karen Katz and Robert MacIntyre. 1995. *Bracketing Guidelines for Treebank II Style. Penn Treebank Project.* Technical Report, University of Pennsylvania.

Bernd Bohnet and Joakim Nivre. 2012. A Transition-based System for Joint Part-of-speech Tagging and Labeled Non-projective Dependency Parsing. In *Proceedings of the 2012 Joint Conference on Empirical Methods in Natural Language Processing and Computational Natural Language Learning.* Jeju Island, Korea, 1455–1465.

Lou Burnard and Syd Bauman. 2008. *TEI P5: Guidelines for Electronic Text Encoding and Interchange.* Available at: http://www.tei-c.org/Guidelines/P5/.

Raffaella Cribiore. 2001. *Gymnastics of the Mind: Greek Education in Hellenistic and Roman Egypt.* Princeton, NJ: Princeton University Press.

Long Duong, Trevor Cohn, Steven Bird and Paul Cook. 2015. A Neural Network Model for Low-Resource Universal Dependency Parsing. In *Proceedings of the 2015 Conference on Empirical Methods in Natural Language Processing (EMNLP2015).* Lisbon, 339–348.

Roy Thomas Fielding. 2000. *Architectural Styles and the Design of Network-based Software Architectures.* PhD Thesis, University of California, Irvine.

David Frankfurter. 1998. *Religion in Roman Egypt: Assimilation and Resistance.* Princeton, NJ: Princeton University Press.

James Goehring. 1999. The Fourth Letter of Horsiesius and the Situation in the Pachomian Community Following the Death of Theodore. In James Goehring (ed.), *Ascetics, Society, and the Desert.* Harrisburg, PA: Trinity Press, 221-240.

Eitan Grossman. 2013. Greek Loanwords in Coptic. In Georgios K. Giannakis (ed.), *Encyclopedia of*

Ancient Greek Language and Linguistics. Leiden: Brill, 118–119.

Andrew Hardie. 2012. CQPweb - Combining Power, Flexibility and Usability in a Corpus Analysis Tool. *International Journal of Corpus Linguistics* 17(3):380–409.

Erhard W. Hinrichs, Marie Hinrichs and Thomas Zastrow. 2010. WebLicht: Web-Based LRT Services for German. In *Proceedings of the ACL 2010 System Demonstrations*. Uppsala, 25–29.

Young-Bum Kim, Benjamin Snyder and Ruhi Sarikaya. 2015. Part-of-speech Taggers for Low-resource Languages using CCA Features. In *Proceedings of the 2015 Conference on Empirical Methods in Natural Language Processing (EMNLP2015)*. Lisbon, 1292–1302.

Bentley Layton. 2011. *A Coptic Grammar*. Third Edition, Revised and Expanded. (Porta linguarum orientalium 20.) Wiesbaden: Harrassowitz.

Marie-Catherine de Marneffe, Timothy Dozat, Natalia Silveira, Katri Haverinen, Filip Ginter, Joakim Nivre and Christopher D. Manning. 2014. Universal Stanford Dependencies: A Cross-Linguistic Typology. In *Proceedings of 9th International Conference on Language Resources and Evaluation (LREC 2014)*. Reykjavík, Iceland, 4585–4592.

Joakim Nivre. 2009. Non-Projective Dependency Parsing in Expected Linear Time. In *Proceedings of the Joint Conference of the 47th Annual Meeting of the ACL and the 4th International Joint Conference on Natural Language Processing of the AFNLP*. Singapore, 351–359.

Tito Orlandi. 2004. Towards a Computational Grammar of Sahidic Coptic. In Mat Immerzeel and Jacques van der Vliet (eds.), *Coptic Studies on the Threshold of a New Millennium. Proceedings of the Seventh International Congress of Coptic Studies*. . Vol. 1. Leiden: Peeters, 125–130.

Michael Piotrowski. 2012. *Natural Language Processing for Historical Texts*. Morgan & Claypool. San Rafael, CA.

Martin Reynaert, Iris Hendrickx and Rita Marquilhas. 2012. Historical Spelling Normalization. A Comparison of Two Statistical Methods: TICCL and VARD2. In *Proceedings of the Second Workshop on Annotation of Corpora for Research in the Humanities*. Lisbon.

Helmut Schmid. 1994. Probabilistic Part-of-Speech Tagging Using Decision Trees. In *Proceedings of the Conference on New Methods in Language Processing*. Manchester, UK, 44–49.

Caroline T. Schroeder. 2006. Prophecy and Porneia in Shenoute's Letters: The Rhetoric of Sexuality in a Late Antique Egyptian Monastery. *Journal on Near Eastern Studies* 65 (2): 81-97.

Joshua Sosin. 2010. Digital Papyrology. In *26th Congress of the International Association of Papyrologists, 19 August 2010*. Geneva. Available at: http://www.stoa.org/archives/1263.

Liang Sun, Jason Mielens and Jason Baldridge. 2014. Parsing Low-resource Languages using Gibbs Sampling for PCFGs with Latent Annotations. In *Proceedings of the 2014 Conference on Empirical Methods in Natural Language Processing (EMNLP)*. Doha, Qatar, 290–300.

Sofia Torallas-Tovar. 2010. Greek in Egypt. In Egbert J. Bakker (ed.), *A Companion to the Ancient Greek language*. Oxford: Willey-Blackwell, 253–266.

Terry G. Wilfong. 2002. *Women of Jeme: Lives in a Coptic Town in Late Antique Egypt*. Ann Arbor: University of Michigan Press.

David Yarowsky, Grace Ngai and Richard Wicentowski. 2001. Inducing Multilingual Text Analysis Tools via Robust Projection across Aligned Corpora. In *Proceedings of the First International Conference on Human Language Technology Research (HLT '01)*. San Diego, CA, 1–8.

Corpora

Coptic SCRIPTORIUM. 2015a. *apophthegmata.patrum*, urn:cts:copticLit:ap, v1.5, 2015-10-04. http://data.copticscriptorium.org/urn:cts:copticLit:ap.

Coptic SCRIPTORIUM. 2015b. *sahidica.1corinthians*, urn:cts:copticLit:sahidica.1corinthians, v1.2.0, 2015-07-30. http://data.copticscriptorium.org/urn:cts:copticLit:sahidica.1corinthians.

Coptic SCRIPTORIUM. 2015c. *sahidica.mark*, urn:cts:copticLit:sahidica.mark, v1.4, 2015-09-27. http://data.copticscriptorium.org/urn:cts:copticLit:sahidica.mark.

Coptic SCRIPTORIUM. 2015d. *shenoute.abraham*, urn:cts:copticLit:shenoute.abraham, v1.3.0, 2015-09-08. http://data.copticscriptorium.org/urn:cts:copticLit:shenoute.abraham.

Coptic SCRIPTORIUM. 2015e. *shenoute.eagerness*, urn:cts:copticLit:shenoute.eagerness, v1.1, 2015-05-27. http://data.copticscriptorium.org/urn:cts:copticLit:shenoute.eagerness.

Coptic SCRIPTORIUM. 2015f. *shenoute.fox*, urn:cts:copticLit:shenoute.fox, v1.2, 2015-05-28. http://data.copticscriptorium.org/urn:cts:copticLit:shenoute.fox.

Coptic SCRIPTORIUM. 2016a. *besa.letters*, urn:cts:copticLit:besa, v1.4.1, 2016-03-28. http://data.copticscriptorium.org/urn:cts:copticLit:besa.

Coptic SCRIPTORIUM. 2016b. *papyri.info*, urn:cts:copticDoc:papyri_info, v1.3, 2016-03-21. http://data.copticscriptorium.org/urn:cts:copticDoc:papyri_info.

Coptic SCRIPTORIUM. 2016c. *shenoute.a22*, urn:cts:copticLit:shenoute.a22, v1.6.1, 2016-03-28. http://data.copticscriptorium.org/urn:cts:copticLit:shenoute.a22.

Automatic discovery of Latin syntactic changes

Micha Elsner and **Emily Lane**
melsner0@gmail and lane.434@osu.edu
Department of Linguistics
The Ohio State University

Abstract

Syntactic change tends to affect constructions, but treebanks annotate lower-level structure: PCFG rules or dependency arcs. This paper extends prior work in native language identification, using Tree Substitution Grammars to discover constructions which can be tested for historical variability. In a case study comparing Classical and Medieval Latin, the system discovers several constructions corresponding to known historical differences, and learns to distinguish the two varieties with high accuracy. Applied to an intermediate text (the Vulgate Bible), it indicates which changes between the eras were already occurring at this earlier stage.

1 Introduction

In recent years, the study of language variation and change has been aided by a variety of computational tools that can automatically infer hypotheses about language change from a corpus (Eisenstein, 2015). In the domain of syntax, however, computational work is still limited by the necessity of manually choosing interesting hypotheses to study. For example, computational research on the syntax of African-American English (Stewart, 2014) is driven by pre-existing scholarly intuitions about the distinctive features of this dialect, but such intuitions are much harder to obtain for dead (or newly-emerging) language varieties.

This paper adopts a method for unsupervised learning of syntactic constructions previously found effective for native language identification (Swanson and Charniak, 2012), and shows that it can discover a range of historically varying elements in a Latin corpus. In particular, we conduct a case study comparing classical prose (1st century

CE) with the Medieval writing of Thomas Aquinas (c. 1270) and the intermediate stage of the Vulgate Bible (4th century CE). Such a method can be used for the initial "hypothesis discovery" step in a historical research project. Although the method is currently incapable of discovering some (lexically bound) constructions, we demonstrate that it discovers several interpretable and interesting historical changes.

The method (which we review more fully below) induces a Tree Substitution Grammar (TSG) from a constituency treebank. TSG rules are larger than Context-Free Grammar (CFG) rules and thus have the power to represent constructions, including partial lexicalization. We use chi-squared feature selection to rank the TSG rules for their sensitivity to historical change. We evaluate the rules both by building classifiers to identify the historical period of unknown text, and by manual examination and interpretation.

2 Variationist research

Computational methods for studying language variation can enhance both diachronic (historical) and synchronic (sociolinguistic) research. In some cases, the computational contribution is to build a classifier for a particular feature which is already of interest. For instance, Bane et al. (2010) target pre-selected phonetic features for analysis in recorded speech. Other computational systems are exploratory: capable of discovering new hypotheses about geographical or social variation in the data. But existing systems of this type are lexicographic. For instance, Eisenstein (2015) detects previously unknown local slang terms, such as "deadass" in New York City. Rao et al. (2010) discover words and ngrams correlated with gender and other social attributes, as do later papers such as Bamman et al. (2014).

Proceedings of the 10th SIGHUM Workshop on Language Technology for Cultural Heritage, Social Sciences, and Humanities (LaTeCH), pages 156–164,
Berlin, Germany, August 11, 2016. ©2016 Association for Computational Linguistics

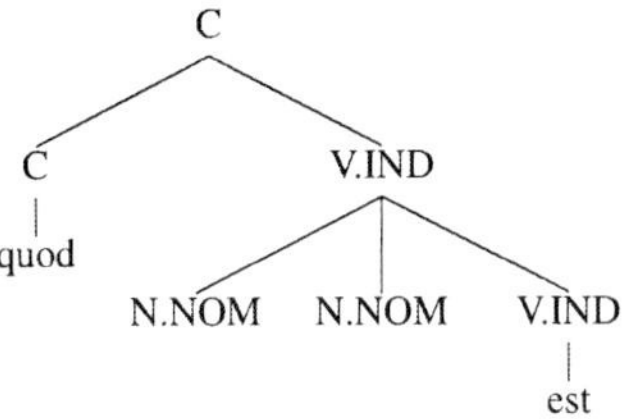

Figure 1: A TSG fragment with the root symbol *C* (complement clause), introducing an indicative subclause headed by *quod* which contains two nominals and the verb *est* "is".

Work on syntactic variation is much rarer. For the most part, it is confirmatory rather than explanatory; computational systems are designed to find examples of specific constructions in order to support investigations driven by pre-existing hypotheses. Such systems do not suggest new hypotheses from the data. Stewart (2014) detects African-American copula deletion and auxiliary verb structures; Doyle (2014) investigates "needs done" and double modals. We know of one exploratory project using syntactic features: Johannsen et al. (2015) use universal dependencies to extract "treelets" correlated with age and gender. Our TSG fragments are similar to their treelet features, but have the potential to be larger and are partly lexicalized.

3 Tree substitution grammars

A Tree Substitution Grammar (TSG) generalizes Context-Free Grammar (CFG) by allowing rules to insert arbitrarily large tree *fragments* (Cohn et al., 2009). Each fragment has a root symbol (analogous to the left-hand-side category in a CFG) and a *frontier* which can consist of terminals (words) and non-terminal symbols to be filled in later in the derivation. An example tree fragment is shown in figure 1; this fragment describes a particular complement clause structure which can be interpreted as the construction "that X is Y".

A single treebank tree may have multiple TSG derivations (depending on how it is split up into constructional fragments), so TSGs must be induced from the data. The Data-oriented Parsing (DOP) method (Bod and Kaplan, 1998) was criticized by Johnson (2002) for its poor estimation procedure. Newer methods select a set of fragments either using Bayesian models (Cohn et al., 2009; Post and Gildea, 2009) or using so-called Double-DOP (Sangati and Zuidema, 2011), which

creates a TSG rule for every maximal fragment which occurs more than once in the dataset. For instance, the fragment in figure 1 would be extracted from the trees for *dicit quod Cicero consul est* and *quod Caesar dux est scimus*,[1] since it is shared between them both, but cannot be further expanded without adding an unshared element. TSGs are equivalent in expressive power to CFGs and can be efficiently parsed using the same algorithms (Goodman, 1996).

TSGs have been used effectively for native language identification (Swanson and Charniak, 2012): determining the native language of a writer with intermediate proficiency in English, given a sample of their English writing. (Two closely related approaches are Wong and Dras (2011) and Wong et al. (2012).) Swanson and Charniak (2014) show that the rules learned by their system can be interpreted as transferring features or constructions from their native language. In this work, we argue that TSG is also useful for detecting the forms of change which occur in historical corpora.

4 Classical and Medieval Latin

Lind (1941) divides Latin roughly into Classical (250 BCE to 100 CE), Late (100-600 CE), Medieval (600-1300) and Neo-Latin (1300-1700). Though these divisions are heuristic, they do correspond to episodes of lexical and grammatical change. Medieval Latin was an educated language used by clerics and scholars. It diverges from its Classical roots partly due to the influence of the evolving Romance languages and of Church texts (themselves often influenced by Hebrew and Greek) (Lind, 1941; Löfstedt, 1959).

Scholars debate the nature and origins of variability within Medieval Latin. Löfstedt (1959, ch. 3) surveys this research. For instance, an early theory that African Late Latin was syntactically distinct was rejected on the grounds that the supposedly African constructions represented a distinct rhetorical style rather than a dialect. Similar questions have been raised about dialectal differences between France and Spain and the influences of Germanic languages on their local varieties of Latin.

A robust computational method could help to resolve controversies like these. In many cases, the dispute is centered around some construction

---

[1] "He says Cicero is consul" and "That Caesar is a general, we know".

which is claimed to be a regional variant. For instance, Hanssen (1945) claims that *mittere pro* may be a calque of English "send for", a claim which Löfstedt (1959) rebuts by providing a variety of examples from elsewhere. The constructions involved may be quite rare, and a specialist in one region or period may be unaware that a construction of interest is attested elsewhere, especially in obscure texts. An automatic method for discovering cases which vary across regions or periods could not only help to reject this type of spurious claim, but also find genuine examples of regional variation which may not have been previously noticed.

5   Case study

To demonstrate the effectiveness of our method, we use it to construct a classifier which differentiates between single utterances of Classical and Medieval Latin. The classifier features are a set of TSG fragments. We induce the TSG from training data, then run a feature selection procedure to limit their number. We show that the learned classifier is fairly effective, and analyze two sets of its learned features by hand, connecting them to the literature on known historical changes.

As a secondary question, we investigate the placement of the Vulgate Bible: is it more similar to Classical or Medieval Latin? The Vulgate is often seen as an intermediate between the two periods. Sidwell (1995, p.30) says that it:

> "sanctified usages such as changes in the use of cases and the subjunctive, and the more frequent use of *quod/quia* clauses in reported speech. ... It is linguistically a central text."

But while the Vulgate has a strong influence on Medieval tradition, its compiler, St. Jerome,[2] was classically educated; in a famous letter, he actually chastised himself for being "a Ciceronian, not a Christian" (Wright, 1933) because of his preference for classical prose over the "uncultivated" Biblical style. Running the classifier on sentences from the Vulgate can reveal how the text balances these two affinities.

---

[2] Our sample, the book of Revelation, was "slightly revised" (Sidwell, 1995) by Jerome from an older Latin translation of the 2nd century CE (Hornblower et al., 2012).

Author	Text	Sents.	Date
	Classical (Perseus)		
Cicero	In Catalinam	327	63 BCE
Sallust	Bellum Catalinae	701	c. 42 BCE
Caesar	de Bello Gallico	71	c. 57 BCE
Petronius	Satyricon	1114	c. 54-68 CE
	Late (Perseus)		
Jerome (editor)	Vulgate Bible (Revelation)	405	c. 380 CE
	Medieval (Thomisticus)		
Thomas Aquinas	Summa Contra Gentiles	9859	c. 1250-70

Table 1: Authors and texts used in the current study; dates from (Shipley et al., 2008; Hornblower et al., 2012).

6   Data and preprocessing

Our case study uses two Latin treebanks, Perseus (Bamman and Crane, 2011) and Index Thomisticus (Passarotti, 2011), each of which contains dependency-parsed Latin prose (Bamman et al., 2007). Table 1 provides a list of authors, dates and sizes. Unfortunately, the Late and Medieval groups are represented by a single author each; this represents a weakness of this project, since it will be impossible to distinguish Medieval Latin in general from the specific style of Aquinas. The data is also somewhat unbalanced, with Aquinas representing much more text than any other author. These limitations are imposed by the system's requirement for parse trees, and the unavailability of other parsed Latin data.

Both source treebanks use non-projective dependency trees. To employ the TSG technique, we convert these to constituency trees. Our conversion introduces a phrasal projection over every head word with children; following Klein and Manning (2004), we give this projection the same label as the head word's part of speech. Non-projective edges are converted to projective ones by reordering the words so that the descendants of every head are contiguous. When a subtree is moved for this purpose, its tag is marked with a diacritic, so that the grammar can learn separate

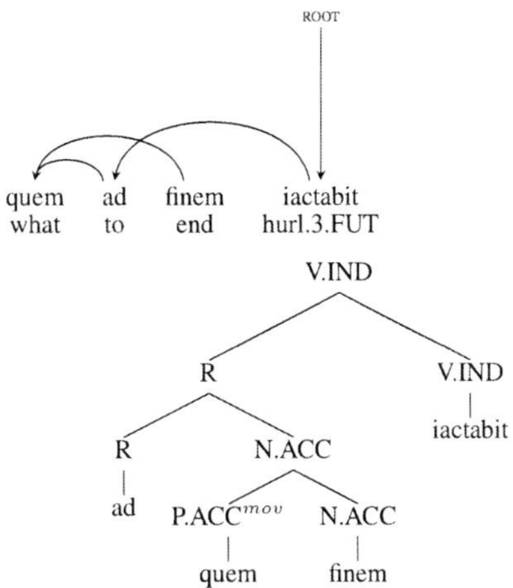

Figure 2: Transformation of the non-projective construction *quem ad finem iactabit* ("how far will [your audacity] hurl [itself]") from the Perseus Treebank into a constituency structure. ^{mov} is the "moved element" diacritic.

rules for non-projective constructions.[3] See figure 2 for an example.

The treebanks use multidimensional part of speech tags, with slightly different tagging conventions. We use only the top-level part of speech tag for most words, converting the Thomisticus tags deterministically into the Perseus tags. We use the remaining dimensions to annotate nominals with their case and verbs with their mood (indicative, subjunctive, imperative or infinitive).

Finally, again following Swanson and Charniak (2013), we selectively delexicalize the trees. This prevents the "syntactic" patterns our system learns as markers of variation from being dominated by lexical items marking different topics (Sarawgi et al., 2011). For instance, Aquinas frequently uses the adjective *Christiana* "Christian", while the Classical authors do not. But this is a change in culture, rather than in language.

We remove all lexical items except prepositions (POS tag *R*), conjunctions (*C*), and a short list of adverbials (*D*), *ne, non, tam, tamen, ita, etiam* ("lest, not, so, however, thus, besides"). We replace all forms of the verb *esse* ("to be"), which is often used as an auxiliary, with the Perseus Treebank lemmatized form *sum1*. For example, the phrase *ad quem finem* is delexicalized to *ad UNK*

UNK, although the part of speech tags remain as a guide to the grammatical form.

Finally, we split our data into random train/dev/test sections, with $\frac{1}{10}$ of each era for development, $\frac{2}{10}$ testing and the rest training. Since we do not train or develop on the Vulgate, we set this data aside as a single set.

7   Learning and ranking constructions

We extract a set of TSG rules using Double-DOP (Sangati and Zuidema, 2011). As stated above, this process yields the set of all maximal TSG fragments which occur in more than one treebank tree. It is usually more exhaustive than the Bayesian extractors (Cohn et al., 2009), although it can be slow for large corpora.

As in Swanson and Charniak (2013), we then match each rule against each treebank sentence, deciding whether that rule can occur in any derivation of the sentence. We assemble these decisions into a $(rule \times sentence)$ binary co-occurrence matrix. To compute variants which change between Classical and Medieval Latin, we sum across sentences in the training set to compute the four-way contingency table of counts: sentences with and without the rule in each era. We compute the χ^2 statistic for each table and use this to rank the rules for feature selection. Swanson and Charniak (2013) recommend χ^2 because it tends to retain moderately rare rules with good predictive power, rather than focusing on generally-applicable rules with weak predictions (as is the case for Information Gain).

We select rules for which the χ^2 probability is less than .00001 (tuned on development experiments; the corresponding χ^2 statistic is about 19). In our dataset, this method selects 357 TSG fragments. We use the Megam (Daumé III, 2004) maximum entropy classifier to learn a predictor for the era (Classical or Medieval) of a sentence given the binary feature vector indicating presence or absence of these 357 fragments. Results are shown in table 2. The classifier overpredicts the majority class (Medieval) but still achieves 77% accuracy on the minority class, indicating that its features are reasonably informative about language change.

7.1   Analysis

We will discuss two interpretable patterns discovered by our system: a known historical change in

---

[3]Unlike the construction of Nivre and Nilsson (2005), this tag is intended to *describe* non-projective constructions but does not give enough information to *parse* them.

Era	N	Correct	Acc
Classical	442	341	77%
Medieval	1972	1931	98%
Majority	2414	1972	82%
Overall	2414	2268	94%

Table 2: Classifier accuracy on test data.

the use of complement clauses, and a stable but hard-to-interpret pattern in adjective/noun ordering. Finally, we discuss our failure to detect the decline of a parenthetical construction called the ablative absolute. In each case, we have manually grouped together TSG fragments selected by the system and imposed an interpretation on them by doing additional linguistic analysis.

Classical Latin verbs like *dicere* "to say" typically take nonfinite complement clauses (Pinkster, 1990). In Medieval Latin, these verbs more commonly take finite complement clauses, often with the complementizer *quod* "that" (Sidwell, 1995, p.368). The two sentences below (the first from Cicero, the second from Aquinas) exemplify these different structures:

(1) Lepidum   te   habitare
     Lepidus.ACC you.ACC live.with.INF
     velle   dixisti
     want.INF say.2.PFV

     "You said you want to live with Lepidus."

(2) Dicitur   quod   sapientia
     say.3.PASS COMP wisdom.NOM
     infinitus thesaurus est
     infinite treasury be.3

     "It is said that wisdom is an infinite treasury."

Table 3 shows a collection of tree fragments related to this change, along with their χ^2 statistic values. The system clearly identifies the Medieval complementizer *quod* "that" with both indicative and subjunctive clauses, along with *autem* "however" and *igitur* "therefore". Although these do occur in Classical prose, the high values of the χ^2 statistic show that they are clearly much more widely used in Medieval Latin. The system also identifies the decline of the Classical complementizer *cum* ("when" with indicatives, "since" with subjunctives). The low χ^2 value (46) for the infinitival complement clause, however, must be accounted as a partial failure of the system; this fragment appears low in the selected list of features.

Fragment	χ^2	hits
More Classical		
(V.INF N.ACC V.INF)	46	69
(C (C cum) V.SBJV)	299	68
(C (C cum) V.IND)	102	24
More Medieval		
(C igitur)	353	1575
(C (C autem) V.IND)	351	1475
(C (C quod) V.IND)	161	990
(C (C quod) V.SBJV)	150	738

Table 3: Hand-selected features related to changes in complement clauses.

The system's failure to extract this construction with high confidence stems from an inability to generalize over the contents of the subclause. Due to the flat tree structure, a subclause with a temporal modifier, for example: *dico te **priore nocte** venisse* "I say that you came **last night**" cannot be unified with a subclause without. This leads to data fragmentation, and therefore to a low frequency for the construction, which reduces the system's confidence in associating it with the Classical period.

A second interpretable set of TSG fragments governs adjective ordering. It consists of all the rules *(N.case N.case Adj.case)* (a nominal, headed by a noun with a postnominal adjective) and *(N.case Adj.case N.case)* (prenominal adjective). Table 4 shows the statistics. With the exception of the ablative case, the Classical data slightly prefers postnominal adjectives, while the Medieval data strongly prefers prenominals. Ledgeway (2012) states that Classical Latin used postnominal adjectives in unmarked contexts, with prenominals serving some semantic and pragmatic functions. This preference is claimed to be stable throughout the Middle Ages, leading to modern Romance languages with mainly postnominal adjectives. Our Medieval corpus data does not follow this pattern, since prenominals are more typical. But whether this reflects an actual localized or temporary change, or Aquinas's personal style, cannot be determined without further investigation.

The ablative absolute is an adverbial modifier that is frequently used to denote a time, or the cause of an action, and often takes the place of a subordinate clause. However, the ablative absolute is not grammatically dependent on any word in its sentence (Allen and Greenough, 1983, p. 263).

Case	% postnominals		χ^2
	Classical	Medieval	
Nom	53	26	135
Gen	56	25	115
Dat	65	8	90
Acc	57	34	413
Abl	35	36	228

Table 4: Percent of postnominal adjectives in noun-adjective phrases, and χ^2 value for the postnominal rule. The Classical data contains more postnominals, while the Medieval data contains more prenominals.

It normally consists of a noun and a passive participle, (although another noun or an adjective can replace the participle):

(3)   Omni   pacata   Gallia
       All.ABL pacified.PAST.PART Gaul.ABL
       ad   eos   exercitus   noster
       against them army.NOM our.NOM
       adduceretur
       lead.3.SBJV

       "With all of Gaul having been pacified, our army would be led against them"

There is current speculation that the ablative absolute descends from either an instrumental or a locative origin (Allen and Greenough, 1983). Ramat (1991) argues that it developed from a very colloquial style of speech, as a way to compensate for a lack of "complementizers, auxiliaries, and determiners" (p. 261). Furthermore, Ramat argues that the construction is "more pragmatic than syntactic", and thus declined as Medieval Latin became more formal and syntactically rigid.

The system finds several rules for ablative noun/participle phrases, but none with a χ^2 value above 40. We detect 56 uses in the Classics and 65 in the Medieval corpus. This construction is hand-annotated in the treebanks, however, so we can check our accuracy. In fact, the Classical corpus contains 105 ablative absolutes, while the Medieval corpus has none. Our system underdetects the Classical cases due to modifiers and reorderings, as discussed above. It overdetects the Medieval ones; Medieval constructions that appear to be ablative absolutes often contain gerunds rather than passive participles, an issue hidden by delexicalization and the use of coarse tags. Additionally, Thomas favors a construction similar to the abla-

tive absolute, but which is actually a prepositional phrase:

(4)   Quem in rebus   cognoscendis
       That   in things.ABL known.PART
       quotidie experimur
       daily   experience.1.PL

       "That we experience daily **in the knowing of things**"

Thus, we miss this historical change because the ablative absolute is quite varied in form, and because our representation fails to distinguish it from similar constructions.

7.2   Late Latin: The Vulgate

We run the Classical/Medieval classifier on the Vulgate, with results shown in table 5. Despite the classifier's overall bias towards the Medieval class, we find that the Vulgate is generally more Classical. However, the proportion of sentences labeled in this way (64%) is not comparable to the 77% of Classical sentences labeled as Classical, indicating that the Vulgate is indeed intermediate between the two eras.

To determine which features most typify the Classical and Medieval components of the Vulgate, we compute the summed contribution of each feature to the entire set of decisions. If a feature f_i has weight θ_i, we compute its importance $M(i)$ over a set of examples x:

$$M(i) = \sum_x |f_i \theta_i| \qquad (1)$$

The top 5 features for each class are shown in table 6. Several features represent changes in adjective ordering (discussed above) and the use of complementizers or clause-initial markers. A few, such as the occurrence of conjunctions and adverbs, do not represent real historical changes and are presumably markers of specific topics or styles. The importance attached to the preposition *in* may reflect either a stylistic difference, or the Medieval tendency to use a preposition where Classical Latin uses the bare ablative case (Sidwell, 1995, p. 367). We believe these results show that the system can aid a linguist in finding language change, but that the output still needs to be analyzed and interpreted by hand.

With the exception of *cum*, the clausal features discussed above have little impact on the classification of Vulgate sentences. To determine whether

	N	%
Total	405	100
Labeled Classical	258	64
Labeled Medieval	147	36

Table 5: Classifier results on the Late Latin Vulgate.

Classical	$M(i)$	Medieval	$M(i)$
Postnominal adj. (abl)	868	Genitive pronouns	757
Any conjunction	768	Preposition *in* "in"	713
Preposition *super* "on"	725	Clause-initial *et* "and"	601
Postnominal adj. (acc)	631	Any adverb	559
Conjunction *cum* "when"	600	Postnominal adjective in PP	507

Table 6: Features important in the classification of Vulgate sentences, ranked by importance $M(i)$.

this represents a failure to generalize, or genuine ambiguity, we search the Vulgate Book of Revelations by hand for verbs with clausal complements; these are not particularly frequent, accounting for their small importance weights. However, both types of complements appear:[4]

(5)   his,   qui se   dicunt
      those.ABL who REFL.ACC say.3.PL
      Judaeos   esse,   et non sunt
      Jews.ACC be.INF and not be.3.PL
      "those who say that they are Jews and are not"

(6)   quia   dicis quod dives sum … et
      because say.2 DEM rich be.1 … and
      nescis   quia tu es   miser
      not.know.2 COMP you be.2 poor
      "For you say, "I am rich, … " You do not realize that you are wretched"

(7)   diabolus … sciens   quod modicum
      devil   … knowing COMP short
      tempus habet
      time   has.3
      "the devil [has come down to you with great wrath], because he knows that his time is short"

Example 5 shows the Classical infinitive clause and 7 the Medieval *quod*-clause. Example 6 ap-

[4]Translations from the New Revised Standard Edition.

pears to be a transitional form, in which the first *quod* is not a complementizer, but a demonstrative introducing a direct quote ("you say *this*: I …"). This is evident from the following first-person verb, where an indirect quote ought to be in second person. The use of *quod* here echoes the Greek text and is an instance of the well-known influence of the Greek Bible on Christian Latin (Löfstedt, 1959, ch. 6).

8 Discussion

We find that TSGs are effective at identifying several historical changes in a modestly-sized corpus of Latin text. This extends the results of earlier papers which use TSGs to identify the writing of non-native English users. Here, the same features are applied to changes across time; we anticipate that similar results could be obtained in synchronic analysis of different dialects.

The approach does have significant limitations, however. Firstly, the dependence on treebank parses limits the set of texts to which the method can be applied. Parsing historical data may require specialized techniques (Pettersson et al., 2013) and fits within a larger set of cross-domain parsing problems which are notoriously difficult (McClosky et al., 2010). In particular, we suspect that the most difficult constructions will be precisely the ones which are novel in a particular era or region, since these may not appear in the training data. Parsers for Latin of any kind are rare, although working systems (McGillivray, 2013; Passarotti and Dell'Orletta, 2010) do exist.

Secondly, as seen above, the system has trouble unifying different examples of large constructions, such as clauses with and without modifiers. This prevents it from learning constructions larger than one or two context-free rules due to data sparsity. More expressive versions of TSG like Tree Adjoining Grammar (Joshi and Schabes, 1997) have been studied as solutions to this problem, including variants reducible to TSG (Swanson et al., 2013). It seems likely that such a more sophisticated grammatical representation could help to address this problem.

Although delexicalization of all content words was effective in controlling for the very different topics represented in our corpus, it also renders the system incapable of recognizing any lexically mediated changes. For instance, the system cannot represent changes in the argument structure or subcategorization of a particular verb. Löfstedt (1959) lists changes such as datives with verbs of asking. Detecting this kind of change would require relexicalizing the trees, and therefore developing more sensitive statistical controls for topic. Due to the rarity of any individual word in a small corpus, however, a solution to this problem would be far less useful without methods for solving the previous ones as well. Only with a large automatically parsed corpus and a method for reducing fragmentations could enough examples of a lexically specific construction be gathered for any but the most common words.

Finally, the system cannot represent any changes involving semantic shifts. For instance, (Sidwell, 1995, p. 364) describes shifts in the tense system, including the use of pluperfect where perfect would be expected. Such changes cannot be detected from trees alone. Discovering them requires an ability to interpret the text and infer the implied time at which actions take place.

9 Conclusion

Despite these limitations, we believe TSGs offer a useful exploratory tool for discovering syntactic variation in corpora. Such a tool can allow historical linguists to learn about possible grammatical changes in dead languages for which they have no native intuition, broadening the kinds of questions they might investigate. This would parallel the recent use of computational systems to learn about lexical variation, allowing similar insights about the nature and history of syntactic change.

Acknowledgments

Ben Swanson, Brian Joseph, Alex Erdmann, Julia Papke and our reviewers, *gratias vobis agimus*.

References

J.H. Allen and J.B. Greenough. 1983. *Allen and Greenough's New Latin Grammar*. Caratzas Publishing Co., Inc., New Rochelle, New York.

David Bamman and Gregory Crane. 2011. The ancient Greek and Latin dependency treebanks. In *Language Technology for Cultural Heritage*, pages 79–98. Springer.

David Bamman, Marco Passarotti, Gregory Crane, and Savina Raynaud. 2007. A collaborative model of treebank development. In *Proceedings of the Sixth International Workshop on Treebanks and Linguistic Theories*, pages 1–6.

David Bamman, Jacob Eisenstein, and Tyler Schnoebelen. 2014. Gender identity and lexical variation in social media. *Journal of Sociolinguistics*, 18(2):135–160.

Max Bane, Peter Graff, and Morgan Sonderegger. 2010. Longitudinal phonetic variation in a closed system. *Proc. CLS*, 46:43–58.

Rens Bod and Ronald Kaplan. 1998. A probabilistic corpus-driven model for lexical-functional analysis. In *Proceedings of the 17th international conference on Computational linguistics-Volume 1*, pages 145–151. Association for Computational Linguistics.

Trevor Cohn, Sharon Goldwater, and Phil Blunsom. 2009. Inducing compact but accurate tree-substitution grammars. In *Proceedings of Human Language Technologies: The 2009 Annual Conference of the North American Chapter of the Association for Computational Linguistics*, pages 548–556. Association for Computational Linguistics.

Hal Daumé III. 2004. Notes on CG and LM-BFGS optimization of logistic regression. Paper available at http://pub.hal3.name#daume04cg-bfgs, implementation available at http://hal3.name/megam/, August.

Gabriel Doyle. 2014. Mapping dialectal variation by querying social media. In *EACL*, pages 98–106.

Jacob Eisenstein. 2015. Written dialect variation in online social media. In Charles Boberg, John Nerbonne, and Dom Watt, editors, *Handbook of Dialectology*. Wiley.

Joshua Goodman. 1996. Efficient algorithms for parsing the DOP model. In *Proceedings of EMNLP*.

Jens T. Hanssen. 1945. Observations on Theodoricus Monachus and his history of the old Norwegian kings, from the end of the XII. sec. *Symbolae Osloenses*, 24.

Simon Hornblower, Antony Spawforth, and Esther Eidinow. 2012. *The Oxford Classical Dictionary*. Oxford University Press.

Anders Johannsen, Dirk Hovy, and Anders Søgaard. 2015. Cross-lingual syntactic variation over age and gender. In *Proceedings of CoNLL*.

Mark Johnson. 2002. The DOP estimation method is biased and inconsistent. *Computational Linguistics*, 28(1):71–76.

Aravind K Joshi and Yves Schabes. 1997. Tree-adjoining grammars. In *Handbook of formal languages*, pages 69–123. Springer.

Dan Klein and Christopher Manning. 2004. Corpus-based induction of syntactic structure: Models of dependency and constituency. In *Proceedings of the 42nd Meeting of the Association for Computational Linguistics (ACL'04), Main Volume*, pages 478–485, Barcelona, Spain, July.

Adam Ledgeway. 2012. *From Latin to Romance: Morphosyntactic typology and change*. Oxford University Press.

L.R. Lind. 1941. *Medieval Latin studies: Their nature and possibilities*. University of Kansas Publications.

Einar Löfstedt. 1959. *Late Latin*. Instituttet for Sammenlignende Kulturforsking.

David McClosky, Eugene Charniak, and Mark Johnson. 2010. Automatic domain adaptation for parsing. In *Human Language Technologies: The 2010 Annual Conference of the North American Chapter of the Association for Computational Linguistics*, pages 28–36, Los Angeles, California, June. Association for Computational Linguistics.

Barbara McGillivray. 2013. *Methods in Latin Computational Linguistics*. Brill.

Joakim Nivre and Jens Nilsson. 2005. Pseudo-projective dependency parsing. In *Proceedings of the 43rd Annual Meeting on Association for Computational Linguistics*, pages 99–106. Association for Computational Linguistics.

Marco Passarotti and Felice Dell'Orletta. 2010. Improvements in parsing the Index Thomisticus treebank. revision, combination and a feature model for medieval Latin. In *Proceedings of LREC*.

Marco Carlo Passarotti. 2011. Language resources. the state of the art of Latin and the Index Thomisticus treebank project. In *Corpus anciens et Bases de donnes, ALIENTO. changes sapientiels en Mditerrane*, pages 301–320. ALIENTO.

Eva Pettersson, Beáta Megyesi, and Jörg Tiedemann. 2013. An SMT approach to automatic annotation of historical text. In *Proceedings of the Workshop on Computational Historical Linguistics at NODALIDA 2013, NEALT Proceedings Series*, volume 18, pages 54–69.

Harm Pinkster. 1990. *Latin Syntax and Semantics*. Routledge.

Matt Post and Daniel Gildea. 2009. Bayesian learning of a tree substitution grammar. In *Proceedings of the ACL-IJCNLP 2009 Conference Short Papers*, pages 45–48. Association for Computational Linguistics.

Paolo Ramat. 1991. On Latin absolute constructions. *Linguistic Studies on Latin: Selected Papers from the 6th International Colloquium on Latin Linguistics*, pages 259–268.

Delip Rao, David Yarowsky, Abhishek Shreevats, and Manaswi Gupta. 2010. Classifying latent user attributes in Twitter. In *Proceedings of the 2nd international workshop on Search and mining user-generated contents*, pages 37–44. ACM.

Federico Sangati and Willem Zuidema. 2011. Accurate parsing with compact tree-substitution grammars: Double-DOP. In *Proceedings of the Conference on Empirical Methods in Natural Language Processing*, pages 84–95. Association for Computational Linguistics.

Ruchita Sarawgi, Kailash Gajulapalli, and Yejin Choi. 2011. Gender attribution: tracing stylometric evidence beyond topic and genre. In *Proceedings of the Fifteenth Conference on Computational Natural Language Learning*, pages 78–86. Association for Computational Linguistics.

Graham Shipley, John Vandespoel, David Mattingly, and Lin Foxhall. 2008. *The Cambridge Dictionary of Classical Civilization*. Cambridge University Press.

Keith Sidwell. 1995. *Reading Medieval Latin*. University of Cambridge.

Ian Stewart. 2014. Now we stronger than ever: African-american syntax in Twitter. *EACL 2014*, page 31.

Ben Swanson and Eugene Charniak. 2012. Native language detection with tree substitution grammars. In *Proceedings of the 50th Annual Meeting of the Association for Computational Linguistics: Short Papers-Volume 2*, pages 193–197. Association for Computational Linguistics.

Ben Swanson and Eugene Charniak. 2013. Extracting the native language signal for second language acquisition. In *HLT-NAACL*, pages 85–94.

Ben Swanson and Eugene Charniak. 2014. Data driven language transfer hypotheses. In *EACL*, pages 169–173.

Ben Swanson, Elif Yamangil, Eugene Charniak, and Stuart M Shieber. 2013. A context free TAG variant. In *ACL (1)*, pages 302–310.

Sze-Meng Jojo Wong and Mark Dras. 2011. Exploiting parse structures for native language identification. In *Proceedings of the Conference on Empirical Methods in Natural Language Processing*, pages 1600–1610. Association for Computational Linguistics.

Sze-Meng Jojo Wong, Mark Dras, and Mark Johnson. 2012. Exploring adaptor grammars for native language identification. In *Proceedings of the 2012 Joint Conference on Empirical Methods in Natural Language Processing and Computational Natural Language Learning*, pages 699–709. Association for Computational Linguistics.

F.A. Wright. 1933. *Letter to Eustochium: Select letters of St. Jerome*. Harvard University Press.

Information-based Modeling of Diachronic Linguistic Change:
from Typicality to Productivity

Stefania Degaetano-Ortlieb
Saarland University
Campus A2.2
66123 Saarbrücken, Germany
s.degaetano@mx.uni-saarland.de

Elke Teich
Saarland University
Campus A2.2
66123 Saarbrücken, Germany
e.teich@mx.uni-saarland.de

Abstract

We present a new approach for modeling diachronic linguistic change in grammatical usage. We illustrate the approach on English scientific writing in Late Modern English, focusing on grammatical patterns that are potentially indicative of shifts in register, genre and/or style. Commonly, diachronic change is characterized by the relative frequency of typical linguistic features over time. However, to fully capture changing linguistic usage, feature productivity needs to be taken into account as well. We introduce a data-driven approach for systematically detecting typical features and assessing their productivity over time, using information-theoretic measures of entropy and surprisal.

1 Introduction

The analysis of diachronic corpora is of great interest to linguistics, history and cultural studies alike. The challenges in dealing with diachronic material are manifold, ranging from corpus compilation and annotation to analysis. Here, we address questions of analysis, notably the data-driven detection and evaluation of linguistic features marking shifts in register, genre and/or style (Halliday, 1988; Halliday and Hasan, 1985). Specifically, we focus on the *productivity* of features over time, i.e. the property of a grammatical pattern to attract new lexical items and to spread to new contexts (cf. Barðdal (2008)).

In terms of methods, we propose a systematic approach to feature detection and evaluation based on information-theoretic measures such as entropy and surprisal. These measures are based on probability in context, where that context may be the ambient context (as in n-gram models) or the extra-linguistic context (here: time, register) (cf. Section 3 for details). While we investigate diachronic linguistic change in English scientific writing, our methodology can easily be applied to other scenarios analyzing differences/similarities across registers/genres/languages/time and the like in terms of typicality and productivity.

To detect features, we employ *relative entropy* or Kullback-Leibler Divergence (KLD), a well-known measure of similarity/dissimilarity between probability distributions used in natural language and speech processing and information retrieval (see e.g. Dagan et al. (1999); Lafferty and Zhai (2001)). Using KLD, we compare different time periods and obtain typical features of scientific texts for further analysis. As features, here, we use part-of-speech (POS) 3-grams to approximate grammatical patterns. To capture productivity, we apply the notion of *average surprisal* (AvS). Using surprisal, we compare differences in probabilities for selected units (here: parts-of-speech) and contexts across different time periods and registers (here: scientific vs. "general" language), which allows us to evaluate their contribution to change in terms of productivity. For example, passive voice is considered a typical feature of scientific writing (compared to other registers) (cf. Biber et al. (1999)). Diachronically, its productivity may have been low in the beginning and increasing later on or it may first have been high and then decreasing over time. For example, in scientific writing passive may have initially been used with only a few verbs (e.g. BE + *made/seen/found*) and in few contexts (e.g. *as/it may be seen*) and then extended to more verbs (e.g. BE + *made/seen/found/observed/determined/produced*) and spread to more contexts (e.g. *as/it/that may/will/must* + VERB), which would indicate a

Proceedings of the 10th SIGHUM Workshop on Language Technology for Cultural Heritage, Social Sciences, and Humanities (LaTeCH), pages 165–173,
Berlin, Germany, August 11, 2016. ©2016 Association for Computational Linguistics

shift from a lower to a higher productivity.

In the following, we describe related work (Section 2) as well as the data, methods and analytic procedures (Section 3), followed by selected analyses and results (Section 4). We conclude with a summary and envoi (Section 5).

2 Related Work

Existing work on diachronic change in scientific language typically focuses on short-term change (e.g. work on the ACL anthology corpus; (Hall et al., 2008)) and mostly investigates lexis-related change (e.g. topical shifts). Here, we address long-term change and grammatical patterns, focusing on their productivity.

Productivity has a long history in the field of derivational morphology, i.e. the word formation processes employed by speakers to generate new words. Different methods have been proposed to measure productivity of affixes (e.g. Baayen and Lieber (1991); Hay and Baayen (2002)). More recently, there is also some interest in modeling syntactic productivity, i.e. the combination of syntactic patterns or constructions with lexical items, with approaches ranging from simple measures such as proportional preference (Biber, 2012) to collostructions (Stefanowitsch and Gries, 2003) and distributional semantics (Perek, 2014, 2016).

In corpus linguistics, existing approaches to diachronic change are essentially frequency-based and work from predefined features known to be involved in linguistic change (e.g. Biber and Gray (2011); Gray and Biber (2012); Taavitsainen and Pahta (2012); Moskowich and Crespo (2012)). While frequency is clearly a major indicator of change, it does not provide a full picture. To investigate syntactic productivity, we clearly need an approach which accounts for context of use. Perek (2014), for instance, considers the semantic context of a specific lexical phrase (V *the hell out of* NP) in diachrony (from 1930 to 2009 in the COCA corpus (Davies, 2008)) by applying distributional semantic models. He shows how the different verbs filling the lexical phrase are semantically related and how visualization techniques and statistical modeling can be used to analyze the semantic development of a construction in terms of syntactic productivity.

We model the productivity of grammatical patterns that become increasingly typical over time by using the notion of *surprisal*. Surprisal is rooted in information theory (Shannon, 1949) and is widely applied in psycholinguistic studies (e.g. Hale (2001); Levy (2008); Demberg and Keller (2008)) to assess cognitive processing effort. We apply surprisal to calculate a unit's probability in context to analyze diachronic shifts in productivity considering a unit's probability in a given context as well as the probability of a context with a given unit (see more details in Section 3).

3 Data and methods

Data The corpus of scientific writing we use consists of the first two centuries of publication of the Royal Society of London (1665-1869; RSC), altogether 35 million tokens (Kermes et al., 2016). It is encoded for text type (article, abstract), author and date of publication. For analysis, the corpus can be flexibly chunked up in different time periods (e.g. decades). Linguistic annotation of the corpus has been obtained by using existing tools: VARD (Baron and Rayson, 2008) for normalization and TreeTagger (Schmid, 1994, 1995) for tokenization, lemmatization and part-of-speech (POS) tagging. For training and evaluation, we created a manually annotated (normalization, part-of-speech tags) subcorpus ($\sim$56.000 tokens). The trained model for VARD exhibited a 10% increase (61.8% to 72.8%) and double the recall (31.3% to 57.7%). For TreeTagger we obtained 95.1% on normalized word forms (Kermes et al., 2016). This procedure ensured a relatively reliable part-of-speech tagging of historical texts.

For comparative purposes, we employ a register-mixed corpus, the Corpus of Late Modern English Texts, version 3.0 (CLMET) (Diller et al., 2011), which has a similar size and roughly spans the same period (1710-1920) as the RSC.

Methods and analytic procedures For feature detection, we create KLD models for RSC on the basis of part-of-speech (POS) 3-grams[1]. Kullback-Leibler Divergence (or *relative entropy*) measures the difference between two probability distributions by calculating the difference in the number of bits between the cross-entropy of two data sets A and B and the entropy of A alone, i.e. $H(A; B) - H(A)$. The more additional bits are

---

[1] To further avoid possible POS tagging errors, in the extraction procedure nouns were restricted to a size of >2 characters. Furthermore, we exclude POS 3-grams consisting of characters constituting sentence markers (e.g. fullstops, colons), brackets, symbols (e.g. equal signs), and words tagged as foreign words.

needed for encoding a given unit (here: POS 3-gram), the more distinctive (and thus typical) that unit is for a given time period vs. another time period. On this basis, we compare the probabilities of 3-grams across the five time periods in RSC[2], aiming to obtain those 3-grams that become increasingly typical of scientific language over time. For this, we create four KLD models for each (fifty years) time period, starting with 1700 vs. its preceding time period based on 1184 POS 3-grams. We then inspect the ranking (based on KLD values) of 3-grams typical of one time period vs. a previous time period. Thus, we obtain the 3-grams typical of 1700 vs. 1650, 1750 vs. 1700, 1800 vs. 1750, 1850 vs. 1800.

We then further analyze selected typical 3-grams in terms of relative frequency, comparing their distributions across RSC. In addition, to confirm typicality within scientific language, we also compare the use of these 3-grams within a general language corpus (CLMET) (cf. Section 4.2).

For studying productivity we apply *surprisal*, a measure of information calculating the number of bits used to encode a message. The amount of bits being transmitted by a given linguistic unit in a running text depends on that unit's probability in context. Formally, surprisal is quantified as the negative log probability of a unit (e.g. a word) in context (e.g. its preceding words):

$$S(unit) = -\log_2 p(unit|context)$$

In corpus analysis, we are interested in the surprisal of all occurrences of a given linguistic unit, i.e. its *average surprisal*:

$$AvS(unit) = \frac{1}{|unit|} \sum_i -\log_2 p(unit_i|context_i)$$

For instance, using words (uni-grams) as units, we can inspect whether a given word is more "surprising" in one context vs. in another context. We create AvS models for RSC and CLMET on the basis of uni-grams in the context of three preceding tokens and compare the AvS of the selected 3-grams across RSC and CLMET. For assessing their productivity, we inspect the AvS ranges of their lexical heads in the preceding context of three tokens as well as their type-token ratios (cf. Section 4.3).

---

[2](1650: 1665–1699, 1700: 1700–1749, 1750: 1750–1799, 1800: 1800–1849, 1850: 1850–1869)

3-gram	example	type
DT.JJ.JJ	*the same general*	nominal
NN.TO.DT	*respect to the*	
TO.DT.JJ	*to the same*	prepositional
IN.VVG.DT	*for determining the*	gerund
DT.NN.VBZ	*the latter is*	verbal; BE
VV.DT.JJ	*produce the same*	verbal; base form
VV.IN.DT	*account for the*	
MD.VB.VVN	*will be found*	
VB.VVN.IN	*be considered as*	verbal; passive
VBD.VVN.IN	*were made with*	
VBZ.VVN.IN	*is composed of*	
VVN.TO.VV	*found to contain*	verbal; to-inf

DT: determiner, JJ: adjective, IN: preposition, MD: modal verb, NN: common noun, TO: to-particle/preposition, VB: verb *be*, VBD: verb *be* past, VBZ: verb *be* present, VV: verb base form, VVG: ing-verb, VVN: past tense verb

Table 1: List of 3-grams increasingly typical in RSC obtained from KLD ranking

4 Analysis and results

4.1 Typicality

From the KLD models (built as described in Section 3), we obtain altogether twelve 3-grams which become increasingly typical over time (see Table 1). A subset of these clearly reflect particular (sets of) grammatical patterns.

Consider, for example, the gerund 3-gram consisting of a preposition followed by an *ing*-verb and a determiner (IN.VVG.DT). According to previous historical linguistic studies (cf. De Smet (2008); Fanego (2004, 2006)), this grammatical pattern reflects the verbal gerund, which has been shown to have developed from Middle English onwards. By our method, we can show that it becomes increasingly typical in scientific writing over time, confirming also Gray and Biber (2012)'s frequency-based results. Another grammatical pattern that becomes increasingly typical in our data is passive voice (reflected by four 3-grams; see again Table 1), which is in line with standard reference works on English Grammar, such as Biber et al. (1999). In addition, there are also two nominal patterns which become increasingly typical over time (DT.JJ.JJ and NN.TO.DT) as well as a prepositional pattern (TO.DT.JJ) and other verbal patterns (DT.NN.VBZ, VV.DT.JJ, VV.IN.DT, and VVN.TO.VV).

In the following, we focus on the two grammatical patterns gerund and passive (overall five 3-grams).

4.2 Frequency-based diachronic changes

All five 3-grams increase in frequency up until 1800 in RSC (see Figure 1 showing frequencies per million in the five time periods). The gerund then drops from 1800 to 1850. The past passive decreases from 1800 to 1850, while the present passive increases. This may indicate a replacement of past tense with present tense for the passive in RSC. The modal passive and BE passive seem to develop a stable distribution from 1750 onwards.

Comparing RSC with CLMET (compare Figure 1 with Figure 2), while there is generally a frequency increase in RSC, CLMET shows a decreasing tendency. Nevertheless, the past passive increases both in RSC and CLMET from 1700 to 1750 to a similar level, but then while in RSC it keeps increasing till 1800, in CLMET it decreases.

Considering the gerund 3-gram, it shows similar frequencies across RSC and CLMET around 1700, while it clearly drops in use in CLMET compared to RSC around 1850. Passive 3-grams show a similar tendency: all 3-grams are less frequently used in CLMET than in RSC around 1850, even though around 1700 3-grams with the verb *be* in base form (modal passive, BE passive) were used to similar extents in RSC and CLMET. Finally, the present passive is less frequently used over time in both RSC and CLMET.

In summary, scientific writing and general language become increasingly distinct over the given time period: Overall, in RSC the gerund as well as the passive increase in frequency, in CLMET their frequencies decrease. This indicates an increasingly more formal, expository and abstract style of scientific written English in comparison to "general" English.

4.3 Productivity

In our discussion of productivity, we focus on the gerund (IN.VVG.DT) and the modal passive (MD.VB.VVN) 3-grams.

4.3.1 Number of types/tokens

To inspect degree of lexical variation, we consider how many types a 3-gram has per tokens over the time periods of RSC and CLMET. We observe that RSC uses fewer types over time, while in CLMET the number of types is fairly stable from 1750 onwards. See Figure 3 and Figure 4 showing the gerund and the modal passive 3-gram, respectively. Thus, in scientific writing the lexical variation of these typical 3-grams goes down over time, giving rise to a more conventionalized use (lower productivity). In general language, instead, lexical variation in these 3-grams increases. Note that overall, the variation is mainly due to the lexical units in the two 3-grams, i.e. VVG and VVN, since the other parts-of-speech are function words.

4.3.2 Preceding contexts

To inspect variation in context, we consider the average surprisal (AvS) of the individual verbs filling

Figure 1: Diachronic frequency distribution of gerund (dashed line) and passive 3-grams in RSC

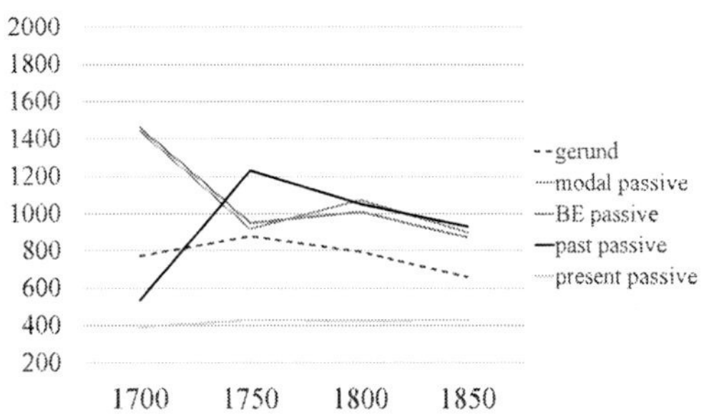

Figure 2: Diachronic frequency distribution of gerund (dashed line) and passive 3-grams in CLMET

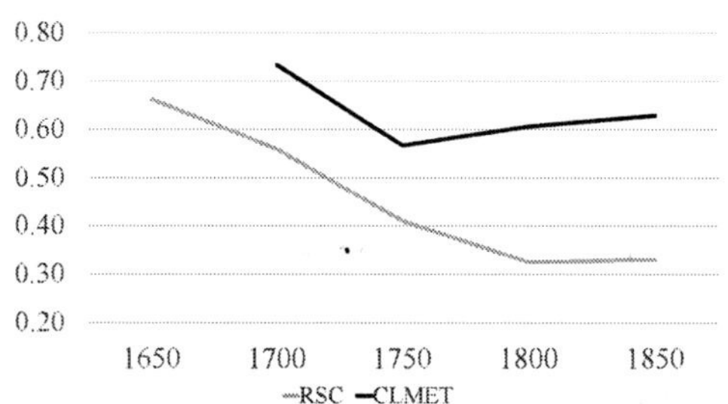

Figure 3: Types per tokens for the gerund 3-gram (IN.VVG.DT)

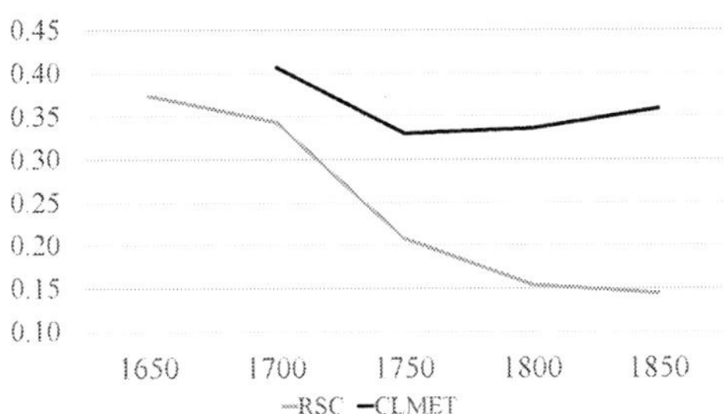

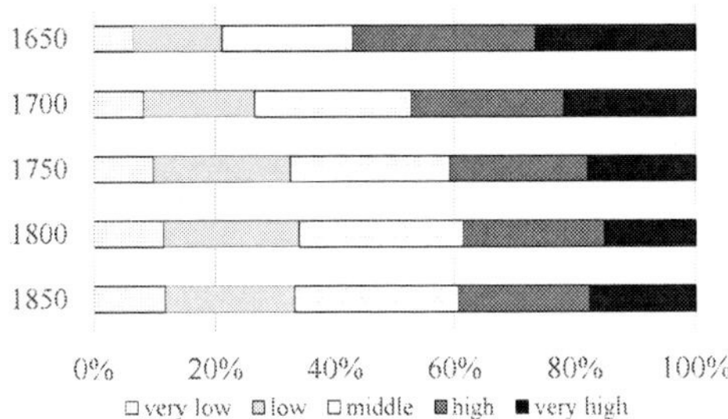

Figure 4: Types per tokens for the modal passive 3-gram (MD.VB.VVN)

Figure 5: AvS values of lexical verb in the gerund 3-gram (RSC)

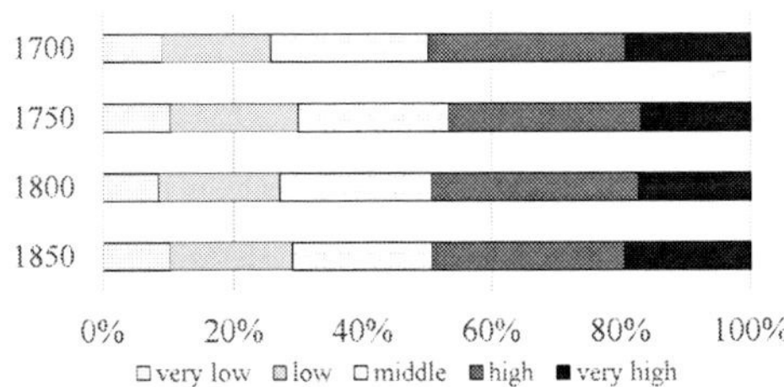

Figure 6: AvS values of lexical verb in the gerund 3-gram (CLMET)

VVG and VVN in their preceding contexts of three words:

$$AvS(verb) = \frac{1}{|verb|} \sum_i - \log_2 p(verb_i | w_{i-1} w_{i-2} w_{i-3})$$

Here we want to see whether these verbs obtain rather low or rather high AvS values. Low values would indicate a relatively conventionalized use of the verb in its context, i.e. a low degree of productivity, because based on its preceding words the verb is quite predictable. High AvS values would point to verbs which are hard to predict by their previous context (e.g. new verbs entering the vocabulary, which would indicate a higher degree of productivity).

The AvS values range from 0 to 22. For comparison, we define a scale based on five quantiles.

Gerund (VVG) Figure 5 shows the AvS distribution of the lexical verbs realizing the gerund 3-gram. Diachronically, in RSC an increasing number of verbs have very low to low AvS values (from ~20% in 1650 to ~30% in 1850, see light gray shades) but a decreasing number have high to very high AvS values (from ~60% in 1650 to ~40% in 1850, see dark shades). This seems to indicate that an increasing number of verbs are used over time in the same context pointing to lower productivity, while rare, untypical or new verbs become less frequent. The middle range (white shade) remains relatively stable over time. Comparing this to the AvS of the lexical verbs realizing the gerund in CLMET, a different tendency is observed (see Figure 6). In general, there is less variation in the distribution of the AvS values in CLMET in comparison to RSC, i.e. productivity does not seem to change diachronically.

To test whether AvS can really be a measure showing effects of productivity, we inspect the lex-

ical realizations of the preceding context of the gerund in RSC considering again the distribution according to five quantiles and the number of types over tokens for each time period. Thus, a low AvS value of the full verb would be an indicator of low productivity in terms of preceding context and vice versa a high AvS value would be an indicator of high productivity. Figure 7 shows how very low to low AvS values (light gray shades) of the verb have also a low number of types over tokens in the preceding context (~0.4–0.6) and high to very high AvS values (dark shades) have a high number of types over tokens (~0.9–1.0). This relation is relatively stable over time. Thus, AvS can be used to distinguish higher vs. lower productivity.

We then inspect the concrete lexical items that have very low to low AvS, i.e. which are quite predictable given the previous context (preceding three words). This allows us to see which items are used in relatively fixed expressions and how this changes over time. Thus, we can inspect how the unit (gerund) changes over time as well as how the context changes (see Table 2). In 1650 and 1700 a relatively general verb, *making*, is used, while over time more specific verbs appear (*determining*, *examining*, *obtaining*). Moreover, the

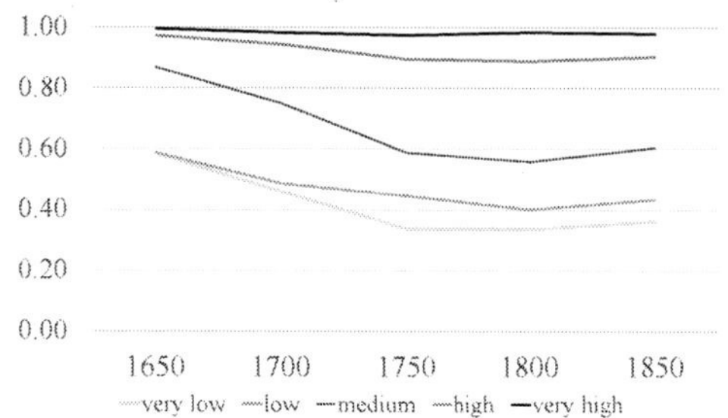

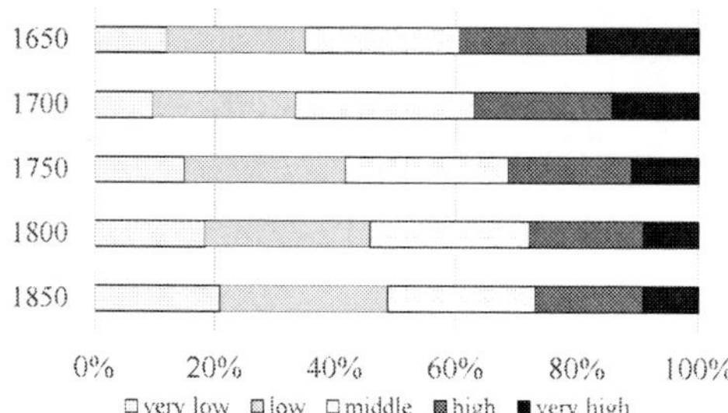

Figure 7: AvS of lexical verb and type-token ratio of preceding context of the gerund 3-gram (RSC)

Figure 8: AvS values of lexical verbs in the modal passive 3-gram (RSC)

context becomes more restricted over time, i.e. the same lexical realization for the preceding context is used (e.g. *an opportunity of* and *the purpose of*) in combination with different verbs. Thus, diachronically lexical variation of the gerund may increase, while its context of use gets increasingly restricted.

Passive (VVN) Considering the modal passive 3-gram (MD.VB.VVN), we observe a similar pattern (see Figure 8). The very low to low AvS values for RSC of the past tense verb (VVN) rise up to around 50% in 1850, while the number of high AvS values decreases over time (to around 30%). Again, this indicates lower productivity over time in RSC. Comparing this to the distribution in CLMET (see Figure 9), it again remains fairly stable over time in comparison to RSC. Thus, also for the modal passive 3-gram, productivity in CLMET remains stable.

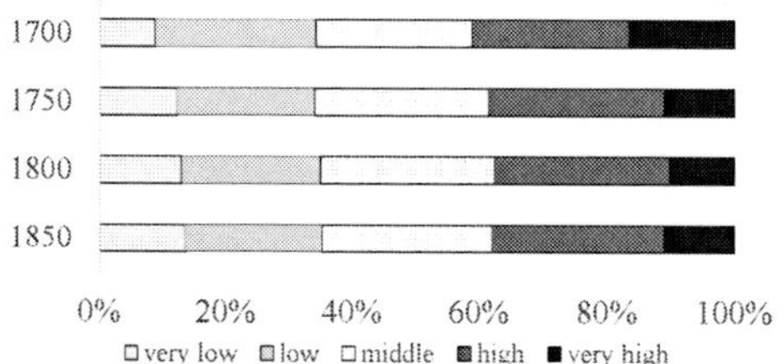

Figure 9: AvS values of lexical verbs in the modal passive 3-gram (CLMET)

From Figure 10, we again observe how low to high AvS values correlate with low to high number of types over tokens, respectively. This confirms that AvS is an indicator of productivity.

Further, we inspect the concrete lexical items that realize the full verb for the passive and which are relatively predictable given the previous context (low to very low AvS). We can see from Ta-

period	context + VVG	freq	%
1650	the way of **making**	12	3.40
	the opportunity of **making**	5	1.42
	the way of **measuring**	3	0.85
1700	be made by **multiplying**	11	1.45
	be capable of **producing**	4	0.53
	the pleasure of **seeing**	3	0.40
1750	an opportunity of **examining**	15	0.64
	be capable of **producing**	12	0.51
	the manner of **making**	11	0.47
1800	the purpose of **determining**	37	0.83
	the purpose of **ascertaining**	36	0.81
	an opportunity of **examining**	17	0.38
1850	the purpose of **ascertaining**	24	0.63
	the purpose of **determining**	23	0.61
	the purpose of **obtaining**	20	0.53

Table 2: Gerund verbs in the gerund 3-gram for very low to low AvS (RSC)

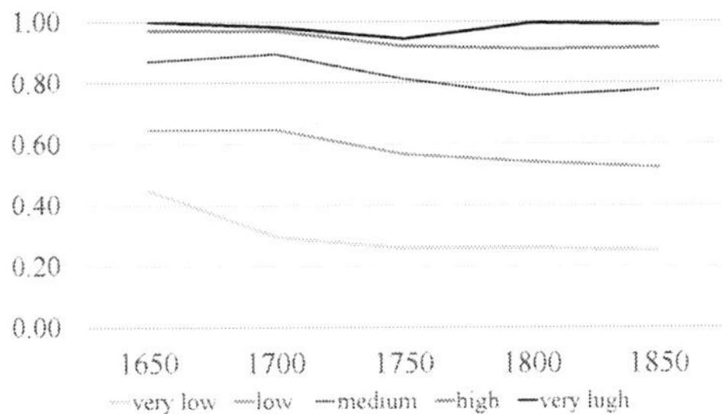

Figure 10: AvS of lexical verb and type-token ratio of preceding context of modal passive 3-gram (RSC)

ble 3 that the verbs used are basically the same diachronically (*found, observed, seen*). What changes is the context they appear in, which becomes progressively restricted over time and develops into a relatively fixed expression by 1850 (*it will be* VVN).

period	context + VVN	freq	%
1650	as may be **seen**	48	5.17
	that may be **made**	21	2.26
	it will be **found**	16	1.72
1700	as may be **seen**	48	4.56
	it will be **found**	26	2.47
	it may be **observed**	24	2.28
1750	it will be **found**	117	2.97
	it must be **observed**	93	2.36
	it may be **observed**	74	1.88
1800	it will be **seen**	351	4.76
	it will be **found**	257	3.48
	it may be **observed**	95	1.29
1850	it will be **seen**	494	5.68
	it will be **observed**	244	2.81
	it will be **found**	227	2.61

Table 3: Passive verbs in the modal passive 3-gram for very low to low AvS (RSC)

5 Conclusions

We have presented an approach to long-term diachronic change — here: in scientific writing — combining typicality and productivity of features involved in changing language use. While relative frequency is clearly a major indicator of change, also productivity, i.e. the lexical extensibility of a linguistic unit and the degree of variation in its immediate context, may change. To address productivity, we have suggested to employ the no-

tion of (average) surprisal, which measures the predictability of a linguistic unit in context. Predictability in context is a function of frequency of a unit, variation of the unit and variation of its context. In a given context, the more frequent a given unit (e.g. a particular part-of-speech) and the less varied its realizations (e.g. lexical types) are, the less surprising that unit is (and vice versa). Also, the contexts in which a unit occurs may change over time, they may expand or become more restricted. More contextual variation makes the unit less predictable, less variation makes it more predictable.

We have investigated a set of POS 3-grams becoming increasingly typical of scientific writing diachronically (mid 17th to mid 19th century), as determined by KLD and feature ranking. We then inspected the relative frequency of the selected 3-grams as well as their productivity over time by means of AvS. Compared to "general language", the analyzed 3-grams become more frequent over time, while their productivity diminishes. Both gerund and passive (with modal verb) exhibit fewer types over time and the contexts in which their lexical heads are used become more restricted. Such restricted language use has been noted before as a property of specialized sublanguages and is confirmed by our analyses (cf. Biber and Gray (2013)).

As the feature detection approach using KLD is based on part-of-speech tags, it can be applied to various other scenarios of comparison (e.g. different languages, registers, modes, etc.). Moreover, depending on the goal of analysis, other kinds of units, at all linguistic levels, and contexts can form the basis of (average) surprisal modeling (see e.g. Asr and Demberg (2015) on the predictability of discourse markers or Schulz et al. (2016) on vowel space and surprisal). In our ongoing work, we analyze the 3-grams that have not been considered here to determine whether they show similar productivity patterns or not. Given that scientific language is said to become increasingly nominal over time (cf. Halliday (1988); Biber and Gray (2011)), we would predict that nominal patterns (e.g. DT.JJ.JJ, NN.TO.DT; cf. Table 1) become more productive over time to ensure a sufficient level of expressivity in scientific language.

References

Fatemeh Torabi Asr and Vera Demberg. 2015. Uniform Information Density at the Level of Discourse Relations: Negation Markers and Discourse Connective Omission. In *Proceedings of the 11th International Conference on Computational Semantics (IWCS 2015)*. London, UK, page 118.

Harald Baayen and Rochelle Lieber. 1991. Productivity and English Derivation: A Corpus-based Study. *Linguistics* 29(5):801–844.

Jóhanna Barðdal, editor. 2008. *Productivity: Evidence from Case and Argument Structure in Icelandic*. John Benjamins, Amsterdam/Philadelphia.

Alistair Baron and Paul Rayson. 2008. VARD 2: A Tool for Dealing with Spelling Variation in Historical Corpora. In *Proceedings of the Postgraduate Conference in Corpus Linguistics*. Aston University, Birmingham, UK.

Douglas Biber. 2012. Register as a Predictor of Linguistic Variation. *Corpus Linguistics and Linguistic Theory* 8(1):9–37.

Douglas Biber and Bethany Gray. 2011. The Historical Shift of Scientific Academic Prose in English towards Less Explicit Styles of Expression: Writing without Verbs. In Vijay Bathia, Purificación Sánchez, and Pascual Pérez-Paredes, editors, *Researching Specialized Languages*, John Benjamins, Amsterdam, pages 11–24.

Douglas Biber and Bethany Gray. 2013. Being Specific about Historical Change: The Influence of Sub-register. *Journal of English Linguistics* 41:104–134.

Douglas Biber, Stig Johansson, Geoffrey Leech, Susan Conrad, and Edward Finegan. 1999. *Longman Grammar of Spoken and Written English*. Longman, Harlow, UK.

Ido Dagan, Lillian Lee, and Fernando Pereira. 1999. Similarity-based Models of Word Cooccurrence Probabilities. *Machine Learning* 34(1-3):43–69.

Mark Davies. 2008. The Corpus of Contemporary American English: 520 Million Words, 1990-present. Available online at http://corpus.byu.edu/coca/.

Hendrik De Smet. 2008. Functional Motivations in the Development of Nominal and Verbal Gerunds in Middle and Early Modern English. *English Language and Linguistics* 12(1):55–102.

Vera Demberg and Frank Keller. 2008. Data from Eye-tracking Corpora as Evidence for Theories of Syntactic Processing Complexity. *Cognition* 109(2):193–210.

Hans-Jürgen Diller, Hendrik De Smet, and Jukka Tyrkkö. 2011. A European Database of Descriptors of English Electronic Texts. *The European English Messenger* 19:21–35.

Teresa Fanego. 2004. On Reanalysis and Actualization in Syntactic Change: The Rise and Development of English Verbal Gerunds. *Diachronica* 21(1):5–55.

Teresa Fanego. 2006. The Role of Language Standardization in the Loss of Hybrid Gerunds in Modern English. In Leiv Egil Breivik, Sandra Halverson, and Kari Haugland, editors, *'These things write I vnto thee...': Essays in Honour of Bjorg Bækken*, Novus Press, pages 93–110.

Bethany Gray and Douglas Biber. 2012. The Emergence and Evolution of the Pattern N + PREP + V-ing in Historical Scientific Texts. In Isabel Moskowich and Begoña Crespo, editors, *Astronomy 'playne and simple'. The Writing of Science between 1700 and 1900*, John Benjamins, Amsterdam, pages 181–198.

John Hale. 2001. A Probabilistic Earley Parser as a Psycholinguistic Model. In *Proceedings of the Second Meeting of the North American Chapter of the Association for Computational Linguistics on Language Technologies*. Pittsburgh, volume 2 of *NAACL '01*, pages 159–166.

David Hall, Daniel Jurafsky, and Christopher D. Manning. 2008. Studying the History of Ideas Using Topic Models. In *Proceedings of the Conference on Empirical Methods in Natural Language Processing*. Association for Computational Linguistics, Stroudsburg, PA, USA, EMNLP '08, pages 363–371.

M.A.K. Halliday. 1988. On the Language of Physical Science. In Mohsen Ghadessy, editor, *Registers of Written English: Situational Factors and Linguistic Features*, Pinter, London, pages 162–177.

M.A.K. Halliday and Ruqaiya Hasan. 1985. *Language, Context, and Text: Aspects of Language in a Social-semiotic Perspective*. Oxford University Press, Oxford.

Jennifer Hay and Harald Baayen. 2002. Yearbook of Morphology 2001. Springer Netherlands, Dordrecht, chapter Parsing and Productivity, pages 203–235.

Hannah Kermes, Stefania Degaetano-Ortlieb, Ashraf Khamis, Jörg Knappen, and Elke Teich. 2016. The Royal Society Corpus: From Uncharted Data to Corpus. In Nicoletta Calzolari (Conference Chair), Khalid Choukri, Thierry Declerck, Marko Grobelnik, Bente Maegaard, Joseph Mariani, Asuncion Moreno, Jan Odijk, and Stelios Piperidis, editors, *Proceedings of the Tenth International Conference on Language Resources and Evaluation (LREC 2016)*. European Language Resources Association (ELRA), Paris, France.

John Lafferty and Chengxiang Zhai. 2001. Document Language Models, Query Models, and Risk Minimization for Information Retrieval. In *Proceedings of the 24th Annual International ACM SIGIR Conference on Research and Development in Information Retrieval*. ACM, New York, NY, USA, SIGIR '01, pages 111–119.

Roger Levy. 2008. A Noisy-channel Model of Rational Human Sentence Comprehension under Uncertain Input. In *Proceedings of the 2008 Conference on Empirical Methods in Natural Language Processing*. Honolulu, EMNLP '08, pages 234–243.

Isabel Moskowich and Begoña Crespo, editors. 2012. *Astronomy 'playne and simple'. The Writing of Science between 1700 and 1900*. John Benjamins, Amsterdam.

Florent Perek. 2014. Vector Spaces for Historical Linguistics: Using Distributional Semantics to Study Syntactic Productivity in Diachrony. In *Proceedings of the 52nd Annual Meeting of the Association for Computational Linguistics*. Association for Computational Linguistics, Baltimore, Maryland, USA, ACL '14, pages 309–314.

Florent Perek. 2016. Using Distributional Semantics to Study Syntactic Productivity in Diachrony: A Case Study. *Linguistics* 54(1):149–188.

Helmut Schmid. 1994. Probabilistic Part-of-Speech Tagging Using Decision Trees. In *International Conference on New Methods in Language Processing*. Manchester, UK, pages 44–49.

Helmut Schmid. 1995. Improvements in Part-of-Speech Tagging with an Application to German. In *Proceedings of the ACL SIGDAT-Workshop*. Kyoto, Japan.

Erika Schulz, Yoon Mi Oh, Zofia Malisz, Bistra Andreeva, and Bernd Möbius. 2016. Impact of Prosodic Structure and Information Density on Vowel Space Size. In *Speech Prosody*. Boston, pages 350–354.

Claude E. Shannon. 1949. *The Mathematical Theory of Communication*. University of Illinois Press, Urbana/Chicago, 1983 edition.

Anatol Stefanowitsch and Stefan Th. Gries. 2003. Collostructions: Investigating the Interaction between Words and Constructions. *International Journal of Corpus Linguistics* 8(2):209–243.

Irma Taavitsainen and Päivi Pahta, editors. 2012. *Early Modern English Medical Texts. Corpus Description and Studies*. John Benjamins, Amsterdam.

Author Index

Adesam, Yvonne, 32
Alegria, Iñaki, 100

Barteld, Fabian, 52
Bhattacharyya, Pushpak, 95
Blessing, Andre, 134
Bouma, Gerlof, 32
Budassi, Marco, 90

Carman, Mark, 95
Coll Ardanuy, Mariona, 63

Degaetano-Ortlieb, Stefania, 165
Dethlefs, Nina, 128

Elsner, Micha, 156
Etxeberria, Izaskun, 100

Frank, Anette, 74

Glavaš, Goran, 12

Hahn, Udo, 111
Hellrich, Johannes, 111
Hiippala, Tuomo, 84
Hulden, Mans, 100
Hulden, Vilja, 140

Iglesias-Franjo, Estíbaliz, 22

Joshi, Aditya, 95

Karan, Mladen, 12
Keller, Mareike, 43

Lane, Emily, 156
Le, Dieu-Thu, 134

Opitz, Juri, 74
Özgür, Arzucan, 106

Passarotti, Marco, 90

Saraswati, Jaya, 95
Schoene, Annika Marie, 128
Schröder, Ingrid, 52
Schroeder, Caroline T., 146
Schulz, Sarah, 43

Schumann, Anne-Kathrin, 1
Shukla, Rajita, 95
Simon, Eszter, 118
Sirinic, Daniela, 12
Šnajder, Jan, 12
Sönmez, Çağıl, 106
Sporleder, Caroline, 63

Teich, Elke, 165

Uria, Larraitz, 100

van den Bos, Maarten, 63
Vilares, Jesús, 22
Vincze, Veronika, 118
Vu, Ngoc Thang, 134

Yörük, Erdem, 106

Zeldes, Amir, 146
Zinsmeister, Heike, 52

Association for Computational Linguistics
209 N. Eighth Street
Stroudsburg, Pennsylvania 18360

ISBN 978-1-5108-2773-8